Human Resource Management in Developing Countries

Increasing globalisation and competitiveness have brought to the fore the importance of effective human resource management for national and international organisations. In recent years, there has been a remarkable development in HRM throughout the world, however, the majority of research has focused on HRM in advanced industrial societies. This book redresses the balance by providing a thorough analysis of HRM in thirteen developing countries in Asia, Africa and the Middle East.

Contributors examine the influence of core national factors on the determination of HRM policies and practices in China, South Korea, Taiwan, India, Nepal, Pakistan, Iran, Saudi Arabia, Algeria, Nigeria, Ghana, Kenya and South Africa. These factors include:

- national culture
- national institutes
- business environment
- industrial sector

A common framework is used by all authors throughout the work to analyse not only the 'context-specific' HRM functions in these countries, but also the diverse and unique configurations of national factors which impact on HRM in cross-national settings.

This work will prove valuable for human resource management practitioners, as well as scholars and students involved in teaching and researching HRM and International Business.

Pawan S. Budhwar is Lecturer in OB and HRM at Cardiff Business School, University of Wales. He received his PhD from Manchester Business School and has published in the fields of international HRM, comparative management, managerial cognition and research methods. **Yaw A. Debrah** is a Senior Lecturer in Management at Cardiff Business School. He teaches courses in Human Resource Management and Comparative Management at both undergraduate and graduate levels. He has lived and worked in Africa, North America, Asia and Europe, and has published numerous articles and book chapters.

Routledge Research in Employment Relations
Series editors: Rick Delbridge and Edmund Heery
Cardiff Business School

Aspects of the employment relationship are central to numerous courses at both under-graduate and postgraduate level. Drawing from insights from industrial relations, human resource management and industrial sociology, this series provides an alternative source of research-based materials and texts, reviewing key developments in employment research.

Books published in this series are works of high academic merit, drawn from a wide range of academic studies in the social sciences.

Human Resource Management in Developing Countries

Edited by
Pawan S. Budhwar
and Yaw A. Debrah

London and New York

First published 2001
by Routledge
11 New Fetter Lane, London EC4P 4EE

Simultaneously published in the USA and Canada
by Routledge
29 West 35th Street, New York, NY 10001

Transferred to Digital Printing 2002

Routledge is an imprint of the Taylor & Francis Group

Typeset in Baskerville by
Keystroke, Jacaranda Lodge, Wolverhampton
Printed and bound in Great Britain by
Biddles Ltd, Guildford and King's Lynn

British Library Cataloguing in Publication Data
A catalogue record for this book is available from the British Library

Library of Congress Cataloging in Publication Data
Human resource management in developing countries / edited by Pawan
S. Budhwar and Yaw A. Debrah.
      p. cm.
   Includes bibliographical references and index.
   1. Personnel management–Developing countries.   2. Human capital–Developing
countries–Management.   I. Budhwar, Pawan S.   II. Debrah, Yaw A.

HF5549.2.D48 H859 2001
658.3′009172′4–dc21   00–051780

ISBN 0–415–22333–4

To Laxmi and Gaurav, who gave me the freedom to complete this task.

To Dorothy, Denise, Lorraine and Derek with all my love.

To those who are interested in international HRM and its progress in developing countries.

Contents

Figures

Tables

Contributors

Dev Raj Adhikari Reader, Central Department of Management, Tribhuvan University, Kathmandu, Nepal.

Augustine K. Ankomah Senior Lecturer, School of Health, University of Teesside, UK.

Mohamed Branine Lecturer, Department of Management and Organization, University of Stirling, Scotland.

Pawan S. Budhwar Lecturer, Cardiff Business School, Wales.

Yaw A. Debrah Senior Lecturer, Cardiff Business School, Wales.

Tung-Chun Huang Professor, Institute of Human Resource Management, National Central University, Taiwan.

Ken Kamoche Associate Professor, City University of Hong Kong, Hong Kong.

Shaista E. Khilji Assistant Professor, Department of Management, McGill University, Montreal, Canada.

Kamel Mellahi Senior Lecturer, Coventry Business School, University of Coventry, England.

Michael Muller Senior Research Fellow, Leicester Business School, University of Leicester, England.

Franca Ovadje Lagos Business School, Nigeria.

Won-Woo Park Assistant Professor, College of Business Administration, Seoul National University, Seoul, Korea.

Monir Tayeb Reader, Department of Business Organization, Herriot-Watt University, Edinburgh, Scotland.

Malcolm Warner Professor and Fellow, Wolfson College and Judge Institute of Management Studies, University of Cambridge, England.

Geoffrey T. Wood Senior Lecturer, Coventry Business School, University of Coventry, England.

Foreword

The importance of managing human resources has been growing over the past twenty years, both in academia and in practice. As a consequence, there has been a great deal written on the topic. In addition, new avenues of investigation have developed, including strategic human resource management and international human resource management. All this has been supported and encouraged by the introduction of several new journals. However, one aspect that has been missing in all of these developments is the perspective of the developing countries of the world. While we know a great deal about managing human resources, it is primarily from the perspective of writers in the developed and Western countries. The perspective of managing human resources in the developing countries would not only be informative, but helpful in understanding human resource management policies and practices in the developed countries.

Pawan Budhwar and Yaw Debrah have given us this perspective with *Human Resource Management in Developing Countries*. These experts in developing countries have gathered together fifteen authors to describe human resource management in thirteen major developing countries of the world, accounting for almost one half of the world's population! These authors, most of whom are indigenous to the countries they are analysing, provide a most insightful review of human resource management as practised in their country. In addition, because of their local knowledge, in combination with knowledge of human resource management in developed countries, they are able to offer a special and unique understanding of human resource management in their developing countries. Furthering the utility of this book is the use by the authors of a common model of human resource management that is offered by Budhwar and Debrah. Thus, each of these original chapters offers insights and understandings that are comparable across countries.

Without doubt the authors have achieved their main objectives of filling a much needed gap in our knowledge of human resource management and providing a book that can be used as a textbook in graduate and undergraduate courses. Indeed, this book should also prove useful to practitioners in multinational companies as well as those who want to prepare themselves and their organizations to work in new and developing countries. For all of us, this knowledge about human resource management in developing countries should be helpful in understanding and improving human resource management in developed countries.

Randall S. Schuler
Rutgers University
New Brunswick,
New Jersey,
USA

Preface

The rapid increase in the globalisation of business and the growing significance of emerging markets suggest that the success of managers in this new century will depend on the degree to which they develop an understanding regarding the dynamics of managing human resources (HRs) in different parts of the globe. We have plenty of information regarding the management of HRs in the developed countries. However, there is a lack of information regarding the dynamics of human resource management (HRM) in developing countries. Global managers have now realised that HRM strategies vary significantly from country to country and that the strategies used to manage human resources in one country are sometimes ineffective or irrelevant in another country. With the growing significance of developing countries in the global world (as suppliers of cheap resources, buyers, competitors, capital users and home for the majority of MNCs' foreign direct investment), both academics and practitioners need to know how HRs are managed in developing countries. This will contribute both to better theory and practice development. Hence, this book.

The challenges of management of HRs in developing countries are complex and demanding. Academics can play a significant role in this regard by providing relevant information to policy-makers and researchers. It is also important for business students – as future business leaders, to gain an understanding of the different issues relating to the management of HRs in developing countries.

The aim of this book is to provide the reader with an understanding of the dynamics of HRM in thirteen developing countries – China, South Korea, Taiwan, India, Nepal, Pakistan, Iran, Saudi Arabia, Algeria, Nigeria, Ghana, Kenya and South Africa. It is intended that the reader should acquire not only an understanding of the HRM functions in these countries, but more awareness of the diverse and unique configurations of national factors (cultural, institutional and business environments) which dictate HRM in cross-national settings. Such awareness will enable the reader to better understand the 'context-specific' nature of HRM in these countries and the need to acknowledge the strength of cross-national HRM differences.

To achieve our objective, all the contributions have been written around a set framework. It examines the influence of core national factors (i.e. national culture, national institutions, dynamic business environment and business sector) on HRM policies and practices in the mentioned countries. This enabled us to consolidate in a single text the dynamics of management of human resources in developing countries, that is questions pertaining to the 'what', 'why' and 'how' of HRM in the various countries. It is hoped that this volume will serve as a catalyst for the development of further theoretical insights and appropriate techniques of HRM in this area. Moreover, there is also the possibility of extending the framework for similar investigations in other countries.

Two main reasons gave birth to this book. First, is the scarcity of material on HRM in developing countries which can be used on relevant courses. Second, this is a product of long discussions with a number of colleagues, other researchers and academics over the years on the need for such a book. This book, then, fills a gap in the area. Hence, most of the chapters in this volume are original contributions to the field and were specially commissioned for the book.

The subject area of the book is suitable for both undergraduate and postgraduate HRM and International Management courses. Moreover, this book will be of interest to cross-national HRM researchers and practitioners.

We would like to thank all those who have in various ways helped to make this project a success. Special thanks to our colleagues at Cardiff Business School who devoted considerable time and effort to the review of the manuscripts. We would also like to thank Stuart Hay (formerly with Routledge), Michelle Gallagher and Joe Whiting at Routledge for their help and assistance.

Pawan Budhwar
Yaw Debrah

Acknowledgements

The editors and the publishers wish to thank the following for permission to use copyright material:

Gabler Verlag for Pawan Budhwar and Paul Sparrow (1998) 'National factors determining Indian and British HRM practices: an empirical study'. *Management International Review*, 38 (Special Issue 2), 105-121.

Elsevier Science for Ken Kamoche (1997) 'Managing human resources in Africa: strategic, organizational and epistemological issues'. *International Business Review*, 6 (5), 547.

1   Introduction

Pawan S. Budhwar and Yaw A. Debrah

Introduction

This chapter, first of all, provides the reader with a brief overview of the developments in the field of human resource management (HRM). Second, it highlights the need to understand HRM in developing countries. Third, it introduces a framework for conducting cross-national HRM evaluations and, finally, it presents the structure of the book and introduces each of the chapters.

Developments in HRM

The developments in the field of HRM are now well documented (see for example, Legge, 1995; Poole, 1999; Poole and Warner, 1998; Schuler and Jackson, 1999; Sisson and Storey, 2000). Nevertheless, the debate on HRM issues continues even though its focus has changed over time. The main issue which occupied academics in the 1980s was the evolution of HRM. In this regard, the debate was mainly on the exploration of the salient aspects of the transformation of personnel management into HRM. Having done so, it moved on to issues pertaining to the incorporation of industrial relations into HRM (Guest, 1991); then the integration of HRM into business strategies, devolvement of HRM to line managers (Brewster *et al.*, 1997; Budhwar and Sparrow, 1997), and finally seeing HRM as a source of competitive advantage for organisations (see, for example, Barney, 1991; Schuler and MacMillan, 1984; Wright *et al.*, 1994). Currently, there is an ongoing debate regarding the contribution of HRM to a firm's performance (Guest, 1997; Huselid, 1995; MacDuffie, 1995; Schuler and Jackson, 1999). With these developments the nature of Human Resource (HR) function has changed from being reactive, prescriptive, and administrative to being proactive, descriptive and executive (Boxall, 1994).

While some seminal HRM research findings have been produced in recent years, research has often been based on a single country or the researchers look at issues in Western Europe or North America. Essentially, these studies have focused on HRM in advanced industrial societies in the West. As relatively very little work on comparative HRM research in developing countries has been done, some researchers have suggested the need for more comparative cross-national

HRM studies (Brewster *et al.*, 1996; Budhwar and Sparrow, 2002; Clark *et al.*, 1999; Pieper, 1990; Poole, 1990).

This is all the more important because of the increasing levels of globalisation and internationalisation of business, the growth of new markets (such as in Africa, Eastern Europe, China, India, South-East Asia and Latin America), the growth of new international business blocs (such as NAFTA, the European Union, ASEAN) and an increased level of competition among firms at both national and international level. As the world develops into a 'global business village', there is a greater need to know how managers in various parts of the world cope with issues and problems related to management of human resources. Thus, we must highlight the major factors that impact on HRM policies and practices in different contexts as such an evaluation will contribute to the development of HRM theories and relevant policies and practices (Budhwar and Debrah, 2001).

Although academics have responded positively to the challenges raised by the globalisation of business by investigating a number of issues and problems related to international business (Hendry, 1996), again the comparative perspective has been put on the back burner. However, the typical questions pursued by comparative HRM researchers that require further attention include the following:

1   How is HRM structured in individual countries?
2   What HRM strategies are developed by organisations?
3   Do organisations implement such strategies?
4   What are the similarities and differences in the HRM systems in different countries?
5   What are the reasons for such similarities and differences?
6   What is the influence of national factors such as culture, government policy and education systems on national patterns of HRM?
7   Is HRM converging or diverging at cross-national level?
8   To what extent are HRM models established in Western nations applicable to other parts of the world?

One possible way to investigate such questions is by identifying and examining the influence of the main factors and variables that impact on HRM in different cross-national settings. Several scholars note that national HR practices are determined by both 'culture-free' factors (such as age, size, and nature of organisation) and 'culture-bound' factors (such as national culture and institutions) (Budhwar and Sparrow, 1998; 2002; Fisher and Shaw, 1992; Easterby-Smith *et al.*, 1995; Hofstede, 1993; Jackson and Schuler, 1999). It is now accepted that management practices including HRM are not universal but are 'socially constructed' in each society (Boxall, 1995).

If the nature of HRM is known to be 'context-specific' (Boxall, 1995; Brewster, 1995; Jackson and Schuler, 1999), then the degree and direction of influence of both culture-bound and culture-free factors on HRM vary from country to country and are responsible for the context-specific nature of HRM (Jackson and Schuler, 1999; Locke and Thelen, 1995). For example, the strong impact of unions and

other pressure groups on HRM in India presents the context-specif
such practices. On the other hand, the influence of competitive press
by the downsizing of the workforce in the United Kingdom highlights
specific nature of the UK HR function (Budhwar and Sparrow, 1998,
the response of unions to competitive pressures such as the introduction of new
production technologies, large-scale restructuring and increasing work flexibility
varies across countries. Union membership has declined significantly in countries
such as the UK, France and the United States, whereas it has remained quite stable
in Canada and Germany. The above examples show that institutional configurations can mediate between environmental pressures and their effects on HR
practices (Locke and Thelen, 1995).

Investigators have identified how important contingency variables such as
the size, age, nature, life cycle stage of an organisation, level of technology used
and presence of formal HR department can influence HR practices (Budhwar and
Debrah, 2001; Jackson *et al.*, 1989; Tayeb, 1988). However, other researchers in
the field (such as Brewster 1995; Budhwar and Sparrow, 1998; Easterby-Smith
et al., 1995; Hofstede, 1993; Sparrow and Hiltrop, 1997) while acknowledging
the role of contingency factors, have noted that more complex culture-bound
arguments must be applied to the field of HRM.

Research on the influence of the main factors on HRM in a cross-national
context is therefore crucial for the growth and development of the field of HRM.
This is particularly so in view of the major developments taking place in developing
nations which have liberalised their economies and opened their doors to foreign
investors. It is essential for practitioners to know the pattern of HRM systems
prevalent in such developing countries. However, the achievement of such an
objective does require more research. Focusing on developing nations would add
a new impetus to HRM research and allow researchers to go beyond the current
predominant emphasis on research in countries in the European Union and North
America. Such an approach would also help researchers to examine the transferability of management systems and practices.

Until the 1970s, the view that management theories are universally applicable
was quite pervasive. However, the influence of the 'convergence hypothesis' has
now waned as sufficient evidence has been gathered against it (Hofstede, 1993).
But the question still remains, to what extent does this contingency view apply
to the relatively new field of cross-national HRM, given that most HRM models
have been developed in the Anglo-Saxon world?

McGaughey and De Cieri (1999) argue that organisations are becoming more
similar in terms of macro-level variables (convergence), but are maintaining their
culturally based dissimilarities in terms of micro-level variables (divergence). This is
a significant finding which perhaps can be applied to HRM in developing countries.

Although both contingent variables and national factors (mentioned above) are
known to influence cross-national HRM, it is suggested that more meaningful cross-
national HRM comparisons can be made by examining the influence of national
factors on HRM (see, for example, Brewster *et al.*, 1996, Boxall, 1995; Budhwar
and Sparrow, 1998; Murray *et al.*, 1976). This thesis is based on the premise that

national factors such as national culture and national institutions form the very basis of HR functions in any country. Therefore, in order to evaluate and highlight the context-specific nature of HRM in different national or regional settings, we need to delineate the major national factors that influence HR practices in such settings. The dilemma of which factors to include under broad concepts of 'national culture' or 'institutions' then needs to be resolved (Budhwar and Sparrow, 2002; Sparrow and Hiltrop, 1997).

Later in this chapter we will present a framework suitable for examining cross-national HRM. First, we highlight the need to examine the scenario of HRM in developing countries.

Need to examine HRM in developing countries

The term 'developing countries' is used in a broad generic sense and is used to represent all countries other than advanced industrialised societies which we refer to as developed countries. Some authors have used other terms such as 'less developed countries', 'newly industrialised countries', 'third world countries', 'emerging nations', 'emerging markets', and 'transitional economies' interchangeably for developing countries (Austin, 1990; Kiggundu, 1989; Warner, 2000). For us, developing countries are the ones which are in their early growth stages of economic development and are in the process of industrialising or are still non-industrialised (Napier and Vu, 1998). This is an ideal-type description as we know that all developing countries are at different stages of economic development.

The existing literature shows that apart from a few journal articles dealing with single countries and the work of a few researchers (see Austin, 1990; Jaeger and Kanungo, 1990; Kanungo, 1995; Kiggundu, 1989; Kiggundu *et al.*, 1983; Warner, 2000), relatively very little has been written about HRM in developing nations. This was probably due to the limited number of researchable topics in mainly small economies with small companies and small wage employment sector. However, over the past two decades, foreign direct investment (FDI) has come to the developing parts of the world, bringing its share from 23 per cent in the mid-1980s to 37.2 per cent in 1997 (United Nations, 1998: 9). Though this amount decreased to 28 per cent in 1998 due to the financial crisis in Asia, FDI to Latin American countries has been rising continuously and is projected to rise in Asia (UNCTAD, 1999). As a consequence, of 53,000 multinational corporations (MNCs) with 450,000 affiliates operating around the world, a total of 230,696 affiliates are now based in developing countries (United Nations, 1998). As a result of such developments, there is now a sudden research interest in management in developing countries (see, for instance, Special Issue of *Academy of Management Journal*, June 2000).

Further, the majority of the world's population live in developing countries. Apart from this, developing countries also perform the following functions:

1   significant buyers;
2   important suppliers of different resources (both natural and human) to industrialised nations;

3   competitors to developed countries with lower labour costs;
4   strategic regional centres for expansion of MNCs;
5   production sites for MNCs;
6   capital users, i.e. from private creditors such as international banks, FDI, and
    foreign official governmental assistance.

(Austin, 1990; Kanungo, 2000; Napier and Vu, 1998)

The above facts highlight the great extent to which both developed and developing countries have now become interdependent on each other. This is also evident from the creation of various economic international trading blocs and 'growth triangles' (Debrah *et al.*, 2000). However, it is important to recognise that the 'state-of-the-art' management practices and techniques which are dictated by unique configurations of different cultural and institutional factors, developed in the context of Western cultural values, cannot be uncritically adopted in developing countries (Mendonca, 2000). Therefore, there is now a need to research and highlight what kind of HR policies and practices are relevant for developing countries.

Considering the above, what decision-makers in developing countries do, or fail to do, is of significant interest to both academics and practitioners in the rest of the world (Blunt and Jones, 1991; Kiggundu *et al.*, 1983). Therefore, for the development of appropriate theory and practice, it has now become important for researchers to understand how HRs are managed and what key factors determine HRM in developing countries.

Framework for examining HRM in developing countries

In order to develop a conceptual framework to examine HRM in developing countries, it is important to define HRM in the broadest sense. There are several reasons for this. First, the existing literature suggests that the concept of HRM is relatively new and possibly non-existent in some regions of the developing world. Second, because several distinctive HR models can exist within firms in a particular country, each of which depends (along with a number of other factors, such as different institutions and national culture) on a number of distinct 'internal labour markets' (Boxall, 1995; Hendry, 1996; Osterman, 1994). Within each labour market, HRM incorporates a range of sub-functions and practices which include systems for workforce governance, work organisation, staffing and development and reward systems (Begin, 1992). HRM is therefore concerned with the management of all employment relationships in the firm, incorporating the management of managers as well as non-management labour.

In line with these views, different scholars in the field of HRM have put forward a number of frameworks for conducting international HRM research (Begin, 1992; Gronhaug and Nordhaug, 1992; Hiltrop, 1996; Jackson and Schuler, 1999; Miles and Snow, 1984; Murray *et al.*, 1976; Negandhi, 1983; Schuler *et al.*, 1993; Tayeb 1995; Welch, 1994). However, these frameworks are found to be normative nature and many of them present a complex set of variables that cannot be t empirically. On the contrary, Austin (1990) suggests an environmental analysis framework to enable managers in developing countries to practise effective management.

Based on a critical analysis of the existing frameworks in the field and over seven years of research in the HRM field, recently Budhwar and associates (see Budhwar and Debrah, 2001; Budhwar and Sparrow, 1998, 2002) have proposed a framework for examining cross-national HRM. They have identified three levels of factors and variables which are known to influence HRM policies and practices and are worth considering for cross-national examinations (for details, see Budhwar and Sparrow, 2002). These are *national factors* involving national culture, national institutions, business sectors and dynamic business environment; *contingent variables* including age, size, nature, ownership, life cycle stage of organization, presence of trade unions and HR strategies and interests of different stakeholders; *organisational strategies* such as the ones proposed by Miles and Snow and Porter; and policies related to primary HR functions and internal labour markets.

However, considering that HRM in developing countries is in its infancy and the argument that HRM in a cross-national context can best be analysed by examining the influence of national factors, we propose to examine the impact of only four national factors on HRM in developing countries. These factors are: national culture, national institutions, dynamic business environment and industrial sector. These broad factors form the macro environment of organisations in a national context. Figure 1.1 presents the framework.

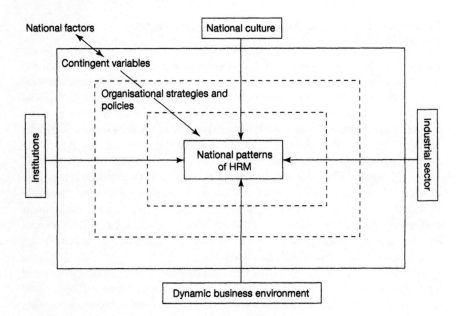

Figure 1.1 Factors determining cross-national HRM practices

Few would question the positioning of national culture, institutional arrange-ments and changing business dynamics in the external context as national factors. Perhaps it is the positioning of the industrial sector which requires justification. The study of national business systems (for example, Rasanen and Whipp, 1992; Whitley, 1992), suggests that the industrial sector is best considered as a country level or national unit of analysis and is worth considering for national level evaluations and comparisons.

This inference is based on the premise that certain sectors (for example, the forest sector in Finland, which is an industrial complex of various businesses that has emerged over the past 130 years) are well connected to similar sectors in other competing countries and to markets all over the world. Examples of such critical sectors include the Finnish forest sector, the Danish milk products sector and the Japanese car sector. All can clearly be distinguished by the very nature of their social networks, ownership control relationships and vertical logistical links. However, all also clearly retain a 'national' character.

It is important to bear in mind that a sector is an accomplishment of many actors who work in different time periods and with diverse logics of action. There are always alternative interpretations and applications of the 'sectoral business recipe', based on simultaneous factions that emerge in the sectoral networks. It is, thus, logical to state that nation–states contain unique configurations of sectors, each trying to develop their own business recipe within the national business system (Rasanen and Whipp, 1992: 48–49). Recent research (for example, Eriksson *et al.*, 1996) has therefore shown how HRM policies and practices are governed by a specific sector. Within the oil-dominating countries (such as Saudi Arabia and Iran), we expect some sector-specific HRM practices.

Table 1.1 provides a detailed breakdown of the main aspects of the four national factors of Figure 1.1. We have made a serious attempt to identify the main compo-nents of the four national factors. However, we are aware that this list is by no means exhaustive. Next, we present a brief discussion on the remaining national factors.

A number of researchers including Easterby-Smith *et al.* (1995), Hofstede (1993), Keesing (1974) Laurent (1993), Schneider (1993), Sparrow (1995) Sparrow and Hiltrop (1997) and Tayeb (1995) have highlighted and explained the influence of national culture on HRM policies and practices. The definition and scope of the concept of culture are, of course, debatable (Tayeb, 1994). It is therefore sensible to examine the impact of those aspects of national culture on HRM which have a sound theoretical base. The important aspects of national culture that have been identified in this regard are shown in Table 1.1.

Moving to the third national factor, researchers in the field of cross-national HRM have considered in detail the impact of different national institutions on HRM policies and practices (Brewster, 1995; Budhwar and Sparrow, 1998; Jackson and Schuler, 1999; Morishima, 1995; Powell and DiMaggio, 1991; Scott, 1995; Sparrow, 1995; Sparrow and Hiltrop, 1997; Zucker, 1987). There are a number of institutional systems whose influence on HRM in a cross-national context must be interpreted. For details see Table 1.1.

Table 1.1 Details of sub-components of national factors determining cross-national HRM

National Culture	Institutions	Industrial Sector	Dynamic Business Environment
Socialisation process	National labour laws	Common strategies,	Competition
Common values,	Trade unions	business logic and	Business Alliances
norms of behaviour	Politics	goals	Changing
and customs	Educational and	Regulations and	composition of
Influence of pressure	vocational training	standards	workforce
groups	set up	Sector-specific	Restructuring
Assumptions that	Labour Market	knowledge	Focus on total
shape managers'	Professional Bodies	Informal and formal	customer
perceptions, insights	International	benchmarking	satisfaction
and mindsets	institutions	Cross-sector	Facility of
Management style	Industry by itself	co-operation	information
Meaning of work	Employers Federation	Common	Technological
and values	Consulting	developments in	change
Personal dispositions,	organisations	business operations	Globalisation of
attitudes and	Placement	Labour or skill	business
manners	organisations	requirements	
Approaches to	Trade bodies	Merger activity	
cultural diversity	Government	Workforce mobility	
Match to the	institutions	Capital mobility	
organisation culture	Local authorities		
	Voluntary bodies		

Finally, a number of the existing frameworks in the field do indicate the impact of a competitive business environment on HRM (Budhwar and Sparrow, 1998; Cappelli, 1995; Hendry and Pettigrew, 1992; Hiltrop, 1993; Soeters and Schwan, 1990; Sparrow, 1995; Torrington, 1993). However, like the factor of national culture, none of the existing frameworks in the field provide the main aspects of the competitive environment which can help to assess its impact on cross-national HRM. Those aspects of a dynamic business environment that have been identified as influencing HRM policies and practices in a cross-national context are shown in Table 1.1. Although many of these dynamics are unique to each nation, a series of developments are pan-national and have been identified as major determinants of international HRM activity.

The structure of the book

Most of the contributors are natives of the country whose HRM practices they discuss. We believe this helps to minimise the Western bias in such projects and has enabled us to present a more realistic picture of HRM in the various countries. This volume is divided into two parts: Part I deals with HRM in Asia and Part II deals with HRM in Africa. The need to cover HRM in Eastern and Central Europe and Latin America could not be accommodated in this volume and would probably require a separate volume.

In Chapter 2 Malcolm Warner highlights how over a period of five decades or so, the People's Republic of China has emerged as an economic power. He suggests that HRM practices based on a unique configuration of national culture and institutions, along with economic reforms have contributed a great deal in this regard. Warner also illuminates our understanding about the rapidly changing dynamics of the labour market in China. The rapidly changing business environment there has contributed to the movement from state-owned enterprises to joint venture and private-owned enterprises. Warner discusses the growth of market socialism and the end of the 'iron rice bowl' industrial employment framework. He succinctly highlights the main factors responsible for such changes and summarises the development of the HR function in China.

Chapter 3 details the dynamics of HRM in South Korea. Here, Won-Woo Park discusses the miraculous economic development in South Korea over the past thirty years and how South Korea has managed to tackle the problems emanating from the recent Asian economic crisis. He highlights the foundations of Korean corporations – the *chaebols* – and how they manage employment relations. In addition, Park discusses the key characteristics of Korean management style and how a number of hidden factors such as family relationships, alumni and region play a critical role in the management of HRs in Korea. Finally, the three main stages of transition of HRM in Korean companies are analysed.

In Chapter 4, Tung-Chun Huang presents the past and present of HRM in Taiwan. He asserts that Confucian work principles still dominate working relationships in Taiwan. Like Park in Chapter 3, Huang also discusses the three stages of development of HRM in Taiwan. Warner, in Chapter 2 indicated similar developmental stages of HR function in China, but a few years behind Taiwan. Huang's chapter reveals that in comparison to China and Korea, Taiwan seems to have a more formal and established HRM function. He also indicates the growing strategic nature of Taiwanese HRM. Huang has enriched his discussion by providing empirical studies and important statistics for Taiwanese industries, sector-specific employment patterns and labour under-utilisation in Taiwan.

Chapter 5 is on HRM in India. Here, Pawan Budhwar presents an overview of the socio-economic environment of India and its impact on Indian HRM. Using the framework introduced in this chapter, he provides questionnaire survey results from 137 large Indian organisations and the survey findings are discussed in light of the existing literature. Budhwar highlights the impact of the socio-cultural set-up and the recent economic reforms on Indian HRM. He delineates the configuration of the main institutions, the cultural aspects and the dynamic business environment which dictate Indian HRM. Highlighting the latest developments in the Indian economy (such as the initiation of the 'second generation' reforms), he points out the main challenges facing Indian HRM in the newly liberalised environment.

In Chapter 6 Dev Raj Adhikari and Michael Muller present the evolution and development of the HRM function in Nepal, and they contend that HRM is not yet established in Nepal. In spite of this, they have attempted to discuss the impact of different factors (such as business environment, Nepalese national culture and prominent institutions) on Nepalese HR function. They present three case studies of HRM in Napalese organisations to show the diverse nature of HRM practices there. In this respect, the authors caution against the adoption of Western-type prescriptions in Nepalese organisations.

Chapter 7 provides an examination of HRM systems and practices in Pakistan. Shaista Khilji shows how a mixture of different social institutions, Islamic principles and Western models (mainly through MNCs and Western training mode) impact on Pakistani HRM. Like India, Pakistan is also finding it hard to get rid of the British legacies in its administrative set-up and influence on employment practices. Khilji nicely summarises the impact of the national factors on Pakistani HRM. Interestingly, she does not suggest a very strong impact of Islam on Pakistani HRM systems. Her discussion is based on a large number of in-depth interviews and thorough literature analyses. Khilji reports that the nature of HRM is more strategic in MNCs than other national and local organisations and also states that Pakistani firms are making a serious attempt to adopt the Western HRM philosophy. Like Adhikar and Muller, she warns against it.

In Chapter 8 Monir Tayeb discusses the dynamics of HRM in Iran. She highlights the role of history, ecology and economy in the development of national patterns of HRM and discusses the significant impact of Islam and Iranian work-related values on Iranian employment policies and practices. It is apparent from Tayeb's presentation that Iranian organisations, like many in other developing countries, do not have a formal and established HRM system. She also highlights the lack of HRM research in Iran and indicates the lack of valid information in this respect.

Chapter 9 is about HRM in Saudi Arabia. Kamel Mellahi and Geoffrey Wood assess the impact of five key factors (i.e. the structure of the Saudi economy, its political environment, the Saudi labour market, the national human resource development (HRD) strategy and the Saudi national culture) on Saudi HRM policies and practices. They highlight a number of significant differences between different categories of employees (such as local versus foreign and males versus females) and note the strong imbalance between public and private sector organisations in favour of the former. They also discuss the key role of national culture and the '*Shari'a* law' in the development of HR policies in Saudi Arabia. Finally, Mellahi and Wood summarise the main challenges facing Saudi HRM.

In chapter 10 Mohamed Branine details HRM in Algeria. He introduces the socio-economic and political system of Algeria and then discusses the labour market and the main factors affecting it. He notes the two main labour market regulations, i.e. 'the self-management' (1962–9) and 'socialist management of enterprises' (1971–90), which significantly affected Algerian enterprises. The HRM situation both before and after the reforms is discussed, and the main problems of managing employees in Algeria and how they are intertwined with unclear policies and practices which are strongly dictated by Algerian national culture, history, political and socio-economic development are expounded.

Chapter 11 is about HRM in Nigeria. Here, Franca Ovadje and Augustine Ankomah discuss HRM in Africa's most populous nation. The chapter explores within a socio-economic context the factors which influence HR policies and practices in Nigeria and throws light on the emerging issues in HRM in the country. A survey of the economy, the dominance of the oil sector and the rapid de-industrialisation since the 1970s are all discussed. This is followed by an analysis of the role of HRM in Nigerian organizations. In particular, the discussion touches on education and HR planning as an essential aspect of human capital development. Recruitment and retention practices are also examined. The next section focuses on the impact of labour laws on HRM policies and practices in Nigeria. The various labour laws are mentioned and the role of trade unions in organizations is highlighted. This is followed by a section on culture and HRM in Nigeria. Making reference to the work of Hofstede, the chapter examines both the positive and negative aspects of national cultures on HRM in Nigerian organizations.

In Chapter 12 Yaw Debrah discusses HRM in the Ghanaian context. He starts the chapter with key statistical information regarding the Ghanaian economy and its impact on Ghana's work employment system. In this section, Debrah explains about the main policy programmes (such as the 'structural adjustment programme', 'vision 2000') initiated over the years and their impact on the HRM function in Ghana. Next he discusses the impact of historical developments (such as the colonial era) on Ghanaian HRM. Debrah clearly highlights how the unstable economic and political environment of Ghana has significantly influenced its HRM. Then he details the impact of national culture on HRM. In the later parts of the chapter, Debrah discusses the HRM functions and IRs system prevalent in the contemporary organisations in Ghana. Finally, he cautions policy-makers against the adoption of Western-style management in the Ghanaian context.

Chapter 13 discusses HRM in Kenya. Ken Kamoche initially highlights the prevalence of traditional administrative procedures and personnel management in Kenyan organisations whose roots were sown during the colonial era. He explains how the colonial rulers encouraged foreign investments and systematically stifled indigenous enterprises. Next, Kamoche discusses the main national factors (such as national culture, political–economic environment) which significantly influence HRM in Kenya. He also explains the various phases (militancy to tripartite agreements) through which industrial relations in Kenya have progressed over the past sixty years. Finally, Kamoche illustrates how the 'resource-based view' of the firm can be adopted to understand the role of strategic management of HRs in the Kenyan context.

In Chapter 14 Geoffrey Wood and Kamel Mellahi present the scenario of HRM in South Africa. They start their chapter with the sensitive discussion of the apartheid era and the management of HRs. Next, they present a concise brief on the political context of South Africa and its impact on unions. This is followed by a discussion on national culture and its impact on HRM. Then, Wood and Mellahi highlight the dynamics of the South African labour market. Main labour legislation and key reforms related to the management of human resources in South Africa and the resultant changes in the unions and work organisation are discussed. Later, the authors talk about contemporary HRM in South African organisations. Finally, they highlight the main challenges facing HRM in South Africa in the new millennium.

The final chapter summarises issues related to HRM in developing countries. Debrah and Budhwar point out the key messages emerging from the volume. They also highlight the main forces creating change in developing countries, the impact of globalisation and FDI on employment in these nations, and finally, the main challenges facing HRM in developing countries.

References

Academy of Management Journal (2000) Special Research Forum on Emerging Economies, 43 (3), 249–517.

Austin, J. E. (1990) *Managing in Developing Countries*, New York: The Free Press.

Barney, J. B. (1991) 'Firm Resources and Sustained Competitive Advantage', *Journal of Management*, 17 (1), 99–120.

Begin, J. P. (1992) 'Comparative HRM: A Systems Perspective', *International Journal of Human Resource Management*, 3, 379–408.

Blunt, P. and Jones, M. (1991) 'Editorial: Human Resource Management in Developing Countries', *International Journal of Human Resource Management*, 2 (1), 3–5.

Boxall, P. F. (1994) 'Placing HR Strategy at the Heart of Business Success', *Personnel Management*, July, 32–35.

Boxall, P. F. (1995) 'Building the Theory of Comparative HRM', *Human Resource Management Journal*, 5, 5–17.

Brewster, C. (1995) 'Towards a European Model of Human Resource Management', *Journal of International Business Studies*, 26, 1–22.

Brewster, C., Larsen, H. H. and Mayrhofer, W. (1997) 'Integration and Assignment: A Paradox in Human Resource Management', *Journal of International Management*, 13, 1–23.

Brewster, C., Tregaskis, O., Hegewisch, A. and Mayne, L. (1996) 'Comparative Research in Human Resource Management: A Review and an Example', *The International Journal of Human Resource Management*, 7, 586–604.

Budhwar, P. and Debrah, Y. A. (2001) 'Rethinking Comparative and Cross-National Human Resource Management Research', *The International Journal of Human Resource Management*, 12 (3).

Budhwar, P. and Sparrow, P. (1997) 'Evaluating Levels of Strategic Integration and Devolvement of Human Resource Management in India', *The International Journal of Human Resource Management*, 8, 476–494.

Budhwar, P. and Sparrow, P. (1998) 'National Factors Determining Indian and British HRM Practices: An Empirical Study', *Management International Review*, 38, Special Issue 2, 105–121.

Budhwar, P. and Sparrow, P. (2002) 'An Integrative Framework For Determining Cross National Human Resource Management Practices', *Human Resource Management Review* (forthcoming).

Cappelli, P. (1995) 'Rethinking Employment', *British Journal of Industrial Relations*, 33, 563–602.

Clark, T., Gospel, H. and Montgomery, J. (1999) 'Running on the Spot? A Review of Twenty Years of Research on the Management of Human Resources in Comparative and International Perspective', *The International Journal of Human Resource Management*, 10 (3), 520–544.

Debrah, Y. A., McGovern, I. and Budhwar, P. (2000) 'Complementarity or Competition: The Development of Human Resources in a Growth Triangle', *The International Journal of Human Resource Management*, 11 (2), 314–335.

Easterby-Smith, M., Malina, D. and Yuan, L. (1995) 'How Culture Sensitive is HRM? A Comparative Analysis of Practice in Chinese and UK Companies', *The International Journal of Human Resource Management*, 6, 31–59.

Eriksson, P., Fowler, C., Whipp, R. and Rasanen, K. (1996) 'Business Communities in the European Confectionery Sector: A UK–Finland Comparison', *Scandinavian Journal of Management*, 12, 359–387.

Fisher, C. D. and Shaw, J. B. (1992) 'Establishment Level Correlates of Human Resource Practices', *Asia Pacific HRM*, 30 (4), 30–46.

Gronhaug, K. and Nordhaug, O. (1992) 'International Human Resource Management: An Environmental Approach', *The International Journal of Human Resource Management*, 3, 1–14.

Guest, D. E. (1991) 'Personnel Management: The End of Orthodoxy?', *British Journal of Industrial Relations*, 29 (2), 147–175.

Guest, D. E. (1997) 'Human Resource Management and Performance: A Review and Research Agenda', *International Journal of Human Resource Management*, 8, 263–276.

Hendry, C. (1996) 'Continuities in Human Resource Processes in Internationalization and Domestic Business Management', *Journal of Management Studies*, 33, 475–494.

Hendry, C. and Pettigrew, A. M. (1992) 'Patterns of Strategic Change in the Development of Human Resource Management', *British Journal of Management*, 3, 137–156.

Hiltrop, J. M. (1993) 'Strategic Pressures Deriving European HRM', *European Management Journal*, 11, 424–434.

Hiltrop, J. M. (1996) 'A Framework for Diagnosing Human Resource Management Practices', *European Management Journal*, 14, 243–254.

Hofstede, G. (1993) 'Cultural Constraints in Management Theories', *Academy of Management Executive*, 7 (1), 81–94.

Huselid, M. A. (1995) 'The Impact of Human Resource Management on Turnover, Productivity, and Corporate Financial Performance', *Academy of Management Journal*, 38 (3), 635–672.

Jackson, S. E. and Schuler, R. S. (1999) 'Understanding Human Resource Management in the Context of Organizations and their Environment', in R. Schuler and S. Jackson (eds) *Strategic Human Resource Management*, London: Blackwell, 4–28.

Jackson, S., Schuler, R. and Rivero, J. C. (1989) 'Organisational Characteristics as Predictors of Personnel Practice', *Personnel Psychology*, 42 (4), 727–786.

Jaeger, A. M. and Kanungo, R. N. (eds) (1990) *Management in Developing Countries*, New York: Routledge.

Kanungo, R. N. (ed.) (1995) *Employee Management in Developing Countries*, Greenwich, CT: JAI Press Inc.

Kanungo, R. N. (2000) 'Business Culture: The Emerging Countries', in M. Warner (ed.) *Regional Encyclopedia of Business and Management: Management in the Emerging Countries*, London: Thomson Learning Business Press, 60–67.

Kanungo, R. N. and Jaeger, A. M. (1990) 'Introduction: The Need for Indigenous Management in Developing countries', in A. M. Jaeger and R. N. Kanungo (eds) *Management in Developing Countries*, London: Routledge, 1–19.

Keesing, R. M. (1974) 'Theories of Culture', *Annual Review of Anthropology*, 3, 73–97.

Kiggundu, M. N. (1989) *Managing Organizations in Developing Countries*, Connecticut: Kumarian Press.

Kiggundu, M. N., Jorgensen, J. J. and Hafsi, T. (1983) 'Administrative Theory and Practice in Developing Countries: A Synthesis', *Administrative Science Quarterly*, 28, 66–84.

Laurent, A. (1993) 'The Cross-Cultural Puzzle of Global Human Resource Management', in V. Puick, N. M. Tichy and C. K. Barnett (eds) *Globalizing Management*, New York: John Wiley and Sons, Inc., 174–184.

Legge, K. (1995) *Human Resource Management: Rhetorics and Realities*, Chippenham: Macmillan Business.

Locke, R. and Thelen, K. (1995) 'Apples and Oranges Revisited: Contextualized Comparisons and the Study of Comparative Labor Politics', *Politics and Society*, 23, 337–367.

MacDuffie, J. P. (1995) 'Human Resource Bundles and Manufacturing Performance: Organizational Logic and Flexible Production Systems in the World Auto Industry', *Industrial and Labor Relations Reviews*, 48, 197–221.

McGaughey, S. L. and De Cieri, H. (1999) 'Reassessment of Convergence and Divergence Dynamics: Implications for International HRM', *The International Journal of Human Resource Management*, 10 (2), 235–250.

Mendonca, M. (2000) 'Human Resource Management in the Emerging Countries', *Regional Encyclopedia of Business and Management: Management in the Emerging Countries*. London: Thomson Learning Business Press, 86–94.

Miles, R. E. and Snow, S. S. (1984) 'Designing Strategic Human Resources Systems', *Organization Dynamics*, 16, 36–52.

Morishima, M. (1995) Embedding HRM in a Social Context', *British Journal of Industrial Relations*, 33, 617–640.

Murray, V. V., Jain, H. C. and Adams, R. J. (1976) 'A Framework for the Comparative Analysis of Personnel Administration', *Academy of Management Review*, 1, 47–57.

Napier, N. K. and Vu, V. T. (1998) 'International Human Resource Management in Developing and Transitional Economy Countries: A Breed Apart?', *Human Resource Management Review*, 8 (1), 39–77.

Negandhi, A. R. (1983) 'Cross-Cultural Management Research: Trend and Future Directions', *Journal of International Business Studies*, 14, 17–27.

Osterman, P. (1994) 'Internal Labor Markets: Theory and Change', in C. Kerr and P. D. Staudohar (eds) *Markets and Institutions*, Cambridge, MA and London: Harvard University Press, pp. 303–339.

Pieper, R. (ed.) (1990) *HRM: An International Comparison*, Berlin and New York: Walter de Gruyter.

Poole, M. (1990) 'Editorial: Human Resource Management in an International Perspective', *International Journal of Human Resource Management*, 1, 1–15.

Poole, M. (ed.) (1999) *Human Resource Management: Critical Perspectives on Business and Management*, Vols I, II and III, London: Routledge.

Poole, M. and Warner, M. (eds) (1998) *The IEBM Handbook of Human Resource Management*, London: International Thomson Business Press.

Powell, W. W. and DiMaggio, P. L. (eds) (1991) *The New Institutionalism in Organizational Analysis*, Chicago: The University of Chicago Press.

Rasanen, K. and Whipp, R. (1992) 'National Business Recipes: A Sector Perspective', in R. Whitley (ed.) *European Business Systems: Firms and Markets in their National Contexts*, London: Sage Publications.

Schneider, S. C. (1993) 'National vs. Corporate Culture: Implications for HRM', in V. Puick, N. M. Tichy and C. K. Barnett (eds) *Globalizing Management*, New York: John Wiley and Sons, Inc., 160–173.

Schuler, R. S., Dowling, P. J. and DeCeri, H. (1993) 'An Integrative Framework of Strategic International Human Resource Management', *The International Journal of Human Resource Management*, 4, 717–764.

Schuler, R. S. and Jackson, S. E. (eds) (1999) *Strategic Human Resource Management*, London: Blackwell.

Schuler, R. S. and MacMillan, I. C. (1984) 'Gaining Competitive Advantage Through HRM Practices', *Human Resource Management*, 23 (3), 351–365.

Scott, R. W. (1995) *Institutions and Organizations*, London: Sage Publications.

Sisson, K. and Storey, J. (2000) *The Realities of Human Resource Management*, Buckingham: Open University Press.

Soeters, J. L. and Schwan, R. (1990) 'Towards an Empirical Assessment of Internal Market Configurations', *International Journal of Human Resource Management*, 1, 272–287.

Sparrow, P. R. (1995) 'Towards a Dynamic and Comparative Model of European Human Resource Management: An Extended Review', *The International Journal of Human Resource Management*, 6, 481–505.

Sparrow, P. R. and Hiltrop, J. M. (1997) 'Redefining the Field of European Human Resource Management: A Battle between National Mindsets and Forces of Business Transition', *Human Resource Management*, 36, 201–219.

Tayeb, M. (1988) *Organisations and National Culture*, London: Sage.

Tayeb, M. (1994) 'Organizations and National Culture: Methodology Considered', *Organization Studies*, 15, 429–446.

Tayeb, M. (1995) 'The Competitive Advantage of Nations: The Role of HRM and its Socio-cultural Context', *The International Journal of Human Resource Management*, 6, 588–605.

Torrington, D. (1993) 'How Dangerous is Human Resource Management? A Reply to Tim Hart', *Employee Relations*, 15, 40–53.

UNCTAD (1999) *World Investment Report 1999*, http//www.unctad.org/accessed September 2000.

United Nations (1998) *World Investment Report 1998: Trends and Determinants*, New York: United Nations.

Warner, M. (ed.) (2000) *Regional Encyclopedia of Business and Management: Management in the Emerging Countries*, London: Thomson Learning Business Press.

Welch, D. (1994) 'Determinants of International Human Resource Management Approaches and Activities: A Suggested Framework', *Journal of Management Studies*, 31, 139–164.

Whitley, R. (ed.) (1992) *European Business Systems: Firms and Markets in their National Contexts*, London: Sage Publications.

Wright, P. M., McMahan, G. C. and McWilliams, A. (1994) 'Human Resources and Sustained Competitive Advantage: A Resource-Based Perspective', *The International Journal of Human Resource Management*, 5 (2): 301–326.

Zucker, L. G. (1987) 'Institutional Theories of Organisation', *Annual Review of Sociology*, 13, 443–464.

Part I

Human resource management in Asia

2 Human resource management in the People's Republic of China

Malcolm Warner

Introduction

The People's Republic of China (hereafter referred to as the PRC) recently celebrated its fiftieth birthday in 1999. Its growth over the period since the 'Liberation', when the Communists took over the mainland in 1949, has by any account been impressive. After the Civil War and Japanese occupation, China was in a dire state; grinding agricultural and urban poverty were the norm. Mao Zedong set out to 'modernize' China, with Soviet aid for a while, building on a relatively small urban industrial base, with a labour force largely composed of illiterate and uneducated peasants (see Naughton, 1995). It was a colossal exercise in 'mass mobilization' or 'people-management' on a scale hitherto not undertaken. The way the Chinese went about it colours the description of how human resources are managed in the People's Republic.

Background

First, we will sketch out some basic statistics about China. It is a big country, with 22 per cent of the world's population but only 7 per cent of its land surface. It has a population of over 1.2 billion people (expected to rise to 1.6 billion by 2050), with a life expectancy of 71 years, with literacy over 80 per cent. The PRC has a huge workforce of over 700 million, most still living in rural areas and in townships and villages. It has a 'one-child policy' in most of the country to restrict population numbers as new citizens as well as existing ones have to be fed, housed and employed, no easy challenge. Half the workforce are employed on the land but about 200 million of these are estimated to be surplus to economic requirements and already over 100 million are already in the towns as part of the 'floating' migrant population known as *mingong*. Over one-third of the population live in urban areas. Those out of work in the towns are officially calculated at 3.5 per cent but in reality this could be over 10 per cent, even 20 per cent in the Northern rust-belt areas.

The PRC nonetheless has enjoyed two decades of economic growth since Deng Xiaoping initiated the Open Door policy in 1979. It has recently been hailed as a potential 'economic superpower' by agencies like the World Bank. Living standards have risen greatly but the distribution of benefits has been uneven. By mid-2000,

Table 2.1 Background statistics on the Chinese economy, mid-2000

Feature	Figure
Population	1,275.9 m.
Population increase	1.0%
GDP (PPP)	$US4,114b
GDP per capita (PPP)	$US3,275
GDP per capita	$US783
Inflation	−0.2%
Exports	$US195b
Current account balance	$US12.0b

Source: Miscellaneous; World Bank; Chinese Government, *Asiaweek*, 29 May 2000

real GDP growth was 8.1 per cent. Industrial production grew at 9.5 per cent. Per capita GDP was US$783 but with purchasing power parity, US$3,275. Inflation in that year was −0.2 per cent. Those living in towns have done better than those inland; urban workers have benefited *vis-à-vis* the peasants. A new middle class has also emerged (*Asiaweek*, 29 May 2000: 26). Table 2.1 shows the background statistics on the Chinese economy, mid-2000.

People management in the Chinese context

The form and style of managing all these human resources in the PRC have many special characteristics which distinguish it from most of the descriptions to be found elsewhere in this book. The application of the theoretical framework set out in the first chapter may, however, be appropriate if taken flexibly. We will examine in turn the influence of national culture and institutions as well as other variables, such as the business sector or the business environment. It would not be appropriate to elaborate this model further at this juncture, as it is more than adequately and elaborately set out elsewhere in the work by the editors.

Initially, the People's Republic of China managed its workforce via a system of personnel management (*renshi guanli*) which endured for half a century, as we shall later see. Studies of Chinese economic management in the critical years after 1949 (such as Schurmann, 1966) show the links between Chinese Communist practice before 1949 as well as the Soviet influence after that date. In addition, established Chinese capitalist and foreign-owned businesses before these were 'nationalized' in the 1950s left a legacy of personnel procedures. Other influences came from the Japanese public and private enterprises set up in Manchuria from the turn of the century (Warner, 1995).

Personnel management was basically a bureaucratic device to run the large state-owned enterprises which were set up in the 1950s. It was probably 'Weberian' rather than 'Marxist' in nature but above all it had to be 'Chinese'. It was basically concerned with the 'bread and butter' activities of recruitment and selection, reward systems, disciplinary procedures, and so on. Any organization, whatever of ownership or whatever kind of social system it is located in, has to a set of procedures of this kind.

Whatever concept evolved in the People's Republic, whether related to personnel or human resources management (the evolution of such practices we will outline in greater detail later), it had perforce to be endowed with 'Chinese characteristics'. It is to the determinants of this cultural flavouring that we now turn.

National culture

National culture in China is probably the most important variable in our analysis. It is almost impossible to discuss any aspect of Chinese life without invoking it. As elsewhere, the cultural variables pre-determine the institutional ones. They permeate social relations both at work and outside the basic work unit (*danwei*).

Chinese culture, as we know it, dates at least as far back as 3,000 years (see Fairbank and Goldman, 1998). Its main influences are probably more recent but even so it is one of the longest and most durable around. 'Sinicization' (by which we mean the conversion of foreign influences into 'Chinese' versions) became the rule and Chinese 'culturalism' welded the many nations the Han conquered into one cultural entity (ibid.: 117). One of the most important influences was Confucianism. The three bonds of loyalty bound the society (loyalty to the ruler, filial obedience and fidelity of wife to husband). Two of these loyalties were within the family and all were 'between superior and subordinate' (ibid.: 19).

Chinese society today is thus the result of a long process of adaptation to changes in this cultural environment. Its core structures have perhaps persisted as the 'bedrock' of the Chinese system on the mainland but had arguably been submerged for many decades by newer layers of institutional change. Such a core of cross-segmental characteristics was actively suppressed for many years under Mao but was, we would argue, so strong it prevailed in many important ways and re-appeared in recent decades as the system became more 'open' under the post-1978 reforms.

A vivid example which comes to mind is 'relational networking' based on inter-personal connections (known in Chinese as *guanxi*) as a co-ordination mechanism which we find in both socialist and capitalist Chinese organizations. This behavioural pattern is basically East Asian and very much ascriptive, communitarian, and particularistic and thus quite distinct from the *Gesellschaft* type of social integration in the West. It illustrates the persistence of Chinese societal patterns, in spite of changes from Imperial rule to Republican, from Revolutionary to Reformist. Indeed, such is the *continuity* that it has been seen as 'Confucian Leninism' (cited in Warner, 1995: 147).

Guanxi, for example, has been deep-rooted in China since Confucius codified the societal rules over 2000 years ago which welded the hierarchical structures holding national Chinese (and overseas Chinese) social structures together, such that clan-like networks have been the main links in the societal chain. Together with *guanxi* (relationships), *li* (rite), *mianzi* (face) and *renqing* (obligations) reinforce the social bonds which make the Chinese system function smoothly. In organization theory, this represents the elements of a reciprocal informal system which acts as neither market nor hierarchy; it acts reciprocally with the existing bureaucratic structures and makes these hierarchies work.

Early modernization involved both Western and Japanese influences on those parts of Chinese society which had seen initial industrialization at the margins, especially in major ports like Canton (now Guangzhou) and Shanghai, as well as in Dalian (in Manchuria). At the end of the nineteenth century, factories were built by foreign capitalists to take advantage of cheap labour and raw materials in the port towns, as well as inland. By the turn of the twentieth century, public education institutions had been set up on Japanese lines, with a subsequent wave of French and Prussian models, but always with a Chinese imprint. Although a primary to university-level system was introduced after 1911, most adults remained illiterate, a challenge which persisted for many years to come. By the inter-war years, the fragile shoots of industrialization and modernization had been planted.

By 1914, a 'critical mass' of Chinese workers and technicians was emerging. During the First World War, 140,000 Chinese workers obtained new skills in munitions factories in France, coming into contact with Communist Party and union militants, with some on their return to become the leaders of the emergent Chinese Communist Party (CCP) and All-China Federation of Trade Unions (ACFTU). By the end of the Second World War in 1945, there were many more craftsmen (over 60 million) than factory workers (less than 4 million). Self-employed craftsmen, family businesses and co-operatives are today still to be found in good number in the urban collective sector, as well as in rural industries, although they are not predominant.

Continuity, in spite of innovation, links past with present. Such stylized economic and work institutions follow a discernible 'Chinese' pattern to a recognizable degree. Although the smaller enterprises were overshadowed by the larger state enterprises in the period of centralized economic planning, under the economic reforms, the older and more flexible structures have come to the fore.

National culture and industrialization

The Liberation in 1949, when Mao led his troops into Beijing, was a major step in the transformation of China. Not only did a Communist government take power over the whole of the mainland, but it also attempted to change a predominantly peasant economy into an industrial one. Schools were set up to train skilled workers and technicians, together with engineering universities. Soviet influence on the new regime was apparent but in the end mostly superficial. 'Let's be Soviet and Modern' became the slogan of the day. The Chinese tried to copy what they thought was their mentor's 'best practice' but were, in fact, misled (Kaple, 1994). They also had considerable Soviet economic and technical aid, with expatriate experts at hand. However, 'modernism' was tempered by 'particularism'.

From the early 1960s to the early 1970s, with the Cultural Revolution ongoing, China was a land in turmoil. Schools and factories alike were shut down, although the economy still grew somewhat, in spite of the disorder. Whatever Mao Zedong tried to impose on the society in term of egalitarian experimentation was, in the end, short-lived. Even so, the criterion of 'better red than expert' was both regressive and inefficient. Technical training had come to a halt and young school-leavers were dispatched to work in rural areas. It was not until the mid-1980s that apprenticeships were restored, using the traditional master (*shifu*) and apprentice (*tudi*).

Deng Xiaoping's economic reforms here launched a new phase in China's development. After 1979, China embarked on a new road involving the 'Open Door' strategy and 'Four Modernizations' policy. The former promised greater trade with the outside world, while leading to the latter which stressed the reform of the four main sectors of the Chinese economy, namely Agriculture, Industry, Science and Technology and, finally, Defence. This was a major attempt to transform the Chinese economic strategy and structure. It was set in motion by the earlier Prime Minister, Zhou Enlai, who died in 1976 but was actually put into practice by Deng a little later.

In order to implement these 'strategic choices' (see Child, 1994, on this concept) enterprise and management decentralization was introduced in the mid-1980s. The economy changed from one based on central planning to one based on market socialism (Naughton, 1995). Over the same period, Chinese industry and its management have been transformed. State-owned enterprises ('owned by the whole people', in the official jargon) had been the mainstay of Chinese industry since the 1950s (see Warner, 1995). They were and are still mainly found in large industrial cities like Beijing, Dalian, Guangzhou, Shanghai, Shenyang, Wuhan, and so on. Large and medium-sized state-owned enterprises (SOEs) in this sector once produced the bulk of total gross value of industrial output, nearly 80 per cent in 1978 but now down to around 25 per cent of this total, although still growing in absolute terms, the same level as in the 1950s. Employing over 100 million workers in all by the late 1990s, state enterprises were generally seen as inefficient and over-manned. At least 40 per cent or possibly more are said to be 'in the red' and many are now to be sold off or made bankrupt. Such firms have the full stereotypical apparatus of Chinese labour–management relations, although the 'iron rice bowl' (*tie fan wan*) system – providing jobs for life and 'cradle-to-the-grave' welfare – is now in question.

'Today, China's patterns of continuity with its pre-1949 past are now re-emerging; the non-state-owned sector (comprising urban collectives, town and village industries, joint ventures, wholly foreign-funded firms and privately owned enterprises) now accounts for the largest part of China's industrial output and employs more workers than the SOEs (*The Economist*, 2000)! The share of collectively owned enterprises (that is, locally owned firms, many of which are family businesses in all but name) in this output grew to over one-third. The officially private sector of very small firms grew to over 5 per cent; with foreign-funded firms (many joint ventures) producing over a quarter of exports. Since 1978, over 350,000 joint-venture and similar agreements have been signed, of which under half have been implemented; foreign capital is now once again a motor of change (ibid.: 16).

Institutions

Institutional developments shaping current Chinese HRM date from more recent times, although social institutions stemming from the national cultural inheritance described above have much deeper roots and go back much further, of course. The embedded institutional values inter-acted with the institution-building of the Communist era and hence the resilience of the 'Chinese characteristics'. Moreover, the deeper values have a surprising residual influence and as the Party's role weakens, they spring back to the forefront.

The period which most affected workplace relations and personnel adminis-tration in terms of institution-building in post-Liberation China, however, was the 1950s. This seminal period set up the key institutions copied, as the Chinese believed, from Soviet example. The Chinese took the Soviet template – they, for example, emulated Soviet personnel practices – but, however, adapted it to Chinese circumstances. The Stalinist paternalist enterprise model became *de rigueur*.

The Chinese worker in the 1950s saw the implementation of the 'jobs for life' and 'cradle-to-the-grave' welfare arrangements, for those working in the urban industrial state-owned enterprises (SOEs). This system was widely known in China as the 'iron rice bowl' (*tie fan wan*) and is now a widely used short-hand term for the management status quo among informed outsiders interested in what is happening in that country (Child, 1994). The system was partly derived from earlier Chinese Communist experience in the liberated zones, and Soviet practice, but in addition may have had roots in Japanese precedents in Occupied Manchuria, as noted earlier. It is clear that there were a variety of influences which shaped the evolution of the 'iron rice bowl', but it had become fully institutionalized by the mid-1950s. Several writers (Walder, 1986; Warner, 1995; Francis, 1996; Lu and Perry, 1997) have perceived the 'iron rice bowl' relationship as 'organizational dependency'. The 'mind-sets' associated with this dependency became deep-rooted and, we will argue, difficult to modify or change. Even so, with the beginnings of reform, the guarantees of the 'iron rice bowl' began to be eroded (Chan, 1995; Cook and Maurer-Fazio, 1999).

Organizations in the PRC tend to be strongly hierarchically-based (another example of the cross-segmental characteristics) in spite of the allegedly egalitarian practices of the Maoist period. Empirical evidence such as found in Laaksonen's (1988) empirical work, one of the pioneering Western pieces of management research in the field, suggests that Chinese enterprises score comparably on orga-nizational variables with many European ones as far as hierarchy is concerned but may be more centralized in many decision-making areas. Top managers in China, for example, kept more decisions in their hands than their counterparts in Europe and even Japan (ibid.: 300). He found clear evidence of 'one-man management' at the time. Interest groups in the Chinese enterprises had less influence than elsewhere. In the late 1980s, managers in Chinese state-owned enterprises gained additional autonomy in investment, personnel and marketing decisions. Hierarchical determinants were later blended with greater market influences (Child, 1994: 103–105). Even so, hierarchical characteristics arguably do still prevail, related to the older, Confucian structures on to which the model copied from the Soviet Union in the 1950s was grafted, albeit with varying degrees of adaptation.

Workers in state-owned plants were enrolled in the only trade union at hand, namely the All-China Federation of Trade Unions (ACFTU) with its 100 million plus members (see Chan, 1995). Since there was often no alternative to being a union member, it is often said that there was widespread passivity rather than activism for most of the time. China's trade unions are, on paper at least, the largest in the world in terms of their membership. They have currently over 103 million members in all, belonging to the official state-sponsored union federation, in more than 586,000 primary trade union organizations. This was (and still remains) the only body permitted to represent Chinese workers since the 'Liberation' (when the Communists took power nationally) in 1949; independent unions may not freely organize; if they do, they are suppressed. There is also no 'right to strike' and the hypothetical 'right' to do so was deleted from the Chinese Constitution in 1982; but there is an elaborate arbitration and conciliation machinery for dealing with whatever disputes occur. Since the rate of unionization varies between one SOE and another, one may rightly conclude that membership, while socially encouraged, is not mandatory. Indeed, the Trade Union legislation of 1993 gives the worker scope to opt out. Even so, many of the state-owned plants have ACFTU union membership of as much as 100 per cent; the average is held to be 92 per cent. It is also worth noting that only full-time urban industrial workers are permitted to join unions, as opposed to temporary workers or peasants. The ACFTU therefore in principle mostly represents the so-called 'avant-garde' of the working class, rather than all Chinese workers, irrespective of the sector of the economy in which they are to be found, with the vast agricultural part excluded.

It is stated in the Constitution of the ACFTU that:

> membership in trade unions is open to all manual and mental workers in enterprises, undertakings and offices inside China whose wages constitute their principal means of livelihood and who accept the Constitution of the Chinese Trade Unions irrespective of their nationality, race, sex, occupation, religious belief or educational background.
>
> (ACFTU Constitution, 1993; see Ng and Warner, 1998)

The ACFTU was set up in 1925, although the earliest labour congress had met in 1922. This set an organizational pattern which continues to the present day of organizing workers on industrial lines, although there were also to be occupational groupings. After 1949, this industrial logic prevailed and was perpetuated in the Trade Union Law of 1950, the first in the Chinese Communist state, which systematized the trade union structure and the ACFTU was designated as its highest body.

At the time, the Soviet Union was China's role-model and the ACFTU was designed as on Leninist lines. It was supposed to be a 'transmission belt' between the Party and the 'masses'. This relationship was explicitly stated. Trade union organizations, at least *prima facie*, represented the institutionalized power of the workers as 'masters' (*zhuren*). They not only had the role of assisting enterprise management to boost production output (and this was a persistent theme through most of the unions' existence in the PRC, including the present) but were also to help them provide adequate collective welfare services, and to organize workers and staff in spare-time cultural and technical studies, vocational training and recreational activities. To this end, they had – and still – retain, considerable funds since enterprises deduct 2 per cent of payroll for ACFTU welfare and associated purposes. However, it should be pointed out that their growth in the 1950s was short-lived, for although they had succeeded in building up their membership and expanding the number and scale of their primary union units, they were formally dismantled during the Cultural Revolution in 1966.

With the onset of the economic reforms at the end of the 1970s, the All-China Federation of Trade Unions (ACFTU) workers' organizations were encouraged to become more involved in promoting economic development and maintaining social stability (White 1996; Ng and Warner, 1998). The trade union structure was formally re-introduced in 1978, through the influence of Deng Xiaoping. It gradually built up its influence over the 1980s, helping to support the economic reforms. Today, its goals remain consistent with those laid down in 1950, at least on paper. It is worth noting that the 'right to work' is still included (unlike the 'right to strike') in its goals, although many Chinese workers are being 'downsized', particularly in the SOEs (see Lee *et al.*, 1999) where trade unions are most strongly represented and when 'unemployment' is no longer a phrase used only in Western capitalist economies.

Worker representation, such as it was, was integrally linked with the above institutional framework of the 'iron rice bowl'. Wages were predictable under this pre-reform system; the pace of work steady; dismissals were rare (see Takahara, 1992). Everyone, there it was said, ate 'out of one big pot' (*daguo fan*); incentives were minimal in many plants. In fact, in reality only about one in seven Chinese workers out of the huge workforce, whether urban or rural, enjoyed this protected status, some with greater protection than others. Whether the other workers were quite happy with this scheme of things is hard to say. They were probably not but it is indeed hard to generalize about 'the workers' as such anyway. For many years, independent studies of these living and work conditions were not possible. Those in SOEs and urban collectives appeared at least to have a relatively cosseted life until fairly recently, compared with those in the villages and the peasants on the land.

Business environment

The Open Door policy which Deng initiated in 1979 set in train a major change in the business environment and a process of modernization. It was to attempt to set up a novel yet hybrid formula of 'market socialism' in the early 1980s, which was to link the PRC with the international community, particularly by building up trade with the outside world and inaugurating the 'Four Modernizations', noted earlier. Numerous economic, ideological, legal, political, social and other reforms followed, allowing China to 'evolve' into an increasingly market-driven but still nominally 'socialist' state, run by the Party. This state of affairs may be contrasted with that in the former Soviet Union which pursued a pluralistic path, albeit with limited results, in both its economic and political domains (see Nolan, 1995). Deng, until his death in 1996, went on to take an essentially pragmatic route, unlike his predecessor.

An important feature of the transformation in the Chinese economy leading to the latest policy initiatives has been the enterprise and labour reforms that had largely occurred in the 1980s and 1990s, directed at phasing out the 'iron rice bowl' which we have discussed above, in particular the 1992 personnel reforms and the 1994 Labour Law, which placed most key labour regulations and sub-legislation in one document (see Josephs, 1995). This latter piece of legislation is an all-encompassing, portmanteau codification of items relating to employment contracts (both individual and collective), industrial disputes, health and safety, industrial disputes, workers' welfare, and so on, under thirteen headings (see Warner, 1995). There is little significant legislation affecting workers not covered by this, although the Ministry of Labour issues new regulations quite frequently.

The lifetime employment system was generally believed by economists to be associated with weak people management and to remove factor mobility and efficiency (Warner, 1995). The general view of such economists working on China as an academic field of study was that the status quo which Deng attempted to reform was highly wasteful and was holding back economic development. He set in train the management initiatives of 1984, for example, particularly with the 1992 personnel reforms. Managers were now allowed more autonomy, particularly in SOEs to hire and fire; decision-making was to become more decentralized in not only personnel but also marketing and purchasing domains. The most important reforms were certainly designed with factor rigidities in human resources allocation in mind.

Already, many joint ventures and non-state-owned firms had incorporated new personnel practices into their own management systems. Most foreign-funded, as well as town and village (as well as privately owned) enterprises had much more autonomy in their people management compared to their state-owned equivalents. This was to unleash motivational energies, for example, as rewards became more performance-linked. Under the old system, it was said 'we pretended to work and they pretended to pay us' (anon). A Western-inspired workplace practice, amidst all this, adopted nation-wide since the mid-1980s, has been the implementation of 'labour contracts' (see Korzec, 1992; Warner and Ng, 1999). By defining the duration of the contract, the period of employment is sharply defined and hence displaces, by implication, the previously enshrined practice of permanent 'lifetime employment'.

Parallel wage system reforms have also been in process since the latter half of the 1980s, as the state's centrally administered pay grade hierarchy withered away, giving way to enterprise-specific wage adjustment processes. Performance-based pay has also been popularized recently, either to supplement or to replace the existent system of seniority pay. At the same time, both the Party and the Labour Ministry have withdrawn from a direct role, leaving these matters to be dealt with by enterprises at their management's discretion.

Business sector

The question of business sector relates to the differential diffusion of new management practices in China. The growth of joint ventures with foreign firms, for example, has led to the inflow of new personnel and HR practices into Chinese enterprises.

Foreign capital has poured in on a large scale over the last two decades, much of it from the Overseas (*Nanyang*) Chinese but substantial amounts also from the West and Japan, aimed at facilitating 'technology transfer' and more efficient management practices (see Child, 1994). The Chinese market retained a fatal attraction for such foreign capital, even if many companies were disappointed with profits, if any, they were able to repatriate from those investments. Although progress towards a more open form of market socialism has not advanced in a straight line, China was acclaimed by the end of the 1990s as a potential economic 'superpower', by economists in the International Monetary Fund, the World Bank and similar global institutions. This new policy was essentially 'top-down' and was largely engineered by the state. The pervasive theme on its human resources agenda has been a serious attempt to get rid of the personnel system of centralized and permanent allocation to the employing units inherited from the pre-reform era and to institute, in its place, a nascent labour market (see Warner, 1995).

The move from the pre-reform configuration to the reform agenda is set out in Table 2.2. However, the emergent pattern of economic and labour relations in post-reform China here features a character of 'dualism', with a boundary commonly drawn between the sector predominated by the multinationals and

Table 2.2 The Chinese industrial and labour relations system

Pre-reform model	Post-reform model
State ownership	Diffused ownership
Resource-constrained	Market-driven
Technical criteria	Allocative efficiency
Economic cadres	Professional managers
Iron rice bowl	Labour market
Jobs for life	Employment contracts
Work assignment	Job choice
Personnel administration	Human resource management
Egalitarian pay and perks	Performance-related rewards
Enterprise-based training	External courses
Company flats	Rented housing market
In-house social services	External social provision
Free medical care	Contributory medical insurance
Central trade union role	Weaker union influence
High institutional dependency	Low institutional dependency

capital investment from overseas, generally labelled as the foreign and overseas-funded sector and an essentially 'home' sector of the state-owned enterprises (see Goodall and Warner, 1997).

We have tried in a recent article (Ding *et al.*, 2000) to empirically show where and how these mixes of personnel management and HRM occurred, using a substantial sample of 62 enterprises, half state-owned enterprises and half joint ventures. The following main points emerged:

1   First, there are significant differences in HRM practices between firms of different ownership. Joint venture partners did have a positive impact on the changes in HRM practices in Chinese enterprises. Recent years have witnessed a large number of multinational companies entering the Chinese market, concentrating in coastal city areas such as the Pudong district in Shanghai.[1] They have brought into China not only substantial amounts of investment with advanced technology and updated products, but also sophisticated management systems and expertise. Their success and efficiency will, we feel, have an important influence on other domestic firms in changing traditional people management practices.
2   Regional differences were found to be significant with regard to average wages and trade union participation. The speed of convergence of HRM practices throughout the country tends to be accelerated with the removal of the barriers to labour mobility, the development of a mature labour market, and the rapid technological progress in telecommunication, transportation and other infrastructural elements.
3   The larger firms (mostly SOEs in our sample) experienced greater organizational inertia in changing HRM practices. The convergence of HRM practices in firms of different size, we believe, depends on the success of the reform of SOEs that are currently experiencing serious difficulties.

Discussion

With the reforms of the employment system, a new type of human resource management (HRM) came to China in the mid-1980s (see Child, 1994; Warner, 1995, 1999). In fact, HRM was said to be rooted in both Western and Japanese management systems and later adopted and modified in the USA and Europe. In an outstanding text, Mabey *et al.* (1998) offer the reader a model of what they dub 'Strategic Human Resource Management' or SHRM. They sketch out the development of these new ways of managing employees through the 1980s and 1990s and how they are distinguished from traditional 'industrial relations'. They then elaborate how faced with a rapid globalization, Western corporations began to significantly switch their people-managing policies and systematize them in new directions. 'Personnel management' thus gave way to HRM, or even SHRM, particularly as a result of Japanese example. Many US multinational corporations took on a set of practices which were 'a new way of managing', harmonizing human resources practices with the strategic objectives of the organization.

As Poole (1997) indicated, this new and strategic HRM is a relatively new term even in Western society: it only developed in its most recent and best known form in the USA in the late post-war years and arrived in the mid-1980s in the UK and much of Europe. In China, HRM as an academic concept emerged via joint teaching arrangements between Chinese and foreign universities but was also apparent in the management practice of larger foreign-funded enterprises, mainly from Japan, the USA and Europe (Warner, 1992, 1995). It can be distinguished from straightforward personnel terminology as follows. The translation of HRM into Chinese pinyin is '*renli ziyuan guanli*' (with the same Chinese characters as in Japanese) which means 'labour force resources management'. However, many people, both managers and academics (and alas most students) now misleadingly use it as a synonym for 'Personnel management' (*renshi guanli*) and indeed treat it as an achieved practice. The reality is that the older form of PM practice is still more common in Chinese enterprises, especially in SOEs where a decidedly conservative air continues to pervade the administration of personnel. PM is largely the norm even in many JVs, as one HR Director noted 'we are still the policemen of the *danwei*', which meant their role was applying personnel rules and regulations to control employee behaviour. Thus, apart from its usage in the large JVs and wholly owned MNCs in China, it is still very far from the initial concept of HRM as understood in the international academic HRM community (Verburg, 1996; Goodall and Warner, 1997; Pange, 1999). The importance of personnel administration in China, however, cannot be over-estimated. It pervades the residual elements of the *danwei* institutional framework and the mind-set it engendered

The larger foreign-funded enterprises, mostly MNCs, hitherto admired as the pattern-setting employers are in the main the firms practising human resource practices, such as HRM borrowed from the West. In many cases, their HR managers are expatriates or, if Chinese, are recruited from the prestigious MBA programmes emerging in China like the one at CEIBS (the China-Europe International Business School) based in Shanghai. Such graduates speak the language of modern management and, if relevant, HRM. They follow 'best practice' in HRM and SHRM, as exemplified in their own corporation internationally or in other MNCs operating in the PRC. They may of course have to adapt their practices to Chinese conditions but this is the nearest one may get to HRM *in strictu sensu*.

We may here compare the role of Personnel and HRM in China with that in Taiwan, as noted elsewhere in this volume. The People's Republic has also followed the three stages of HRM as set out in Chapter 4. However, there has been a much greater time-lag in the case of China and the earlier stage of personnel management has lingered on longer on the mainland due to the later date of reform. Much of the practice in the PRC follows the first stage of the three noted by Huang (see Chapter 4). There is now a move to the second and third stages but it has been slower.

Conclusion

First, we may conclude that the role of national culture and institutions weighs heavily in the balance when we look at how human resources are managed in the PRC as national culture is pervasive in the Chinese case.

Second, institutions have a crucial role to play because, among other reasons, there is a great deal of institutional and organizational inertia in the Chinese employment system. We have seen the importance particularly of the post-1949 institutions, set up largely in the 1950s. This provided the framework for the 'iron rice bowl' which set the standard for urban industrial employment for many years and is only now being dislodged from the Chinese workplace.

Next, the business environment; here, China has moved from predominance by the state-owned sector to a sectoral pluralism where there are SOEs, JVs and other foreign-funded firms, privately owned companies, TVEs, and so on. The business environment is one of market socialism 'with Chinese characteristics'.

Finally, if we look at the role of the business sector associated with the above, we have seen the specific differentiation of personnel and HR practices in China in recent years. It is clear that there is a strong division between the state-owned and non-state sectors, and within the latter the importance of location, ownership and employee size.

To sum up: since the Chinese working class is after all the largest in the world, at least in sheer weight of numbers, the transformation of their working lives from a planned top-down system to a more market-driven one is clearly of serious concern to anyone interested in this huge country, which has within its borders, one in four of the human race.

Moreover, what happens in China could have huge implications economically, and politically, not only in Asia-Pacific but much further afield in this increasingly inter-connected globalizing society. The state there, as we have seen, is no longer the main employer, is becoming less and less important in the labour market and will be less able to 'organize' workers at arm's length via dependent bodies like the ACFTU as its role becomes more detached.

Outside the ACFTU's orbit, no independent trade unions are allowed; labour dissent is quickly stamped upon. If the official unions do not organize the newly proliferating foreign-financed or domestic privately owned plants, there are no unions at all for growing numbers of workers, as in SMEs in Hong Kong and probably elsewhere in East Asia. Individual labour contracts are already the norm in most Chinese firms, although some workers in the privately owned enterprises do not even have them; job security is basically poor, with a fair amount of temporary posts; welfare increasingly is now becoming the responsibility of the worker (see Warner, 2000).

It is not all bad news but more and more cases of real hardship are coming to light. Since there is a ready supply of migrant labour from the drudgery of the fields into the towns and villages, let alone the cities, employers can easily call the shots. More and more state-sector workers are officially marked out for the ranks of the unemployed in the year 2000. Conversely, the non-state-sector is expanding, providing more jobs, and is generally in better shape, albeit with sluggish growth in the deflationary conditions of the current economic malaise. The relative change in the balance between these two sets will dominate Chinese HRM for many years to come.

Note

1   A concentration of MNCs in Shanghai earmarks the city as one place where Western-style HRM may be readily found.

References

Asiaweek (2000) 29 May, 26, 91.

Chan, A. (1995) 'The Emerging Patterns of Industrial Relations in China and the Rise of the Two New Labour Movements', *China Information: A Quarterly Journal*, 9 (4), 36–59.

Child, J. (1994) *Management in China During the Age of Reform*, Cambridge: Cambridge University Press.

Cook, S. and Maurer-Fazio, M. (1999) 'Introduction', in Special Issue, 'The Workers' State Meets the Market: Labour in Transition', *Journal of Development Studies*, 35 (3), 1–15.

Ding, D. Z., Goodall, K. and Warner, M. (2000) 'Beyond the Iron Rice Bowl: Whither Chinese HRM?', *International Journal of Human Resource Management* 11 (2), 217–236.

Economist, The (2000) *The Economist: A Survey of China*, 8 April, 18pp.

Fairbank, J. K. and Goldman, M. (1998) *China: A New History*, Cambridge, MA: Harvard University Press.

Francis, C. B. (1996) 'Reproduction of Danwei Institutional Features in the Context of China's Market Economy: The Case of Haidian District High-Technology Sector', *China Quarterly*, 147, 839–859.

Goodall, K. and Warner, M. (1997) 'Human Resources in Sino-Foreign Joint Ventures: Selected Case Studies in Shanghai and Beijing', *International Journal of Human Resource Management*, 8 (5), 569–594.

Josephs, H. K. (1995) 'Labour Law in a "Socialist Market Economy": The Case of China', *Columbia Journal of Transnational Law*, 23 (3), 561–581.

Kaple, D. (1994) *Dream of a Red Factory: The Legacy of High Stalinism in China*, Oxford: Oxford University Press.

Korzec, M. (1992) *Labour and the Failure of Reform in China*, London: Macmillan and New York: St Martin's Press.

Laaksonen, O. (1988) *Management in China During and After Mao*, Berlin: de Gruyter.

Lee, G. O. M, Wong, L. and Mok, K. (1999) *The Decline of State-Owned Enterprises in China: Extent and Causes*, Occasional Paper, no. 2, Hong Kong: City University, December.

Lu, X. and Perry E. J. (1997) *Danwei: The Changing Chinese Workplace in Historical and Comparative Perspective*, Armonk, NY: and London: M. E. Sharpe.

Mabey, C., Salaman, G. and Storey, J. (1998) *Human Resource Management: A Strategic Introduction*, Oxford: Blackwell.

Naughton, B. (1995) *Growing out of the Plan: Chinese Economic Reform 1978–93*, Cambridge: Cambridge University Press.

Ng, S. H. and Warner, M. (1998) *China's Trade Union and Management*, London: Macmillan and New York: St Martin's Press.

Nolan, P. (1995) *China's Rise, Russia's Fall*, London: Macmillan and New York: St Martin's Press.

Pange, L. (1999) 'Human Resistance or Human Remains?: How HR Management in China Must Change', *China Staff: The Human Resources Journal for China and Hong Kong*, V, 8, July/August, 8–11.

Poole, M. (1997) 'Industrial and Labour Relations', in M. Warner (ed.) *IEBM Concise Encyclopaedia of Business and Management*, London: International Thomson Business Press, 264–282.

Schurmann, F. (1966) *Ideology and Organization in Communist China*, Berkeley, CA: University of California Press.

Takahara, A. (1992) *The Politics of Wage Policy in Post-Revolutionary China*, London: Macmillan and New York: St Martin's Press.

Verburg, R. (1996) 'Developing HRM in Foreign-Chinese Joint Ventures', *European Management Journal*, 14 (5), 518–525.

Walder, A. G. (1986) *Communist Neo-Traditionalism: Work and Authority in Chinese Industry*, Berkeley, CA: University of California Press.

Warner, M. (1992) *How Chinese Managers Learn*, London: Macmillan and New York: St Martin's Press.

Warner, M. (1995) *The Management of Human Resources in Chinese Industry*, London: Macmillan and New York: St Martin's Press.

Warner, M. (1996) 'Chinese Enterprise Reform, Human Resource and the 1994 Labour Law', *International Journal of Human Resource Management*, 7 (7), 779–796.

Warner, M. (ed.) (1999) *China's Managerial Revolution*, London: Frank Cass.

Warner, M. (ed.) (2000) *Changing Workplace Relations in the Chinese Economy*, London: Macmillan and New York: St. Martin's Press.

Warner, M. and Ng, S-H. (1999) 'Collective Contracts in Chinese Enterprises: A New Brand of Collective Bargaining Under "Market Socialism"', *British Journal of Industrial Relations*, 37 (2), 295–314.

White, G. (1996) 'Chinese Trade Unions in the Transition from Socialism: Towards Corporatism or Civil Society?', *British Journal of Industrial Relations*, 34 (4), 433–457.

3 Human resource management in South Korea

Won-Woo Park

Introduction

Thirty years of South Korea's miraculous economic development, which began in the early 1960s, hauled the then underdeveloped South Korea (hereinafter Korea) into the ranks of developed countries. As a result, per capita Gross National Product (GNP) was over $10,000 in 1995. However, behind the rapid economic growth lie inconsistencies and irregularities not only in sociopolitical aspects but also in economic aspects. Corporate growth, which had formed the basis of the economic growth, was also full of problems despite its quantitative growth.

Beginning in the early 1990s, Korean firms were burdened outwardly with the need to compete simultaneously with the firms in the advanced countries and of the least developed among developing countries (LDDC) and inwardly with the need to change their organizational structure and human resources systems from the ones fit for rapid growth to the ones for the low growth era. In addition, the increase in income was accompanied by noticeable changes in the mentality and attitude of the people, and since the early 1990s, Korean companies have strived to innovate and transform their HRM systems under the name of 'New Human Resource Management (New HRM) Systems'. Such efforts, however, failed to significantly increase the corporate competitiveness mainly due to organization's feeble attempts at innovation and by opposition from the employees. In these circumstances, rapid economic downturn due to the shortage of foreign currency in the end resulted in the bail-out of Korea by the International Monetary Fund (IMF) in 1997.

The IMF bail-out was an extremely shameful experience for Koreans who had courage and were proud not only of having joined the ranks of developed countries with the most rapid economic growth in the history of the world, but also of having achieved democratization on their own. However, the foreign currency crisis can be regarded as a blessing in disguise since it brought rapid transformation in hard-to-change aspects such as mentality, attitude, behavior and systems. The recent economic trials etched in the minds of the people the importance of competitiveness based on transparency, rationality, and capability, and provided a chance for the people to change their quantity-oriented way of thinking to a quality-oriented one. As people's way of thinking and behavior go through rapid transformation, so do the contents of the organization's HRM.

The aim of this chapter is to explain the characteristics of HRM in Korea. However, as Korea has gone through drastic changes in a short period of time, the present-day HRM in Korea is also going through a significant transformation. The rest of the chapter is divided into four parts; explanations of the past and the present of Korean economy and its companies, internal and external factors influencing HRM in Korea, characteristics of HRM in Korea, and, finally, changes in HRM-related matters due to the recent economic crisis and the outlook on HRM in Korea.

The Korean economy

Past: unprecedented growth

Since the late nineteenth century when imperialism reigned supreme and international politics was changing rapidly, Korea (then Chosun, to put it correctly) chose national isolation and closed the door to foreigners rather than accept the modern Western civilization. In comparison, the neighboring country of Japan absorbed modern civilization from the West with enthusiasm. Consequently, Chosun was relegated to the unfortunate state of being a Japanese colony from 1910 to 1945. After independence, the Korean peninsula was split into two parts due to the differences in ideology of the USA and the former USSR in the Cold War. Shortly after, the country was left in ruins by a war that began in 1950 and lasted for three years. Economically, post-war Korea, was one of the poorest countries in the world. Although it was an agricultural country, most people had rice meals only for their birthday or ancestor worship, and many starved to death.

The late President Park Chung Hee, who came into power through a military coup in 1961, devised a five-year economic development plan to become 'a wealthy nation' and implemented it for several consecutive terms starting in 1962. Succeeding leaders followed such plans, and as a result, Korea's per capita GNP leapt from $82 in 1961 to $10,543 in 1996, the year the seventh development plan was completed. From 1962 to 1996, Korea's real annual growth rate in GNP was 8.41 percent, the highest in the world, and its annual export growth rate was 26.49 percent (Bank of Korea, 2000). Thus, by the mid-1980s, many began to call Korea's rapid economic growth 'The Miracle on the River Han'.

Present: the IMF bail-out and the transition to a developed country

Of the many factors that contributed to Korea's wondrous economic growth, systematic support from the government, abundant cheap labor, and the efforts made by both the company and the employee played the most important roles. This attests to the fact that Korea has the economic system of a typical developing country. However, the democratization movement in the late 1980s resulted in significant wage increase and by the 1990s, Korea's advantage of low labor cost had disappeared. Furthermore, LDDCs such as China and Malaysia started to compete with Korea using the cheap labor strategy, which Korea had used in the past. Consequently, Korea had no choice but to change its economic system rapidly to that of an advanced country. The problem was that before the Korean companies had adapted themselves to the new strategy of placing high quality before low price, the support and protection from the government they had counted on disappeared. As Korea became a member of the World Trade Organization (WTO) in 1995 and the OECD in 1996, the country was forced to adopt a fundamental change in the relations between government and business. And the stark economic reality that soon followed was too much for the weak structure of Korean companies to handle.

In 1961, Korea's per capita annual income was US$82. Since domestic savings were minimal, borrowing money from foreign countries was the only way to rescue the country from extreme poverty. Overseas financial institutions refused to accept the credit of Korean firms at the time, and the Korean government had to guarantee the repayment of foreign loans. As Korean companies gradually gained their international credit standings, the government stopped extending the direct payment guarantees. Korean companies, however, kept signaling to foreign lenders that the government would in effect guarantee repayment, while encouraging these lenders to think of Korean industry, especially the *chaebol* as immune to bankruptcy.

As Korea became a member of WTO and OECD, the Korean government promised that it would refrain from supporting the private business sector by means of unfair practices for the sake of economic development. In March 1997, the new Finance-economy Minister made a strong statement in support of a market-based economy. As a result, international financiers, who had lent money to the Korean *chaebol* despite their average debt-equity ratio of 450 percent, were forced to reconsider their lending activities after such a strong stand advocated by Korea's top economic policy-maker.

The bankruptcy of Kia Motors, the Hanbo Group, and their subcontractors in 1997, served as a clear warning to foreign financial institutions. Now the time had come for these foreign financial institutions to apply to Korean companies the same credit conditions as are applied to companies in the developed countries. Not being able to simply rely on the government's repayment guarantees, the lenders will have to seriously evaluate the creditworthiness of potential borrowers. In particular, lenders will closely examine a company's debt-equity ratio. As of 23 November 1997, the day that the Korean government requested bail-out from the IMF due to the shortage of foreign currency to repay its debt, none of Korea's thirty largest *chaebols* have maintained a debt-equity ratio below 150 percent – a ratio kept by international 'blue chip' companies (Cho, 1998). Since then Korean companies have had to go through a severe financial restructuring and structural reform to increase their debt-equity ratio and to fulfill the requirements asked by the IMF. Due to the foreign currency crisis, the exchange rate of Korean won to one US dollar rose from 761.12 in October 1997 to 1,512.22 in December 1997. This caused the plunge of per capita GNP of Koreans from $10,543 in 1996 to $9,511 in 1997. Korea had to experience a falling growth rate (6.0 percent in 1997 and −5.8 percent in 1998) for the first time since the end of the Korean War in 1953 (Bank of Korea, 2000).

However, despite the evaporation of self-confidence, the crisis was an opportunity for Koreans to rethink the importance of frugality, competence, and international competitiveness. Millions of Koreans stood in lines to hand over their gold jewelry to boost foreign reserves. Thanks to the efforts of Koreans, their nation is expected to graduate from the IMF bail-out in the shortest time period in IMF history. Just two years after Korea received the bail-out loan from the IMF, foreign exchange holdings rose from US$3.94 billion (in December 1997) to US$61.9 billion (in December 1999), and 68.71 percent of the money borrowed from the IMF was repaid in less than one year while the economic growth rate reached 10.7 percent in 1999 (Bank of Korea, 2000).

The Korean corporations

Past: chaebol-*centered external expansion*

Despite the fact that strong leadership with a stable political environment, sound economic planning by the government, and the high productivity of abundant well-educated, low-cost workers were important elements in the remarkable economic growth of Korea, the efforts of the private business sector, especially those of the *chaebols* have often been cited as the real catalysts in Korea's economic success (Kang, 1996; Lee and Yoo, 1987; Lee *et al.*, 1991; Steers *et al.*, 1989).

A *chaebol* is a family-owned and managed business group consisting of large companies in many diversified areas (Yoo and Lee, 1987). Although similar in structure, Korean *chaebols* are somewhat different from either *zaibatsu* or *keiretsu* of Japan (*zaibatsu* first appeared when Mitsubishi was formed in 1893) in terms of ownership, culture, and strategy (Lee *et al.*, 1991). Although the oldest *chaebol* (i.e., Doosan) was founded in 1896, most big *chaebols* of today were formed around the middle of the 1950s. The Japanese occupation of Korea from 1910 to 1945 stifled any potential entrepreneurial class in Korea, and the Korean War had devastating effects on all sectors of Korean society. Not until Korea began its economic development plan in the early 1960s did entrepreneurial power first emerge in Korea (Kang, 1996).

Since the total sales of top thirty *chaebols* account for 91.85 percent of Korean GDP, and the total exports by the five largest *chaebols* (i.e., Samsung, Hyundai, LG, Daewoo, SK) constitute 54.4 percent of all Korean exports in 1998 (Bank of Korea, 2000), it is clear that the state of the Korean economy reflects the success of the *chaebols*. Therefore, the history of Korea's economic development is itself the history of the development of the *chaebols*.

However, the growth of the *chaebol* is often criticized since it focused more on quantity than on quality. As mentioned above, none of the top thirty *chaebols* maintained a debt-equity ratio below 150 percent as of December 1997. The 'octopus arm'-style expansion of most *chaebols* has been largely based on government policy, with the primary goal of increasing total sales volumes rather than profitability (Lee *et al.*, 1991).

Present: increased focus on competitiveness and profitability

The main reasons for the IMF bail-out of the Korean economy are government's misjudgment in policy, people's over-expenditure, the labor unions' demands for higher wages and extreme activities, and the management's errors in decision-making. The present debt-dependent financial structure of Korean companies is the product of thirty-six years of government policy that encouraged private companies and financial markets to depend on foreign loans as a means of achieving artificially high growth in the absence of sufficient domestic capital. In fact, it would otherwise have been impossible for Korea to rise from the level of a least-developed economy to a middle-income economy, with a per capita income of $10,000, within a span of a single generation (Cho, 1998).

Korean companies weakening of competitive power, however, had been already cited as a source of problems in the late 1980s when wages began to rise. Therefore, by the early 1990s, many of the Korean companies were already striving for transformation though the transformation during this period was a little different in its nature and effects from that of the late 1990s after the IMF bail-out. The transformation of the early 1990s was a voluntary one from within, in order to adapt to the external environment, and the tendency was to leave the size of the organization and the human resource alone while transforming the structure and the system by blending what was from the West with that from the East. This resulted in slow changes and superficial effects. On the contrary, the transformation in the late 1990s was in part self-imposed and in part mandatory, bringing about in a very short period of time not only corporate financial restructuring and structural reform, but also fundamental changes in the mentality and attitude of the employees. It is characterized by the adoption of management practices that are generally based on Western (especially American) principles. In sum, the innovation of Korean companies started in the early 1990s, and the speed and depth of the innovation were expedited by the foreign currency crisis.

Korean companies underwent significant changes in their fundamental approach to management in the early 1990s. This grew out of the turmoil (following the democratization) of the late 1980s and the need to reshape organizations for quicker responses to changes in the business environment.

The example of Samsung is worth looking at in this regard. Samsung was one of the first companies to start the innovation of the early 1990s. In 1993, Chairman Lee challenged his managers to prepare themselves for major, sustained organizational change. Lee argued that if Samsung wished to survive to the year 2000, it would have to increase its efforts in globalization, product innovation, and quality management. Only first-class companies will survive, he said. How does a company become first class? According to Lee, by emphasizing quality over quantity, by reaching out to every corner of the globe, and by having good timing. Then in 1994, Chairman Lee announced a reduction of the number of corporate subsidiaries by half and a reorganization of Samsung's diverse business activities into four core sectors: electronics, machinery, chemicals, and finance and insurance.

The chairman of each core subgroup was given wide-ranging autonomy. Lee said such dramatic changes were necessary if the company was to compete effectively in the twenty-first century, adding, 'Change everything but your wives and children.' Everything was to be questioned. Usually, managers had typically remained at work until after 10 p.m. each evening; Lee decreed that everyone had to leave the building by 4 p.m., after only eight hours at work. Anyone found in the building after 4 o'clock risked termination. Lee also decreed that making defective parts was 'a cancerous and criminal act on the part of management'. And above all, Lee insisted that all employees undergo what he called a 'mind reformation' to become more creative and global in their thinking (Ungson *et al.*, 1997).

Despite the efforts to innovate themselves, Samsung had to experience a serious economic crisis as did all the other Korean companies. However, with the eruption of an economic crisis and the borrowing of bail-out money from the IMF, the corporate strategy of most Korean companies has changed dramatically. For example, many companies have changed their focus from sales volume to profitability. Putting profitability before gross sales is basic business common sense in the West but it was a radical concept for most Korean companies, which for decades had been obsessed with market share and setting production and export records.

Samsung Electronics, which set a record-breaking profit in 1999 after showing a deficit for three consecutive years, attributes its remarkable corporate comeback to the Presidents Yun's profits-first decree. Since Yun took the helm of the sprawling Samsung Group's electronics businesses in January 1997, he has been reversing many practices that have long characterized Korea's *chaebols*. Samsung Electronics has dramatically reduced its debts, sold or spun off dozens of assets unrelated to its core businesses, set up financial and managerial fire walls between itself and other Samsung companies, and cut a third of its workforce (Moon and Engardio, 1999).

While Korean companies were going through corporate financial restructuring and corporate structural reform, tens of thousands of employees were laid off from banks, which were known for their job security. Furthermore, Daewoo, the third-largest *chaebol* in Korea went bankrupt. All these phenomena have had a great impact on the mentality of Koreans, and there has been a tremendous decrease of loyalty towards the organization as the myth of lifelong employment was shattered. Therefore, HRM in Korean companies is also experiencing a great change within a short period of time.

Factors affecting HRM in Korea

Many variables could have had an effect on the characteristics of HRM in today's Korea. Broadly, they are divided into external and internal factors.

External factors

This section discusses Korea's national culture, labor force, industrial structure, government–business relationship, labor union, labor laws, and vocational education and training set-up and their impact on Korean HRM.

National culture

Twenty-six percent of Koreans are Christians (National Statistical Office, 1998a). The largest church in the world is located in Seoul. Nevertheless, Christianity may not yet have had a profound impact on the formation of characteristics of the Korean people (Chang and Chang, 1994).

Both Buddhism and Confucianism have been generally accepted as religions in Korea and have become an integral part of the lives of the Koreans, but there is a major difference between them: Buddhism is understood and practiced as a pure religion while Confucianism is understood more as a moral philosophy with moral teachings. Confucianism is associated more with the contemporary world, rather than emphasizing the afterlife. Having a meaningful, moral, and virtuous life in this world is an end itself; it does not serve as a precondition to the life after death. Shamanism has been integrated into the lives of the Koreans through ancestor worship. Koreans, as living offspring, accept blessings in return from the spirits of their ancestors. The practice of shamanism in Korea shows the importance of the family system, which was emphasized and integrated fully into the teachings of Confucianism. Koreans are one of the most family-oriented people in the world. Maintaining family tradition and enhancing family prestige are the most important obligations to each family member. Although Korean Christians formally discontinue this process of shamanism ritual, they still informally maintain the tradition of ancestor worship.

It is difficult to understand the Korean management system clearly without understanding the importance of its family system. Koreans work for their business to preserve their family tradition and to enhance their family prestige through successful businesses. Through the ancestor-worship ritual, the living offspring proudly report to their ancestors of their success and thank the spirits for their blessings. As was mentioned above, the teachings and the value system of Confucianism have prevailed in the minds of Koreans. This means that Confucianism has been accepted as a set of moral teachings and ethical values, but not as a religion. Based on Confucianism, Korean society has the following characteristics: orderly society (understanding and maintaining your position in society); free society (no religious caste system, no food restrictions except for health reasons, ability and determination determine your ultimate rank); family-oriented society (filial piety to your parents, loyalty to superiors, paternalistic society); group-oriented society (individualism in a group setting, *hwa* [harmony] among members); and education-oriented society (career success = f [level of education] mentality, respect for scholars) (Chang and Chang, 1994).

Labor force

The economic growth of Korea has been built on a foundation characterized by an abundance of human resources and a scarcity of natural resources. Korea must import most of the natural resources necessary for its products and exports, and this has served to intensify the need to develop the country's human resources.

South Korea has a population of 46.8 million, and its population density (463 people per km²) is among the highest in the world (UN, 1998). However, Koreans are generally well educated and disciplined. Some 98 percent of Koreans can read and write, 80 percent of the population graduate from high school, and the majority of high school graduates go to colleges (63.5 percent of the graduates) or vocational training schools. Total expenditure for education amounted to 13.3 percent of GNP in 1998 (Ministry of Education, 1998).

In addition to the Confucian culture that emphasizes success through education, military training is known to have contributed a lot to the development of disciplined workers of Korea. A Korean male, unless physically handicapped, must spend about three years in military service. The compulsory military training instills discipline, preparing the young populace to function effectively in a complex industrial society.

A significant trend in the Korean labor force is the increase of women and foreigners. The proportion of women in the labor force has increased from 31.8 percent in 1980 to 39.9 percent in 1998 (National Statistical Office, 1998b) due to the increase in the cost of living, the change of values regarding women's role in the society, the increase in the number of well-educated women, and the Gender-Equality Employment Act.

Many small and medium-sized firms are experiencing a shortage of labor, especially in the so-called '3D (dirty, dangerous, and difficult)' jobs. These jobs are often filled by migrant workers as 'industrial trainees'. Most of these workers come from South-East Asia, and many remain in Korea as illegal immigrants after their 'training' period has expired. There were 266,000 migrant workers in Korea as of December 1997, and 55.6 percent of them were staying illegally in Korea (Ministry of Justice, 1998).

Industrial structure

The core of Korea's seven five-year economic development plans (1962–96) was the stimulation of economic growth through exports. From the outset, economic planners were keenly aware of the need to export manufactured goods to pay for imports of foods, raw materials, and intermediate industrial goods. With the absence of natural resources and a sizeable domestic market, Korea had to depend on overseas resource supplies and markets for its products. In the early 1960s, primary goods such as silk, tungsten, and fishery products were exported. As industrialization progressed, light-manufactured goods such as textiles, footwear, synthetic products, and plywood replaced primary goods. By the early 1980s, labor-intensive light-manufactured goods were replaced by capital-intensive products, including steel products, ships, petroleum products, and tires. In the second half of the 1980s, the export of manufactured goods gave way to the export of technology-intensive industrial products such as automobiles, computers, consumer electronics, and semi-conductors.

The change in Korea's export structure is reflected in the change of its industrial structure. As exports moved from primary goods to light manufacturing goods, and then to capital and technology-intensive products, the proportion of the primary sector (especially agriculture) in the nation's GNP had declined from 41 percent in 1965 to under 7 percent in 1995. In comparison, the manufacturing sector increased from under 19.3 percent to 27.5 during the same period. The service sector increased from 39.7 percent to 65.5 for the same period (Chung *et al.*, 1997).

Korea's industrial structure is unique in two respects. First, the proportion of the manufacturing sector in Korea's GDP is substantially higher than that of other advanced nations in Western Europe and North America, where the manufacturing sector accounts for about 20 percent of their GDP. Only Japan (30 percent) and Germany (22 percent) share a similar industrial structure. Second, the industrial structures in other developing nations normally moved from 'early industries' such as foods and textiles to 'middle industries' such as wood products, rubber products, and chemicals, and then to 'late industries' such as heavy machinery, metal, and petro-chemical products (Chenery and Taylor, 1968). Korea, however, moved from the early industries directly to late industries as a result of the government's heavy and chemical industries drive in the 1970s (Song, 1997).

Government–business relationship

The phenomenal growth of the Korean economy since the early 1960s was the result of the joint effort of the government and business. The government planned for the economy, and business implemented these plans. Thus, there was a strong tie-up relationship between the government and business. However, this government–business relationship was not reciprocal. The government leaders exercised great control over the economy, but the businessmen had little impact on politics. This phenomenon is still true today. Traditionally, Koreans have observed a culture based on the mentality 'government officials first, and the civilians last', and the Korean government has had undisputed authority over business.

The government's supremacy was particularly evident between the 1960s and the 1980s as the government implemented successive five-year economic plans that produced the so-called 'miracle on the River Han'. In order to achieve rapid economic growth under 'guided capitalism', the Korean government has adopted a policy of concentrating wealth in the hands of a few capable businessmen in order to accelerate the saving and investment sequence. This policy, however, also resulted in producing a few wealthy and powerful *chaebols* in Korea during the last thirty years (Chang and Chang, 1994).

It is very difficult for a Korean company to become a *chaebol* without the support of government and political leaders. In a real sense, the *chaebols* are the products of a government–industry mix. It is critically important for *chaebols* to raise sufficient capital in the form of loans from banks. The Korean banking system is under tight control of the government. The simple truth is that one cannot continue business unless one has loans from banks, and one cannot have loans from banks unless one maintains a good relationship with the government; no loans can be obtained without government approval, making *chaebols* and other corporations somewhat at the mercy of the government for their financing (Chang and Chang, 1994).

Labor union

In Korea, a labor union is basically formed at the enterprise level, and workers in a company, regardless of their job categories, join the same union. Local unions in the same industry establish an industrial federation. These federations constitute the Federation of Korean Trade Unions (FKTU). Unitl 1997, the FKTU was the sole national union organization authorized by the government since the 1960s. The Korea Confederation of Trade Union (KCTU), or *Minjunochong*, was not recognized as a legal entity by the government till 1997. Despite allowing many unions at the national level, however, a decision on many unions at the enterprise level has been postponed until the year 2002.

By law, collective bargaining is carried out at the enterprise level, and the KFTU and KTUC propose the general guidelines for their affiliated unions. Because of the in-house structure of labor unions, the influence of these national centers is limited to general economic and political issues, and firm-specific issues are negotiated by local unions. The national and industrial federations can assist local unions in organizing and educating workers in the process of developing bargaining strategies (Chung *et al.*, 1997).

Union membership in Korea was at an all-time high in 1989 when nearly 2 million workers were represented by the labor organization. It was the political events (democratization) of 1987 that had brought about this profound change in the labor movement. Between July and September 1987, there were over 3,200 strikes, more than had taken place in the preceding five years. Most of these were fought over demands for higher wages and the freedom to establish the union of a worker's choice.

In the period since 1987, therefore, the labor union movement has begun to enjoy a quite different sociopolitical environment. It enjoyed an era of reluctant acceptance if not *de facto* guarantee of union organization. In the period between 1987 and 1993, unions, along with other progressive social forces, played the role of a major political force that helped restore democratic rule in Korea. Union activities, therefore, were generally backed by popular support, and carried some political weight as well.

Prior to this change, union membership was largely restricted to production workers. Since 1987, however, union membership has expanded into a number of other industries and occupations. These include clerical and professional employees, the media, primary and secondary teachers and researchers.

Largely due to the unprecedented increase in union membership and the revitalization of its activities that were often accompanied by work stoppages, the organized workers have succeeded in raising their wage on an average of 15 percent a year for ten consecutive years until the eruption of foreign currency crisis and the beginning of bail-out loan from the IMF. The real wage of workers in the manufacturing industry, for example, increased more than two and a half times during this period.

With the rapid increase of wage rates and the accompanying industrial unrest in particular, a wave of hostile sentiment towards the union once again began to build up among business and the conservative political forces. Claiming that in this era of global competition, confrontational type of labor relations could not be afforded, businesses began to advocate a new system of labor relations that would help improve labor market flexibility and put an end to adversarial-type labor relations. Though there were no attempts to amend the Labor Law, the government, by means of adjudication, executive orders and guidelines, once again stressed the importance of issues related to national competitiveness and said they were more important than trade union rights. As a civilian government that didn't need to prove its legitimacy was launched in 1993, the government formally began to reassess its labor policies that had become lenient towards workers' organized activities, to the extent of accepting collective bargaining and workers' collective activities. The government's rhetoric was that in order to maintain the competitive edge in this new world economic order, it was imperative for government to promote the free play of the market mechanism and to minimize all the negative effects of institutions that work against improving the competitiveness of the Korean economy in the global market.

Imbued with these ideas, the government began to introduce measures designed to discourage workers' attempts to organize for collective bargaining. Hence, since early 1990, the official interpretation of the laws stopped supporting the cause of workers and helped to discredit some of the legitimate functions of organized workers. With the change of government policies from protecting workers' rights to overseeing or often discouraging collective activities of the workers in the name of free play of market mechanisms, private firms also joined the campaign to challenge and discredit workers' organized activities.

Largely due to the change in the politico-economic climate, which began in early 1989, union membership began to decrease considerably. It has decreased from 1,932,000 in 1989 to 1,599,000 workers by the end of 1996 and the density from 18.6 percent to 12.2 percent during the same period (Park, Y., 1998).

Labor laws

Most aspects of labor relations in Korea, from minimum terms and conditions of employment to the conduct of collective bargaining, are governed by statute and administrative decrees and regulations. Although violations of mandatory provisions of these laws are criminal offenses punishable by fines and sometimes but rarely imprisonment, Korean employers have traditionally not strictly adhered to the many requirements. However, as the Korean labor movement gathers strength, such violations expose companies to the risk of criminal complaints during periods of labor unrest of collective bargaining.

The main Korean labor legislations are detailed briefly below:

- *Labor Standards Act* (1953) prescribes minimum terms and conditions of employment.

- *Industrial Accident Compensation Insurance Act* (1963) prescribes the mandatory employees' compensation program.
- *Labor Relations Commission Act* (1963) prescribes the formation and operation of the Labor Relations Commission for the security and development of labor relations.
- *Employment Security Act* (1967) establishes placement services and promulgates rules on recruitment.
- *Act on the Prevention of Pneumoconiosis and Protection, etc. of Pneumoconiosis Workers* (1984) describes the protection of employees' health and the promotion of their welfare by identifying pneumoconiosis and employees engaged in dusty work and grants consolation benefits to such employees and their bereaved family.
- *Certified Labor Affairs Consultant Act* (1984) establishes a certified labor affairs consultant system for the smooth operation of labor-related matters and autonomous labor management.
- *Minimum Wage Act* (1986) establishes an administrative body to set minimum wage levels for certain employees.
- *Gender-Equality Employment Act* (1987) generally requires employers to afford equal employment opportunities and treatment to male and female employees.
- *Industrial Safety and Health Act* (1990) establishes the basic statutory framework for the regulation of health and safety in the workplace.
- *Act Relating to Employment Promotion, etc. for the Handicapped* (1990) prescribes obligations of employers who employ a certain number of employees to also employ at a certain percentage of physically handicapped persons.
- *Employee Welfare Fund Act* (1991) grants some tax benefits to a business enterprise making a contribution of 5 percent of its earnings before tax to its employee welfare fund.
- *The Aged Employment Promotion Act* (1991) prescribes obligations of certain employers hiring aged employees whose number will be decided on the basis of a standard employment ratio to the total number of employees.
- *Act on Promotion of Welfare of Workers in Small and Medium Enterprises* (1993) prescribes the systematic welfare activities of small and medium-sized enterprise employees.
- *Basic Employment Policy Act* (1993) describes the formation and the implementation of the employment policy for employment security.
- *Employment Insurance Act* (1993) grants benefits to the unemployed to promote employment and job-seeking activities.
- *Trade Union and Labor Relations Adjustment Act* (1997) prescribes procedures for the formation and management of unions, rules for collective bargaining, lists of unfair labor practices, procedures for governmental mediation efforts and rules on labor disputes.
- *Act Concerning the Promotion of Worker Participation and Cooperation* (1997) prescribes the mandatory formation of labor management councils in companies meeting certain criteria and functions.
- *Vocational Education and Training Promotion Act* (1997) prescribes the matters necessary for the promotion of vocational education and training.

- *Wage Claim Guarantee Act* (1998) establishes the pay-guarantee fund in order to pay retired employees deferred wages or severance pay on behalf of bankrupt employers.   (Park, J.H., 1998; Ministry of Labor, 2000)

Vocational education and training

The vocational education and training system in Korea is divided into two subsystems. One is the vocational education system, which is under the control of the Ministry of Education. The other is the vocational training system, which is under the control of the Ministry of Labor.

The current vocational education is provided by vocational high schools, two-year junior colleges, and polytechnic universities. Vocational high school is three-year educational institutions after six-year elementary schools and three-year middle school. It provides vocational education at secondary level, and is composed of six types; agricultural school, industrial school, commercial school, marine and fishery school, vocational school, and comprehensive school. While curricula of vocational schools are diverse, depending on individual schools or types, in general, the curriculum of vocational schools is composed of two-year school-based learning and six months to one year work-based training. The number of vocational high schools has increased from 605 in 1980 to 771 in 1998. In 1998, there were 960,000 students, which comprises up to 40 percent of whole population of high school students (Jin, 1999).

Two-year junior colleges provide vocational education at post-secondary level. They aim to produce the manpower with strong basic competencies and high technology, which can adjust to rapidly changing industrial society. In Korea, junior colleges were established as vocational schools to correspond to the increased demand for medium-level technicians in the mid-1970s along with industrialization based on heavy industry. Presently, fields of studies in the two-year colleges are humanities, social sciences, natural sciences, arts and physical education, medical and pharmacy, and the teaching profession. In 1998, there were 158 junior colleges and 800,000 students which constitutes up to 28 percent of total post-secondary students (Jin, 1999).

Polytechnic universities aim to provide continuing education and upgrading education for adult workers and thus contribute to enhance the quality of manpower. In 1998, there were 18 polytechnic universities and 15,000 students. In 1998, one-third of the entrants were currently employed and one-quarter were over 24 years.

Vocational training system out of schools is composed of public institutions and private institutions. Public institutions are managed by KOMA (Korea Manpower Agency) under the Ministry of Labor and local governments. They provide diverse training programs, which aim to produce semi-skilled and skilled manpower. Vocational training in the private sector is provided by companies. Companies have a duty to pay 'employment insurance' fees, which are increased by the number of employees. Employment insurance fees are collected and are redistributed to the training programs, which enhance vocational competencies of employees. Those programs are very diverse in terms of training periods. They range from few-day programs to two-year programs.

Private vocational training academies provide supplementary training for vocational school students and vocational training to high school dropouts or adult job changers. In 1998, the number of private vocational training academy students was 58,134 (Jin, 1999).

Internal factors

The internal factors affecting HRM in a company are now discussed, with explanations of the common characteristic of Korean companies, and its hidden background. Korean management style is in the process of change, and the recent developments are summarized below.

Korean management style

The corporate cultures of Korean companies are noticeably different from one another. Any Korean businessman will easily tell the difference between the corporate cultures of the two largest *chaebols* in Korea, for example, Hyundai and Samsung. However, no matter how different the corporate cultures are, there certainly is a common denominator that makes the Korean management style unique.

Based on a thorough review of literature (see for example Chang and Chang, 1994; Chung *et al.*, 1997; Lee and Yoo, 1987), the characteristics of the Korean management style can be summarized as: management by owner-managers, clan management, lifetime employment with some qualifications, interorganizational mobility, based on Confucian work ethics, top-down decision-making, paternalistic leadership, loyalty, individualism in group settings, compensation based on seniority and merit rating, and a close government–business relationship.

One of the unique aspects of Korean management is management by family. Many founder-owners have handed over the company to the eldest son in the family because of their Confucian belief that the company can be managed more effectively with the loyalty of and hierarchy within the family. Also, various social connections based on clan, home town or school have a substantial impact on various levels of relationship within the company.

Lifetime employment is evident in many Korean organizations. However, some of the more talented employees will leave the company to obtain better positions or opportunities elsewhere, especially in the high-tech industry. This can be expressed as a high degree of mobility in comparison to the immobility of Japanese. As a result, the concept of lifetime employment in Korea is quite flexible (Lee and Yoo, 1987).

One of the most striking features of Korean organizations is the high degree of centralization and formalization of their managerial practices (Chung *et al.*, 1997). Important decisions are usually made at the top level, then filtered down to lower levels, and there is little evidence of consensus decision-making. However, there is no visible resistance to this type of decision-making, primarily because of the Confucianism, which entails paternalism, loyalty, and respect for elders and seniors (Lee and Yoo, 1987).

Individualism in a group setting is a unique feature of Korean management systems. Individual aspiration is as important as organizational goals for most Korean employees. In the Korean management system, group harmony or consciousness is strongly emphasized. It is one of the most popular mottos for many organizations. Nevertheless, it is not permitted to stifle individual aspirations in the context of group settings. One of the most important roles of superiors is, therefore, to promote individual aspirations in order to achieve organizational goals (Chang and Chang, 1994).

Hidden factors of Korean management style

In the HRM aspect of Korean management system, relationships of family, alumni, region, and the state (government) are critically important. Without comprehending these relationships, no one can truly understand the HRM of Korean organizations. *Chaebols* and other business and non-business organizations (military, government, schools, hospitals, etc.) have been using these relationships for their survival and expansion (Chang and Chang, 1994).

As part of the Korean management system, family relationship is a critical factor in most companies. In almost all the *chaebols*, the family members of the founders play key roles in the management of the *chaebol*. In most cases, children of the founders hold the key positions in their organizations and one of them, usually the eldest son, succeeds his father once he retires or dies. Sons-in-law, fathers-in-law, uncles, brothers, and nephews also participate in the management of *chaebol*. There are, however, some *chaebols* in which the family relationship is not a crucial factor, but these groups are an exception to the rule.

Schools are important in any society, but in Korea they are crucial. On the whole, a Korean's career success depends mostly on the schools from which he or she graduates. There are a number of very prestigious universities. *Chaebols* recruit management trainees mostly from the graduates of these prestigious universities. Among the top executives of the seven largest *chaebols*, the alumni of Seoul National University account for 62.3 percent, and the three most prestigious universities (Seoul National University, Yonsei University, and Korea University) account for 84 percent of the top executives. This trend also applies to the middle and lower management levels of *chaebols*, although the number of the graduates from other universities has increased among the top executives (Chang and Chang, 1994).

Historically, the regional relationship is extremely strong in Korean society, and this tradition also applies to the management system. Although the importance of the regional relationship has been somewhat weakened *vis-à-vis* family and alumni relationship, it is still significantly relevant in understanding the management of Korean corporations. In many cases, top level executives of *chaebols* are from the same region as the founders. When *chaebols* recruit college graduates, regional relationship is not as strongly emphasized as the capacity and talent. However, college graduates will notice a subtle regional relationship as they climb up the organizational ladder of *chaebols*.

The changes in Korean management style

Although Korea is recovering very quickly from its economic crisis that began with the foreign currency crisis in November 1997, this event had a tremendous impact on people's values, on the policy of Korean government, and on the management system of Korea. Nobody knows for sure how far-reaching these changes will be. However, some very important characteristics of Korean management have already changed.

Koreans have witnessed phenomena they never thought possible in Korea, for example, massive lay-offs from banks and the sudden fall of the third-largest *chaebol* in Korea. After a blood-shedding structural reform, the loyalty of Koreans towards their organization decreased very much. Lifetime employment is no longer taken for granted. Even with the quick recovery of the Korean economy, the newly changed perceptions or values still persist. Therefore, thousands of people have voluntarily left once-admired *chaebols* to start their own business. To stop the brain drain, Korean companies have no other way but to change their long-held HRM systems from seniority-based HRM to competency and performance-based ones.

Korean HRM

A well-educated and diligent labor force fueled the aforementioned rapid economic growth of Korea. However, when one considers how Korean companies had valued their human resources as the core source of their competitiveness, nothing much positive can be said about it. While Korea showed miraculous economic growth, it failed to make significant progress in HRM.

HRM in the 1960s and 1970s was traditional HRM in the primary stage of striving for economic growth through modernization based on traditional sociocultural values permeating society. Though the 1980s witnessed increasing efforts to adopt Western HRM as rapid growth and globalization occurred, traditional HRM was still the dominant management style at that time. Korean companies up to this time considered low wages to be the major business strategy for cost reduction and did not realize the need for human resource development.

Already in the early 1990s, the need for changes in Korean HRM was raised. Korean HRM before then had assumed an ever-growing economy. In a growing economy, unreasonableness and shortcomings in HRM pose little problems regarding promotion and increase in wages due to the increase in the organization's earnings and economy of scale, especially for those who were determined to free Korea from persistent poverty. With low economic growth, however, the organizational growth weakened as well and the opportunity for promotion decreased due to HR backlog. Increase in wages failed to meet the increase in consumption. Furthermore, even though the steep increase in wages after the 1987 democratization was an unsatisfactory one for the employees, the increased wage level was high enough to adversely affect the companies' competitiveness and consequently called for a change in the system under the name of 'New HRM' system (see Bae, 1998 for a good description of New HRM).

As foreign, especially Western (American) HRM spread in the 1990s, a clash with traditional HRM occurred, bringing about a period of chaos due to the lack of common standard. In the early 1990s, many companies adopted results-based performance appraisal systems, ability- and performance-based payment and incentive systems, team-basis slim organizations, recruiting and promotion irrespective of the academic background, and strengthening the specialist training and management education programs, all under the name of 'New HRM'. But in the early 1990s, perhaps due to the afterglow of the economic success in the 1980s, the efforts at transforming HRM were not fruitful since the organization failed to realize the need for change and the employees were resistant to change. Since the late 1990s, the Western HRM system, which is fundamentally different from the traditional HRM of the past, such as early retirement and lay-offs following the IMF bail-out and the introduction of an annual salary and stock options, has been implemented. Since the will of the organization to change is great and the resistance to change on the part of employees is scarce, it is high time that HRM system reform were carried out.

The change in Korean HRM

The transition of Korean HRM up to the 1990s is summarized in Table 3.1. Since the phenomena in the 1990s were very complex and dynamic despite the short timespan, the phenomena will be divided into three stages (Kim, 1999).

Stage 1: 1990–94

After the Korean government's Declaration of Democratization on 29 June 1987, labor disputes that bordered on violent illegal strikes spread like wildfire in all the industries throughout the nation and kept HRM in most Korean companies from changing to meet the various needs of the employees.

In addition, the labor movement spread even to the white-collar workers and the disputes lasted for ten to nineteen days. This resulted in the development of the 'no work, no pay' system. The need for a new pay system arose, as well as the need for the change from seniority-based to ability-based pay system. As the civilian government set out in 1992, the pay system that reflected the military dictatorship till then changed to a new system that put autonomy and harmonious labor relations before everything.

Stage 2: 1994–97

This stage is when the HRM in Korea enters a new phase, for most companies adopted the New HRM as if in competition and introduced the ability-based HRM. This was aimed at proving the past seniority-based system was inefficient

Table 3.1 The transition in the characteristics of HRM of Korean companies

	1960–70s *Take-off stage*	1980s *Restoration stage*	1990s *Transformation stage*
Development stage of Korean economy			
Characteristics of Korean HRM	*Rule under the traditional culture*	*Partial introduction of foreign HRM skills*	*Blending of Western and the traditional HRM*
Job analysis	Concept of job analysis yet undefined	Attempts at rudimentary job analysis	Dispersion of job analysis (Tendency to be misused in the name of staffing and downsizing)
Selection	Selection based on personal connection and academic background	Academic background-oriented public selection	Ability-oriented selection (diversified selection methods)
Performance appraisal	Subjective top-down appraisal	Control-oriented performance appraisal	Diversification of performance appraisal methods and introduction of ability- and performance-based factor
Training and development	Intended to cultivate the employees	Intended to bring up well-rounded employees	Intended to bring up professionals
Promotion	Seniority-based system	Seniority-based system (Need for ability-based system realized)	Efforts at ability-based promotion system (Implementation of selective promotion system)
Job rotation	The concept of job rotation undefined	Job rotation accommodating the superior	Job rotation reflecting partially the opinions of subordinates
Pay	Pure seniority-based pay system	Seniority-based pay system with single pay class	Partial adoption of ability-introduced pay system (annual salary)
Incentives	Non-existent incentive structure	Poor management of incentive system	Introduction of incentive system such as profit sharing
Benefits	Paternalistic benefits	Efforts to increase benefits quantitatively	Efforts to improve the quality of work life through benefits
Outplacement	Non-existent outplacement	Need for outplacement raised	Expulsion-centred outplacement (early retirement/lay off)

Source: Modified from Shin (1998: 200)

without a proper evaluation. However, such task-oriented HRM became person-oriented in the process of implementation while the recruitment and selection of employees were still based on the academic backgrounds of the candidates. Even though the New HRM system boasted that it was based on ability, academic background and seniority could not be ignored in reality. The seniority-based HRM system once again became common and the Korean companies faced confusion in introducing New HRM in their company.

Stage 3: 1998–99

Under the reign of the IMF, HRM in Korean companies lost sight of its way and faced massive unemployment caused by early retirement and restructuring, together with a structure that is costly and less efficient. Thus, the situation called for a new type of HRM that would help to overcome the management crisis.

Some companies were forced to accept the *yonbongjae*, i.e. annual salary system intended to simplify the complicated pay structure and set employee compensation on the basis of job-related skills and performance and retirement system. This instigated labor disputes and HRM in Korean companies became a complex mix of various systems and forms based on customs and the rational HRM system of the advanced countries. Korean companies at present are still without a clear comprehensive HRM system.

Korean HRM in the twenty-first century

The three biggest *chaebols* in Korea (Hyundai, Samsung and LG) announced in December 1999 that they would all be adopting the stock option system beginning in the year 2000. What had been previously implemented only partially in financial institutions such as securities companies and banks or in venture companies spread and such a phenomenon forecasts a great transformation of formerly seniority-based selection and pay systems. Automatic promotions based on seniority or the 'same grade, same pay' principle have been transformed into a performance-based system. This means that the company will give out the fruits of its success according to the contribution of the employees. In addition, colleagues who are in the same field with the same grade will differ greatly in their bonuses based on the contributions they have made.

The reason the big companies want to adopt the stock option system is partially because they would like to raise the efficiency level, but more importantly because they found it imperative to stop the brain-drain prevalent at present. The recent enthusiasm over venture companies caused an exodus of quality manpower from the big companies, all set out to join the small and medium-sized companies or start one themselves. The big companies had been in need of more people so that they could enter the Internet and telecommunications market, but now they are losing their valuable people.

LG Group began to offer, along with stock option, new incentives such as a signing bonus, a special bonus, and a digital bonus from 2000. When the much-needed quality human resource joins the company, the company pays a lump-sum signing bonus that has no upper limit, a special bonus that reflects the performance, a digital incentive that pays out 100 million won (about US$87,000) in one payment to the best performer, and a refresh vacation that offers extra vacation time, also to the best performer. Based on work performance, there is a difference not only in promotion and pay, but also in vacation.

Should such new HRM system be taken up fully by the three biggest *chaebols* in Korea, it is expected that the others will soon follow *en masse*. As a result, American-style HRM system will take root in Korean economy for sure. Table 3.2 summarizes the transformation underway at present.

Table 3.2 Past and future of Korean HRM

HRM element	Past	Future
Selection	Public selection oriented Recruitment of new graduates	Recruitment on the basis of vacancies Recruitment of experienced employees
Performance appraisal	Internal competition oriented For promotion and compensation Top-down goal setting Short-term performance oriented Direct superior	Market competition oriented For leading to achieve business goal Cascading style of goal setting Mid- to long-term performance oriented Direct superior, colleague, subordinate, committee
Reward	Importance of internal equity Individual management of reward factors Fixed-cost characteristic Short-term reward oriented	Importance of market value Total compensation package management Variable-cost characteristic Mid- to long-term compensation mix
Organizational structure and management	Efficiency valued Vertical organization Corpulent headquarters Hierarchical organization Insourcing	Effectiveness valued Horizontal network organization Slim headquarters Flat organization Outsourcing
Corporate culture	Closed and hierarchical Unilateral communication	Open and democratic Real-time bilateral communication

Source: Modified from Kong (1999: 20) and Lee (2000: 12)

The transformation of Korean HRM system is a result of the simultaneous impact of the two forces: the foreign currency crisis and the digital revolution. The former has forced Korean companies to pursue a global standard whereas the latter has called for a fundamental restructuring in the HRM system. The transformation process shows that the importance of human resources as the core success factor of the organization is at last being realized by the Korean companies. If such a transformation in HRM system occurs, Korean HRM will no longer follow the economic growth as it did in the past but will be an engine of growth for the Korean economy and the companies. This will in future make the people realize that the IMF bail-out that succeeded the recent economic crisis, what they had once thought of as a disgrace to the nation, was in fact 'a timely gift from God'.

References

Bae, J. (1998) 'Beyond Seniority-Based Systems: A Paradigm Shift in Korean HRM?', in C. Rowley (ed.) *Human Resource Management in the Asia Pacific Region: Convergence Questioned*, London: Frank Cass.

Bank of Korea (2000) *Korean Economy*, Seoul.

Chang, C. S. and Chang, N. J. (1994) *The Korean Management System: Cultural, Political, Economic Foundations*, Westport, CT: Quorum Books.

Chenery, H. B. and Taylor, L. (1968) 'Development Patterns Among Countries and Over Time', *Review of Economics and Statistics* 50 (4), 391–416.

Cho, D. (1998) 'Korea's Economic Crisis: Causes, Significance and Agenda for Recovery', *Korea Focus*, January–February, 15–26.

Chung, K. H., Lee, H. C. and Jung, K. H. (1997) *Korean Management: Global Strategy and Cultural Transformation*, New York: de Gruyter.

Jin, M. (1999) 'System of Vocational and Technical Education and Training', *Economic Development and Educational Policies in Korea*, Seoul: Korea Educational Development Institute, 99–116.

Kang, M. H. (1996) *The Korean Business Conglomerate: Chaebol Then and Now*, Berkeley, CA: Institute of East Asian Studies, University of California.

Kim, S. S. (1999) 'The Changes and Characteristics of Human Resource Management in Korean Corporations in the 1990s' (in Korean), *The Magazine of Human Resource Management*, September, 14–17.

Kong, S. P. (1999) 'New Paradigm of Korean Human Resource Management and the Global Standard' (in Korean), *The Magazine of Human Resource Management*, September, 18–2.

Lee, J. I. (2000) 'HR Revolution in Digital Era' (in Korean), *CEO Information*, 234, Seoul: Samsung Economic Research Institute.

Lee, S. M. and Yoo, S. (1987) 'The K-type Management: A Driving Force of Korean Prosperity', *Management International Review*, 27 (4): 68–77.

Lee, S. M., Yoo, S. and Lee, T. M. (1991) 'Korean Chaebols: Corporate Values and Strategies', *Organizational Dynamics*, 19 (4), 36–50.

Ministry of Education (1998) *Statistical Yearbook of Education*, Seoul: Ministry of Education.

Ministry of Justice (1998) *Statistical Yearbook on Departure and Arrivals*, Seoul.

Ministry of Labor (2000) Law and Regulations, http:\\www.molab.go.kr (accessed March 2000).

Moon, I. and Engardio, P. (1999) 'Samsung: How a Korean Electronics Giant Came out of the Crisis Stronger than Ever', *Business Week*, 20 December, 44–48.

National Statistical Office (1998a) *Population and Housing Census*, Seoul.

National Statistical Office (1998b) *Economically Active Population Survey*, Seoul.

Park, J. H. (1998) 'An Overview of Korean Labor Law', *Korean Labor and Employment Laws: An Ongoing Evolution*, Seoul: Korea Labor Institute and Kim & Chang Law Offices.

Park, Y. (1998) 'Labor Relations and the Future of Work Society in Korea', paper presented at international seminar on Industrial Relations of Korea, US and Japan, The Institute of Industrial Relations, Seoul National University.

Shin, Y. K. (1998) 'The Evaluation and Prospects of Human Resource Management of Korea' (in Korean), in W. D. Lee (ed.) *Labor of Korea in the 21 Century*, Seoul: Korea Labor Institute, pp. 163–219.

Song, B. (1997) *The Rise of the Korean Economy*, Hong Kong: Oxford University Press.

Steers, R. M., Shin, Y. K. and Ungson, G. R. (1989) *The Chaebol: Korea's New Industrial Might*, New York: Ballinger.

UN (1998) *Demographic Yearbook*, New York: United Nations.

Ungson, G. R., Steers, R. M. and Park, S. (1997) *Korean Enterprise: The Quest for Globalization*, Boston: Harvard Business School Press.

Yoo, S. and Lee, S. M. (1987) 'Management Style and Practice of Korean Chaebols', *California Management Review*, 24 (4), 95–110.

4 Human resource management in Taiwan

Tung-Chun Huang

Socio-economic and cultural background

The island of Taiwan is located at the western edge of the Pacific Ocean, adjoining Japan in the north and the Philippines in the south. Although only 36,129 square kilometers in area, Taiwan has a population of 22 million, making it one of the most densely populated areas in the world. Lacking natural resources, Taiwan has relied heavily on human resource to develop its economy. As a result of sustained and rapid economic growth over the last five decades, the per capita GNP of Taiwan has risen from US$97 per year in 1950 to US$13,235 in 1999, one of the fastest rates of growth in the world. Taiwan now has transformed itself from an agricultural economy into a newly industrialized economy. Although many factors have contributed to the outstanding economic achievements of Taiwan, the effective utilization of its human resources has been particularly crucial to the island's success (Huang, 1997a).

In the mid-1980s, the global economic boom greatly accelerated the growth of the Taiwan economy and the growth rates were in double digits. The booming export trade spurred on the vigorous development of manufacturing industry, which accounted for 39.4 percent of GDP in 1986 and 38.9 percent in 1987, each a higher ratio than ever before. From 1987 onwards, export expansion slackened while domestic demand strengthened. The dampening of exports reversed industrial growth, resulting in an appreciable reduction in its share of GDP. The rapid expansion of domestic demand had led to the rapid development of the service sector whose relative importance in the economy rose tremendously (see Table 4.1).

The population growth rate during the periods of 1950s and 1960s was very high. However, as a result of the successful implementation of the family planning programs, the rate decreased dramatically to less than 2 percent in the 1970s and kept decreasing to around 1 percent in the 1980s. In 1998 it stood at 0.86 percent. Because of the baby boom in the 1950s and 1960s, the percentage of the population consisting of working-age people has continued to increase. However, it is expected that the ageing of the population will be accelerated in the coming years. The labor participation rate (LPR) was 67.6 percent in 1951, then dropped yearly and remained at 58.0 percent in 1998. While the LPR rate for males showed a downward trend, that for females moved in the opposite direction.

Table 4.1 Structure of industry as percentage of GDP in Taiwan

Period	Agriculture	Industry	Service	Total
1970	15.5	36.8	47.7	100
1975	12.7	39.9	47.4	100
1980	7.7	45.7	36.0	100
1985	5.8	46.3	47.9	100
1986	5.6	47.1	47.3	100
1987	5.3	46.7	48.0	100
1988	5.0	44.8	50.1	100
1989	4.9	42.3	52.8	100
1990	4.2	41.2	54.6	100
1991	3.8	41.1	55.1	100
1992	3.6	39.9	56.5	100
1993	3.7	39.0	57.3	100
1994	3.6	37.3	59.1	100
1995	3.5	36.3	60.2	100
1996	3.3	35.5	61.2	100
1997	2.7	34.9	62.4	100
1998	2.5	34.6	62.9	100
1999	2.6	33.1	64.3	100

Source: Council for Economic Planning and Development, Executive Yuan. *Industry of Free China*, various years.

The employment structure also showed a dramatic shift. Agricultural employment declined from 56.7 percent in 1951 to 8.9 percent in 1998. Industrial employment increased from 16.3 percent in 1951 to a peak of 42.8 percent in 1987, but by 1998 it had dropped to 37.9 percent. Service employment has grown at a relatively stable pace over the years. It has been the largest share since 1988, increasing its share of total employment from 27.0 percent in 1951 to 54.5 percent in 1999 (see Table 4.2).

The average monthly working hours of all industry decreased from 203.9 in 1985 to 190.6 in 1998. The average monthly earning in manufacturing increased from NT$253 in 1951 to NT$37,686 in 1999 (see Table 4.3). The fast growth of labor cost resulted in the decline of the manufacturing sector, especially the labor-intensive companies. Many of them transferred the whole plant to Mainland China or South East Asia countries and some of them were switched from labor-intensive to technology-intensive production.

After stabilizing at around 4 percent in the early 1960s, Taiwan's unemployment rate by the late 1960s had fallen to below 2 percent. During the twenty-five years that followed, Taiwan enjoyed a very low unemployment rate. However, unemployment jumped to 2.60 percent in 1996 and remained at 2.69 in 1998. Underemployment is another important issue of human resource development in Taiwan. As shown in Table 4.4, between 15.0 percent and 27.4 percent of the labor force in Taiwan was underutilized during the period 1977 to 1998. Low productivity and lack of skills are the two chief reasons for inadequate pay. Mismatch between occupation and educational attainment was the second reason for inadequate utilization.

Table 4.2 Employed people by industry structure

Period	Agriculture, forestry and fishing (%)	Industry (%)	Service (%)
1951	56.7	16.3	27.0
1960	50.2	20.5	29.3
1970	36.7	27.9	35.3
1980	19.5	42.5	38.0
1985	17.5	41.6	41.0
1986	17.0	41.6	41.4
1987	15.3	42.8	42.0
1988	13.7	42.5	43.8
1989	12.9	42.1	45.0
1990	12.9	40.8	46.3
1991	13.0	39.9	47.1
1992	12.3	39.6	48.0
1993	11.5	39.1	49.4
1994	10.9	39.2	49.9
1995	10.6	38.7	50.7
1996	10.1	37.5	52.4
1997	9.6	38.2	52.3
1998	8.9	37.9	53.2
1999	8.3	37.2	54.5

Source: Council of Labor Affairs, Executive Yuan, Republic of China, *Monthly Bulletin of Labor Statistics*, various years.

Table 4.3 Working hours and monthly earnings

Period	Average monthly working hrs of all industry			Average monthly earning in manufacturing	
	Regular	Overtime	Total	NT$ *	Increase rate %
1951				253	—
1960				621	1.2
1970				1,553	1.1
1980				8,040	1.2
1985	194.3	9.6	203.9	12,697	4.3
1986	193.5	11.8	205.3	13,983	10.1
1987	193.6	11.6	205.2	15,356	9.8
1988	192.1	10.4	202.5	17,012	10.8
1989	189.6	9.9	199.5	19,461	14.4
1990	187.5	9.5	197.0	22,048	13.3
1991	187.3	9.5	196.8	24,469	11.0
1992	187.1	9.3	196.4	26,972	10.2
1993	187.1	9.2	196.3	28,892	6.9
1994	186.3	10.3	196.6	30,727	6.6
1995	184.7	9.8	194.5	32,441	5.6
1996	184.0	9.7	193.7	33,765	4.1
1997	183.9	10.3	194.2	35,275	4.5
1998	181.0	9.6	190.6	36,244	2.7
1999	180.5	9.9	190.4	37,686	4.0

Source: Same as Table 4.2.
Note: * 1US$=30.5NT$

Table 4.4 Profile of labor underutilization in Taiwan

Item	May 1977	May 1980	May 1985	May 1990	May 1995	May 1998
Labor force (1,000)	5,864	6,566	8,569	8,318	9,158	9,501
Inadequate labor force utilization (1,000)	1,604	986	1,867	1,734	1,544	1,707
As a proportion of the labor force (%)	27.4	15.0	24.7	20.4	16.9	18.0
Inadequate working hours (%)	0.5	1.1	2.7	1.6	2.1	2.5
Too low pay (%)	17.9	7.5	12.2	9.1	7.4	6.5
Mismatch (%)	7.6	5.2	7.2	8.7	5.7	6.7
Unemployment (%)	1.4	1.2	2.6	1.5	1.6	2.4

Source: Directorate-General of Budget, Accounting and Statistics, Report on the Manpower Utilization Survey, various years.

In Taiwan, Confucianism is the cornerstone of cultural tradition. Harmony and consensus are the basic tenets of Confucian philosophy. The principle of harmony and consensus reflects an aspiration towards a conflict-free, group-based system of social relations. In addition, Confucian principles advocate respect for work, discipline, thrift, protecting 'face', ordering relationships by status, duty to family and economic egalitarianism. Protecting face is related to harmony, both emphasize the avoidance of conflict in interpersonal relationships (Pelled and Xin, 1997).

Chinese culture values a strong sense of family obligation. In traditional Chinese business organizations, the decision-making is very often guided by family influence. Employees' attachment and loyalty towards their organizations are very important (Chow, 1994). On the other hand, Chinese managers feel that companies should look after the welfare of employees and their families, and that companies should do as much as possible to help solve society's problems. Chen (1990) suggested that a good manager should follow the guidelines set out in traditional Chinese literature: thus, be morally upright; behave properly as a model for their subordinates; establish rules for their subordinates to follow; have authority and power; be fair in providing rewards and punishment; and create an harmonious atmosphere.

However, the external and internal environment of Taiwanese business has changed dramatically, and the influence of traditional culture seems to be declining. For example, Leung (1995) has suggested that when Chinese corporations increase in size and complexity, their traditional management style might need to change. Merchant *et al.*'s (1995) study suggested that several variables seem to be more important than national culture in explaining differences between US and Taiwanese firms in management practices. These include the company's stage of economic development, the senior manager's education and experience, the company's type of business, and the use of consultants.

Economic development and human resources

The recent economic crisis in East Asia has served to underscore the inherent economic resilience of Taiwan. The economic crisis that rocked the economies of Indonesia and Thailand in late 1997 continued to spread throughout the region in 1998 but Taiwan's economy has shown great resilience. Even though Taiwan's economic growth for 1998 was affected by the financial troubles of Asia, it still grew by 4.8 percent, higher than the other three little tigers (Hong Kong, South Korea, and Singapore).

Many reports have discussed the factors that have contributed to Taiwan's successful results in 1998, despite the economic crisis. Tanzer (1998) stated that Taiwan diversifying its booming high-tech industry has helped it weather the Asian economic storm. He noted that the combination of US know-how and Taiwanese entrepreneurship, engineering and manufacturing skills are creating enormous new wealth on this island. *The Economist* (1998a) suggested a couple of important factors, including a light foreign debt burden, better banking regulations, and a more flexible economy that helped insulate Taiwan from the regional turmoil. Taiwan's educational system has also attracted praise for the role it plays in turning out highly-educated, motivated workers skilled in today's technology (*The Economist*, 1998b). According to statistics, Taiwan spent about 19.5 percent of its national budget in 1997 on education. From another viewpoint, Flanigan (1998) said that the most important lesson for Asia is Taiwan's enthusiastic embracing of democracy. He in particular praised Taiwan's adaptability.

Apart from the successful factors mentioned above, the development of human resources also played a critical role in Taiwan's economic development (Liu, 1998). Using an econometric model to analyse Taiwan's economic growth, Lee *et al.* (1994) suggested that human capital evolution played the most important role in driving growth. Tallman and Wang's (1994) results also proved the importance of labor skill in enhancing growth. Examining industrial development and structural adaptation in Taiwan, Liu (1998) concluded that learning capability and human capital determine the endurance of Taiwan's industrial success.

When we investigate the change of labor cost and productivity of manufacturing in Taiwan, we can find the reasons for success. The growth rate of labor cost in the four years (1995–1998) are all negative (between –0.34 percent and –2.68 percent), while the growth rate of labor productivity is positive and in good shape (between 4.81 percent and 6.97 percent). Labor productivity increases and keeping cost down mean that the effective utilization of human resource has improved the competitive advantage of Taiwanese business in world competition. In an empirical study of the machinery firms in Taiwan, Kao *et al.*, (1996) found that management has a stronger effect than technology on productivity. They argue that the largest holding companies and the international movement of capital and personnel in Taiwan are part of the reasons that pressure firms to formalize and centralize their HR practices.

All this evidence leads us to believe that the practices of human resource management (HRM) in Taiwanese business must have some vital characteristics that we may learn. Therefore this study aims to explore the practices of people management in Taiwan's business sector. Specifically, it examines the following elements: the percentage of time consumption on various HR functions; the influence of HR functions on establishment of policy formulation and execution; the importance of HR activities in contributing organizational objectives; and to what extent has this importance changed? Finally, what are likely to be the most important HR activities in the future?

Development of human resource management practices

In 1973, Negandhi (1973) conducted a study and found that the manpower management practices of local Taiwanese firms were less developed than those of US and Japanese subsidiaries. His findings indicated that in Taiwanese firms no manpower policies were stated and documented, there were no independent personnel departments, rarely job evaluation, no clear criteria for selection and promotion, most promotion based on age and experience, training programs focused on operatives only, and financial rewards were the main incentives. Therefore, he concluded that the people management practices in local Taiwanese firms were unable to effectively utilize their high-level manpower.

In 1985, Yeh (1991) conducted another survey and suggested that the human resource management practice of Taiwanese firms was a kind of mixture of practices that were imported from Japan and America. He argued that local firms in Taiwan have adapted very well in people management and can no longer be considered as the least developed. Yeh also suggested that adaptation and learning from US and Japan subsidiaries have increased the managerial ability of local Taiwanese firms to utilize their human resources.

Recently, Yao (1999) in a keynote address divided the development process of HRM in Taiwan into three stages. Stage I took place before the mid-1960s. In that period, HRM was only a part of the administrative function. Its major responsibilities were attendance and leave administration, payroll and employee welfare, hiring, and performance appraisal administration.

Stage II was from mid-1960s to the late 1970s. In that time, some US multinationals (e.g. IBM, RCA, TI) and Japanese multinationals (e.g. Matsushita, Mitsubishi) established operations in Taiwan and transplanted their home-country personnel management practices. During the 1970s, some informal professional personnel managers organizations were formed to meet regularly to exchange personnel information (Farh, 1995). During this period, the function of HRM was operational and reactive. The major responsibilities were hiring and retention, competitiveness of the job package, providing basic training programs, and maintaining harmonious industrial relations.

After the 1980s, HRM in Taiwan gradually moved into stage III, and some HR departments were even involved in the formulation of business strategies (Yao, 1999). In this period, two human resource professional organizations (the Chinese Human Resource Management Association and the Human Resource

Development Association of ROC) were formed. Both of them organize and sponsor a number of seminars, workshops, and training programs to promote modern HRM practices. In addition, two academic institutes of HRM were established at National Sun Yat-sen University and National Central University, respectively. Both of them offer Master and PhD programs in the field of human resource management. Now, the HRM department in Taiwan business begins to play a stronger functional role. Its major responsibilities include personnel planning and control, management training, career development, and providing advice and counsel for line managers.

The role and function of human resource management

In 1995, this author conducted a survey about the HR role and function of 315 firms in Taiwan. One question asked the HR managers to estimate the approximate percentage of time their departments spent on each HR matter. The result indicates that the greatest area of personnel work on which HR departments spend time is recruitment and selection, accounting for 14.6 percent (see Table 4.5). The second largest area is training and development, around 13.7 percent, followed by compensation and benefit, which spends 12.65 percent of the department's time. Other personnel work such as 'organizational structure and personnel rules', 'performance appraisal', and 'human resource planning' each take 8 to 9 percent of the HR department's time.

Compared to the time spent in different sectors, Table 4.5 shows that the HR departments in industrial sectors spend a greater percentage of their time on 'training and development', 'human resource information system', and 'health, safety and working conditions' than their counterparts in the service sector. On the other hand, the service sector spends a great percentage of their time on 'business culture and organizational morale management' work than that in industrial sector.

As to firm size, the only differences are in the areas of 'job analysis and job design' and 'business culture and organizational morale management'. One interesting finding is that although small (less than 100 employees) and medium firms (100–299 employees) still spend the highest percentage of time on recruitment and selection, the large firms (more than 300 employees) spend most in the area of training and development. This may be due to the fact that large firms can attract more candidates, therefore they can transfer more resources from recruiting people to train and develop human resources.

'Health, safety, and working conditions' and 'industrial relations and grievances' are the only two HR areas that show a significant difference among nationality of capital sources. American-owned firms spent more time handling labor–management relations and grievances than Japanese-owned and local firms. On the other hand, Japanese-owned firms spent more time on the work of health, safety and working conditions than their counterparts.

This author also asked the HR managers to evaluate the rank of the HR activities in terms of their importance to the contribution to organizational

Table 4.5 Approximate percentage of time spent on HR matters

HRM practices	Total	Trade sectors		Firm size			Nationality of capital source		
		IND	SER	S	M	L	TAI	JAP	AME
Recruitment and selection	14.6	14.8	14.3	14.6	15.9	12.7	15.0	15.5	14.8
Training and development	13.7	12.5	15.7	13.0	13.7	14.6	13.3	11.1	14.8
Compensation and benefit	12.6	12.7	12.3	11.9	13.6	11.9	11.8	14.3	12.8
Organizational structure and personnel rules	8.6	8.6	8.6	8.2	8.0	10.1	8.7	7.6	7.6
Performance appraisal	8.3	8.0	8.6	8.1	8.5	8.0	8.1	8.8	8.5
Human resource planning	8.2	8.0	8.7	8.1	8.0	8.6	8.5	7.7	8.3
Human resource information system	6.9	7.4	5.7	6.0	7.0	8.0	7.4	7.0	5.4
Discipline and separation	5.8	5.9	5.6	6.4	5.5	5.4	6.2	6.0	5.0
Health, safety and working conditions	5.6	6.8	3.2	5.6	5.8	5.5	5.2	8.3	5.5
Industrial relations and grievance	5.1	5.0	5.3	5.5	5.0	4.6	4.6	4.6	6.3
Job analysis and job design	5.5	5.6	5.4	6.4	4.4	6.0	5.9	5.2	4.8
Business culture and organizational morale management	5.3	4.7	6.6	6.3	4.6	4.7	5.4	3.8	6.3

objectives; 1 stands for the most important while 12 the least important. Table 4.6 shows that the most important contribution of the HR department to business is training and development, followed by compensation and benefit, and the work of human resource planning third. 'Recruitment and selection', 'Performance appraisal', and 'Organizational structure and personnel rules' are ranked fourth to sixth, respectively. The ranking in industrial sector differs a little from that in the service sector. In the industrial sector, 'Compensation and benefit' is the most important HR function and 'Recruitment and selection' the second. However,

Table 4.6 The rank of the activities in terms of their importance in the contribution made by the HR function to organizational objectives in the last three years

HRM Practices	Rank overall	Trade sectors		Firm size			Nationality of capital source		
		IND	SER	S	M	L	TAI	JAP	AME
Training and development	1	3	1	3	1	2	1	3	3
Compensation and benefit	2	1	3	1	3	1	3	1	1
Human resource planning	3	4	4	4	2	6	4	6	5
Recruitment and selection	4	2	5	2	4	3	2	2	4
Performance appraisal	5	5	2	5	5	4	5	4	2
Organizational structure and personnel rules	6	6	6	6	6	5	6	7	8
Job analysis and job design	7	8	8	8	8	7	8	9	7
Human resource information system	8	7	10	10	7	9	7	5	11
Business culture and organizational morale management	9	10	7	7	9	8	9	11	6
Discipline and separation	10	11	9	9	11	10	10	10	10
Industrial relations and grievance	11	12	11	11	12	12	12	12	9
Health, safety and working conditions	12	9	12	12	10	11	11	8	12

Note: 1 = most important; 12 = least important.

in the service sector, the most influential HR activity is 'Training and development' and 'Performance appraisal' is the second. The ranking order of importance of HR function also differs in terms of firm size and the nationality of the capital source.

Table 4.7 shows that the importance of HR functions' contribution to organizational objectives has changed in the last three years: 1 stands for increase, 0 for no change and –1 for decrease. All the means of listed HR activities are positive. This implies that the role and status of HR department are becoming more important in Taiwan. Among the HR activities, the biggest share in importance increase

Table 4.7 The extent to which the importance of the HR function contribution to organizational objectives has changed in the last three years

HRM practices	Total	Trade sectors		Firm size			Nationality of capital source		
		IND	SER	S	M	L	TAI	JAP	AME
Human resource planning	.67	.68	.65	.64	.62	.78	.71	.39	.68
Training and development	.67	.67	.66	.63	.48	.69	.67	.61	.66
Performance appraisal	.54	.52	.58	.60	.45	.53	.52	.44	.62
Human resource information system	.53	.53	.54	.46	.60	.55	.55	.39	.58
Organizational structure and personnel rules	.52	.54	.48	.48	.49	.64	.60	.41	.45
Compensation and benefit	.48	.52	.39	.48	.45	.53	.47	.36	.61
Business culture and organizational morale management	.44	.44	.47	.45	.41	.49	.45	.10	.66
Recruitment and selection	.39	.41	.34	.29	.46	.42	.34	.41	.53
Job analysis and job design	.37	.36	.41	.41	.32	.39	.38	.19	.26
Health, safety and working conditions	.31	.38	.12	.27	.27	.40	.34	.36	.26
Industrial relations and grievance	.24	.24	.25	.15	.29	.29	.24	.00	.26
Discipline and separation	.18	.19	.16	.15	.17	.24	.26	.04	.05

Note: 1 = increase; 0 = no change; −1 = decrease.

is human resource planning (0.67), training and development (0.67), followed by performance appraisal (0.54). The change in the importance of HR function does not appear to be significant in terms of trade sector, except the increase in health, safety and working conditions is remarkably higher in the industrial sector than that in the service sector. Table 4.7 also shows that the change in the activities of 'Human resource planning', 'Business culture and organizational morale management', and 'Job analysis and design' are significantly different in terms of the nationality of the capital source. In these three HR areas, the increase in the importance seems higher in local and American-owned firms than that in Japanese-owned firms.

The strategic level of human resource management in Taiwan

The emphases in the study of HRM in recent years have shifted from the operating efficiency of individual employees to the managerial efficiency of entire industries. To be effective, HRM policies must be closely linked to human resource systems, and must fit in with the overall aims and functional requirements of businesses (Fombrun *et al.*, 1984; Foulkes, 1986; Kochan *et al.*, 1984; Tichy *et al.*, 1982). Companies that have no definite HRM policy, or that do not take human resources into consideration when selecting a business strategy, are seen to suffer a competitive disadvantage relative to those firms that do (Cook and Ferris, 1986; Gomez-Mejia *et al.*, 1995). HRM literature has recently taken to using the term 'strategic' to describe the type of HRM that makes human factors an integral part of broad-based, long-term planning to implement an organization's aims (Beaumont, 1993).

Recently, discussion of strategic human resource management (SHRM) has been increasing in Taiwan. Several textbooks have also been written on the subject (e.g., Ho and Young, 1994; Chang, 1996), which is gaining importance in the Academy of Management. This growing interest has raised a number of questions, such as: Are strategic concerns given sufficient emphasis in HRM in Taiwan? To what extent is SHRM carried on by Taiwanese businesses? Does the practice of SHRM differ according to industry, organizational size, and the amount of capital resources available?

SHRM implies a managerial orientation that ensures that human resources are employed in a manner conducive to the achievement of organizational goals and missions (Gomez-Mejia *et al.*, 1995). Another critical requirement of SHRM is the full involvement of line departments in HRM functions and activities. SHRM emphasizes close coordination between such internal HRM functions as recruiting, selection, training, development, performance appraisal, and compensation. At the same time, HRM must be integrated with functions external to HRM departments, such as marketing, finance, production, and research and development (Anthony, *et al.*, 1996; Cook and Ferris, 1986).

Fomburn *et al.* (1984) divided firms into operational, managerial, and strategic types, according to the HRM stage of evolution they had reached. Boxall (1994) also classified firms into three types: the operational type; the type which fits with business strategy, and the strategic type, on the same bases. In 1998, Huang (1998) conducted an empirical investigation into the strategic level of HRM in Taiwan.[1] He designated operational firms as those that take little account of human resource when selecting a business strategy and that do not attempt to promote close links between HRM and other functions. Strategic firms are defined as those that give careful consideration to human resource factors in their business strategies and that ensure close links between HRM and organizational goals and priorities. Managerial firms are described as being in transition between the operational and strategic categories.

The results indicated that nearly 44 percent of the companies sampled have HRM practices that are close to the strategic category. Their HRM is closely linked to business strategy, their line departments are fully involved in HRM activities, and there is close integration between HRM and external functions. Another 44 percent are on a transitional path to SHRM but are still far from attaining a strategic orientation. The remaining 12 percent of the companies are still in the functional operation stage: their personnel management is without a strategic orientation at all.

The data also revealed that, although a greater proportion of larger firms adopt SHRM than smaller ones, there is no statistically significant difference according to size. However, this study discovered that the HRM methods practiced by US-owned businesses in Taiwan were more strategically oriental than those employed by Japanese-owned and Taiwanese-owned businesses. This finding implies that the national source from which a firm obtains capital will influence the type of approach it takes to people management.

Why do Japanese firms in Taiwan adopt such a low strategic orientation? One reason may be that the managerial decisions of Japanese businesses are formed by group discussion and consensus, but not in conjunction with any specific business strategy. As a result, their human resource plans lack formal procedures and definite rules. Besides, since employees previously were evaluated on the basis of seniority but not on performance, it was difficult to achieve a close link between HRM and other functions, and the management of people in Japanese-owned businesses remained at the personnel administration level. Regarding the people-management practices of Taiwanese businesses, although some follow the Japanese style, many have been attracted to new HRM concepts recently originating in the United States. As a consequence, the strategic level of Taiwanese HRM practices is higher than that of Japanese-owned businesses.

Training and development

The development of human resources may be carried out, by and large, via two approaches: formal academic education and vocational training. While academic education attempts to convey to citizens a core basis of general knowledge, vocational training seeks to raise the level of workers' skills, making them more employable and better equipped to meet the needs of the workplace.

A nine-year compulsory education program is currently being implemented in Taiwan. Approximately 86 percent of those who complete this program opt to continue their schooling. Those who at this stage wish to seek employment, or who do not intend to pursue higher education, are encouraged to participate in one of the vocational-training programs offered by training institutes in order to acquire specialized skills needed in the job market.

ʃThe types of training can be classified into two categories: public training and enterprise training. Public training is available to society at large, although, in a narrow sense, it is limited to training provided by vocational training institutions. Participants in public training are not pre-identified, and training opportunities are open to the public. Institutional and operational expenditures are borne in whole or in part by the government. The expenses of participants in pre-employment or job-transfer training programs, including tuition, sundry expenses, materials, and insurance, are fully paid by the government (Huang, 1997a). There are currently thirteen public training centers operating in Taiwan, which provide a total of 8,425 public training slots in more than 100 different trades. In 1998, there were 29,823 individuals taking part in public training programs.

A number of larger private-sector business firms have taken the initiative in setting up training departments to conduct employee training. In the meantime, the government, in cooperation with trade associations, has been helping small and medium-sized enterprises to pool their resources and set up centers offering training in various specialties. According to a survey by Huang (1997b), the typical business firm in Taiwan spends an average of US$141,200 annually on training and development (T&D), roughly US$265 per employee. The annual training expenditure per employee in the industrial sector was estimated at US$242, below the US$331 spent per employee in the service sector. Furthermore, the differences in annual T&D spending according to the nationality of firm ownership are significant: the annual T&D spending per employee is US$224 in Taiwanese-owned firms, US$208 in Japanese-owned companies, and US$182 in US-owned firms, respectively.

Training expenditure as a percentage of total staff payrolls is around 2.79 percent for business firms in Taiwan. However, 46.2 percent of firms in Taiwan spend less than 1.5 percent of payroll on T&D, a larger proportion of firms than in Australia (21.0 percent), among foreign-invested enterprises in China (30.1 percent), and 34.5 percent in Hong Kong (Huang, 1997b). This implies that many Taiwan firms must devote more money and effort to T&D if they are to be competitive in international markets.

Findings also indicate that companies provided more training days for managerial/ professional (11.7) and foreman/supervisory staff (9.0) than for manual/technical (6.3) and clerical/staff (7.6) employees. It also shows that firms in the industrial sector provided more training days for their clerical/staff and managerial/ professional employees than the service sector. By contrast, firms in the industrial sector provided fewer training days for their manual/technical and foreman/ supervisory staff than service-sector firms. US-owned companies provide a significantly greater number of days than Japanese-owned and Taiwanese-owned firms for the mean number of training days for foreman/supervisory employees.

Firms in Taiwan collected information on training effectiveness from trainees (97.3 percent) and trainers (92.9 percent), and from trainees' supervisors (88.4 percent). A slightly smaller number of companies received feedback from trainees' subordinates (72.5 percent) and trainees' clients (64.2 percent). The three conventional methods of evaluating training effectiveness were obtaining feedback from questionnaires submitted to trainees (66.9 percent), conducting appraisals of trainee performance (46.2 percent), and interviewing trainees' supervisors (43.3 percent).

Career development and succession planning

Succession planning is widely believed to help business organizations with internal resourcing, to reduce attrition of the workforce caused by job-hopping high-fliers, and to prepare qualified candidates for appointment to senior management positions (Wallum, 1993). It is further known that when organizations fail to treat their succession plans as living documents, they may not only threaten their own continuity but also lose the opportunity to revitalize themselves (Getty, 1993). Even so, succession planning has been slow to take root in traditional Chinese businesses, which have been noted for their informal organization, top-down decision-making, and emphasis on personal ties and relationships. However, rapid growth and increasingly tougher competition may force these firms to change their style of management.

The results of another survey show that approximately one-third of Taiwanese firms fail to adopt any type of formal succession arrangement (Huang, 1999). Respondents cite small organizational scale, lack of a human resources department equipped to handle succession matters, an insufficient number of personnel skilled in planning, and possible negative side effects of the planning process as major reasons dissuading their companies from adopting a plan. The results of logistic regression analysis indicate that the adoption of a successful plan is strongly related to firm size. Firms with fewer than 300 employees are less likely to implement a succession plan than those with a substantially larger workforce; however, once the number of employees surpasses 1,000, further increases in size are seen to have little effect on planning. In addition, the subsidiaries of US and Japanese multinationals operating in Taiwan were seen as more likely to implement a succession plan than local firms were.

Evidence shows that the adoption of formal succession plans is somehow related to management culture. The traditional Chinese management style seems to militate against the adoption of new management practices such as succession planning, especially when they may weaken the paternalistic authority of managers. Even so, this does not mean that Chinese management cannot change. In fact, although proportionately fewer Taiwanese business firms have adopted succession plans than their foreign counterparts, this study finds that up to 60 percent of locally owned firms have already introduced a formal plan. As Taiwanese firms increase in size and are more closely integrated with the global economy, and as the number of publicly held corporations in Taiwan continues to grow, it is expected that the adoption of formal succession systems will become more widespread.

Industrial relations

In past decades Taiwan has been famous for her harmonious industrial relations in achieving successful economic development. Government intervention, cultural tradition, Confucian tenets, social networks, and patriarchal orientation have been claimed to be the major determinants in peaceful labor–management relations (Lin, 1997). Trade unions are regulated by the Trade Unions Act (TUA), which was enacted in 1929 and last amended in 1975. According to the TUA, workers could organize a union where a workplace employees over thirty, and when the workplace has a union, union membership is mandatory for workers.

Trade unions in Taiwan are categorized into two types: industrial unions and craft unions.[2] The organization rate at the end of 1998 is 41.09 percent; however, the rate for industrial unions is only 22.06 percent while for craft unions it is 52.12 percent. Even though craft unions have a higher organization rate, their role in industrial relations is less important. This is because the major reason for a worker to join craft union is to join the labor insurance program[3] which is subsidized by the government (Chen, 1998a). The low organization rate of industrial unions can be attributed to the high proportion of small and medium-sized enterprises and the high turnover rates in business (Chen, 1998b). Furthermore, that unions did not play an important role in collective bargaining and the settlement of labor disputes may be a major reason for this.

The Collective Agreement Act stipulates the rights and obligations of collective bargaining between unions and employers. In 1998 only 300 out of 3,732 unions, around 8.04 percent, signed collective agreements with their employers. One reason for the low percentage is that the Collective Agreement Act contains many provisions that are considered to discourage the development of bilateral negotiations (Kleingartner and Peng, 1991). Another major reason is that the Labor Standard Act has regulated very high working conditions[4] for employees, which resulted in very little room for employers to concede (San, 1993). Even though there is an agreement between union and employer, many union members get only a tiny benefit such as one more day with-pay holiday from the employers. It is suggested that unions in Taiwan are concerned more with the provision of services and social activities for members and rarely involve themselves in collective bargaining or promoting improvements in working conditions (Lin, 1997). Another major function of the unions in Taiwan is to mobilize workers to help KMT (the ruling party) candidates win elections (Chen and Taira, 1995).

According to the Settlement of Labor Dispute Act, labor disputes are categorized into rights dispute or interests dispute. Rights dispute can either be settled by mediation or by the courts. Mediation or arbitration is applied to resolve interests dispute. Before 1987, strikes were illegal under the martial law. After the lifting of martial law, the number of strike is increasing but is still far less than Korea and Japan. Most of the labor disputes are resolved via informal conciliation instead of mediation or arbitration as prescribed by the law. The reason is that the procedure of mediation and arbitration is more complicated than informal conciliation. For example, there were 4,138 cases of dispute in 1998. The highest number pertained to dispute over labor contract (1,945) the second pertained to wages (1,321), while disputes over occupational hazards (493) were the third. Among them, 3,641 were resolved by informal conciliation and 461 were resolved by mediation. Some 86 cases were unresolved. Trade unions do not play an important role in resolving disputes between labor and management (Chen, 1998b).

Conclusion

This chapter aimed to explore the practice of people management in Taiwanese firms. It first presented the socio-economic and cultural background of Taiwan, the Republic of China. The Confucian principles such as respect for work, discipline, thrift, ordering relationships by status, duty to family, and conflict-free, group-based systems of social relation still dominate the working relationship in Taiwanese firms. However, the traditional management style is changing while the corporations increase in size, complexity, and competition from overseas.

HRM practices in Taiwan have been remarkably improved. In 1973, Negandhi suggested that the people management practices in local Taiwanese firms were unable to effectively utilize its manpower. A decade later, Yeh (1991) conducted another survey in 1985 and concluded that the adaptation and learning from US and Japan subsidiaries had increased the managerial ability of local Taiwanese firms to develop their human resource. Another decade later, Huang's (1998) findings show that though there are still 12 percent of firms in Taiwan in the traditional personnel management stage, there are 44 percent on a transitional path to strategic orientation. The remaining 44 percent of companies are closely linked to business strategy, their line departments are fully involved in HRM activities, and there is a close integration between HRM and external functions.

This chapter also presented the role and functions of HRM in Taiwan. Specifically, it examined the percentage of time spent on various HR functions such as the influence of HR functions in the establishment of policy formulation and execution, the importance of HR activities in contributing organizational objectives, and to what extent has this importance changed? It also described training expenditure and provision, career development and succession planning, and industrial relation systems. All of this profiles the current practices of HRM in Taiwan. As to the future challenges, in replying to the question,[5] What are the three most important HR activities in the next three years? HR professionals expressed the view that training and management development, human resource planning, performance management, compensation and benefit, and job design were the most important. Beyond these, some specific HR issues such as HR reengineering, downsizing, flexibility management, expatriate management, and quality of working life were also raised. This shows that the role and function of HRM in Taiwan are becoming more important than before; however, HRM also faces a serious challenge at present.

Notes

1   That study selected members of two HRM professional groups – the Chinese Human Resource Management Association and the Human Resource Management Association of the Republic of China as research subjects. Of the 873 questionnaires sent out to the members of these two associations, the author received 315 replies, for an effective response rate of 36.1 percent. The average number of employees per sample firm was 868. In 36 percent of the firms sampled, employees were represented by trade unions; in 64 percent there was no union representation. Sample firms had been in business an average of 20 years, and the average age of their employees was around 33.6 years.

2 The term 'industrial union' means the union organized by workers of different crafts in various divisions of one and the same industry; whereas the term 'craft union' means the union jointly organized by workers of one and the same craft.

3 According to the Labor Insurance Act, members of a craft union who have no definite employer or who are self-employed shall be insured under this program as an insured person. For them, 40 percent of the insurance premium shall be defrayed by the provincial or municipal government concerned, and the remaining 60 percent by the insured person. Since the labor insurance program is a kind of benefit, many workers who have no definite employers or the self-employed want to be craft union members. Their major aim is to be insured instead of negotiating with employers.

4 In Taiwan, the Labor Standard Act regulates many important working conditions such as circumstances of terminating a labor contract, holidays and vacations, overtime pay, with and without pay leave-taking, compensation for occupational accidents, and retirement payments, etc.

5 Data source comes from the survey mentioned in note 1.

References

Anthony, P. A., Perrewe, P. L. and Kacmar, K. M. (1993) *Strategic Human Resource Management*, Fort Worth: The Dryden Press.

Beaumont, P. B. (1993) *Human Resource Management: Key Concepts and Skills*, London: Sage Publications.

Boxall, P. (1994) 'Placing HR strategy at the Heart of Business Success', *Personnel Management*, July, 32–35.

Chang, H. C. (1996) *Strategic Human Resource Management*, Taipei: Yanze Ltd (in Chinese).

Chen, C.-S. (1990) 'Confucian Style of Management in Taiwan', in J. M. Putti (ed.) *Management: Asian Context*, McGraw-Hill, pp. 177–197.

Chen, S.-J. (1998a) 'The Development of HRM Practices in Taiwan', in C. Rowley (ed.) *Human Resource Management in the Asia Pacific Region: Convergence Questioned*, London: Frank Cass, pp. 152–169.

Chen, S.-J. (1998b) 'Union Loyalty and Union Participation: The Case of Taiwan', *Journal of Labor Studies*, 8, 183–204.

Chen, S.-J. and Taira, K. (1995) 'Industrial Democracy, Economic Growth and Income Distribution in Taiwan', *American Asian Review*, 4, 49–77.

Chow, I. (1994) 'Organizational Commitment and Career Development of Chinese Managers in Hong Kong and Taiwan', *The International Journal of Career Management*, 6 (4), 3–9.

Cook, D. S. and Ferris, G. R. (1986) 'Strategic Human Resource Management and Firm Effectiveness in Industries Experiencing Decline', *Human Resource Management*, 25 (3), 441–458.

The Economist (1998a) 'The flexible tiger', 3 January, 7.

The Economist (1998b) 'Taiwan and the Asian Crisis', 24 January, 66–67.

Farh, J. L. (1995) 'Human Resource Management in Taiwan, the Republic of China', in L. F. Moore and P. D. Jennings (eds) *Human Resource Management on the Pacific Rim: Institutions, Practices and Attitudes*, Berlin: Walter de Gruyter.

Flanigan, J. (1998) 'Taiwan – Asia's Improbable New Strongman', *The Los Angeles Times*, 26 April, p. D1.

Fombrun, C. J., Tichy, N. M. and Devanna, M. A. (1984) *Strategic Human Resource Management*, New York: Wiley.

Foulkes, F. K. (1986) *Strategic Human Resource Management*, Englewood Cliffs, NJ: Prentice-Hall.

Getty, C. (1993) 'Planning Successfully for Succession Planning', *Training and Development*, 47 (11), 31–33.

Gomez-Mejia L. R., Balking, D. B. and Cardy, R. (1995). *Managing Human Resources*, New York: Prentice Hall International, Inc.

Ho, Y. F. and Young, K. A. (1994) *Strategic Human Resource Management*, Taipei: Sun-Min Book Company (in Chinese).

Huang, T. C. (1997a) 'Vocational Training in Taiwan: Current State and Future Challenge', *Industry of Free China*, August, 61–78.

Huang, T. C. (1997b) 'Employee Training and Management Development in Taiwan', *Industry of Free China*, December, 107–123.

Huang, T. C. (1998) 'The Strategic Level of Human Resource Management and Organizational Performance: An Empirical Investigation', *Asia Pacific Journal of Human Resource Management*, 36 (2), 59–72.

Huang, T. C. (1999) 'Who Shall Follow? Factors Affecting the Adoption of Succession Plans in Taiwan', *Long Range Planning*, 32 (6), 609–616.

Kao, C., Kuo, S., Chen, L. H. and Wang, T. Y. (1996), 'Improving Productivity via Technology and Management', *International Journal of Systems Science*, 27, 315–322.

Kleingartner, A. and Peng, H. Y. (1991) 'An Exploration of Labour Relations in Transition', *British Journal of Industrial Relations*, 29 (3), 427–446.

Kochan, T. A., McKersie, R. B. and Cappelli, P. (1984) 'Strategic Choice and Industrial Relations Theory', *Industrial Relations*, 23 (1), 16–39.

Lee, M. W., Liu, B. C. and Wang, P. (1994) 'Growth and Equity with Endogenous Human Capital: Taiwan's Economic Miracle Revisited', *Southern Economic Journal*, 60 (2), 435–444.

Leung, F. L. (1995) 'Overseas Chinese Management: Myths and Realities', *East Asian Executive Reports*, 17 (2), 6–13.

Lin, Y. Y. (1997) 'Labour Relations in Taiwan: A Cross-cultural Perspective', *Industrial Relations Journal*, 28 (1), 56–67.

Liu, B. T. (1992), 'Small and Medium-sized Business and Taiwan's Economic Development', *Taiwan's Economy*, 192, 19–45 (in Chinese).

Liu, S. J. (1998) 'Industrial Development and Structural Adaptation in Taiwan: Some Issues of Learned Entrepreneurship', *IEEE Transactions on Engineering Management*, 45 (4), November, 338–348.

Negandhi, A. R. (1973) *Management and Economic Development: The Case of Taiwan*, The Hague: Martinus Nijhoff.

Merchant, K. A., Chow, C. W. and Wu, A. (1995) 'Measurement, Evaluation and Review of Profit Center Managers: A Cross-Cultural Field Study', *Accounting Organizations and Society*, 20 (7/8), 619–638.

Pelled, L. H. and Xin, K. R. (1997) 'Work Values and their Human Resource Management Implications: A Theoretical Comparison of China, Mexico, and the United States', *Journal of Applied Management Studies*, 6 (2), 185–198.

San, G. (1993) 'Industrial Relations in Taiwan', in D. R. Briscoe, M. Rothman and R. C. D. Nacamulli (eds) *Industrial Relations Around the World*, Berlin: Walter de Gruyter.

Tallman, E. and Wang, P. (1994) 'Human Capital and Endogenous Growth: Evidence from Taiwan', *Journal of Monetary Economy*, 34, August, 101–124.

Tanzer, A. (1998) 'Silicon Valley East', *Forbes*, 1 June, 122.

Tichy, N. M., Fombrun, C. J. and Devanna, M. A. (1982) 'Strategic Human Resource Management', *Sloan Management Review*, 23 (2), 47–60.

Yao, D. (1999) 'Human Resource Management Challenges in Chinese Taipei', in *Human*

Resource Management Symposium on SMEs Proceedings vol. II, 30–31 October, Kaoshung: National Sun Yat-sen University.

Yeh, R. S. (1991) Management Practices of Taiwanese Firms: As Compared to Those of American and Japanese Subsidiaries in Taiwan', *Asia Pacific Journal of Management*, 8 (1), 1–14.

Wallum, P. (1993) 'A Broader View of Succession Planning', *Personnel Management*, 25, 42–45.

5 Human resource management in India

Pawan S. Budhwar

Introduction

This introduction highlights three things: background information on India; recent developments in the Indian economy; and a review of Indian human resource management (HRM) literature. The latter part of the chapter presents results from a large-scale HRM survey. Finally, the main conclusions and future challenges facing Indian HR managers are highlighted.

India is a democratic republic, comprising twenty-five states and seven union territories. It borders Bangladesh, Bhutan and Burma in the east, China in the north and north-east, Pakistan in the west and north-west and Sri Lanka in the south. It occupies a strategic location in South Asia for international trade. With an area of 3.3 million square km, India is the second largest country in Asia and the seventh largest in the world. A former British colony, India has emerged as the largest democracy in the world since independence in 1947.

India is the birthplace of three of the world's main religions: Hinduism (about 7000 years BC), Buddhism (487 BC) and Sikhism (1699 AD). Indian society comprises six main religious groups: Hindus (83.2 per cent), Muslims (11 per cent), Sikhs (2 per cent), Christians (2 per cent), Jains and Buddhists (less than 1 per cent). There are over three thousand castes.

India has 179 languages and 544 dialects. The Constitution recognises sixteen languages, Hindi and English being the two official languages. India has one of the largest English-speaking populations in the Asia-Pacific region. The literacy rate for those over 15 years of age is 51 per cent, but literacy is unevenly distributed (Budhwar, 2000a). These facts show the diverse nature of the Indian workforce.

Though rich in culture and natural resources, India currently faces a number of problems: political and religious instability; ever-increasing levels of population; unemployment and poverty; corruption in government offices; castism; a low per capita income; instability of output in agriculture and related sectors; slow privatisation of the bloated public sector; lack of adequate intellectual property protection; excessive bureaucracy; and an increasing gap between rich and poor. The level of corruption in politics is rapidly rising.

After independence, the government set up a 'Planning Commission' in 1950 to formulate national plans. Since then (till early 1990s) a 'mixed economy' approach (emphasising both private and public enterprise) has been adopted. Economic planning is mainly carried out through the five-year plans and industrial policies. Presently, the ninth five year-plan and the industrial policy begun in 1991 are in progress (see Datt and Sundharam, 1999). The next section further highlights the present dynamic business environment and the challenges it has created for the HR function in India.

Economic crisis and liberalisation of Indian economy

Despite the formalities of planning, the Indian economy reached its nadir in 1991. It witnessed a double digit rate of inflation, decelerated industrial production, fiscal indiscipline, a very high ratio of borrowing to the GNP (both internal and external) and a dismally low level of foreign exchange reserves. Foreign reserves had become so low that they were barely sufficient to meet the cost of three weeks' imports (see Ahulwalia, 1994; Budhwar, 2001). The Indian government was forced to pledge gold to the Bank of England to meet the country's foreign exchange requirements. The World Bank and the IMF agreed to bail out India on the condition that it changed to a 'free market economy' from a regulated regime. To meet the challenges, the government announced a series of economic policies beginning with the devaluation of the rupee, followed by a new industrial policy and fiscal and trade policies. A number of reforms were undertaken in the public sector, in trade and exchange policy, in the banking sector, and foreign investment was liberalised. A detailed report on the functioning of these policies is contained in the Special Issue of the *Columbia Journal of World Business* (1994).

Liberalisation of policies has resulted in a huge increase in competition for Indian firms with foreign firms. In addition, Indian firms are now under great pressure to change from indigenous, costly and probably less effective technology to a high, more effective and costly technology (Venkata Ratnam, 1995). There is a strong need to change the infrastructure, the bureaucracy at operating levels and the existing culture (organisational). Current policies imply a switch from labour-intensive to more capital-intensive methods of production, and therefore a new requirement for organisations is to remove surplus labour and to generate new sustainable employment. Indian organisations are attempting to improve quality and match world standards such as ISO 9000. The aim is to increase productivity, reduce costs and over-manning while generating employment, improving quality, and reducing voluntary and involuntary absenteeism (Krishna and Monappa, 1994; Rao *et al.*, 1994).

The brighter side of the new paradigm is that it has changed the thrust of corporate management from 'regulation driven' to 'market driven' and from 'protection' to 'competition'. It has created opportunities for technology up-gradation, resource mobilisation from new sources, expansion, diversification, turnaround and internationalisation (Dixit, 1994).

All the threats and opportunities created by the liberalisation of policies have a significant implication for HRM. This is because the aim of the liberalised policies is to increase productivity, reduce costs, improve quality, generate employment, reduce over-manning in Indian industry (downsizing) and create a significant drop in the incidence of industrial sickness (Krishna and Monappa, 1994). All these aims are closely connected with HR issues.

To Indian HRM academics, the implications of liberalisation are anticipated to be wide-ranging. Those Indian organisations that have upgraded technology now compete against multinational enterprises (MNEs) and are considering the need to develop a highly diverse workforce into well-trained, motivated and efficient employees. Organisations are also having to cope with the subsequent de-skilling, re-skilling and multi-skilling problems, workforce reduction policies, retention and career development issues (Venkata Ratnam, 1995). The faster Indian organisations can modernise and mechanise plants, introduce new technology, revamp plant layout for easier and efficient material handling and eliminate waste, the more successful they will be (Sodhi, 1994). The espoused solution to this problem is to use the HR function to develop a constant awareness of missions, ensure continuous appraisal of internal strengths, enhance innovation, improve compensation schemes, introduce more informal communication and develop better employee relations (Sparrow and Budhwar, 1997). This will require a considerable change in the attitudes, working systems, strategy and human resource skills of Indian organisations. It is also argued that an expansion of the role into areas of strategy development, information system design, cultural development and technical expertise will necessitate a decentralisation of the HRM role, along the lines seen in the West (see Budhwar and Sparrow, 1997).

Since these reforms, the economy has responded positively and India is now considered one of the largest emerging nations, having bypassed the Asian economic crisis of 1997–98. The World Bank forecasts that, by 2020, India could become the world's fourth largest economy. In the last few years, state control and ownership in the economy have been reduced, bold steps have been taken to correct the fiscal imbalance, to bring about structural adjustments and to attract foreign direct investment. Substantial reforms have been made in the telecommunications, financial and shipping sectors, as well as in direct tax and industrial policy. However, India still has a long way to go before it can compete fully with some of the more economically advanced Asian nations (Budhwar 2000a). Human resource development (HRD) is seen as the key to success in such circumstances (see Balaji *et al.*, 1998; Budhwar, 2000a; Rao *et al.*, 1994).

HRM function in India

Formalised personnel functions have been common in Indian organisations for decades. The origins of the personnel function can be traced back to the 1920s with the concern for labour welfare in factories. The Trade Union Act of 1926 gave formal recognition to workers' unions. Similarly, the recommendations of the Royal Commission on Labour gave rise to the appointment of labour officers in 1932 and the Factories Act of 1948 laid down the duties and qualifications of labour welfare officers. These developments all formed the foundations for the personnel function in India (Budhwar and Khatri, 2001; Sparrow and Budhwar, 1996).

In the early 1950s two professional bodies were set up: the Indian Institute of Personnel Management (IIPM) formed in Calcutta and the National Institute of Labour Management (NILM) in Bombay. During the 1960s, the personnel function began to expand beyond its welfare origins with the three areas of labour welfare, industrial relations and personnel administration developing as the constituent roles for the emerging profession. In the 1970s the thrust of the personnel function shifted towards the need for greater organisational 'efficiency' and by the 1980s personnel professionals began to talk about new concepts such as HRM and HRD. The two professional bodies of IIPM and NILM were merged in 1980 to form the National Institute of Personnel Management (NIPM) in Bombay. The status of the personnel function in India has therefore changed over the years (for more details see Jain, 1991; Venkata Ratnam and Shrivastava, 1991). However, presently it is changing at a much more rapid pace than ever, mainly due to the pressures created by the liberalisation of economic policies.

As a result of such pressures, there is a strong emphasis on HRD in Indian organisations. In fact, HRD is the term more often used to denote personnel function than HRM in India (Budhwar, 2000a). Although the recent reforms have created tremendous pressures on the traditional Indian personnel/management system, it is too early to judge whether there is any noticeable change in the way organisations are managed in India. Since the traditional Indian management system developed over a very long time, understandably it will take some time to change. However, some early symptoms of change are appearing. HRM is playing a noticeable role in bringing about changes in Indian organisations. More and more Indian organisations are creating a separate HRM/HRD department. There has been a significant increase in the level of training and development of employees (Budhwar and Sparrow, 1997; Sharma, 1992). Constitutional pressures are forcing organisations to employ people from backward and reserved categories (Jain and Venkata Ratnam, 1994; Venkata Ratnam and Chandra, 1996). There are also indications of a movement towards performance-related pay and promotions. However, these are more evident in the private sector (Bordia and Blau, 1998). Similarly, in comparison to the public sector, the internal work culture of private enterprises now places greater emphasis on internal locus of control, future orientation in planning, participation in decision-making, effective motivation techniques and obligation towards others in the work context (Mathur *et al.*, 1996). There is also an attempt to select new recruits on the basis of merit in the private sectors (at least at the lower and middle levels).

The above discussion presents a broad over-view of the HRM function in India. However, to develop an in-depth understanding it is important to examine the main factors which form the very bases of HRM in India. Based on the framework introduced in Chapter 1, results from a large-scale study are presented here. These results are based on a questionnaire survey run in firms having 200 or more employees in six industries in the manufacturing sector (food processing, plastics, steel, textiles, pharmaceuticals and footwear), carried out between January and April 1995. The respondents were the top personnel specialist (one each) from each firm. The response rate was around 30 per cent (137 out of 450 questionnaires).

The main thrust of the study was to analyse the thinking of personnel specialists on the influence of national factors on their HR function (see Budhwar and Sparrow, 1998).

To examine the influence of national factors on HRM policies and practices, the respondents were asked to allocate a maximum of 100 points to different aspects of the following: national culture, institutions, dynamic business environment and business sector. Since the impact of the national factors on cross-national HRM is under-researched, to gain more insight into the matter an open-ended question after each national factor question was asked. To present a picture of the scene, the mean scores of the respondents' perceptions on the influence of the four national factors on HRM policies and practices were computed. The open-ended questions were content-analysed and percentages were computed to summarise the results. To complement the survey results, support from relevant literature is also provided.

Influence of national culture on Indian HRM

The results in Table 5.1 show that on average Indian managers give a high priority to the importance of cultural assumptions that shape the way employees perceive and think about the organisation (24.4), as well as common Indian values, norms of behaviour and customs (22.9) and the way in which managers are socialised in India (21.7).

Content analysis of the open-ended question shows that 54 per cent of the Indian managers believe that social relations play an important role in managing human resources. Indian managers note that common Indian values, norms of behaviour and customs have an important influence on their HRM policies and practices (48 per cent). Managers' actions are dictated by these values and norms of behaviour. Some 42 per cent of the Indian managers feel that pressure groups (such as unions) act as saviours of employees belonging to the reserved categories, dictate the terms and conditions of certain agreements and most of the time are felt to cause trouble for management.

To a great extent, the present HRM system is a product of a mixture of social, economic, religious and political factors which have now prevailed in India for a long time. Indians are socialised in an environment that values strong family ties and extended family relationships. They are more likely to develop stronger

Table 5.1 Influence of different aspects of national culture on Indian HRM

Aspects of national culture	No. of cases	Mean
1 Way in which managers are socialised	130	21.72
2 Common values, norms of behaviour and customs	130	22.94
3 The influence of pressure groups	118	15.92
4 Assumptions that shape the way managers perceive and think about the organisation	135	24.44
5 The match to the organisation's culture and 'the way we do things around here'	126	20.85

affiliative tendencies or greater dependence on others (see Budhwar *et al.*, 2000). Thus, in the work context, interpersonal relations are more relevant for them and as a result, their job-related decisions might be influenced more by interpersonal considerations than by task demands (Kanungo and Mendonca, 1994). Further, factors such as the long British rule, a strong caste system, religion and an agrarian-based society, the extended family system, a high rate of illiteracy and poverty and weak and unimportant ties between state and individual have created a management system which is based on social and family relationships (Budhwar, 1999).

Several researchers have compared Indian management practices with those of other regions such as the USA, the UK and Japan. For example, in cultural terms compared to an English person, an Indian person is more fearful of people in power, obedient to superiors, dependent on others, fatalistic, submissive, undisciplined, friendly, modest, unreserved, collectivist, caste-conscious and clan-orientated and law-abiding. On the other hand, compared to English people, he is less self-controlled, tenacious and less willing to take account of other people's views (Tayeb, 1988). Similarly, Sharma (1984) in his study contrasted the high efficiency and achievement-oriented US management style with a more fatalistic style in India. Given their daily exposure to scarcity in the economy and an indifferent society in the face of poverty, Indian managers are more inclined to believe events are predetermined by a 'hidden hand' that shapes their destiny. They also demonstrate tough resilience in the face of hazards, reinforced by an infinite capacity to bear sufferings.

Hofstede (1991) found that India has a low to moderate uncertainty avoidance culture. However, in contrast, some analysis by Indian academics characterises the management style as one that demonstrates an unwillingness to accept organisational change or take risks, a reluctance to make important decisions in work-related matters or lack of initiative in problem solving, a disinclination to accept responsibility for job-related tasks and an indifference to job feedback (Kanungo and Mendonca, 1994; Singh, 1990).

Hierarchy and inequality are deeply rooted in India's tradition and are also found in practice in the form of unequally placed caste and class groups. Indian organisational structures and social relations are therefore hierarchical and people are status conscious. They find it comfortable to work in a superior–subordinate relationship which is personalised. India's positioning in Hofstede's (1991) research as a high power distance culture then reflects the hierarchical nature of Hinduism (evidenced by the caste system), the early socialisation process that highlights the importance of the family structure and remnants of British colonial influence. Age also matters greatly in India, and seniority can be expected to play a significant role in decisions about promotion and pay. Apart from these, one's caste, religion and social contacts also matter significantly. Inter-group relationships are characterised by suspicion of other groups, a search for small group identity and a strong inclination to affiliate with people in power (Sahay and Walsham, 1997; Sharma, 1984). Such inequalities have persisted and remained in equilibrium because of organic links between them and ingrained inter-dependence of the different socio-economic groups.

India is also a low masculinity culture in Hofstede's terms. This is reflected in a paternalistic management style and preference for personalised relationships rather than a more divorced performance orientation (Kanungo and Jaeger, 1990). This generates a 'tendermindedness' and 'soft work culture' that is associated with a reluctance to take bold decisions and see them through to the end (Sinha, 1990). Success is judged on a 'moral consideration of the text' and strict observance of ritual, not on actual behaviour, absolute principles or rules. Indian work culture dictates a distinctive style of transformational leadership, which has been called the 'nurturant-task leadership' style (Mathur *et al.*, 1996; Sinha and Sinha, 1990). This draws upon the use of familial and cultural values (such as affection, dependence and need for personalised relationships) to temper the firm and structured task direction expected in situations of high power distance. In such conditions the motivational tools have to have a social, inter-personal and even spiritual orientation (Sinha and Sinha, 1990).

Low individualism (as per Hofstede's results for India) implies that family and group attainments take precedence over work outcomes. The primary purpose of work is not to express or fulfil one's self, but as a means to fulfil one's family and social obligations. Indeed, family and social networking is an important method of obtaining work, securing promotion and advancing pay (Sparrow and Budhwar, 1996; 1997). A self-reinforcing circle exists, whereby culture dictates that political connections and ascribed status, not achievement status, underpin selection, promotion and transfer systems, such that loyalty of appointees is more towards the appointing authorities than the goals of the organisation, and job-related decisions are influenced more by interpersonal relations than by task demands (Kanungo and Mendonca, 1994). Moreover, low social and intellectual mobility forces owners to recruit managers from their own families, castes and communities, reinforcing old customs, values and beliefs. The top Indian industrial houses (such as Tatas, Birlas) are good examples of this. The high prevalence of owner-managers within the business structure fits well with this cultural tendency (see Budhwar, 1999; Budhwar and Khatri, 2001).

Based on a detailed analysis of Indian national culture and its impact on Indian management, Sharma summarises it thus:

> It presents a plausible picture of the average Indian's resistance to change, his willingness to delegate but unwillingness to accept authority, his fear of taking an independent decision, his possessive attitude towards his inferiors and his abject surrender to his superiors, his strict observance of rituals and his disregard of them in practice, his preaching of high morals against personal immorality, and his near-desperate efforts at maintaining the status quo while talking of change.
>
> (1984: 76)

In the light of this characterisation of Indian HRM, one is tempted to ask the question, do Indian managers presently behave in the same way as discussed above? Or have they changed or are trying to change their practices to cope with the pressures thrown up by the recent liberalisation of Indian economic policies? A number of institutions are changing their pre-liberalisation stance, such as trade unions, labour laws, the educational and vocational training set up, and, of course, government policies. What are the effects of such changes on the Indian HRM function?

Influence of national institutions on Indian HRM

Results in Table 5.2 show that Indian managers give a high priority to national labour laws (40.89), trade unions (28.55) and educational and vocational training set up (24.45), regarding their influence on HRM policies and practices.

Table 5.2 Influence of different institutions on HRM

Institutions	No. of cases	Mean
1 National labour laws	132	40.89
2 Trade unions	98	28.55
3 Professional bodies	101	16.06
4 Educational and vocational training set up	120	24.45
5 International institutions	72	11.18

Content analysis of the open-ended answers shows that the majority of Indian managers (61.5 per cent) believe that Indian national labour laws influence their HRM policies and practices the most because they limit the actions that can actually be implemented. Moreover, they are 'pro-labour' and adherence to them is important for maintaining good industrial relations and therefore the survival of organisations. They have a direct impact on personnel policies and act as guiding pillars for 'exit policies' (developed to facilitate retirement in the light of liberalisation) and the downsizing of organisations. Some 28.4 per cent of Indian managers feel that trade unions significantly influence their HRM policies and practices and 16.9 per cent of Indian managers believe that the present educational vocational training set-up of India is helpful in increasing employees' efficiency, contributes to the process of up-dating their skills and facilitates better stress management. Less than 1 per cent of the Indian managers admit that their HRM practices are influenced by professional bodies and international institutions.

At present, there are over 150 state and central laws in India which govern various aspects of HRM at the enterprise level (Budhwar and Khatri, 2001; Venkata Ratnam, 1995). Unfortunately, while there is a proliferation of legislation, the implementation is weak (Budhwar, 1995). However, the legislation still dictates most HRM policies and practices. Some of the prominent labour laws are:

- The Factories Act, 1948;
- The Industrial Employment (Standing Orders) Act, 1946;
- Industrial Disputes Act, 1948;
- Trade Unions Act, 1926;

- Minimum Wages Act, 1948;
- Payment of Wages Act, 1936;
- Payment of Bonus Act, 1965;
- Employee State Insurance Act, 1948;
- Compensation Act, 1923;
- Apprenticeship Act, 1961; and
- Maternity Benefit Act, 1961 (for more details, see Gonsalves *et al.*, 1995).

As expected, the influence of trade unions on HRM is significant. Although in percentage terms unions in India are in decline, in absolute terms there is an increase in union membership (Das, 1999). Moreover, as has happened in the West (for example, in the UK), the Indian unions are now playing a more co-operative role and are less militant (Venkata Ratnam, 1995). Nevertheless, they still greatly influence HR policies and practices in Indian companies, for example, in the recruitment of new employees, payment of bonuses and internal transfers. The unions are strong due to the political support they enjoy and the existence of pro-labour laws in India (Sodhi, 1994; Sparrow and Budhwar, 1997; Venkata Ratnam, 1995).

The educational and vocational training set-up is the third important institution which influences Indian HRM (see Table 5.2). A number of institutes such as the Indian Society for Training and Development, the All India Management Association, the National Institute of Industrial Engineering and the HRD Academy have been established over the years. They provide training to all levels of employees. In 1988, a centrally-sponsored scheme of vocationalisation of secondary education was launched for classes XI and XII. Under this scheme, 150 courses have been introduced in six major areas – agriculture, business and commerce, engineering and technology, health and paramedical, home science and others. In 1993, a Central Institute for Vocational Education was set up in Bhopal to provide technical and academic support to the vocational education programme in the country (Yadapadithaya, 2000: 82).

On the other hand, Indian organisations, both past and present, have made attempts to emulate Western or Eastern (Japanese) patterns of management. This is because Indian managers are often trained in the West and most of the Indian management institutes have adopted the Western education system. However, due to the strong family, social, religious influence, on the one hand, and the Western education on the other, Indian managers internalise two separate sets of values. The first is acquired from their family and community and is related to affiliation, security, dependency and social obligation. The second is drawn from their education and professional training and relates to personal growth, efficiency and collaborative work (Sahay and Walsham, 1997). In practice, the first set of values are more dominant.

Both the results and existing literature show the weak influence of international institutions on Indian HRM (see Table 5.2). There can be two possible explanations for this. First, the type of international institutions existing in the region and, second, their power and influence on HRM in India. For example, the international institutions more relevant to India include the International Labour Organisation (ILO), the General Agreement on Tariffs and Trade (GATT) and the South Asian Association for Regional Co-operation (SAARC). However, their influence on Indian HRM is not significant (Sparrow and Budhwar, 1996). The influence of the ILO on Indian HRM policies is expected to be high, but in practice the provisions of the ILO are not followed to any great extent (Venkata Ratnam, 1995). Institutions such as the SAARC work for mutual co-operation in the region (Whitley, 1992) but hardly influence HRM in India.

Influence of dynamic business environment on Indian HRM

Results from the survey show that, on average, Indian managers give a relatively high priority to customer satisfaction (25.1 out of 100 points) and increased competition/globalisation of business structure (24.3) regarding their influence on HRM policies and practices (for details see Table 5.3).

Results of the content analysis show that the majority of the Indian managers (74.4 per cent) believe that their personnel function is under severe pressure to improve productivity by developing an efficient and responsible workforce. The emphasis is on the need for team work, enhanced training programmes, HRD, skills improvement and retraining of employees by providing technical skills. Some 65.4 per cent of Indian managers believe that due to the dynamic business environment there is a strong need for management to change initiatives (to change attitudes, perceptions and improve the work environment), 60.8 per cent of Indian managers feel that the personnel should contribute more actively in the restructuring of the business, i.e. facilitating de-layering, downsizing, decentralisation and cost reduction. Some 43.5 per cent of Indian managers feel that, because of the dynamic business environment, there is a need for more emphasis on customer

Table 5.3 Influence of dynamic business environment on Indian HRM

Changes in business environment	No. of cases	Mean
1 Increased national/international competition/Globalisation of corporate business structure	125	24.28
2 Growth of new business arrangements e.g., business alliances, joint ventures, and foreign direct investment through mergers and acquisitions	116	17.57
3 More sophisticated information/communication technology or increased reliance on automation	125	18.20
4 Changing composition of the workforce with respect to gender, age, ethnicity and changing employee values	102	14.04
5 Downsizing of the work force and business re-engineering	105	15.45
6 Heightened focus on total management or customer satisfaction	126	25.05

satisfaction, and 33.2 per cent feel that competitive pressures have resulted in enhanced levels of manpower planning to ensure that the right person is in the right place at the right time, and a need to attract and retain labour (with rare skills) and improve the efficiency and quality of their work.

The mean score for downsizing of the workforce and business re-engineering aspect of dynamic business environment (competitive pressures) is high (see Table 5.3). As mentioned above, due to the liberalisation of the Indian economy, there is an increased level of competition from overseas firms. This has put a lot of pressure on the Indian personnel function in domestic companies to prepare and develop their employees so that these companies are able to compete with overseas firms in skills, efficiency and effectiveness (Krishna and Monappa, 1994; Sparrow and Budhwar, 1997; Venkata Ratnam, 1995). Improvement in the quality of goods produced and services provided is also seen as a way to survive in the present competitive business environment, hence, the obvious focus on total customer satisfaction in Indian organisations.

Influence of business sector on Indian HRM

Results in Table 5.4 show that on average Indian managers score high on regulations and standards that are specific to their industrial sector (21.6) as well as the specific requirement/needs of customers or suppliers (supply chain management) that characterise their sector (18.8).

Content analysis of the open-ended answers show that 37 per cent of Indian managers believe that regulations and standards specific to a particular sector (industry) do act as a guideline for HR policies in organisations belonging to that industry and they are required to abide by these. Some 25.9 per cent of the Indian managers feel that specific requirement/needs of customers or suppliers that

Table 5.4 Influence of business sector on Indian HRM

Aspects of business sector	No. of cases	Mean
1 Common strategies, business logic and goals being pursued by firms across the sector	129	15.31
2 Regulations and standards (e.g., payments, training, health and safety) specific to your industrial sector	122	21.55
3 Specific requirement/needs of customers or suppliers that characterise your sector (i.e. supply chain management)	129	18.97
4 The need for sector-specific knowledge in order to provide similar goods/services in the sector	116	12.17
5 Informal or formal benchmarking across competitors in the sector (e.g., best practices of market leaders)	110	11.55
6 Cross-sector co-operative arrangements e.g., common technological innovations followed by all firms in the sector	96	9.94
7 Common developments in business operations and work practices dictated by the nature of the business	102	12.99
8 A labour market or skill requirement that tends to be used by your business sector only	102	13.86

characterise a particular sector act as an important influence on their HRM policies and practices. This is one of the most important means for an organisation's survival, especially in a rapidly changing environment. It is also an important factor influencing HRM policies and practices. Also, 10.2 per cent of the managers think that the common strategies, business logic and goals being pursued by firms across a particular sector influence their HRM policies and practices, along with informal or formal benchmarking across competitors in the sector to ensure that they have best HRM practices (7.1 per cent).

The existing Indian literature on sector-specific HRM practices and policies is fragmented. As such, there is no sector-specific labour legislation. However, some sector-specific HR patterns are reported in the literature (see Budhwar, 2000b). Industries in the steel sector (initiated by the Steel Authority of India) have to train their employees in specific skills, such as mechanical or electrical craftsman skills or both, depending on the level of employee. The Steel Authority of India (which accounts for over 40 per cent of the total crude steel production of India) is working towards making all the employees under the age of 45 years literate. Similar efforts are also being initiated by Tata Steel (another major player in the Indian steel sector). The link between pay and performance is being established in the steel sector through incentive schemes. The industry level machinery for consultation and co-operation is through 'National Joint Consultative Committee for Steel Industry'. At present, most steel plants are being downsized and voluntary retirement or early separation schemes are being adopted. A similar practice of voluntary retirement scheme is followed in the Indian pharmaceutical sector when a plant has to downsize (Venkata Ratnam *et al.*, 1998).

Until 1962, large pharmaceutical companies in India employed unmarried female workers in their manufacturing and packaging areas. This was due to the type of equipment used and the perception that female workers were better suited to the job. However, this trend has now changed, as the pressure to manufacture more has forced the pharmaceutical firms to move to a six-day working week and work is carried out in three shifts. Due to high profitability in pharmaceutical companies, the majority of large firms have a better wage/salary structure compared to other industries (Mehrotra, 1998).

Similarly, there are some sector-specific HR practices prevalent in other sectors. For example, in the booming software and information technology sector, the patterns of HR practices are significantly different from the above discussed traditional sectors. On average, the academic achievements and background needed to get a job in these sectors are much higher and more specific in comparison to other sectors. Due to the tight labour market and rapid growth of these sectors, their salary structure along with different perks offered is very high. Despite handsome salaries, the employee turnover rate in the computer and information technology-related industries is very high. Different mechanisms such as profit-sharing schemes, share option schemes, overseas holidays, company house, company cars, etc. are being offered to retain employees in such sectors (for details see Guha, 1999a). For information on other sector-specific HR practices see Budhwar (2000b) and Venkata Ratnam and Verma (1998).

Conclusions

The adoption of the framework detailed in Chapter 1 has not only helped to highlight the main interplay between the HRM policies and practices and national factors but also the context-specific nature of Indian HRM. For example, the strong impact of unions and pressure groups on Indian HRM clearly presents the context responsible for such practices. Such an analysis contributes to the assessment of the way in which HRM in different nations is becoming similar or remaining different (Budhwar and Sparrow, 1998). Such research is of value to practitioners as it helps to develop an understanding of the main predictors (i.e. national factors) of HRM in different national and regional settings. They can develop their policies and practices accordingly. The information can also be used as a training tool for expatriates.

Considering the sample size, the nature of respondents and the research topics covered, it would be unwise to come to any definite conclusions regarding Indian HRM. It is essential to examine much more closely the regional HRM differences, the Indian industrial relation system, the differences in private and public sector management practices and policies and the issues related to indigenous management approaches in India. Apart from these, to develop a better understanding regarding the influence of national culture on HRM policies and practices, the impact of different dimensions of national culture such as the ones proposed by Hofstede (1991) and Hampden-Turner and Trompenaars (1993) should be examined. The influence of more institutions such as labour markets (Benson, 1995), employers federations and consulting organisations is also worth examining. Similarly, more aspects of the dynamic business environment such as the facility of information (mainly due to the development of the Internet) and the impact of the globalisation of business on cross-national HRM should be examined. Finally, it must be kept in mind that the influence of the business sector on cross-national HRM is under-researched.

With an anticipated GDP growth rate of 6 per cent, India is now projected to be one of the fastest-growing economies in Asia (see Budhwar, 2001). With a parliamentary majority it is likely that the present government can complete its five years, thus providing the much needed political stability at the national level. The present government has been quick to initiate the vital 'second generation' of reforms. If successful, these significant changes could push the growth rate to 9 or 10 per cent. With full ownership allowed, MNCs will no longer need to put up with the constraints of struggling joint ventures, or share the fruits of success with other Indian companies (Guha, 1999b). The success of the Indian software and hardware sectors is now widely acknowledged world-wide. Along with cheap manpower, Indian 'brain power' is now contributing to real cost advantage.

Such a dynamic and competitive business environment presents a number of challenges to Indian HRM. The antagonistic role of trade unions is on the verge of change. However, due to strong political support, the pace of this change is very slow. Commentators in the field (such as Das, 1999) suggest the need for structural adjustments (such as stopping multiple subscription of union membership, reducing inter-union rivalry, reducing political influence on unions and increasing union membership) to make unions more co-operative. This in turn means there is a strong need to amend the provisions of a great deal of labour legislation such as the Trade Union Act of 1926 (which is strongly pro-labour). Understandably, such macro-level structural changes take a long time, therefore, it is the HRM function which should mould things (within the mentioned constraints) to make best use of their HRs.

The giant public sector organisations need to downsize to reduce their surplus labour so as to improve their efficiency. Both the trade unions and labour legislation are the most serious hindrance in this regard (Venkata Ratnam, 1995). Some attempts in this regard in the form of the introduction of 'voluntary redundancy schemes' have been initiated. However, the functioning of such programmes is at present, inadequate. Like the West, Indian work dynamics also suggest that there is a need to encourage flexible work practices. A small shift towards flexible and part-time work is being reported in the literature (see Balaji *et al.*, 1998). HRM can further contribute and speed up this process, especially when it becomes strategic and proactive (Budhwar, 2001).

Considering the pressures (discussed above) created by overseas operators on local operators, there is a strong need for Indian HRM to seriously emphasise issues related to performance-related pay, to stop (or at least reduce the intensity of) the 'brain drain' (serious efforts should be made to absorb and retain the HR talent within the country), to bring women in the mainstream of the workforce, to try to bring in objectivity in appraisals, promotions and transfers (reduce the impact of social and political pressures) and to change the less productive work culture to a more productive one. The suggested changes are not easy to make and implement. However, if the Indian organisations want to compete with their foreign counterparts and if India wants to become a true economic power, then most of the above-mentioned challenges need serious consideration.

Acknowledgement

I would like to thank Syed Akhtar, Ken Kamoche and Malcolm Warner for their useful suggestions on an earlier draft of this chapter.

References

Ahulwalia, M. S. (1994) 'India's Quiet Economic Revolution', *The Columbia Journal of World Business*, Spring, 6–12.

Balaji, C., Chandrasekhar, S. and Dutta, R. (eds) (1998) *Leading Change Through Human Resources: Towards a Globally Competitive India*, New Delhi: Tata McGraw-Hill.

Benson, J. (1995) 'Future Employment and the Internal Labour Market', *British Journal of Industrial Relations*, 33 (4), 603–608.

Bordia, P. and Blau, G. (1998) 'Pay Referent Comparison and Pay Level Satisfaction in Private Versus Public Sector Organisations in India', *The International Journal of Human Resource Management*, 9 (1), 155–167.

Budhwar, P. (1995) 'Awareness of Labour Legislations and Exploitation: A Direct Relationship', *Haryana Labour Journal*, XXVI (2), April–June, 5–9.

Budhwar, P. (1999) 'Indian Management Style and HRM', in M. Tayeb (ed.) *International Business Text*, London: Pitman, pp. 534–540.

Budhwar, P. (2000a) 'Indian and British Personnel Specialists' Understanding of the Dynamics of their Function: An Empirical Study', *International Business Review*, 9 (6), 727–753.

Budhwar, P. (2000b) 'Factors Influencing HRM Policies and Practices in India: An Empirical Study', *Global Business Review*, 1 (2), 229–247.

Budhwar, P. (2001) 'Doing Business in India', *Thunderbird International Business Review*, forthcoming.

Budhwar, P. and Khatri, N. (2001) 'Comparative Human Resource Management in Britain and India: An Empirical Study', *The International Journal of Human Resource Management*, forthcoming.

Budhwar, L., Reeves, D. and Farrell, P. (2000) 'Life Goals as a Function of Social Class and Child Rearing Practices in India', *International Journal of Intercultural Relations*, 24, 227–245.

Budhwar, P. and Sparrow, P. (1997) 'Evaluating Levels of Strategic Integration and Devolvement of Human Resource Management in India', *The International Journal of Human Resource Management*, 8, (4), 476–494.

Budhwar, P. and Sparrow, P. (1998) 'National Factors Determining Indian and British HRM Practices: An Empirical Study', *Management International Review*, 38 (Special Issue 2), 105–121.

Das, H. (1999) 'Trade Union Activism – Avoidable or Inevitable?', *Indian Journal of Industrial Relations*, 35 (2), 224–236.

Datt, R. and Sundharam, K. P. H. (1999) *Indian Economy*, New Delhi: S. Chand and Company Ltd.

Dixit, M. R. (1994) 'New Environment, Corporate Strategy and the HRD Agenda', in T. V. Rao, D. M. Silveria, C. M. Shrivastava and R. Vidyasagar (eds) *HRD in the New Economic Environment*, New Delhi: Tata McGraw-Hill Publishing Company Limited, pp. 15–29.

Gonsalves, C., Bhat, R. and Mathew, M. (eds) (1995) *Cases on Indian Labour Laws*. Vol. 1, New Delhi: Friedrich-Ebert-Stiftung.

Guha, K. (1999a) 'Software Services Lead the Charge, India: Annual Country Report', *Financial Times*, 19 November.

Guha, K. (1999b) 'Parent-owned Competitors Sound the Death Knell. India: Annual Country Report', *Financial Times*, 19 November.

Hampden-Turner, C. and Trompenaars, F. (1993) *The Seven Cultures of Capitalism: Value Systems for Creating Wealth in the United States, Britain, Japan, Germany, France, Sweden and the Netherlands*, New York: Doubleday.

Hofstede, G. (1991) *Culture's Consequences: Software of the Mind*, London: McGraw-Hill Book Company.

Jain, H. C. (1991) 'Is there a Coherent Human Resource Management System in India?', *International Journal of Manpower*, 12 (1), 10–17.

Jain, H. C. and Venkata Ratnam, C. S. (1994) 'Affirmative Action in Employment for the Scheduled Castes and the Scheduled Tribes in India', *International Journal of Manpower*, 15 (7), 6–25.

Kanungo, R. N. and Jaeger, A. M. (1990) 'Introduction: The Need for Indigenous Management in Developing countries', in A. M. Jaeger and Kanungo, R. N. (eds) *Management in Developing Countries*, London: Routledge, pp. 1–19.

Kanungo, R. N. and Mendonca, M. (1994) 'Culture and Performance Improvement', *Productivity*, 35 (4), 447–453.

Krishna, A. and Monappa, A. (1994) 'Economic Restructuring and Human Resource Management', *Indian Journal of Industrial Relations*, 29 (4), 490–501.

Mathur, P., Aycan, Z. and Kanungo, R. N. (1996) 'Work Cultures in Indian Organisations: A Comparison Between Public and Private Sector', *Psychology and Developing Society*, 8 (2), 199–222.

Mehrotra, R. (1998) 'Industrial Relations in the Indian Pharmaceutical Industry', in C. S. Venkata Ratnam and A. Verma (eds), *Challenge For Change: Industrial Relations in Indian Industry*, New Delhi: Allied Publishers.

Rao, T. V., Silveria, D. M., Shrivastava, C. M. and Vidyasagar, R. (eds) (1994) *HRD in the New Economic Environment*, New Delhi: Tata McGraw-Hill Publishing Company Limited.

Sahay, S. and Walsham, G. (1997) 'Social Structure and Managerial Agency in India', *Organisation Studies*, 18, 415–444.

Sharma, I. J. (1984) 'The Culture Context of Indian Managers', *Management and Labour Studies*, 9 (2), 72–80.

Sharma, R. D. (1992) 'Lack of Management Training in India: Causes and Characteristics', *International Journal of Manpower*, 13 (3), 27–34.

Singh, J. P. (1990) 'Managerial Culture and Work-related Values in India', *Organisation Studies*, 11 (1), 75–101.

Sinha, J. B. P. (1990) *Work Culture in Indian Context*, New Delhi: Sage.

Sinha, J. B. P. and Sinha, D. (1990) 'Role of Social Values in Indian Organisations', *International Journal of Psychology*, 25, 705–714.

Sodhi, J. S. (1994) 'Emerging Trends in Industrial Relations and Human Resource Management in Indian Industry', *Indian Journal of Industrial Relations*, 30 (1): 19–37.

Sparrow, P. R. and Budhwar, P. (1996) 'Human Resource Management in India in the New Economic Environment', in Saxena, A. and Devedi, H. (eds) *HRM in the New Economic Environment*, Jaipur: National Publishing House, pp. 28–73.

Sparrow, P. R. and Budhwar, P. (1997) 'Competition and Change: Mapping the Indian HRM Recipe Against World Wide Patterns', *Journal of World Business*, 32 (3), 224–242.

Tayeb, M. (1988) *Organisations and National Culture*, London: Sage.

The Columbia Journal of World Business (1994) Spring. Special issue.

Venkata Ratnam, C. S. (1995) 'Economic Liberalisation and the Transformation of Industrial Relations Policies in India', In Verma, A., Kochan, T. A. and Lansbury, R. D. (eds) *Employment Relations in the Growing Asian Economies*, London: Routledge.

Venkata Ratnam, C. S., Balakrishanan, S. and Rath, J. (1998) 'Steel Industry in India in Transition: A Study of Changes in Some Aspects of Employment Relations', in C. S. Venkata Ratnam and A. Verma (eds) *Challenge For Change: Industrial Relations in Indian Industry*, New Delhi: Allied Publishers.

Venkata Ratnam, C. S. and Chandra, V. (1996) 'Sources of Diversity and the Challenge before Human Resource Management in India', *International Journal of Manpower*, 17 (4/5), 76–108.

Venkata Ratnam, C. S. and Shrivastava, B. K. (1991) *Personnel Management and Human Resources*, New Delhi: Tata McGraw-Hill Publishing Company Limited.

Venkata Ratnam, C. S. and Verma, A. (1998) (eds) *Challenge For Change: Industrial Relations in Indian Industry*, New Delhi: Allied Publishers.

Whitley, R. D. (1992) *Business Systems in East Asia*, London: Sage Publications.

Yadapadithaya, P. S. (2000) 'International Briefing 5: Training and Development in India', *International Journal of Training and Development*, 4 (1), 79–89.

6 Human resource management in Nepal

Dev Raj Adhikari and Michael Muller

Introduction

Like many developing countries, the Human Resource Management (HRM) function is not yet fully established in Nepalese organisations. An attempt is made in this chapter to highlight the main factors which determine HRM policies and practices in Nepal. Business environment, national culture and national institutions all play a significant role in this regard. Three case studies provide empirical support to the discussion.

Business environment

Nepal, a Hindu state is located in the Himalayas between India and Tibet (China). Hindus comprise 90 per cent of its population, the remainder mainly consisting of Buddhists and Moslems. The population of 22 million is further divided into eighteen ethnic groups and traditionally in four main castes. Some 90 per cent of the people live in rural areas, of which many are only accessible by foot. When measured by GNP per person, Nepal is the ninth poorest country in the world. It has the highest fertility (5.3 per cent) and mortality rate (91 per thousand) in South Asia. As 42 per cent of the population lives below the poverty line and 73 per cent are illiterate, poverty and population growth of 2.6 per cent per annum are serious obstacles for the development of the country (World Bank, 1998).

Since its unification in the eighteenth century, Nepal has been an independent kingdom. Unlike India and other countries in South Asia, it was never colonised. During the autocratic rule by the Rana family, from 1816 to 1951, foreigners were generally not allowed to enter the country, so Nepal was almost completely isolated from the outside world. In 1951 Nepal became a constitutional monarchy, however, the real power remained with the King. Although the Constitution theoretically guaranteed freedom of speech, the police apparatus was not publicly accountable and political activists were arrested and tortured. In 1990, a pro-democracy movement, which was motivated by economic problems and discontent with corruption, forced the King to end his rule, and a multi-party democracy was established. Since then the King has retained certain powers, but has dissociated himself from direct day-to-day government activities (Europe Publications, 1999).

Since 1990 Nepal has been struggling to establish a stable government. During the first three years of democracy the centrist Nepali Congress counted on a majority in the parliament, but then, due to inner party conflicts, it lost a mid-term poll. Since then no single party has until recently been able get a clear majority. The main political parties, the Congress, its main challenger the Communist Party of Nepal (Unified Marxist–Leninist), which is a social democratic party, and its rival to the right, the National Democratic Party, were struggling for power. As a result, the government changed six times between 1994 and 1999 (Europe Publications, 1999). This situation has favoured short-term politically motivated promises for holding power at the expense of long-term investments. In 1999, the Nepali Congress won a majority in the 205-seat lower house of the parliament, but factional infighting still diverts attention from social and economic problems.

Similar to other South Asian countries, Nepal remains largely an agrarian economy. More than 80 per cent of the economically active population work in the agricultural sector (see Table 6.1). Some of the serious problems facing this sector are its dependence on the monsoon rain, lack of fertilisers, scarcity of new land, continued environmental degradation and tense relations between landlords and tenants. Moreover, industry mainly depends on agricultural products and most of the industrial output is accounted for by traditional cottage industries such as basket weaving and the production of cotton fabrics. More than 15 per cent of the economically active labour force are unemployed. The small manufacturing industries and the service sector cannot meet the demand for work. Hence, substantial numbers have to work in the informal sector, in jobs such as street vendors, domestic servants and day labourers. Thus, similar to other Third World countries, Nepal has a dualistic economic structure, where a pre-capitalist economic system and a small industrial sector co-exist (Bean, 1994: 215).

In 1956, with the foundation of Nepal Bank Limited, the government started to invest heavily in the establishment of public enterprises. Although sixteen of the sixty-four public enterprises founded since then were privatised in the 1990s,

Table 6.1 Economically active population in Nepal

Economic sector	Number of people employed	Percentage
Agricultural, fishery and forestry	5,961,788	81.2
Manufacturing	150,051	2.0
Electricity, gas and water	11,734	0.2
Construction	35,658	0.5
Business, restaurant and hotel	256,012	3.5
Transportation, communication and storage	50,808	0.7
Finance and real estate	20,847	0.3
Community and social services	752,019	10.2
Others and industry not stated	100,668	1.4
Total	7,339,580	100

Source: Central Bureau of Statistics (1998)

state-owned firms still dominate the economy and in particular the small manufacturing sector. In contrast to the relatively large public sector corporations, private-owned firms are generally small. This sector consists of indigenous firms and joint ventures with foreign firms. Some Nepalese family groups, such as the Jyoti Group, Choudhary Group, Golchha Organisation, Khetan Group and Baidhya Organisation own most of the private sector. Major industries include carpets and rugs, food products, tobacco, textiles, chemicals, cement and bricks.

Turning to foreign trade, Nepal's economy is closely tied to its major trading partner, India. The major commodities imported are petroleum products, fertilisers and machinery. Principal exports are hand-knitted woollen carpets, ready-made garments and soap products. Carpet and garment exports expanded dramatically in the late 1980s and early 1990s. However, due to problems such as poor quality, trade restrictions and increasing hostility in the West to the use of child labour, these industries contracted in the mid-1990s. Despite the growth of craft industries, foreign aid, tourism and remittances from Nepalese working abroad still account for 50 per cent of foreign-exchange earnings. Nevertheless, there is the potential for economic growth not only in agriculture, but also in tourism and hydropower generation (Europe Publications, 1999: 793).

Another factor which has had a significant impact on the Nepalese business context is the deregulation of the economy. In 1991, the government started economic reforms, which aimed to move the country towards a free market economy. The influence and pressure of major foreign aid donors such as India, the United States, Japan, Europe, as well as institutions such as the World Bank played a vital role in the adoption of the reform programme. Public expenditure was cut by reducing subsidies, introducing a value-added tax, privatising companies, and laying off civil servants. The reform programme has also included the freeing of trade and prices, the elimination of public monopolies, the introduction of a convertible currency and the revitalisation of the stock market (American Embassy Kathmandu, 2000). With the liberalisation of the economy, the government aims to encourage trade and foreign investment. After decades of protectionism, Nepal has opened its doors to international investment. Foreign investments in joint venture operations with Nepalese partners or as 100 per cent foreign-owned subsidiaries are allowed. To attract foreign capital, investment procedures have been simplified and business licences and registration requirements have been eliminated. Nevertheless, there are some sectors such as cottage industries, consultancy and legal services which are still not open to foreign investment (HMG Nepal, 2000).

Although liberalisation and privatisation have been supported by all major parties, there have been different degrees of commitment to its implementation. Whereas centre or centre-right governments have moved more rapidly into this direction, Communist-dominated governments have favoured relatively more state control and interference in the economy. However, despite growing foreign investment, much of the Nepalese economy continues to be dominated by state-owned enterprises and corruption continues to flourish. The investment climate is severely distorted by bureaucratic delays, inefficient government administration and state intervention in the economy. Also major problems such as lack of direct access to seaports, few raw materials, inadequate electricity, difficult land transport, and inadequately developed and enforced legislation remain. Add to this, poverty, illiteracy and rapid population growth, one can see that companies in Nepal have to operate in a difficult business context.

National culture

The Nepalese culture has been strongly influenced by its neighbours – India, and Tibet China. India in particular has had a profound influence, as Indian migrants brought the Hindu caste system to Nepal. Today Nepal is the only official Hindu state in the world. Although the caste system was abolished by the Constitution and the cultural and religious rigidity of the caste system has eroded, there is still some correlation between the caste hierarchy and the socio-economic class hierarchy (Savada, 1991). For example, most posts in the civil service, the army and the police are held by members of the two highest Hindu castes and these also dominate the political parties. There is also still a link between occupational specialisation and membership of certain castes or ethnic groups. A further outcome of this cultural legacy is that women occupy a secondary position in business and the civil service. This can at least partly be attributed to the impact of the Rana rule in Nepal. Today, however, qualifications and particularly in the state-owned sector, political affiliations and connections are more important determinants for appointments, promotion and access to training abroad than the caste system.

Between the middle of the eighteenth century and the nineteenth century, Nepal was ruled by one family, the Ranas. Their regime isolated Nepal from the rest of the world. The Rana family attained a monopoly of power and developed a system of feudal culture in the society (Europe Publications, 1999: 784). For example, public appointments were made as a *Baksis* (gift) to those most favoured by the regime. After a brief interlude in the 1950s, many features of the Rana system were incorporated by King Mahandra in the *Panchayat* system, which operated between 1962 and 1990. This centrally controlled partyless council system served as the institutional basis of the King's rule. Since the 1960s, chief executives of public enterprises have been appointed following cabinet decisions. Such appointments are made rather on the basis of compliance with the ruling political system than professional qualifications. In government services, especially in ministries and departments, jobs are not assigned on demand (what a person can do) and on most favoured basis (whom the chief executive most favours). In fact, power sharing and decentralisation of decision-making are made very selectively and there is no valid system of performance management. Furthermore, the cultural legacy may have also contributed to a tendency among management to avoid decision-making (Agrawal, 1975) and responsibility (Shrestha, 1980). However, even after the dramatic political and economic changes of the early 1990s, the long-standing national culture of centralised administration and management has not yet changed. Some of the rules and regulations of the *Panchayat* system are still in place. Nepalese decision-makers still prefer to hold power rather than to delegate and devolve it. The overwhelming belief among them is that the more power you hold, the more you are recognised in society (Adhikari, 1999).

So far we have emphasised historical and traditional influences on Nepalese culture. However, over the last decades Western materialism has become an important influence on Nepalese culture, particularly in the urbanised Kathmandu Valley. Copying Western popular culture and values in general and consumerism in particular has had a profound impact on Nepalese youths.

Nepalese institutions

During the Rana regime only the ruling elite had access to education, the rest of the population remained largely illiterate. Ranas were against any sort of social and institutional development of the country, because they feared that this might threaten their regime. However, despite their isolation policy, already at that time English education had a higher status than the traditional one in the few colleges that existed. In the 1960s, primary education became free for all. Before the advent of democracy Tribhuvan University, Kathmandu University and Mahendra Sanskrit University were established. During the 1970s, vocational training was introduced in high schools. Some of the major institutions that have been established for professional and academic developments since then are: the Centre for Economic and Development Administration (CEDA), the University Research Centre, the Administrative Staff College and the Bankers Training Centre. In the private sector organisations like the Federation of Nepalese Chambers of Commerce and Industry (FNCCI), the Federation of Nepal Cottage and Small Industries (FNSCI), the Management Association of Nepal (MAN), the Hotel Association of Nepal (HAN), the Engineers Association of Nepal, the Trade Promotion Centre, the Social Service Council and the Small Business Promotion Project have played a vital role in the development of vocational and professional manpower. Among these, the Federation of Nepalese Chambers of Commerce and Industry is the main agency in the private sector to promote business and industry in Nepal. With the establishment of democracy in 1990 more educational institutions were opened, among them two new universities, Eastern University and Pokhara University. More than 3,000 community organisations are working in different regions of the country concentrating on human resource management, child labour, micro-financing, social awareness programmes, education and training. Despite these efforts, the literacy rate is low and vocational and technical training is not widely offered. The national system of higher education has to deal with a large number of students. The majority of jobs in Nepalese manufacturing firms are low skill ones requiring little formal qualification or experience. The skills needed are learned on the job and there is no labour shortage for these types of job. In contrast, people with higher education and skills are often unable to find employment in positions commensurate with their qualifications. In the past, educated people found good employment upon graduation in the expanding bureaucracy or development consultancy firms established by foreign donors (Savada, 1991). Today job opportunities in both of these employment outlets are more limited.

The low skill Nepalese economy in conjunction with poverty at least partly explains why child labour is still a major problem in Nepal. After the restoration of the multi-party democracy in 1990, Nepal ratified the UN Convention on the Rights of the Child and ILO Convention 138 which is concerned with the rights of working children. As a consequence, Nepal adopted the Child Act of 1992 which provides legal protection for children in the workplace and the Labour Act of 1992 which prohibits the employment of children under the age of 14. However, both Acts are good examples of laws which have not been effectively implemented yet. In the rural economy and the informal sector, child labour is widespread and children are employed in agriculture, mines, factories and domestic services (Pradhan, 2000; Suwal, 1998).

The most important law for the management of human resources in Nepal is the Labour and Trade Unions Act of 1992, which applies to any establishment employing ten or more people. This makes detailed provisions for the employment of workers and the operation of trade unions. The main provisions include that every job has to be classified, every employee has to receive an employment contract, that non-Nepalese citizens cannot normally be employed, and that a file has to be kept for every employee. It also regulates that working hours are fixed at forty-eight per week and that overtime work is remunerated at one and a half times the normal wage. The Act also stipulates that employers have to provide welfare funds, compensation in case of accident, a pension scheme, medical insurance and other social benefits. It permits strikes, except for employees in essential services, but also gives the government the opportunity to halt a strike. Finally, it makes provision for the settlement of grievances. If individual and collective labour conflicts cannot be settled at the company level, a labour office can be approached for the resolution of the conflict. If any party is dissatisfied with the outcome at this level, appeals to the Labour Court can be made. Similar to other areas of the law, the rapid turnover of governments during the last decade has meant that a complete code of labour law has not yet been developed. Furthermore, the Labour Courts have not been effective in enforcing the existing law. This is one explanation why a system of collective bargaining has not yet evolved in Nepal.

The state not only exerts its influence via the law, but also by other means. The government has a direct influence not only on the management of organisations in the public sector, but also on the state-owned enterprises. Top managers of these firms are directly appointed by the cabinet. In these decisions political affiliation is often more important than knowledge of the business. Furthermore, the government not only directly sets terms and conditions for all those employed in the public sector, but also for the private sector. Among these are maximum working hours, compulsory retirement age and minimum holidays. There is also a minimum wage with different rates for unskilled, semi-skilled, skilled and highly skilled employees. Furthermore, in 1974 a compulsory employee bonus of 10 per cent of annual profits was introduced.

In contrast to the state, trade unions are not very powerful in Nepal. Trade unions were banned during the *Panchayat* regime. Today, trade union membership is very low, only about 30,000 workers are organised. The benefits of collective bargaining are not widely appreciated by a workforce which has little knowledge of it (Ojha, 1993). Hence, similar to other developing countries there is only limited trade unionism in Nepal. Moreover, there are thirteen different unions which are split along party political lines. The three main unions are the sister organisations of the Nepal Communist Party, the Nepali Congress and the National Democratic Party. The unions are not only 'rivals' of each other, but also 'political enemies', as the labour movement is used by political parties as an electoral and political agent in the struggle for state power. This is illustrated by figures on industrial unrest provided in Table 6.2. They indicate that the number of disputes and the extent of days lost due to strike was the highest in 1991–92 when democracy was just established. After calming down during the mid-1990s, growing political instability has led to an increase in labour unrest, albeit not to the level of the early 1990s.

The above discussion suggests that environmental factors have a strong potential influence on the management of human resources in Nepal. The following case studies will illustrate the impact this has in practice. They were conducted during three months of field research in 1999 and are based on interviews with senior managers, employees and trade union representatives of three companies. For the interviews a check list was prepared. Among the issues covered were the role of personnel departments and trade unions as well as human resource planning, recruitment and selection, performance management, training and development activities, pay and benefit packages, employee relations and communication.

Table 6.2 Number of disputes and man-days lost in Nepal

Description	1991–92	1992–93	1993–94	1994–95	1995–96	1996–97
Strikes	128	47	25	27	20	36
Lockouts	31	5	1	4	1	15
Total	159	52	26	31	21	51
man-days lost due to:						
Strikes	140,375	38,652	25,129	33,944	26,696	68,746
Lockouts	15,301	8,758	3,325	1,814	9,535	25,132
Total	155,676	47,410	28,454	35,758	36,231	93,878

Source: HMG, Department of Labour (1998)

Case studies

Nepal Transit and Warehousing Company (NTW)

NTW is a state-owned company which provides transit and warehousing facilities for importers and exporters. It was founded in 1971 and today employs about 200 employees. The head office is located in the capital, Kathmandu, and there are branches at transit points in Nepal and India. The company has to compete with private firms and agents and is only making a small profit.

Similar to other state-owned firms, NTW is under direct control from the government. Any major organisational change or investment has to be approved by the respective ministry. Furthermore, although internal guidelines prohibit employees from being a member of a political party, political affiliation plays an important part in recruitment and promotion decisions. The general manager is directly appointed by the government and it appears that political beliefs rather than professional expertise often guide the recruitment for this position. Each of the seven changes of government in the 1990s has led to a change in the general manager. As a result of this unstable situation, there is generally little trust between the general manager and other company employees. This situation has prevented the company from addressing major problems such as overstaffing.

NTW does not offer any internal training. Every employee can obtain leave to attend outside training courses. However, the application process is highly bureaucratic, so that only very few employees have taken this opportunity. The company has an internal pay scale. Although high performing employees can get a merit increase, there is no formal system of individual or group-based performance-related pay. Similar to other public sector organisations, the company provides a number of social benefits such as medical allowances, company loans, house rents and transport allowances. In the absence of a state pension scheme, the company's retirement benefits are of particular importance for employees. Since 1997 a trade union has been organising some of the employees. So far the union and management have a good working relationship. Nevertheless, there appears to be a growing dissatisfaction among employees with the management of the company. Employees perceive a lack of inter- and intra-departmental co-operation.

Nepal Bank

Nepal Bank is the largest and oldest bank in Nepal. Founded in 1938, it has 218 branches all over the country. Until 1998, the state owned more than 50 per cent of the shares, since then it only holds 48 per cent. However, the government retains a strong influence on the bank as four of the nine board members are directly or indirectly appointed by it. This explains why the employee rules and regulations are still guided by the ones for the civil service. Currently Nepal Bank employs 6,600 people, more than one-third of all those working in the Nepalese financial sector. In 1990 the bank reduced its workforce by 800 people. This was achieved by a combination of voluntary redundancy and early retirement fostered by a generous incentive.

Every year conferences are held at the regional level of the bank where all managers discuss problems and strategies for future improvement. Problems and solutions identified are then further discussed at the local, regional and central level of the bank. Nevertheless, morale of the bank employees is not very high. One indicator is that, similar to the civil service, there is a distinction between 'first and second hours practices'. This means that although there is no flexitime, employees are only expected to be on duty during first hours between 10.30 and 14.00, but avoid duties and take doubtful leaves for the remainder of the day. Managers also complain about a strong bureaucracy in the bank.

Among the nine staff departments is a personnel administration department and a training department. The establishment of a separate training department at the end of the 1980s was an attempt to institutionalise human resource development within the organisation. The training department identifies training needs and organises courses for bank employees. The bank has its own training centre, but this lacks minimum logistic facilities such as computers, photocopying machines and a library. Before 1990, most external recruitment took place without a formal vacancy notice. Although today every vacancy is publicly announced and written examinations and interviews are conducted, there is still scope for politicians and relatives to exert their influence in the recruitment and selection process. In the absence of a formal human resource development system, promotion mainly depends on seniority. This situation has led to dissatisfaction among ambitious and innovative young employees who can progress only slowly through the ranks.

With regard to pay, the bank has to operate under the restrictions of the government. This means that it cannot, for example, implement a performance-related salary system. However, depending on the annual profit of the bank, all bank employees receive a bonus in the form of a certain percentage of their monthly salary. Similar to the first case study company, bank employees also receive a wide variety of allowances.

There are three main banking unions in Nepal, each affiliated to a political party. In Nepal Bank the unions affiliated to the Congress and to the Unified Marxist–Leninist Communist Party are active. The unions exert a particularly strong influence in promotion and transfer decisions, as members ask them to represent their interests. The relationship between the unions and management is perceived by both sides as unsatisfactory. Management complains about constant interference by the unions in the banking operations and that unions are highly political and criticise mismanagement in the bank.

Nepal Arab Bank (NABIL)

Nabil was established in 1984 as the first joint venture bank in Nepal; 50 per cent of its capital is held by the National Bank of Bangladesh, 20 per cent by Nepalese institutional shareholders and the rest by private ones. The bank is widely known for its prompt and efficient service and it is operating highly profitably. Currently it employs about 400 employees in twelve different branches.

Employee selection is based on a written test which is organised by an independent recruitment agency. New employees are usually recruited for the junior assistant level and from there promotion is mostly internal. There are nine hierarchical levels between the entry level, the junior assistant, and the executive director. Hence, similar to other Nepalese organisations, Nabil has a strong hierarchy. To facilitate internal promotion, there is a job rotation policy which makes it compulsory to change a job every two years.

Every year the performance of each employee is assessed. There are three types of appraisal, one for officers, one for non-officers and one for employees who are not professional bankers. Directly linked to the rating is a system of merit increases.

Whereas for 'sub-standard' or 'acceptable' ratings there will be no increment, salaries are increased for the others. As a result, pay is not only more differentiated than at other banks, but also higher. In addition, every bank employee can receive an annual bonus which depends on the profits of the bank. Finally, social benefits are also more generous than in other banks.

Unlike other organisations, employee morale seems to be quite high. Moreover, the second hour practices do not exist. However, a problem is the relatively high labour turnover. Nabil employees are often targeted by other joint venture banks. Unlike Nepal Bank, the industrial relations climate at Nabil is one of high trust. At least partly this is explained by the fact that the workforce is organised by a company union which is not affiliated to any political party.

Conclusion

From the above discussion, it appears that contradictory contextual factors affect the HRM of Nepalese organisations. Over the last decades the government has implemented several legal changes to promote investments by indigenous and foreign-owned firms, but a relatively unstable business environment still does not favour investment in human resources. On the one hand, the Nepalese culture fosters the adoption of traditional managerial practices such as centralised management and administration, but, on the other, it is quite open to modern Western-type management practices. Depending on factors such as the degree of state intervention and the openness to foreign influences, HR practices in Nepalese firms differ widely as the three sample firms demonstrated.

The example of Nepal suggests that there are opportunities and challenges for a transfer of Western-type HRM prescriptions to developing countries. Nepalese managers and policy-makers are generally not convinced about the benefits of investment in human resources. In particular there is no recognition that people should be treated as valuable assets. Therefore, it is important to make Nepalese decision-makers aware of the Western literature which demonstrates the performance impact of HRM practices. However, the Nepalese context does not appear favourable to many aspects of American or European HRM concepts. Prescriptions for the devolvement of human resource responsibility to line managers are one example. This is difficult because of the limited knowledge and skills of many managers. Furthermore, Nepalese decision-makers often prefer to hold the power rather than delegate and devolve it. Therefore, there is a need to develop HRM concepts and prescriptions that are more attuned to the business context of Nepal.

References

Adhikari, D. R. (1999) *Human Resource Management in Nepal: Policies and Practices*, Innsbruck: Leopold-Franzens-University.

Agrawal, G. R. (1975) 'Management: The Critical Constraint in the Development of Nepal', *Nepal Journal of Management*, 21–29.

American Embassy Kathmandu (2000) *Country Commercial Guide 2000*, American Embassy, Kathmandu http://www.south-asia.com/USA/, (accessed 10 April 2000).

Bean, R. (1994) *Comparative Industrial Relations* 2nd edn., London: Routledge.

Central Bureau of Statistics (1998) *Statistical Pocket Book*, Kathmandu: Central Bureau of Statistics.

Europe Publications (1999) *The Far East and Australia 2000*, 31st edn, London: Europe Publication.

HMG Nepal (1998) *Facts on Industrial Relations*, Kathmandu: Department of Labour.

HMG Nepal (2000) *Foreign Investment Board*, http://www.info-nepal.com/fips/policy.hml, *(accessed 8 February 2000)*.

Nepal Home Page Business and Economy Directory (2000), wysiwyg://6/http://www.nepal-homepage.com/dir/business/business.html, (accessed 8 February 2000).

Ojha, P. K. (1993) 'Workers' Participation in Industry: Nepal Experience', in P.R. Pant and N. Manandhar (eds), *Industrial Relations in Nepal: A Book of Reading*, Kathmandu: Friedrich Naumann Foundation and Industrial Relations Forum.

Pradhan, G. (2000) *Challenging Child Labour*, http://www.south-asia.com/cwin/child-labour.html, (accessed 31 January 2000).

Savada, A. M. (1991) *Nepal*, Federal Research Division Library of Congress, Washington, http://lcweb2.loc.gov/frd/cs/nptoc.html, (accessed 10 April 2000).

Shrestha, J. B. (1980) 'Role of Entrepreneurs and Managers in Nepal', *Management Dynamics*, 1, 1.

Suwal, B. R. (1998) *Child Labour Situation in Nepal*, Kathmandu: Tribhuvan University.

World Bank (1998) *World Development Report, 1998*, Washington, DC: World Bank.

7 Human resource management in Pakistan

Shaista E. Khilji

Introduction

Despite its unique cultural set-up, a large and capable workforce educated and well versed in English, liberal privatization and investment policies, and strategic geographical importance (the gateway to the Central Asian Republics, bordering China and Russia in the North and adjoining India on its eastern borders), Pakistan has been largely ignored in management research. This chapter intends to fill this void by providing an overview of the issues facing Pakistani managers and by exploring management approaches appropriate to the specific environment they encounter. The main aims of this chapter are threefold: first, to discuss the nature and status of HRM in Pakistan; second, to analyse the influence of key national factors on Pakistani HRM; and, third, to study the impact of prevalent HRM approaches (both traditional and present) on employees.

To achieve these aims, an analysis of the following topics is conducted:

1 The key economic and business environment
2 The status of HRM in Pakistan
3 The national factors unique to the understanding of HRM in Pakistan.

The chapter will conclude by drawing out implications for further research and discussing the possible future of HRM in Pakistan.

Some basic facts about Pakistan

Pakistan is the seventh most populous country of the world, with a total population of 138 million (World Bank, 2000). At 2.18 percent, it has one of the world's highest population growth rates, such that in the next two decades its population is expected to surpass 260 million. The total employed labor force is estimated at 38.18 million, which is only 27.66 percent of the total population. In effect, 41 percent of the total population is under the age of 14 years (CIA, 2000). Due to slow economic growth for the past two years, 2.36 million people are unemployed (Government of Pakistan, 1999).

The economy is agrarian in nature as 46 percent of the labor force is employed in the agricultural sector. The contribution of the agricultural sector to gross domestic product (GDP) is 24.5 percent (see Table 7.1 and Table 7.2). Manufacturing sector employs 17 percent of the labor force. Although its share to GDP is only 19.1 percent, it is growing faster than any other sector (at a rate of 5 percent) and if it continues to grow at this rate, it is expected to bypass the agricultural sector in the next ten years, both in its contribution to the GDP and in terms of the labor force employed.

There are 766 companies listed on the Karachi Stock Exchange (Karachi Stock Exchange, 2000). The textiles sector is the largest, with 224 listed firms and foreign investment is most active in sectors such as chemicals/fertilizers, pharmaceuticals, banking, auto, fuel and energy.

Since the early 1990s, Pakistan has been implementing a comprehensive program of deregulation and fostering a climate for private investment by opening up activities previously monopolized by the public sector. Bold steps have been taken to privatize the entire public sector, including financial institutions and industrial units and lucrative incentives have been offered for private investment. These efforts, aimed at reversing the trend of nationalization and improving economic growth, have created a suitable business environment in the country.

Table 7.1 Sectoral distribution and its percentage share of GDP in Pakistan (1998–99)

Sectors of the economy	Percentage share of GDP
Agriculture	24.5
Manufacturing and mining	19.1
Wholesale and retail	15.4
Transport and communication	10.2
Services	8.9
Public administration and defence	6.1
Electricity and gas	4.1
Construction	3.6
Finance and insurance	2.3
Others	5.8

Source: Government of Pakistan (1999). Pakistan Economic Survey. Available at http://www.pak.gov.pk

Table 7.2 Employment by occupation in Pakistan (1998–99)

Major occupations	Percentage
Agriculture	47.0
Manufacturing and mining	17.0
Services	17.0
Professional	5.0
Administrative	1.0
Clerical	4.6
Others	8.4

Source: Government of Pakistan (1999). Pakistan Economic Survey. Available at http://www.pak.gov.pk

Public sector organizations have been marked by a passive management culture. Political patronage rather than sound business decisions have often determined their operations. Therefore, from the onset, the private sector was encouraged to develop forward-looking management systems. However, it was not until 1997 that the government undertook the task of changing the prevailing corporate culture of public sector enterprises by doing the following:

1   Appointing professional teams of managers at the top-most hierarchical levels whose task was to change the HRM culture by making it meritocratic, decentralized and responsive to employees' needs (Khilji, 1999b).
2   Outlining a unique Pakistan 2010 Program that distinctly outlined the need to refashion a new work culture whose building blocks are characterized by innovation, quality and discipline (Government of Pakistan, 1997).

The initial success of invigorating the economy was dampened by nuclear tests, subsequent imposition of sanctions by the G-7 countries and frequent changes of governments, with the result that the economy started to stagnate and the public began to grow disillusioned with the state of affairs. A detailed discussion of these factors is covered in the following sections.

Human resource management in its infancy

Khilji (1995) and Siddiqui (1997) provided the evidence which indicates that a majority of businesses in Pakistan (both local and foreign) have restructured their personnel divisions as human resource divisions. However, they do not provide any information about what this change entails. A more recent survey by Khilji (1999b) explores the content and context of these changes, mainly in the private sector, in local as well as in multinational firms. As this survey is more comprehensive (523 questionnaire responses and 186 in-depth interviews in fifteen organizations) and up-to-date, findings from this survey will be cited throughout this chapter.

Khilji (1999b) argues that HRM in Pakistan is passing though an embryonic stage. Of the fifteen organizations in her sample, only three (all of which were multinationals) had embraced an integrated and focused approach to HRM, taking cultural and structural changes into consideration. In these organizations the role of HRM had been broadened, HR departments had been brought up to par with other business areas and communication channels had been opened up. The other twelve organizations were following a piecemeal approach whereby only certain HR activities had been introduced in installments. All organizations had adopted 'pay for performance' and were making concerted attempts to expand the role of their training programs. In addition to this, six organizations had also adopted 'Management by objectives' (MBO) and 'open' appraisal systems. Despite these efforts, most of these organizations suffer from lack of communication, a gap between managers' promises and implementation of policies and an inconsistency of HRM practices among employees and the centralized structure of the organizations. Employees expressed dissatisfaction with the existing norms. They clearly understood the vital role that HRM played in adding value to the work environment and building their long-term careers and they aspired for a pro-active, professional and participatory approach to people management. Some of these elements will be further discussed in the next section as various national factors are identified and explained.

National factors

Over the years, a number of researchers have highlighted the significance of national factors (like national culture, work-related values and external environment) in understanding HRM systems, following which many studies have been conducted to determine their impact on HRM policies and practices (Easterby-Smith *et al.*, 1995; Gill and Wong, 1998; Hannon *et al.*, 1995; Horwitz and Darren, 1998; Lawler *et al.*, 1995; Newman and Nollen, 1996; Rosenzweig and Nohria, 1994). Budhwar and Sparrow (1998) have categorised these as *national culture, dynamic business environment, institutions* and *specific business sectors*. They also provide a detailed list of the aspects constituting each of these four factors. This framework is adopted in this chapter.

National culture

Research in HRM has shown that social institutions (such as family, education through socialization process) influence companies' strategies and organizational practices in a systematic way, with the result that companies' structures and processes reflect typical national patterns (for details see Hofstede, 1980, 1991; Jaeger and Kanungo, 1990; Mueller, 1994; Tayeb, 1995).

Based upon the above premise, in a systematic analysis of the work-related values of employees in Pakistan, many influences from early childhood are evident. Khilji (1995, 1999b) has described Pakistani culture as a mixture of *religion, Indian origins, British inheritance* and *American influences*. The following discussion will describe each of these influences and their impact on Pakistani HRM systems.

Religion: the foregone influence

Some 96 percent of the Pakistani population is Muslim (Government of Pakistan, 1999). Assumptions about religion seem to be prominent in the minds of people because the ideology of the creation of Pakistan emerged from the belief that Muslims of the Indian sub-continent were a separate nation based on their religion and their Islamic cultural heritage. Consequently, they should be given the independence to form their own state in which they could freely practice Islam and formulate systems that would emanate from the teachings of the Holy Book, the Quran.

However, since independence became a reality, Pakistani rulers have repeatedly chosen to give lip service to the importance of Islamic symbols (Malik, 1996) while confining religious beliefs to the private domain. The only exception was General Ziaul Haq, a military ruler who believed Pakistan would continue to strive only if it sticks to Islam (James, 1993). As a consequence, the Islamization of socio-economic systems began which seems to have left an impact on economic, legal and educational systems of the country. For example, in schools and colleges (up to graduate level), teaching of Islamic Studies was made a compulsory subject. Zia's aim was to fuse together religious and secular teachings so that they would be based on Islamic principles in every domain and at every level. In other words, for future generations of Pakistanis, thinking should be fashioned to reflect and be derived from rules of thought and action laid down in the Quran.

Tayeb (1997) argues that in a predominantly Muslim country, Islam, through national culture, influences organizations. It follows that in countries where Islam plays such a role, there would be an extensive influence on HRM. However, this is not the case in Pakistan. Khilji's (1999b) research shows Islamization of macro institutions (to facilitate Islamic practices within the society) extends only to a limited degree to organizations. Examples would include the allocation of prayer rooms where employees could say their prayers during office hours, extended lunch breaks for Friday prayers and shorter office hours during Ramadhan (the month of fasting). It has been argued that the Islamization program in Pakistan is concerned only with the outer shell and not the core of Islam (Ahmad, 1996; James, 1993; Lyon, 1993; Malik, 1996). As well, in Pakistan (as in certain other Muslim countries) Islam has become localized due to the overshadowing impact of other influences (Latifi, 1997; Tayeb, 1998). These other influences will be elaborated upon in the following sections.

Indian origins: some lasting impressions

Most people of Pakistan are originally from the Indian sub-continent (although some have Turkish, Afghani, Arab and Iranian ancestors[1]). Therefore, many of the prevailing customs and tradition, that form the edifice of the society, can be traced back to Indian origins. The social set-up in Pakistan is family-centered. Obligations to family include both financial and ritual practices. In a typical working family set-up, great care is taken in the choice of a child's education. He is expected to be obedient to his parents, teachers and other elders. This pattern of dependence (upon elders or seniors) pervades all human contact and people carry a strong need for 'dependence/security' (Lyon, 1993). The educational system also requires surrendering to authority. Personal initiative, originality and independence in decision-making are met with disapproval. As a result, people generally accept authority unquestioningly.

It is important to mention that many of the above characteristics of the Pakistani social set-up are contrary to the very principles of Islam. For example, Islam calls its believers to meditate and probe, promotes 'achievement' and holds each individual responsible for his actions (Khilji, 1999b). However, as many social characteristics have been incorporated into the 'Islamic' codes of conduct, Islam in Pakistan (like other Muslim countries) has become localized (Latifi, 1997; Tayeb,

1998). This explains why the Islamic value system does not appear to be the guiding norm of behavior for society in general.

British legacies: not changing with times?

The British, who established a colony on the sub-continent for almost a century, are thought to be responsible for creating elite classes in the society, notably feudal and civil servants. In the past few decades, a relatively small, educated elite has increasingly been displaced by an educated middle class, but without bringing an essential change of attitude. Just like their counterparts in the colonial era, the elite symbolize money, power and status and do not respond to the needs of people. In practice, the law or the law-enforcing bodies also protect the affluent and the powerful. The rich or powerful can commit a crime and go unpunished, either through bribe or *gaunxi* (connections) (Hussain, 1999; Khilji, 1999b). The resulting two-track system has widened the gap between the haves (elites) and the have-nots (the general public). The best of schools and other facilities are available only to the elites, while a majority of ordinary people still struggle to obtain the basic necessities of life, such as electricity and clean drinking water. In the minds of the public there are no longer any checks and balances to curb the power of the influential (Hussain, 1999).

A manifestation of elite culture is also exhibited within organizations. HR policies and practices, in all sample organizations, favor marketing or business graduates over other employees, and managers over non-managers (Khilji, 1999b). Salary differentials between entry-level employees and executives are as high as 800 percent. Employees in marketing are given preferential treatment with better perks, greater training opportunities, higher bonuses and far more frequent promotions than other employees. Biases reflected in various HR policies (especially in training and rewards) create a work environment that hampers cooperation between these groups. For example, certain experienced workers were unwilling to devote the time expected to train fresh university graduates and to resolve problems that arose (ibid.). They resented the fact that the young university graduates were being given better salaries because of their education, even though they lacked the experience to perform the job well.

American influences: the way forward?

Since the creation of Pakistan, the United States has been the most significant foreign player in its politics and probably the most vital element in the formulation of various economic and foreign policies (Hussain and Hussain, 1993). Moreover, in the 1980s, with the Russian invasion of Afghanistan, American help for Afghani refugees, rehabilitation and defense purposes reached the US$ 2 billion mark. Simultaneously, cultural influences also peaked. Americans came to Pakistan and conversely Pakistanis found the gateway to America. The exposure brought American ideas into the schools and the workplace. Meanwhile, electronic media also played its role. Today many affiliates of American business schools are seen in every neighborhood of major cities. The two most well-respected business schools of the country[2] are run like top-class North American business schools (Khilji, 1999a). Management faculties of government universities also follow American syllabi. Many training institutes (like PIM-Pakistan Institute of Management) were also established with the aid from Ford Foundation and Harvard, both in terms of money and content of training programs.

Zakaria (1994) and Khilji (1995, 1999a) have observed that Pakistani managers want to follow American management style. American management is considered to be more progressive and result-oriented, whereas British managers are hailed as slow and bureaucratic, trademarks which the Pakistani civil service seems to have inherited from them.

Corporate culture: the changing perceptions

The corporate culture of Pakistan, like many developing countries, has been characterized as *collectivist, associative* and having a *high uncertainty avoidance* and a *high power distance* (Hofstede, 1980, 1991; Khilji, 1995; Trompenaars, 1994). This implies that there is a general unquestioning respect for authority, people are integrated as cohesive groups and they are emotional. On the masculinity index, Pakistanis are found exactly half way, i.e., possessing both masculine and feminine qualities (Hofstede, 1991: 84). This means people exhibit both the tougher qualities usually associated with men (i.e. being aggressive, ambitious and competitive) as well as the feminine qualities such as modesty, caring for others and a non-ambitious nature. However, evidence from Khilji's (1999b) recent research suggests (and it will be highlighted in following discussion) that the inclination is definitely towards masculine qualities.

Organizations have a formal and hierarchical structure (Khilji, 1999b). Consequently, HRM is also centralized. Policies formulated at head offices are cascaded down to each office/division for a uniformity of objectives and culture. Employees cannot approach their HR departments directly. Going though the proper channel is always stressed. Autonomy given to employees is low and they are not often encouraged to rely on themselves or to learn new things. There is a communication gap between management and employees. Typically, HR policies and practices are made in isolation; feedback from employees during formulation process or afterwards is not sought. Employees seldom know what decisions are being made at their HR departments as communication between employees and HR departments is kept to a minimum. The 'talk' of management does not always match their 'walk'. HR managers are generally praised for their policies but employees expressed dissatisfaction with their role and impact (Khilji, 1999a).

Jamal (1998) and Khilji (1999b) report a low level of trust among Pakistani employees. Khilji's (1999b) describes how Pakistani employees are detached from their work organizations and have an individualistic relationship to their workplace. There is a clear-cut distinction between in-group and out-group members (Triandis, 1995). Organizations are seen as out-groups while families, and at times co-workers (or managers), form in-groups. Whenever there is a conflict between the two, ties with the latter take precedence over the former. She gives the example of group turnover (whereby managers tend to take along employees with whom they have formed in-groups when they join another organization) which was stated as the most common cause of a high exit from the organizations.

From the above discussion it follows that Pakistani society holds three distinct types of ethos which sometimes conflict. The first comes from the *social set-up*, the second from *religion* and the third from the *West*. The first two are deeply rooted in the emotional experiences of growth during childhood and permeate in a pervasive subconscious manner. The third is an acquired knowledge. The actions chosen are invariably influenced by these types of ethos. Depending on a given situation, one of them becomes a major determinant of choice. However, as the previous discussion states, Islam appears to be the least significant influence at work, despite the strong feelings of allegiance people have for it (see Table 7.3).

The business environment

Deregulation: lessons learned from the public sector

Economic policies followed in Pakistan can be termed as liberal; they have sought to make maximum use of market mechanisms. The role of public investment has been to supplement rather than to displace private investment. The only exception was the 1971–77 period of nationalization which created a setback to the growth of the economy. The country had developed a sound industrial base during the 1960s, but suddenly went into slump. The problems were compounded by the low level of output due to bureaucratic management, heavy over-staffing and political interference in the management of establishments (Mirza, 1995). Rigid personnel practices were the norm and decisions were largely beyond the control of management. Chief executives were hired or fired by successive governments (Klein, 1992). Managers were often forced to hire staff, not necessarily on the basis of merit, but on the recommendations of union leaders. Unions, which had special political protection and did not necessarily represent workers' interests, made it very difficult to lay off excess staff. Performance-based remuneration was forbidden. Wages and salaries were not competitive with those of foreign competitors (Khilji, 1999b). Despite an increasingly large availability of training institutes dedicated to employee development, many organizations failed to benefit because of a lack of planning. Seniority, contacts or using training as a reward for those employees close to management or union leaders often determined those chosen (Eldridge, 1992). Management failed to develop or implement systems that were fair, led by assessment of training needs and linked to career development plans of individual employees.

Consequently, in 1990, a government privatization program was introduced. This program was deemed a success as investors' interest was sparked and many new enterprises (especially in the banking sector) were set up. At the same time, multinationals that had long been operating with a low profile, started reinvesting

Table 7.3 Important national factors and their impact on HRM in Pakistan

Factor	Aspect	Impact
National culture	Social set-up Social clouts	All spheres of HRM are affected; referrals and knowing the management is the most common source of recruitment, rewards and a good performance appraisal. In the minds of people, maintaining a good relationship with managers is far more important than the actual tasks they perform. The impact is negative as it prevents organisations from living up to the expectations of changing business conditions and leads to frustration amongst employees.
	Hierarchy/ large power distance	Results in centralised decision-making, causes communication gap, lowers autonomy and stifles participation. Managers are unwilling to share power or information. Employees are not used to questioning authority.
	Low trust	Organisations are seen as out-groups. Results in low organisational commitment and high turnover rate.
	British inheritance: Elitism/distinct social classes	Those in power/influential positions are favoured in terms of higher salaries, better training opportunities and more frequent promotions.
	Culture of public sector enterprises	There is desire to part with the past and to build a progressive culture. By contrast, in smaller organisations, where HRM lacks initiative, the culture has been duplicated.
	American influences	These expose people to American management systems/ideas, like use of MBO and feedback oriented appraisals. Management training is largely based upon American ideas.
Business environment	Competition	Forces organisations to redesign their management structures and to adopt new HRM practices in order to remain competitive. Increase in training programmes led by an organized needs-assessment. Job opportunities being available for employees, creates a high turnover.
	Economic conditions: High unemployment	Problems in recruitment; large pools of unsolicited applications, vacancies are not announced and advertisements are avoided or blind ads are used. There is a large supply of labour hence some smaller companies have no difficulty recruiting and do not really understand the need to retain employees.
	Instability	Causes reduced trust amongst employees. Organisations hesitate to expand and are afraid to commit resources for HR development.
	Political uncertainty	Causes disillusionment and lack of trust amongst employees. Organisations hesitate to commit to HR development.

Table 7.3 (continued)

Factor	Aspect	Impact
	Technology Use of internet	Exposes employees to new ideas and helps build high expectations.
Institutions	Multinationals	These are agents of change; they bring in new ideas for local organisations to follow; they set standards in the field of HRM. Market surveys and adoption of performance based rewards have been copied by large and more successful local organisations.
	Unions	The union's laws influence termination, dismissals, safe and healthy work environment. Past experience compels organisations to avoid formation of unions at workplaces. Job titles redesigned to give clerks officer status Employees asked to sign an agreement not to form unions at work.
	Article 27b	Marginalises union influences
Business sector	Benchmarking	Local organizations look up to Multinationals in pursuit of new HRM practices.
	Common strategies	These evolve out of a competitive environment. They foster customer/employee orientation and develop participatory management cultures.

in the market through expansion of services or diversification of products. The government also took initiatives to foster a business-driven culture and to encourage the use of professional and modern management practices. This created a healthy, profitable and competitive business environment making the private sector more progressive than the public sector (Bokhari, 1996). In a recent survey, *The Economist* reported: 'There are remarkable examples of private sector taking over the duties of a corroded state and performing them well' (Unger, 1999).

It is apparent that Pakistani organizations and their culture are undergoing a dramatic change. The public sector organizations that were run on colonial patterns are being revamped. The private sector is a valuable addition to the business environment, it has added impetus to the economy, made it more competitive and added a fresh perspective to HRM systems.

Political culture causing disillusionment

Pakistan's political history has always symbolized a tug-of-war between the ruling elite of the country, namely military, bureaucracy and feudal politicians all attempting to monopolize power (Malik, 1994). In the past decade, the row has toppled five democratically elected governments. Despite that, politicians (representing this elite) have not won the sympathies of their electorates because not only have they failed to deliver their promises but they have also proven to be corrupt (Amir, 1999). A noted Pakistani columnist wrote:

> Wherever we look – from the railways to the police; and from civil bureaucracy to parliamentary democracy – an unbroken vista of rubble, broken promises and failed potential meets the eye. Wherever there has been progress, it has been largely due to individual initiative and determination. The management skills and institutional support needed to run infrastructure have virtually been eradicated through nepotism and corruption.
>
> (Hussain, 1999)

This pattern has caused unrest, as well as feelings of insecurity and disillusionment for the public. So strong is the pessimism that Burki (1993), begins his analysis of Pakistan's economy by saying, 'I was struck by the extraordinary amount of *pessimism* with which people seem to view their future.'

Similarly, Unger (1999) and Khilji (1999b) shed light on the disgruntled outlook of Pakistanis. Being exposed to hollow promises of politicians and their failure to deliver, it is hardly surprising that people have developed a distrustful and skeptical outlook. The same attitude is carried over to organizations where employees refuse to buy the words of management and want to see results. An employee was quoted remarking about her HR department, 'They all spin tales . . . You know what it is like in our country!' (ibid.).

Economic instability one step forward and two steps back

The change in predisposition and priorities of the people has already been mentioned. Economic hardship may be at the helm of it. Economic uncertainty, led by political instability and vindictiveness, has acted as a major deterrent to the stable growth of the economy (Barron and Higgins, 1995; *Euromoney*, 1989). Every Prime Minister appoints a new cabinet and an entourage of advisers. Together they eliminate programs undertaken by previous governments. Although new programs are put into practice aiming to solve the same economic problems, they, too, are duly changed when the next government takes office without sparing a thought for the amount of resources that may have gone into implementing these programs. Despite abundant land, cheap labor and low office costs,[3] Pakistan lags behind other developing countries in terms of the amount of foreign investment it has attracted. This is unfortunate because the investment policies have been recognized as 'the best' among emerging markets (*The Economist*, 1995) and in 1993–4 it was declared the winner among emerging markets, in terms of FDI inflow (*Banker*, 1995; *The Economist*, 1995).

Human development record: adding salt to the wounds

The growth record of Pakistan's economy has been quite commendable and compares favorably with other countries of South Asia. A noteworthy feature of economic progress has been the achievement of respectable growth rates (Burki,

1988, 1993; Khan, 1997). However, in the arena of social development, progress has been uneven and mediocre. While various quality-of-life indices do reflect a distinct improvement over the years, but they are still disappointing for a country of Pakistan's economic standing. The literacy rate at 40 percent is one of the lowest in the world. The educational facilities even with substantial expansion over the years, are inadequate and unevenly distributed (Khilji, 1999a). In 1997–8, the budget allocated to education remained a meager 2.25 percent of GNP while during the same period, the country opted to display and detonate nuclear weapons. The current 1999–2000 budget allocated Rs.142 billion for defense purposes and only Rs.116.3 billion to developing the country and its 138 million people (*Dawn*, 1999).

This should, however, not create the wrong impression that Pakistan has a shortage of educated labor. The reality is that the amount spent on the three levels of education (primary, secondary and the tertiary) have been disproportionately allocated; i.e. colleges and universities in urban areas have been expanded to the detriment of elementary education in rural areas (Korson, 1993). This, together with a high population growth rate and the inability of the economy to provide job opportunities for its educated and uneducated labor force, has created a paradoxical situation: an abundance of unemployed graduates and an increase of a million illiterate workers each year. Even though more money has been diverted to tertiary education, it remains insufficient to meet the needs of a population that is growing rapidly and is geographically spread out (Ahmad, 1997). To make things worse, because of limited employment opportunities, the 'brain drain' has not been discouraged.

Workforce: too large to handle

Another major difficulty in Pakistan's situation is the high rate of population growth (2.1 percent). As a consequence, increased national output has not led to improvement in the standard of living. Expansion of the social services has proven insufficient to satisfy the needs of such a large population. If the population growth rate continues in the same way, the labor force will also grow at this rate into the first decade of the twenty-first century (Cameron and Irfan, 1992). It is an alarming situation for the country, because this rate far exceeds domestic employment growth. Currently, about 2.36 million are unemployed at the rate of 6.10 percent (Government of Pakistan, 1999). The distribution of employment by occupation shows that 47 percent of the population is in agriculture and that a mere 34 percent is in service or manufacturing (see Table 7.2). While many developed economies have moved from agriculture to manufacturing to service to knowledge-based industries in the last century, Pakistan still remains an agrarian economy (see Table 7.1).

The above discussion and existing literature point out that a large but unemployed (or underemployed) workforce due to limited job opportunities, unwise budgeting priorities and economic uncertainty have caused frustration and insecurity among the working class. An unstable political system and growing income and social disparities have worsened the situation. Jamal (1998), in his ethnographic study of Pakistanis, argues that traditional and cultural values associated with group life have deteriorated in the past twelve years because of political uncertainty and economic hardship. As a result, there is an ever-increasing trend towards materialism. Khilji (1999b) also argues economic hardship, competition for jobs, retaining these jobs and ambitions to prosper in a status-conscious and materialistic society seem to have strengthened *individualistic* attitudes towards organizations. As a result, commitment to organizations is low and desire to leave is high. Respondents in her survey were clear that they would quit if their organization did not meet their personal needs. This means employees essentially form economic relationships with their organizations and treat them like out-groups. At the same time, relationships to managers are considered important (either for achieving individual or social needs) and here they may form close in-groups.

Multinationals: agents of change

Multinationals, in Pakistan, are seen as a means of bringing in new technology and work practices and providing training grounds for the workforce. They are also expected to set trends in the field of management because confidence in local organizations is low. In one example, a Citibank-trained Pakistani and his team (all of whom have vast experience with multinational banks) were appointed to rescue the biggest nationalized bank and to put the management back on the right track before it was privatized. In a public sector environment that stifles creativity and innovation, multinationals are expected to act as agents of change and some of them seem to live up to the expectations. Khilji's (1999b) research shows that multinationals are gradually disseminating HRM practices to local organizations, practices either borrowed from their parent companies or developed indigenously. Large and profitable local organizations observe practices in multinationals and adopt them in their own settings. Employees in local organizations treat multinationals as benchmarks of developments in the field of HRM and the open management style; they wish a participatory style was also prevalent in their organizations. As a consequence, multinationals also enjoy a high image in the market and are considered 'employers of choice'. They recruit the best from the market and also offer higher salaries and better perks.

Institutions

Labor laws

British bureaucratic systems that persisted after independence have introduced many elements of rationalized systems including a large number of laws regulating HRM practices. Broadly, these laws deal with the provision of a safe and healthy working environment, the employer's liability in case of injury caused by accidents, various welfare measures for workmen, the workmen's fair share in the company's profits and the employer's contributions towards their social security funds. All organizations, irrespective of origin and industry, are required to abide by these laws. For example, termination of regular employees is not permissible for any reason other than misconduct. If a workman is aggrieved by termination of his services, discharge or dismissal, he has the right to apply to a committee for the redress of his individual grievance. Many organizations in the past were taken to court by the dismissed employees. Not only did it tarnish their image in the market, but the majority of court decisions favored the employee. In some instances, organizations were asked to reinstate the employee. Consequently, organizations hesitate to dismiss an employee unless gross misconduct is repeatedly observed. In such a case, full internal investigation into the causes is launched before dismissal takes place.

Unions: diminished significance

Since independence, as the political power has shifted from democratically elected representatives to military regimes, the labor history of Pakistan came to be characterized as a mix of labor concessions and repression. Four different labor reforms were announced in the country. The fourth Labor Policy, introduced in 1972, included comprehensive measures to strengthen trade unions (Saeed, 1995) but 'brought to new heights the familiar mix of labor concessions and repression that have characterized the Pakistani labor history' (Chandland, 1995: 69). Unions received political patronage and the interests of workers were not necessarily represented. In 1977 after martial law was imposed, strikes and lock-outs were banned, as well as student unions and (the registration) of trade unions of some corporations (such as Pakistan International Airlines and Pakistan Television). At the same time, politicization of the labor unions in public sector organizations (as discussed previously) reached notorious levels (Khan, 1989). Even after the martial law was lifted, successive governments failed despite their promises to implement a comprehensive new policy and political patronage of the unions reached new heights, such that in Pakistan unions are instantly equated with corruption and misuse of power by employees and management, alike.

In 1997, the government introduced a new policy, Article 27b, to free the work environment from the influences of unions. As a result, union activities have been deprived of power they once enjoyed and exploited; and the impact of unions on businesses in Pakistan is reduced to an insignificant level. New organizations and multinationals, though previously unionized, now discourage employees from forming unions. Some organizations take extra caution by either obtaining an 'undertaking' from new employees that they will not involve themselves in union activities of any kind or by assigning titles of 'officers' to clerks and computer operators to legally prevent them from forming a union.

Professional bodies and international institutions

HRM in Pakistan has a low status and HR jobs are not considered specialized. There are numerous business schools and universities around the country that offer MBA degrees but none of them offer a degree or diploma in HRM. The perception is that if it is an HR job, anyone can do it (Khilji, 1999b). As a result, there is a scarcity of HR specialists or professionals or professional bodies.

Unlike countries in the West where international institutions like EU and NAFTA have strong influences upon HRM policies and practices, Pakistan does not seriously comply with regulations imposed by international bodies like the ILO and GATT. Hence, the impact of both professional bodies and international institutions on HRM is negligible.

The business sector

Sector-specific HRM policies and practices are only observed in few business sectors. For example, in the banking industry, organizations like Citibank and ABN Amro have especially tailored in-house customer services training programs for existing and new employees in order to socialize them into the emerging culture. Second, a range of modern services, such as evening/Saturday/telephone banking, ATMs and credit cards have been introduced by multinational banks and soon imitated by many local banks. Third, new HRM practices are being introduced to retain the employees who have been trained.

As mentioned above, multinationals have been at the forefront of these initiatives. New technologies have necessitated increased cooperation such as the Master Card arrangement between Bank of America-Pakistan and Askari Bank (a large local bank) or the ATM sharing between Askari Bank and ABN Amro-Pakistan. However, these cooperative arrangements do not extend to HRM. An attempt was made to run a forum by HR managers from the multinationals in order to meet and discuss various HRM issues, however, it was short-lived. On the brighter side, some HR managers do use informal networking in order to learn from the experiences of others and learn about the likely impact before adopting a new policy (Khilji, 1999b).

Impact on HRM practices

In this section, main HRM practices prevalent in several organizations will be examined in order to study the direct impact of the many factors previously discussed (see summarization in Table 7.3).

Culture builders

As has been pointed out, many organizations in Pakistan have reorganized their HRM function. Yet their focus continues to be either on administrative tasks or planning how to control employees to minimize labor costs. There are only a few exceptional cases where multinationals have revised the roles of their HR managers and asked them to take the role of culture builders by bringing management and employees closer to each other. These multinationals are most aggressive in their own industry and have expanded their operations tremendously in the market. The management at these multinationals believes that competitive advantage is found in their people. Therefore, they strive to increase employee productivity by investing in them, adopting a feedback-oriented MBO approach and linking performance evaluation to their career development. They are considered 'employers of choice', hence have an advantage in attracting and selecting only the best candidates.

Other organizations

Among other organizations, two different sets of practices are adopted. The first set is more in line with the practices of multinationals and has been adopted by larger and more successful local organizations. They emphasize the use of merit alone or in conjunction with 'contacts' in the recruitment process. They have also set up in-house training facilities to expose their employees to different ideas. However, unlike the multinationals, training is neither organized nor actually tied to individual career development. Recently, these organizations have also started conducting salary surveys, like their multinational counterparts, in order to attract and retain the best employees. As explained previously, this recent shift is the outcome of the competitive environment in which these organizations find themselves, a trend that has been set by some multinationals and a realization that an effective HRM system is the key to competitive advantage.

The other set of practices, mainly pursued by less successful and smaller local organizations lacks the initiative and promise exhibited by the former. In these organizations, the social status of candidates often guides recruitment decisions. Training is considered an expense and is limited to the bare minimum. For example, in one of Khilji's (1999b) sample organizations, not one employee (out of a total of 264) had been sent for training in the last seven months. Employees are assessed without any input from the appraisee. The concept of feedback is alien to the managers in these organizations (Qureshi, 1995).

At the same time, there are some similarities in all of these organizations. Often, good performance is believed to go unrewarded. The perception that discriminatory management practices exist within organizations produces invisible cleavages and factions leading to covert accusations and counter-accusations. Typically these are claims of favoritism that have resulted in a bonus or large salary increase (Qureshi, 1995). Employee morale is lowered, there is a lack of trust and a lack of striving for excellence. 'If my rewards do not match my efforts, what is the use of a performance evaluation and why should I put in extra for this organization?' (Khilji, 1999b).

These factors tend to create obstacles preventing organizations from building capabilities and identifying role models of performance which are essential to improve their competitive strengths. As a consequence, employee satisfaction and organizational commitment are low. Top management often comments that organizational loyalty is missing. But Khilji (1999b) reports that organizations that observed fairness, implemented policies of employee empowerment, opened up communication channels and adopted a participatory management style had higher employee satisfaction and lower turnover.

Conclusion

HRM holds a promise for employees in Pakistan and is the way forward. Employees recognize the significant role of HRM and aspire towards it. There seems to be a large amount of room for growth for HRM activities as the economy develops further. However, it must be emphasized that the current state of affairs – the uncertain political/economic environment is not conducive to development. Therefore, political stability, along with rules of good governance, should be achieved and sustained if Pakistan wants to recognize its people's needs to enhance their productivity in order to maximize the full potential of the economy.

Notes

1   These were the traders or settlers who brought in the message of Islam.
2   Institute of Business Administration, Karachi, was established in the 1970s with financial and academic assistance from Wharton Business School; and Lahore University of Management Sciences, Lahore, was founded in the late 1980s on patterns of McGill University and Harvard Business School.
3   The office occupation cost in the prime business cities is only US$10 per sq. ft per year (Government of Pakistan, 1997).

References

Ahmad, M. (1996) 'The Crescent and the Sword: Islam, the Military and Political Legitimacy in Pakistan', *Middle East Journal* 50, (3), 235–256.

Ahmad, M. (1997) 'Education', in R. Raza (ed.) *Pakistan in Perspective 1947–1997*, Karachi: Oxford University Press, pp. 238–275.

Amir, A. (1999) 'Out of breath already', *Dawn*, Karachi, Internet edition. Available on http//www.dawn.com (accessed 10 September 1999).

Banker (1995) 'Going global', *Banker*, March, 45–46.

Barron, C. and Higgins, T. (1995) 'The Shock of the New', *Global Investor*, Dec. 94–Jan. 95.

Board of Investment (1999) '*Investment Figures*', Islamabad, Online. email: boipak@isb.com-pol.com (accessed May 1999).

Bokhari, F. (1996) 'Loss of Faith?, *The Banker*, 146 (842), 73–76.

Budhwar, P. and Sparrow, P. (1998) 'National Factors Determining Indian and British HRM Practices: An Empirical Study', *Management International Review*, 38 (2), 105–121.

Burki, S. J. (1988) 'A Historical Perspective on Development', in S. J. Burki, and R. Laporte (eds) *Pakistan's Development Priorities: Choices for the Future*, Karachi: Oxford University Press.

Burki, S. J. (1993) 'Pakistan's Economy in the Year 2000: Two Possible Scenarios', in H. Korson (ed.) *Contemporary Problems of Pakistan*, Oxford: Westview Press.

Cameron, J. and Irfan, M. (1992) 'Enabling People to Help Themselves: An Empirical and Human Resource Development Strategy for Pakistan in the 1990s', *World Employment Program*, ILO, 92–102.

Chandland, C. (1995) 'Trade Unionism and Industrial Restructuring in India and Pakistan', *Bulletin of Concerned Asian Scholars*, 27 (4), 63–78.

CIA (2000) *World Fact Book*, Online, Available at http://www.odci.gov/cia (accessed 5 January 2000).

Dawn (1999) 'Budget 1999–2000', *Dawn*, Online, available at http//www.dawn.com (accessed 13 June 1999).

Easterby-Smith, M., Malina, D. and Yuan, L. (1995) 'How Culture Sensitive is HRM? A Comparative Analysis of Chinese and UK Companies', *International Journal of Human Resource Management*, 6, 1.

Eldridge, D. (1992) 'A Strategic Approach to Employee Development in an Agriculture Bank', *International Sector of Public Sector Management*, 5, 2, 15–20.

Euromoney (1989) 'Pakistan: Not Enough Sockets for Investors to Plug into?', *Euromoney*, 16, 18, 15–16.

Gill, R. and Wong, A. (1998) 'The Cross-cultural Transfer of Management Practices: The Case of Japanese Human Resource Management Practices in Singapore', *International Journal of Human Resource Management*, 9, 1, 116–135.

Government of Pakistan (1997) *Pakistan 2010 Program*, Islamabad: Ministry of Commerce and Industries.

Government of Pakistan (1999) *Pakistan Economic Survey*, Islamabad, Finance Division, Economic Adviser's Wing. Available at http://www.pak.gov.pk (accessed 15 December 1999).

Hannon, J. M. *et al.* (1995) 'International Human Resource Strategy and its Determinants: The Case of Subsidiaries in Taiwan', *Journal of International Business Studies*, 26, 3, 531–554.

Hofstede, G. (1980) *Culture's Consequences*, London: Sage.

Hofstede, G. (1991) *Cultures and Organisations: Software of the Minds*, London: McGraw-Hill.

Horwitz, F. and Darren, A. (1998) 'Flexible Work Practices and HRM: A Comparison of South Africa and Foreign-Owned Companies', *International Journal of Human Resource Management*, 9 (4), 590–607.

Hussain, I. (1999) 'Democracy in the Doldrums', *Dawn*, Karachi, Online, available at http//www.dawn.com (accessed 16 October 1999).

Hussain, M. and Hussain, A. (1993) *Pakistan: Problems of Governance*, Lahore: Vanguard Books.

Jaeger, A. M. and Kanungo, R. N. (1990) *Management in Developing Countries*, London: Routledge.

Jamal, A. (1998) 'Can we Learn Something from the Perceptions and Consumption Practices of Transnational South Asia Communities Living in the West?', paper presented at the Inaugural Conference of Asia Academy of Management, Hong Kong, December.

James, M. (1993) *Pakistan Chronicle*, London: Hurst.

Karachi Stock Exchange (2000) *Past, Present and Future Trends*, Online, available at http://www.kse.com.pk. Email: companyaffair@kse.com.pk (accessed 5 January 2000).

Khan, A. A. (1997) 'Economic Development', in R. Raza (ed.) *Pakistan in Perspective 1947–1997*, Karachi: Oxford University Press.

Khan, S. Y. (1989) 'Trade Unions Revival: Are We Moving in the Right Direction?', *Pakistan and Gulf Economist*, 14–20 January, 12–15.

Khilji, S. E. (1995) 'International Human Resource Management in Pakistan', unpublished MPhil thesis, University of Cambridge.

Khilji, S. E. (1999a) 'Management in Pakistan', in M. Warner *International Encyclopaedia of Business and Management*, London: International Thomson Press.

Khilji, S. E. (1999b) 'An Empirical Study of Human Resource Management in Pakistan: The Case of Pakistan', unpublished PhD Thesis, University of Cambridge.

Klein, M. U. (1992) 'Commercial Banking in Pakistan', in A. Nasim (ed.) *Financing Pakistan's Development in the 1990s*, Karachi: LUMS.

Korson, H. (1993) *Contemporary Problems of Pakistan*, Oxford: Westview Press.

Latifi, F. (1997) 'Management Learning in National Context', unpublished PhD thesis, Henley Management College.

Lawler, H., Jain, H. C., Ratnam, C. S. and Atmiyanandana, V. (1995) 'Human Resource Management in Developing Economies: A Comparison of India and Thailand', *International Journal of Human Resource Management* 6, (2), 319–346.

Lyon, P. (1993) 'Epilogue', in P. James (ed.) *Pakistan Chronicle*, London: Hurst.

Malik, I. (1996) 'The State and the Civil Society', *Asia Survey*, 36, 7.

Malik, I. H. (1994) 'Governability Crisis in Pakistan: Politics of Authority, Ideology and Ethnicity', *Round Table*, 332, 3.

Mirza, S. A. (1995) *Privatization in Pakistan*, Lahore: Ferozesons.

Mueller, F. (1994) 'Societal Effect, Organizational Effect and Globalization', *Organization Studies* 15, 3, 407–428.

Newman, K. L. and Nollen, S. D. (1996) 'Culture and Congruence: The Fit between Management Practices and National Culture', *Journal of International Business Studies*, Fourth Quarter, 753–779.

Qureshi, Z. A. (1995) 'Impact of Management Practices on Employee Effectiveness in South Asia', in R. N. Kanungo (ed.) *New Approaches to Employee Management*, London: JAI Press, Vol. 3.

Rosenzweig, P. and Nohria, N. (1994) 'Influences on HRM Practices in MNCs', *Journal of International Business Studies*, 25 (2), 229–251.

Saeed, K. A. (1995) 'In Search of a Labour Policy', *Pakistan and Gulf Economist* 14 (21), 6–11.

Siddiqui, H. R. (1997) 'Human Resource Development in Pakistan', *Dawn*, Karachi 23 March 1996.

Tayeb, M. (1995) 'The Competitive Advantage of Nations: The Role of HRM and its Socio-Cultural Context', *International Journal of Human Resource Management*, 6 (3) 588–605.

Tayeb, M. (1997) 'Islamic revival in Asia and HRM', *Employee Relations*, 19 (4), 352–364.

Tayeb, M. (1998) 'Transfer of HRM Practices across Cultures: An American Company in Scotland', *International Journal of Human Resource Management*, 9 (2), 332–358.

The Economist (1995) 'Emerging Markets', *The Economist*, 145, 6.

Triandis, H. C. (1995) *Individualism and Collectivism*, Boulder, CO: Westview Press.

Trompenaars, F. (1994) *Riding the Waves of Culture*, London: The Economist Books.

Unger, B. (1999) 'India and Pakistan: A Survey', *The Economist*, 22–8 May.

World Bank (2000) 'Country Profile', online, available at http://www.worldbank.org, (accessed 5 January 2000).

Zakaria, S. (1994) 'Investment Culture in Pakistan', unpublished MPhil thesis, University of Cambridge.

8 Human resource management in Iran

Monir Tayeb

Introduction

Given the dearth of reported studies on Iranian HRM policies and practices, the present chapter focuses on major external macro factors which make up the context of Iranian organisations. It also discusses their implications for micro-level HRM policies and practices. Available studies conducted in Iran at different times are used to paint the picture. The term HRM has not yet taken root in Iran, therefore, in this chapter the term is used to denote the broad personnel function.

This chapter initially details factors which constitute Iran's national context and national character (such as geography, ecology, political and economic institutions, foreign trade, religion and history). Then it highlights the main work-related values and attitudes in Iran. This is followed by a section on HRM in Iran and, finally, concluding remarks are made.

National context of Iran

Iran, situated in the Middle East, almost at the centre of Asia, is the seventh largest country in the world in terms of land mass (1,648,000 sq km). It is situated between the Caspian Sea in the north and Persian Gulf in the south. It has land borders with Iraq, Turkey, Afghanistan, Pakistan and the former USSR republics of Turkmenistan, Armenia and Azerbaijan. The neighbouring countries have over the centuries influenced and been influenced by Iranian culture. Currently the ethnic composition of the nation is: Persian 51 per cent, Azerbaijani 24 per cent, Gilaki and Mazandarani 8 per cent, Kurd 7 per cent, Arab 3 per cent, Lur 2 per cent, Baloch 2 per cent, Turkmen 2 per cent, and others 1 per cent.

The country's population, estimated at over 66 million in 1998, is a young one with 44 per cent under 14 and about 4 per cent over 65 years of age. The literacy rate is around 72 per cent, with the rate being higher in urban areas than rural regions and slightly higher among men than women.

The climatic and other physical conditions of the environment within which a community lives do have some bearing on the way it evolves as a culturally coherent group (Tayeb, 1996). Some of the Arian tribes who, thousands of years ago, migrated from Central Asia and settled in Iran, faced harsh variable seasons, salt deserts and very few rivers. It was not perhaps an accident of history that they became an aggressive nation, fought many nations, conquered their lands and built the Persian Empire which ruled over a vast area for centuries.

In the past, most Iranians used to make their living through agricultural activities, in some thousands of small villages, depending upon their agricultural output. These villages were scattered throughout the land without connecting roads. They were isolated, self-sufficient, closed systems. Wherever there was a small water source, there was also a small village. Agricultural life was difficult in the relatively dry climate of the Iranian plateau. Bani-Asadi (1984) explains that these conditions gradually brought about the qualities of patience and acceptance of hardship among Iranians.

Iran has seen many changes in its social, economic and political make up in the twentieth century, not to mention the previous twenty-four centuries of its recorded history. There have been two revolutions, one of which brought down the Ghajar dynasty in the earlier part of the century and the other, in the late 1970s, changed the country's regime from a monarchy to a republic. In the last quarter of the last century the economy has experienced some extraordinary times: an oil boom, a bloody eight-year war (see also below), and international sanctions. It has been subject to large-scale nationalisation, wide-ranging rationing and privatisation and structural adjustment. National culture and other social institutions have also undergone tremendous changes. There are various elements in this environment which have left their imprints on Iranian organisations and their management, and it is to these that we shall now turn.

The Islamic revolution

The 1979 Islamic revolution was the culmination of many years of growing dissatisfaction with the autocratic rule of the Shah and his 'cronies', which had left the vast majority of people, especially those who lived in the rural areas and the outskirts of larger towns, impoverished and disaffected but had enriched a selected few. After over 2,500 years of absolute monarchy, the country was changed to an Islamic republic, with an elected president and legislature.

The Islamic revolution also had other profound implications for the economy and society as a whole. Islam, it is worth noting, has been the main religion of Iran for almost 1,400 years and has influenced as well as being influenced by the Iranian culture. Throughout the history, this influence has ebbed and flowed considerably; it was perhaps at its weakest during the Shah's regime, whose father secularised the society.

The revolution marked another period of ascendance of Islam, which not only changed the political, economic and cultural fabric of the society but also the private lives and relationships of its people. After all, Islam, unlike many other religions, is an all-encompassing creed and governs every aspect of life, both worldly and spiritual. For instance, almost immediately after the new regime was established, all banks were nationalised and foreign participation in the financial sector was terminated. Later, in 1984, a law was designed to make the banking sector subject to Islamic rules, replacing the payment of interest with profit and risk-sharing schemes. All organisations and institutions, such as the armed forces, universities and other educational establishments, public and private sector companies, the media, the arts and cultural events, are required to conform to Islamic laws and regulations. Women have to follow a strict Islamic dress code at work, and indeed elsewhere. A policy of segregation of sexes is observed in prayers, wedding ceremonies, public transport, schools, sports events, television quiz shows, queues at shops, and so forth.

Although many foreign commentators still speak of an Iran that is obsessed with revolution and radicalism, nevertheless, Iran has been evolving. Social, political and economic realities have caused the radicalism and revolutionary romanticism to subside. A new era of rationalism has dawned in the country (Rouhani, 1998).

The economy

The economy, although it is a capitalist one, is run on a strict protectionist and statist model. Many industries and firms which in a large number of capitalist countries would normally be in private hands, are owned and managed by the state in Iran. It is estimated that the government's share of the ownership of the economy is 80 per cent. The government has tried in recent years to reduce subsidies and price control over certain commodities and food products but the process is inevitably a slow one. Attempts were also made to reform the economy and start a process of privatisation in the early 1990s, but the programme faltered. In the late 1990s the question of privatisation was aired again but could not take a practical shape.

Like other developing countries, Iran's protectionist policy is in part a reaction to political events. Iran has never lost its independence throughout its history, but foreign powers such as the United States and Great Britain influenced the country's foreign and domestic policies, especially for the best part of the twentieth century. The Shah's father, the founder of the Pahlavi dynasty, came to power with the help of the British. Later, during the Second World War, because of his support for Hitler, the Allies, led by the United States and Britain, forced him to abdicate in favour of his son, who ruled the country under their patronage. A *coup d'état* in 1953, which entrenched his position of power in the country further, was conceived by the British and brought to fruition by the Americans. Later, in the 1960s and early 1970s the United States forced through the ill-thought-out so-called White Revolution upon the Shah in an attempt to make him a more acceptable autocrat (see for instance, Goode, 1997). These and similar episodes have created a need and desire in people for real political independence and economic self-reliance.

The constitution of the Islamic Republic of Iran divides the country's economic system into three constituent parts: public, co-operative and private. The public sector includes all major and generative industries such as foreign trade, mining, banking, insurance, power generation, major water distribution networks, radio and television, telecom, airlines, shipping lines and railways. The co-operative sector includes companies, manufacturing and distributive organisations set up in towns and villages on the basis of Islamic guidelines. The private sector includes those parts of agriculture, animal husbandry, industry, commerce and any other services that complement the economic activities of the public and co-operative sectors. During the eight-year Iran–Iraq war, many private and co-operative activities fell under the management of the government. But since then, the private sector's activities have gradually expanded. There is also a parallel underground economy, the size of which is estimated to be around 25 per cent of the GNP (Coville, 1994).

Iran is OPEC's second largest oil producer and accounts for roughly 5 per cent of global oil output. The country holds 9 per cent of the world's oil reserves and 15 per cent of its gas reserves. Crude oil forms 85 per cent of the country's exports with carpets, fruits, nuts, hides, iron, steel making up the rest. Major imports are machinery, military supplies, metal works, foodstuffs, pharmaceuticals, technical services and refined oil products. The GDP growth rate as of 1996 was 3.6 per cent.

The economy was battered massively by the war between Iran and one of its neighbours, Iraq in the 1980s, which lasted for eight years and drained the country of its resources (both natural and human), and brought the country's process of economic development and industrialisation to a grinding halt. The war interrupted the export of oil and left much of the country's oil installation and other industries and the infrastructure in ruins. The total damage is estimated at around $400m in addition to some $90bn of the financial costs of military activities. The country is now slowly recovering from the aftermath of this war (Mazarei, 1996).

Foreign trade

The 1979 revolution brought about changes in the relations between Iran and major Western countries. As a result, there was an almost overnight halt to foreign direct investment which had hitherto provided some of the momentum for the economic growth. Later, for one reason or another, sanctions were piled upon sanctions which aggravated these already uneasy relations, and which in turn had serious implications for Iran's economy in general and its business sector in particular.

Foreign direct investment from non-Western countries, especially those in South East Asia, was the first to flow back again after the end of war with Iraq in the late 1980s and has increased gradually since then. In the late 1990s efforts were made, by all sides concerned, to improve the relations with Western nations. As a result, a few European companies have started to develop business interests in the country. However, because of internal political struggles between various factions and certain unease in the relationships between Iran and the USA and European Union, progress has been very slow on that front. Moreover, existing laws discourage foreign investment, by allowing non-Iranians only 49 per cent of the shares in any venture and no right to own property. Strict labour laws are another deterrent to investment.

The country has nonetheless 'become an object of desire for the international oil and gas industry' (Corzine, 1998: 4). Iran is now fully opening its doors to foreign investment in many sectors, and significantly in its vital oil and gas fields, the latter through 'buy-back' contracts only. 'Buy-back' contracts that form the basis of Iran's plan to open its energy industry to foreign investment are a compromise to overcome the country's constitutional bar on foreigners 'owning' any of its oil and gas reserves. Under the scheme, foreign companies will finance specific projects. Repayment, including an agreed rate of return on investment, will take place over a specified period from a field's output. Developments will probably be around three years, with a similar period for cost recovery. At no time will a foreign company 'own' any of the oil or gas produced, ensuring the arrangement stays within Iran's constitutional framework.

Iran's geographic position, situated between Caspian Sea and Persian Gulf, is also proving to be a draw. The country has embarked upon concerted efforts to establish itself as a transit route for oil from the Caspian Sea region. The prospect of being able to integrate Caspian operations with projects in the country may be especially appealing to big companies. Smaller companies too sense a unique opportunity. Independents such as Monument Oil and Gas of the UK and Saga Petroleum of Norway intended to incorporate Iran into their corporate plans (*Financial Times*, 1 July 1998) but the author has not been able to establish whether or not this has in fact happened.

Culture-building institutions

At the heart of Iranian culture lies its main religion, Islam, a faith to which over 98 per cent of the population belong. Before going any further, it is important to note that Islam, although it has certain precepts and principles which are followed by the believers living in different parts of the world, takes on a great deal of the local 'colour', partly because of genuine local interpretation of some of the principles and partly for political and non-religious considerations. As a result, there are differences in both secular and religious aspects of social life among Muslim nations. Saudi Arabia, for instance, adheres strictly to the Sacred Law (*Shari'a*) in many spheres of life, while Turkey has turned to secular laws for the administration of its economic and social affairs. Recently in Turkey a newly elected member of parliament was barred from taking up her seat because she wished to wear an Islamic head cover – her action was considered as politically undesirable.

For Muslims, Islam is not a man-made institution; the Koran contains the words of God, revealed syllable by syllable to Mohammed some 1,400 years ago. The deeds of its adherents are therefore inseparable from divine commandments. Islam is generally viewed by some non-Muslims as being a fatalist religion. But the Koran specifically asserts that humans are able to choose and to intervene in their destiny, and that they are held responsible for the consequences of their deeds. However, they are not left alone to run their life. God has equipped them with the Koran and the traditions of Prophet Mohammed, which in the Islamic view, are one of the most important sources of guidance that humans can use to steer their actions and beliefs.

Islam permeates people's taken-for-granted values and assumptions as well. Ultimate fear of and trust in God alone, piety and abstinence, decency, truthfulness, helping the poor and weak, respect for age and seniority, hospitality, loyalty, obedience of leaders and looking up to seniors for direction, family-orientation, uncertainty avoidance, and fatalism yet acceptance of responsibility for one's actions, are among the Islamic roots of Iranian culture. Islam also asserts that the nature of relationships between people should be egalitarian, and urges leaders to consult their followers in the running of their affairs.

Islam is not, of course, the only source of Iranian national character. As Bani-Asadi (1984) points out, Iranian culture is a mixture of three different cultures which have co-existed for centuries: Ancient Persian culture, with about 6,000 years of history; Islamic culture, with about 1,400 years of history; and Western culture, with over 200 years of history.

Throughout its long history, the nation has experienced many unpleasant and hard times as well as happy episodes: authoritarian regimes, repression, wars, domination and invasion by foreign powers and loss of territory. Some of these events have created a deep scepticism and distrust in the national psyche and a need to take refuge in the security offered by religion and in the comfort of home and family, which are the only things alongside God that can be trusted.

The way that Iranian people coped with internal dictators and external enemies and occupiers was through either resistance and struggle or 'false adaptation' (Bazargan, 1958). Despite the peculiar adaptability which enabled the Iranians to live with the autocracy and corruption of their kings and rulers or oppressions for centuries, the imposed governments made the people distrustful of governors and unwilling to obey the rules and laws made by lawmakers. In fact, disobedience of the ruler and their rules or commands was a value. Those who did it were perceived as heroes fighting against cruelty and injustice. All this, one can argue, could lead to a culture of unwillingness to carry out orders.

Encounter with the West

Iran's cultural, economic and military contacts with the West go back to the Persian Empire and its wars with the Greeks (under the Achaemenid Persians) and the Romans (under the Sassanian Persians). In more recent times France, especially since the time of Napoleon I, has been a major source of Western influence on Iran. In the twentieth century, the Shah's father, the founder of the Pahlavi dynasty, was instrumental in modelling certain civic institutions, such as the legal system, education, the civil service, and the armed forces on the French pattern. Modernisation was invariably equated with Westernisation. Western engineers and advisers were brought in to build and modernise the country's infrastructure such as railway networks and suspension bridges. Men and women were forced, sometimes brutally by the armed forces and the police, to change their traditional costumes and wear contemporary Western clothes, as part of the process of secularisation as well as the Westernisation of society: women had to abandon their traditional *chador* (veil) and men had to wear ties. Western arts, from theatre to cinema and classical music and later its pop variety, which had been introduced to the country in a limited way before the Pahlavi dynasty, permeated cultural life, especially in cities and other urban areas, alongside the traditional arts. The 'swinging 1960s' were as much alive in Tehran as they were in London and Paris. During the Shah's own reign, American influence in the country's affairs increased and to some extent replaced that of Europe.

This long-term exposure to Western culture, notwithstanding cultural differences between various Western countries, arguably introduced the Iranians to certain secular industrial values and ideas such as economic/material growth, security, individualism, democracy, and comfort and enjoyment. However, what the Shah and his father did not encourage were the West's long fought-for and won democratic practices and respect for individual liberty and human rights.

A final point to make here is that the above major sources of culture have had varying degrees of influence on the cultural make-up of the Iranians over time and at different levels of society. Whereas, for example, one might observe individualistic attitudes and behaviour among employees in relation to their workplace, similar to what the present author found in British and certain Indian companies (Tayeb, 1988), at the family and other in-group levels collectivism prevails. As for the time dimension, across its long history, the nation has gone through both ups and downs and change of collective mind: from being proud and powerful empire builders to being humiliated, for a short period, during the Second World War by being occupied and carved up by the Allied forces; from taking on board many Western values and fashions to rejecting outright anything which came from the West, from being the closest one can get to secularism to being completely engulfed in religious teachings and practices.

Iranian culture and work-related values and attitudes

Latifi (1997), in a study of traditional and modern Islamic texts, identified the following work-related characteristics: equality before God; individual responsibility within a framework of co-operation with others; a view that people in positions of power should treat subordinates kindly, as if they were their own brothers or sisters; fatalism but also a recognition of personal choice; encouragement of consultation at all levels of decision-making, from family to the wider community, to the country as a whole. Having remodelled these values according to Hofstede's dimensions (Hofstede, 1980; Hofstede and Bond, 1988), she concluded that Islamic traditions would place Iranians broadly on a middle point on power distance, uncertainty avoidance, and individualism; nearer the masculinity end of femininity/masculinity dimension; and close to the long-term end of the time-orientation scale.

Other scholars have identified further Islamic values which have their roots in the Koran and the teachings of Mohammed and his successors. Ali (1988), for example, in a study of values of Muslim students in the USA, developed fifty-three statements which he grouped into two sets of values: work ethic and individualism/self-reliance. He argued that in Islam work is obligatory and self-reliance is a source of success. Further, he proposed that although one's loyalty revolves around self and family, within the workplace loyalty to one's superior is necessary for an organisation to survive.

Sherif (1975) identified nobility, patience, self-discipline, good appearance, abstinence, resolve, sincerity, truthfulness, servitude and trust as major Islamic values. Similarly, Endot (1995), following his review of the literature, identified eleven major Islamic values which have consequences for organisations and are also incorporated in the model advocated by the Malaysian government as part of its Islamisation policy. Endot (1995: 436) identified eleven basic values of Islam that lead to a 'respectable nation': trustworthiness, responsibility, sincerity, discipline, dedication, diligence, cleanliness, co-operation, good conduct, gratefulness and moderation.

Human resource management in Iran

It is important to note that HRM in Iran has not yet become a subject of academic investigation and to the present author's knowledge an on-going research into HRM in international joint ventures in Iran, conducted by one of her research students, Pari Namazie (2000), is the first known academic study of HRM in Iran.

Namazie found that, Iran's perception and role of HRM is very different from that of developed countries. Whereas western and many other developed countries view HRM as a strategic function, seeking to achieve competitive advantage by making full use of human resources, in Iran the role of HRM is more basic. As Tayeb (2000) points out, HRM in this country is really the 'old' personnel management with a heavy local colour especially in recruitment and training areas.

In addition, certain socio-political considerations might take precedence over strictly business concerns. For instance, in the public sector, which covers over 80 per cent of the economy, female staff in top managerial positions were made redundant after the initial years of the revolution and large numbers of war veterans were recruited following the eight-year war between Iran and Iraq, as a social welfare measure. Private sector companies, on the other hand, do not have to follow such policies and might therefore have greater flexibility in the management of their human resources.

Islamic values and human resource management

From the discussion of Islamic values one could, to some extent, speculate as to what HRM might look like in a Muslim country like Iran. However, it should be borne in mind that it is not easy to isolate the effects of Islam on HRM from those of other socio-cultural institutions, such as education, political factors like the power of trade unions and the government's economic and industrial policies. Nevertheless, given the pervasiveness of Islam and its influence on various spheres of material as well as spiritual life in a Muslim country like Iran, it is possible to discern certain patterns in the workplace which are compatible with their Islamic origins. Translated into workplace behaviour, certain Islamic values such as respect for age and seniority, loyalty, obedience of leaders and looking up to seniors for direction, should mean a considerable power distance between superior and subordinates. At the same time Islam encourages leaders to consult their followers, so this should encourage a consultative decision-making style. Self-discipline, trustfulness, honesty, resolve, loyalty, and abstinence should encourage managers to trust their subordinates' judgement and integrity, which could in turn lead to delegation of authority to employees further down the hierarchy and a participative management style. They could also reduce the need for external control mechanisms, such as clocking in and out as a means to monitor manual workers. Co-operation, patience, and family-like relationships among people, should encourage teamwork and mutual support within an organisation and care for the community outside it.

This is, of course, a speculative picture of management that one may draw on the basis of Islamic ideals (Tayeb, 1997). The extent to which these ideals are actually translated into practice is a different matter. They are by their nature open to interpretation, and the workplace is a notoriously fertile ground for such interpretations, given its varied constituencies, interests and goals.

Moreover, as was mentioned before, Iranians have experienced a great deal of hardship and hostility over centuries. These experiences and their resultant mistrust in others could have implications for management of organisations in modern times. From the employees' point of view, the workplace does not belong to their in-group, as is the case, for example, in Japan. Their commitment to the company is at best shaky and at worst open to negotiations. As a consequence, corruption in many institutions and organisations, especially in the public sector, is endemic. Also, employees' willingness to participate in the decision-making process and the running of the organisation, particularly at middle and lower levels, is almost non-existent. On the management side, there is a deep mistrust in the subordinates. As a result, organisations tend to be centralised, with power concentrated in the hands of a few and trusted senior managers.

In a study of fourteen organisations in the pre-revolutionary Iran, Tayeb (1979) found that some of the managers who had been educated in American and European universities were aware of the merits of decentralisation of decision-making in their organisations as an appropriate response to their changing environment, but they were reluctant to employ such an approach in their own companies. They did not trust their subordinates' abilities and intentions to carry out their tasks properly. Indeed, these managers argued that they would stand to benefit if they tightened their control over their employees and made important decisions themselves. Some had chosen to appoint their own close friends and relatives to crucial posts, thereby to ensure the proper handling of the organisation's tasks.

In post-revolutionary Iran, Bani-Asadi (1984), Mortazavi and Karimi (1990) and Mortazavi and Saheli (1992) found that organisations were mainly characterised by a paternalistic culture. Mortazavi and Saheli also found a close relationship between this paternalistic behaviour of managers and job satisfaction of their subordinates (see also Mortazavi *et al.*, 1996).

Latifi (1997) closely observed a small sample of Iranian managers at work over a period of time and found that Iranian employees viewed their managers as sympathetic brothers and sisters or compassionate fathers and mothers. In addition, this family-like relationship appears to have been extended to include 'social' roles for the managers. They were frequently involved in their subordinates' private lives and family matters. Some of those interviewed said they would make their time and organisations available for high school and university students who wished to conduct research projects or acquire work experience as part of their courses. They saw this as fulfilling a part of their responsibility to society and to the next generation of managers.

Latifi also found that managers preferred face-to-face, verbal communication with their subordinates, quite compatible with the paternalistic and collectivist culture of Iran. Such findings confirm Hofstede's (1991: 67) point, i.e. the employer –employee relationship in collectivist societies 'is perceived in moral terms, like a family link'. He further argues that high power distance supports the paternalistic pattern of behaviour of the people who live in high power distance countries. In these countries, parents, teachers or managers are supposed to know everything and expected to take all initiatives at home, in the classroom or in organisations. Managers are seen as making decisions autocratically and paternalistically (Hofstede, 1980). Iran, although it is not among the very high power distance countries, it is still high relative to many nations included in Hofstede's (1980) study.

Latifi (1997) also reports that one of the tasks of the Iranian managers was to develop their subordinates. This task is included as a component in the role of leader. The managers were frequently performing the duties of a mentor, coach, teacher, or an adviser.

Research evidence shows that many managers perform such roles regardless of the country in which they work (see for instance Kanter, 1983; Kotter, 1985; Orth *et al.*, 1987). But it seems that, as Latifi (1997) points out, these roles are crucial for the managers who work in less developed countries, such as Iran, where the level of education and skills of the workforce are not very high. Moreover, these roles also fit in with the paternalistic culture of Iran, where managers are expected to be like fathers/mothers to their subordinates.

Management training and education in Iran

The vast majority of Iranian organisations, notwithstanding a growing army of educated managers with MBA and other business degrees from home and abroad, are run by people with little or no managerial qualifications. A study by Amirshahi (unpublished manuscript) found that of over 700 university-educated executives and senior managers surveyed, only 13.7 per cent had a management degree. Even these had probably not received the kind of education which would be needed to operate successfully in the current Iranian economy (Latifi, 1997).

Latifi's research exposed the gap between Iranian managers' professional and skill needs and what is offered in universities and business schools. MBA courses, for instance, are generally modelled on American and British ones, which are primarily designed for their own domestic needs. The appropriateness of such courses for managers working in a protected economy dominated by the public sector is rather doubtful. In fact, the managers who participated in Latifi's study considered such courses to be irrelevant. This is a handicap which holds Iranian companies back with regard to personnel management as well as other techniques such as marketing and forecasting.

Learning from foreign companies

Managers the world over attempt to learn from their more successful counterparts at home and abroad. In this regard, adaptability to socio-cultural and political economic characteristics contributes significantly to the success of such cross-border learning processes. The Japanese, for instance, were very successful in importing certain US-grown management techniques and ideas and adapting them to their own local specifications. It is well known that practices such as quality circles were introduced into Japan by Americans such as Deming and Juran who arguably helped bring about Japan's post-war production miracle. Finding that their ideas about total quality management evoked little interest in the United States, they discovered more fertile ground elsewhere (Hodgson, 1987). It is arguable that in Japan's case this fertile ground was its culture, which could accept and use these US-grown ideas.

One of the prerequisites for the successful implementation of quality circles, for example, is a high degree of commitment by employees to their company and its goals – a characteristics that is attributed to most Japanese employees. But Iran's similar attempts to adopt US models in the 1950s and 1960s were a total disaster. It could be argued that Iranian workplace culture was to some extent responsible for this failure. Practices such as participative decision-making, quality circles, total quality management and multi-skilled teamwork presuppose, among other things, a willingness to participate in group decision-making and decision implementing and a strong commitment to the workplace, on the part of employees. They also assume a certain degree of confidence and trust in employees and willingness to delegate authority to team members, on the part of their managers. Iranian organisations do not appear to be as fertile a ground for such management practices as were those in Japan when Japanese managers successfully imported them from the United States a few decades ago.

However, proper training and willingness on the part of both managers and employees can overcome such local difficulties, but employee and management training programmes can be costly and, unless there is an obvious benefit to the companies, they may not wish to embark on such programmes. In a protectionist economy such as Iran's, domestic firms have a captive market and are sheltered from the rigour of competition by seasoned foreign firms. As a result, there is little or no incentive for them to import successful foreign management techniques and train their workforce to implement them.

Moreover, such a sheltered market, which has not yet been penetrated in any significant numbers by foreign direct investors, deprives Iranian firms of exposure to the latest 'best practices' carried out by successful multinational firms operating in their back garden. Fortunately, Iran, as was mentioned earlier, has in the last few years opened up its market to foreign direct investment, especially in the form of 'buy-back' contracts and joint ventures, and is now actively encouraging inward foreign direct investment. Further developments along these lines will no doubt have managerial as well as economic benefits for the country in due course.

Conclusion

A word of explanation about the absence of discussion on some of the obvious topics and issues in a chapter like this is in order. Micro and macro level issues such as the main labour legislation and unions prevalent in Iran and their impact on specific HRM policies and practices, sector-specific HRM practices, such as in the oil sector, the existence and role of professional bodies (equivalent of the UK IPD), educational vocational set-up and the gender composition of the workforce and its influences on HRM are not discussed in the chapter. The reason is that up-to-date information on these is not readily available and efforts to obtain such information proved futile.

The origins of the national culture were traced through ecological conditions and certain major culture-building institutions such as history and religion. It was argued that various factors have contributed, to varying degrees of intensity, to the cultural make-up of the nation, across different institutional levels and also over a period of time. As if directed by an invisible hand, they have over centuries taken their turn of coming into sharp focus and then fading away only to come back again with renewed vigour.

The implications of Iran's national culture for work-related values and attitudes held by employees and for their organisations' management, especially HRM, were discussed within the country's current political economic context.

The environment within which Iranian managers operate is volatile and intensely political. The economy and indeed society as a whole were reconstructed after the 1979 revolution on an Islamic model, which permeates both private and public lives of peoples and organisations. In addition, managers are constrained by certain problems such as skill shortages, inadequate infrastructure and difficulty of access to advanced technologies, which in turn deprive them of the professionalism they require and limit their scope for innovation and excellence. Also, certain cultural characteristics, such as scepticism and mistrust in others, evolved over hundreds of years and influenced by various historical events, have resulted in centralised organisations with limited scope for participation and cross-fertilisation of ideas.

With the improvement of relations between Iran and her Western partners already appearing on the horizon, and an increase in foreign direct investment that this could entail, the economy might be injected with much needed competition, managerial skills and advanced technologies.

References

Ali, A. (1988) 'Scaling an Islamic Work Ethic', *The Journal of Social Psychology*, 128 (5), 575–583.

Bani-Asadi, H. (1984) 'Interactive Planning on the Eve of the Iranian Revolution', PhD dissertation, University of Pennsylvania.

Bazargan, M. (1958) *Sazgari Irani* (Iranians' Adaptation), Tehran: Yad (in Farsi).

Corzine, R. (1998) 'Investing in Iran: Top Companies Lured by Huge Opportunity', *The Financial Times*, 1 July, p. 4.

Coville, T. (1994) *The Economy of Islamic Iran: Between State and Market*, Tehran: The French Institute for Research.

Endot, S. (1995) 'The Islamisation Process in Malaysia', PhD thesis, University of Bradford.

Goode, J. F. (1997) *The United States and Iran: In the Shadow of Musaddiq*, Basingstoke: Macmillan.

Hodgson, A. (1987) 'Deming's Never-ending Road to Quality', *Personnel Management*, July.

Hofstede, G. (1980) *Culture's Consequences*, Thousand Oaks, CA: Sage Publications.

Hofstede, G. (1991) *Culture and Organizations*, London: McGraw-Hill.

Hofstede, G. and Bond, M. H. (1988) 'Confucius and Economic Growth: New Trends in Culture's Consequences', *Organizational Dynamics*, 16, 4–21.

Kanter, R. M. (1983) 'Change Masters and the Intricate Architecture of Corporate Culture Change', *Management Review*, October, 18–28.

Kotter, J. (1985) *Power and Influence*, New York: The Free Press.

Latifi, F. (1997) 'Management Learning in National Context', PhD thesis, Henley Management College.

Mazarei, A. (1996) 'The Iranian Economy under the Islamic Republic: Institutional Change and Macroeconomic Performance (1979–1990)', *Cambridge Journal of Economics*, 20 (3), 289–314.

Mortazavi, S. and Karimi, E. (1990) 'Cultural Dimensions of Paternalistic Behaviour: A Cross-cultural Research in Five Countries', in S. Iwawaki, Y. Kashima and L. Kwok (eds) *Innovation in Cross-cultural Psychology*, Amsterdam, Berwyn, PA: Swets and Zeitlinger, pp. 147–151.

Mortazavi, S. and Saheli, A. (1992) 'Organisational Culture, Paternalistic Leadership and Job Satisfaction in Iran', paper presented at the 22nd International Congress of Applied Psychology, Erlbaum, UK.

Mortazavi, S., Smith, P. B., Youki, M. and Tayeb, M. H. (1996) 'Paternal and Supervisor Behaviours – A Comparative Study in Iran, Japan and England', presented at the 13th International Congress of Cross-Cultural Psychology, Montreal, Canada, 12–16 August.

Namazie, P. (2000) 'A Preliminary Review of Factors Affecting International Joint Ventures in Iran', paper presented at the 27th Annual Conference of Academy of International Business (UK Chapter) Strathclyde University, Glasgow, April.

Orth, C. D., Harry, E. W. and Benfari, R. C. (1987) 'The Manager's Role as Coach and Mentor', *Organizational Dynamics*, 15, 66–74.

Poole, M. (1990) 'Human Resource Management in an International Perspective', *International Journal of Human Resource Management*, 1 (1), 1–15.

Rouhani, S. (1998) 'When Will We Meet Again?', *Time Magazine*, 17 August, 19.

Sherif, M. A. (1975) *Ghazali's Theory of Virtue*, Albany, NY: State University of New York Press.

Tayeb, M. H. (1979) 'Cultural Determinants of Organizational Response to Environmental Demands', MLitt thesis, University of Oxford.

Tayeb, M. H. (1988) *Organizations and National Culture: A Comparative Analysis*, London: Sage Publications.

Tayeb, M. H. (1996) *The Management of a Multicultural Workforce*, Chichester: Wiley.
Tayeb, M. H. (1997) 'Islamic Revival in Asia and Human Resource Management', *Employee Relations*, 19 (4), 352–364.
Tayeb, M. H. (2000) *The Management of International Enterprises: A Socio-Political View*, Basingstoke: Macmillan.

9 Human resource management in Saudi Arabia

Kamel Mellahi and Geoffrey T. Wood

Introduction

Within global commodity chains, oil represents an important exception to the general rule of transnational or end-user dominance (Czaban and Henderson, 1998: 585–563) as at certain historic moments, primary producers have been vested with extraordinary power. In turn, this has led to the creation of a specific form of growth regime within the oil-producing states in the Middle East. The Saudi accumulation regime is oil-centred, with large sectors of industry remaining heavily dependent on state sponsorship.

The assembly of institutions designed to stabilise what has been a highly uneven growth process has certain defining characteristics: this includes a highly segmented labour market, with a clear distinction drawn between indigenous Saudis and foreign workers. Similarly, any balance that might exist in the Saudi labour market has little to do with supply and demand, but with a codification of wage relations, whereby firms historically have traded off ongoing investment and limited job creation for Saudis in return for state patronage and a relatively free hand in terms of the utilisation of foreigners (cf. Grahl and Teague, 2000: 162). Human resource management in Saudi Arabia represents a product of the nature of the productive system, and the codification of practices in formal legislation and in unwritten rules governing conduct (ibid.). In this chapter, we provide an overview of the development and changing nature of the context within which HRM operates, and actual practices and problems associated with HRM in Saudi Arabia.

Contextual Factors Shaping HRM Practices

How firms manage their human resources is the product of a wider socio-economic context. In Saudi Arabia, five key factors have shaped and continue to shape HRM policies and practices. These are: the structure of the Saudi economy, the political environment, the structure of the labour market, national HRD strategy and national culture.

Economic context and HRM

The Saudi economy centres on the production of oil (see Table 9.1). Oil and oil derivatives make up around 90–95 per cent of total Saudi export earnings, providing over 75 per cent of the country's budgetary revenues (Saudi American Bank, 2000) and account for around 37 per cent of GDP (Azzam, 1993: 14). Kemp (1999) described the Saudi economy as 'buoyed by oil, bound by its uncertainty'. Thus, of all the countries affected by the drop in oil prices since the mid-1980s, Saudi Arabia probably has been among the most affected. The drop in oil prices was further exacerbated by the Gulf War and its high costs. After experiencing almost two decades of high economic growth, Saudi Arabia has suffered a downward plunge since the mid-1980s. This has had a direct effect on job creation. Since the early 1990s, the Saudi economy has been growing at an average rate of 2 to 0 per cent while the population growth rate has been closer to 4 per cent since the 'oil boom baby boom' began in the early 1970s. *The Economist* (2000) estimated that the economy should grow by 6 per cent annually to generate enough jobs for young male Saudis entering the labour market. This disparity in economic growth and population growth has pushed the issue of unemployment to the forefront as baby boomers are now entering the labour market (see Figure 9.1).

Unemployment is not officially measured in Saudi Arabia. However, using demographic data and private sector employment, the Saudi American Bank (2000) estimated unemployment of male Saudis in the 20–29 age group to be around 15–20 per cent. The inclusion of female Saudis would make this average much higher. Gavin (2000) reported that more than 100,000 Saudi males enter the workforce every year, yet the non-oil private sector is only creating enough new

Table 9.1 Saudi Arabia: key economic data (billion US$)

Data	1994	1995	1996	1997	1998	1999	2000
Nominal GDP	117.8	123.5	133.9	143.5	130.0	140.92	149.4
(% change)	1.39	4.86	8.48	7.13	−10.8	8.4	6
Real GDP							
(% change)	0.10	0.00	1.40	1.90	1.60	1.00	2.00
Population (million)	18.20	19.10	20.00	21.00	21.00	21.40	21.80
Saudi	13.20	13.60	14.00	14.50	15.00	15.40	15.80
Non-Saudi	5.00	5.50	6.00	6.50	6.00	6.00	6.00
Saudi oil prices							
($ barrel)	14.50	15.65	19.00	18.25	11.50	17.45	18.50
Government							
budget balance	−9.28	−7.31	−5.07	−4.21	−12.27	−9.07	−7.46
revenues	34.40	39.07	47.76	54.80	38.13	39.20	41.87
expenditures	43.68	46.37	52.83	59.01	50.40	48.27	49.33
Cost of living							
(% change)	0.60	4.80	1.30	0.00	−.20	−1.20	0.00

Source: Saudi-American Bank (2000)

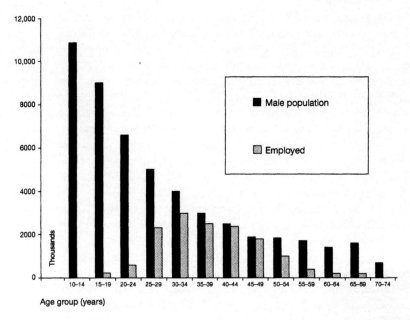

Figure 9.1 Saudi male population: age and employment, 2000
Source: Saudi American Bank (2000)

jobs to absorb about one in three job seekers. According to reports in the Saudi popular media, what is referred to as 'high and persistent' unemployment is straining the very fabric of society, and could lead to a wider upheaval. In neighbouring Bahrain, high unemployment amongst urban youth did indeed lead to political unrest in the 1990s, and there are fears that this pattern could be replicated in Saudi Arabia. Given the persistent birth rates of around 4 per cent per annum in Saudi Arabia, with more than half of the national population under the age of 15 years, job creation for locals is expected to become more crucial in the future.

Although the Saudi government espouses a free market economy, and since the mid-1990s has encouraged the private sector to take up the responsibility of economic development, the fact remains that the government still holds tight control over economic and social development policies and activities: the Saudi mode of regulation remains a heavily state-centred one. Large state corporations, generally monopolies, dominate the Saudi economy. These firms include the oil firm Saudi ARAMCO, the Saudi Basic Industries Corporation (SABIC), The Saudi Telephone Company (STC), and several other large firms. Historically, this reflected the country's small and underdeveloped private sector before and just after the discovery of oil, and the state's desire to promote growth while shoring up existing social structures and political institutions.

Saudi Arabia which possessed little more than a scanty administrative structure up to the early 1960s, frantically encouraged the growth of the government bureaucratic machine to keep pace with the needs of its economic and social prosperity, and of course, to create employment in the aftermath of the oil windfalls of the

1970s and early 1980s. The resultant structures are poorly constructed and, by the government's own admissions, grossly over-staffed. In addition, the recent financial constraints have precluded the expansion of employment in the public sector. This has forced the private sector to assume a greater importance in the Saudi economy, becoming the principal agent in creating new jobs for Saudi nationals (Al Nafii, 1993; Azzam, 1997).

There is little doubt that the frantic development of the public sector has distorted the Saudi labour market. Much of the inflow of the oil revenues in the 1970s and 1980s was ploughed directly into the public sector (Shaban *et al.*, 1995). As a result, the public sector was able to offer employment to locals with generous reward packages and good quality of working life. Meanwhile, due to the fact that it employs predominantly foreign workers, wages in the private sector are very low. Indeed, wages in the public sector are several times greater than private sector wages (*Al-Iktissad Wal-Aamal*, 1997). This distortion affects locals' incentives to work for the private sector. Shaban *et al.* (1995) reported that the government sector became the only option that new entrants to the national labour force considered; a government job is perceived as a citizen's right. Given that governments, as employers, are particularly vulnerable to political pressures – even in an absolute monarchy – public sector wages are not readily adjustable downwards, while large-scale redundancies can be potentially destabilising. Given this, it is likely that the relatively high wages paid by the state will continue to distort the labour market for the foreseeable future.

In order to lessen its dependence on oil and given its desire to join the World Trade Organization (WTO), Saudi Arabia has recently been making genuine efforts to liberalise its economy by giving more responsibility to the private sector, and to speed up integration into the world economy. Saudi Arabia has signalled its commitment to reforms by instituting several laws and policies (e.g. privatisation laws, investment laws, and new FDI laws) to stimulate competition. Although Saudi Arabia made good progress toward achieving WTO membership in 1999, significant work remains before the accession negotiations are brought to a successful conclusion. In August 1999, the Saudi Arabian government established a Supreme Economic Council to accelerate these reforms. The overriding principle of this globalisation policy has been the promotion of increased efficiency through competition, both domestically and internationally, with a view to providing a sounder basis for sustainable and real employment-creating economic growth. Another major aim of these reforms is to speed up the repatriation of Saudi capital held abroad. The prospect of global competition requires Saudi firms to utilise all their available resources in order to survive and succeed in the global economy. Despite the popular enthusiasm and optimism about economic reforms and the integration of the Saudi economy into the global arena (Kemp, 1999), there is a real apprehension and anxiety about the consequences of free, unfettered trading on the survival of so many Saudi firms long sheltered by the government from foreign competition.

Political environment

Saudi Arabia is a theocratic, Islamic, traditional monarchy, based on a tribal system with a large royal family. Within this traditional form of government, the central figure of government is the King, who is head of the House of Saud, the Chief of State and Head of Government. In this form of political system which lacks a written constitution in the political sense, the Koran is considered the constitution and the principles of the *Shari'a* law. The King is the highest authority in the land and challenge to political power in any shape or form is not tolerated. Consequently, employees, both Saudis and foreigners, are not allowed to establish trade unions and/or form similar associations. Strikes are banned by law. Atiyyah (1996) reported that expatriate workers who resort to strike can face imprisonment and summary deportation. Nonetheless, it is expected that management should seek to resolve any dispute through negotiation and mediation. Atiyyah (1999) noted that in this context, one of the key tasks of managers in Saudi Arabia is achieving and maintaining a conflict-free work environment.

Labour market context

In a country of 19 million people, over 6 million were foreigners in mid-1990s (see Table 9.1) representing no less than 60 per cent of the working population and more than 93 per cent of private sector employees (Cooper, 1996). Kemp (1999) estimated that remittances by expatriate workers are around $15,000 to $16,000 million a year. Given the breakdown of the official job machine in the public sector, the need for 'Saudisation' in the private sector has led the economic, social and political debate in Saudi Arabia in recent years.

According to an estimate by the *Al-Iktissad Wal-Aamal* (1997) magazine, no less than 95 per cent of the new jobs in the 1995–2000 period were in the private sector. Moreover, most were manual skilled jobs requiring specific vocational skills. The government introduced legislation in the mid-1990s which compelled private organisations to employ Saudis wherever possible. In addition, firms had to increase the number of Saudis employed by 5 per cent a year or face sanctions (Resolution 50). In practice, so far, despite the laws and regulations, and the media hype about Saudisation, employment of locals in the private sector has not changed significantly. *The Economist* (1997) reported that calls by political leaders to employ locals have been largely ignored, with many firms choosing to obfuscate rather than implement the law letter-for-letter. There are four interrelated reasons for the private sector's resistance to Saudisation.

The first factor is labour cost. The influx of cheap foreign labour during the past three decades led to the development of a labour-intensive private sector, whose continued profitability hinges on being given a free hand in the utilisation of foreign workers. Although, since the mid-1990s, Saudi Arabia has increased the cost of the latter by introducing compulsory health care for foreign workers and increasing the cost of issuing and renewing work visas from SR 1000 to SR 2000 ($533), local workers still are very much more expensive to hire (Montagu, 1995). It has been argued that more than 85 per cent of jobs in Saudi are paid less than what a Saudi would accept as a minimum (Cooper, 1996). It has further been alleged that locals will demand about six times the salary a skilled foreign worker would be prepared to accept and 'will not work as hard' (*The Economist*, 1997). Foreign workers from developing countries accept relatively low salaries because they can still earn more than they could earn in their home countries (Al-Najjar, 1983; Atiyyah, 1996; Owen, 1986). Furthermore, the majority of foreign workers are young male bachelors and therefore do not have a family to support. For local workers, however, the high cost of living in Saudi Arabia makes the level of wages offered by the private sector incapable of providing an acceptable living standard for local workers (Alogla, 1990; Atiyyah, 1996; Lumsden, 1993). Mellahi and Al-Hinai (2000) reported that managers in Saudi Arabia and Oman ranked 'demand for higher salaries' as the key and most important difference between local and foreign workers. More importantly, managers considered the acceptance of lower salaries by Saudis as the most important factor that would make them more employable in the private sector. A similar study by The Council of Saudi Industrial Chamber of Commerce (1993) found that 83 per cent of private firms surveyed turn to foreign workers because locals do not apply for jobs in the private sector and 82 per cent justified it by the low cost of foreign workers.

Second, social and cultural perceptions towards work in the private sector greatly influence companies' ability to recruit and retain qualified local workers (see Table 9.2). In Saudi Arabia, the type of work, sector of employment and social interactions at work determine the social status of the worker and his family (Mellahi, 2000a). Hence, workers place a great deal of importance on the effect of their work on their social recognition. For instance, most of the jobs in the private sector are manual jobs which Saudi society holds in low esteem. Even before the influx of foreign workers, these jobs were allocated to people with a low social status and social interactions with them were severely restricted (Atiyyah, 1996). Baxter (1998) reported that in Saudi:

> For youngsters leaving school the barriers against desirable career paths are almost mythical. They will not accept jobs as salesmen because this does not befit their social status; they will not take workshop jobs where there is a threat of physical danger. Low salaries are an insult . . . the Saudi youth has too much pride to swallow.

The third factor is discipline and control. Research on the management of foreign workers in Saudi Arabia supports the view that foreign workers are easier to control and more disciplined than local workers (Atiyyah, 1994, 1996; Lumsden, 1993). This could be a result of the fact that work permits in Saudi Arabia are often valid for one year and foreign workers do not qualify for permanent residency or naturalisation, regardless of the length of their stay, therefore employers have few obligations towards foreign workers who can be laid off and sent home at short notice. In addition, foreign workers hold work permits for a specific occupation with a specific employer and therefore they cannot move freely between employers

Table 9.2 Comparison between HRM practices for Saudis and non-Saudis

	Non-Saudis	*Saudis (in the public sector)*
recruitment	mainly by foreign agent	HR department
compensation	fixed and very low	negotiated
HRD	very low	extensive
job hopping	very low	extensive
administrative cost	high	low
management style	authoritarian	paternalistic
basis for control	external, mechanistic, coercive	internal, driven normative
basis for compensation	cost	cost and socio-cultural factors
time horizon	short term	long term

or sponsor without the consent of their employer or sponsor – *Kafeel*. Hence, labour turnover and job-hopping among foreign workers do not exist. A study conducted by Saudi Industrial Chambers of Commerce (1993) showed that 91.8 per cent of private firms in Saudi Arabia believe that foreign workers are more disciplined than locals.

It is worth mentioning that some unscrupulous private employers unfairly treat many foreign workers, especially the unskilled (Atiyyah, 1996). These practices exist because of the absence of strong regulative pressure and the low level of enforceability at the firm level (Atiyyah, 1996). Although data on how foreign employees deal with these practices is not publicly available in Saudi Arabia, Sirhan *et al.* (1983) reported that in the United Arab Emirates only 2 per cent of foreign workers go to courts to settle their disputes. This is understandable. Most foreign workers are ignorant of the labour and residency laws and regulations, and fear retaliation from employers if they take action.

The fourth, and perhaps the most important, factor is the inability to integrate in a multi-cultural work environment. Workforce diversity is becoming a more and more important issue in Saudi Arabia. Organizations in Saudi Arabia employ people from diverse cultural backgrounds sharing different attitudes, needs, desires, values and work behaviour. It is commonly argued that workers with diverse cultural backgrounds should be psychologically linked or attracted towards interacting with one another in pursuit of the firm's objective as this is very important. However, this depends on the level of social integration, group cohesiveness and the ability to work together. This requires workers to get to know one another, and replace negative stereotypes (see Al-Qassimi, 1987) with more accurate knowledge of each other as individuals, which reduce prejudice and conflict and promote greater group cohesiveness. According to published research, however, local workers are often not able to integrate in the multi-cultural work environment (Mellahi and Al-Hinai, 2000; Atiyyah, 1996; Daher and Al-Salem, 1985; Al-Salem *et al.*, 1979; Parry, 1997; Baxter, 1998). For instance, from a sample of 8,581 Kuwaitis, 60 per cent described their relationships with foreign workers as being superficial and limited to official or business affairs, and 40 per cent admitted that nationals treat foreign workers condescendingly (Atiyyah, 1994). Thus, it becomes less pleasant and more difficult for a diverse workforce and locals to work together. Baxter (1998) noted that a Saudi worker 'doesn't want to come to a business and work opposite a Korean or a Filipino. He wants a manager's job from day one.'

Saudi Arabia's HRD strategy: education and vocational training

As illustrated earlier, while rich in capital and natural resources, Saudi Arabia has been and continues to be inadequate in developing indigenous supply of skilled and qualified human resources. In an attempt to close the supply–demand gap in indigenous skilled people, over the years, Saudi Arabia has invested heavily in general and vocational education. Since the late 1980s, the Ministry of Education, the Ministry of Labour and Social Affairs, the regional Chambers of Commerce and the General Organisation for Technical Education and Vocational Training (GOTEVT) have allocated significant resources to vocational education and this commitment appears set to continue for the foreseeable future.

The modern structure of the Saudi Arabian education system began in 1954 with the establishment of the Ministry of Education. There was little development in the field of education in the Arab peninsula prior to the discovery of oil; only a small proportion of the population had access to any form of education. Furthermore, education was limited to religious schools teaching Islamic laws and values and basic literacy skills, and was confined to big cities (Tibawi, 1972). However, the large financial surplus from oil revenues in the 1970s and the early 1980s enabled the government to invest heavily in both general and vocational education. In the Fifth Development Plan (1990–4) the government allocated 19 per cent of its total expenditure to general and vocational education, increasing this proportion to 23 per cent in 1998. As a result, Saudi Arabia has established seven universities, eighty-two colleges and more than 18,000 primary and secondary schools. The expansion of education has resulted in an extensive increase in the student population: since the early 1970s, the number of students has increased sixfold and around 4 million students enrolled in Saudi schools in 1996. However, as illustrated earlier, most jobs in the private sector require vocational education skills. Thus, a detailed examination of the vocational education system and training in Saudi Arabia provides some insight into current and future challenges facing Saudi firms in terms of shortage and availability of technical skills.

The first Five Year Development Plan (1970–5) gave birth to the present Saudi Arabian vocational education and training system. Although the number of students enrolled on vocational education and training courses increased 29fold during the 1970–96 period, the vocational education system is still relatively small. Furthermore, only students who could not remain in the general education stream after primary and intermediate education go to the vocational training centres and intermediate vocational colleges, respectively. This is partly due to the fact that secondary vocational education limits students' chances to acquire university education, which has traditionally provided access to highly paid and socially respected white-collar jobs (Mellahi, 2000a).

Meeting the demands of the economy in terms of skilled workers cannot be accurately measured by the quantity and quality of skills acquired, it depends fundamentally on the extent to which skills acquired are used in employment. Mellahi's (2000a) study of vocational colleges of technology in Saudi Arabia revealed that over half of graduates in subjects leading to skilled manual jobs seek office jobs or start their own trade business rather than work for an employer as a skilled worker. The study found that the structure of the wage system and the social attitudes towards vocational education and vocation-based jobs are the key impediments to vocational education expansion and effectiveness. Students rule themselves out of vocational-based jobs on the grounds of low salary and low social status.

National culture and HRM

Culture exerts a profound influence on HRM practices. The cultural values and social attitudes to management and work in Saudi Arabia are very different from those found in the rest of the world (Badawy, 1980; Anastos, Bedos and Seaman, 1980; Al-Twaijiri, 1989; Yavas and Yasin, 1999). This perception is the product of social cultural values and attributes, some deeply rooted in Middle Eastern Islamic and tribal history and as well as the oil-boom experience. The major contemporary cultural and social features of Saudi Arabia that have influenced the practices of HRM can be attributed to two inter-related main factors: the influence of religion, and the influence of tribal and family traditions. Although for the purpose of this chapter we differentiated between Islamic and tribal and family values in Saudi Arabia, it must be mentioned that, in reality, it is difficult if not impossible to draw a clear distinction between the two. Most tribal and family values in Saudi Arabia are a product of Islamic teachings.

The Influence of Religion (Islam)

Islamic laws and values influence management practices in Saudi Arabia. Quranic principles and prophetic prescriptions serve as guides for managers in conducting their business affairs. Islam's influence could be observed in three main areas: employment of women, management style and HRM practices.

Despite the high investment in the education and training of women which resulted in an exponential increase of women in schools and universities in Saudi Arabia, the participation of women in the formal economic and social sectors is still modest. Female employment and unemployment are not included in most national statistics. Saudi Arabian women's share of the labour force is one of the lowest in the world. This is due to the moral and religious belief among the vast majority of people in Saudi Arabia that marriage and child-bearing remain the principal objectives for women (Doumato, 1999). In addition, the high fertility rates impede women's ability to work. Furthermore, the extreme degree of occupational segregation limits women's chances to obtain work. Even for the increasing minority of young women, especially among university graduates, whose aspiration extends beyond the home into a career, their options are limited to home economics, education and nursing. For example, one report summarised the options open for Saudi women as follow '[Saudi women] will not stand in production lines in large factories, and will not work as secretaries in companies and will not work in service industry as hostesses in aeroplanes or sales assistants' (*Al-Iktissad Wal-Aamal*, 1997: 60).

Managerial attitudes and practices in Saudi Arabia are shaped by Islamic values. Islamic values and teaching put strong emphasis on obedience to leaders. The authority of the leader or manager is thus accepted as right and proper and subordinates are expected to show respect and obedience to superiors. In addition, a heavy emphasis is put on forgiveness, kind-heartedness and compassion. Atiyyah (1999) argued that Arab and Islamic values emphasise harmony, co-operation and brotherly relationships. Conflicts should be avoided or suppressed. Alhabshi and Ghazali (1994) listed the following as core Islamic management values: every act should be accompanied by intention (*niyat*); conscientiousness and knowledge in all endeavours (*itqan*); proficiency and efficiency (*ihsan*); sincerity (*ikhlas*); passion for excellence (*al falah*); continuous self-examination; forever mindful of the almighty – piety (*taqwa*); Justice (*'adl*); truthfulness (*amanah*); patience (*sabar*); moderation; keeping promises; accountability; dedication; gratefulness; cleanliness; consistency; discipline; and co-operation.

Islamic practices also influence management–employees interactions. For instance, at least twice a day, Muslim managers and workers meet and pray together side by side regardless of managerial positions and influence. Although, so far no empirical research has been conducted to examine the effect of such daily interactions, it is fair to argue that these interactions could lessen physical and psychological distances between management and employees.

The Influence of tribal and family traditions

The Arab culture is traditional, socio-centric, male-dominated (Badawy, 1980; Abdalla, 1997) and encourages dependence on relatives and friends (Hofstede, 1984). While the tribal traditions promote consultation in decision-making within the same tribe or extended family, *Asabiyah* – intense loyalty to their own tribe or regional group – encourages authoritarianism with non-kin (out-group), such as other tribes and expatriate workers. Research on dominant management styles in Saudi Arabia provides conflicting results. While a body of research (Al-Jafary and Hollingsworth, 1983; Ali, 1989b; Ali and Al-Shakhis, 1985) reported that the consultative and participative styles are predominantly preferred by Saudi Arabian managers, Ali (1993) found that regardless of the contingency factors, managers tended to adopt an authoritarian management style. Ali sought to explain these conflicting results by pointing out that managers in Saudi do not tend to create a situation of real consultation, but rather a feeling of consultation. He argued that the consultative style that prevails in Arab countries such as Saudi Arabia is different from the Western consultative style and he called it a 'pseudo-consultative style' in order to distinguish it from true consultative one. Muna (1980) argues that while subordinates expect to be consulted about decisions in Arab cultures, they do not expect participation in the decision-making process.

Ali (1998a) argues that the authoritarian management style is a result of the process of socialising outside the family's and tribe's environment which does little to prepare individuals to work within groups outside the family and the tribe. Atiyyah (1999) noted that organisations in Saudi Arabia are run much like traditional entities such as clans or tribes in which paternalistic authoritarian managers rely heavily on their social leadership skills to get work done. Managers resort to informal methods and social pressures before turning to punitive steps.

Using Hofstede's taxonomy, Saudi Arabia could be described as high in power distance, high in uncertainty avoidance (Bjerke and Al-Meer, 1993) and collectivist within the in-group and individualist with the out-group. Bjerke and Al-Meer indicated that 'high power distance' could be attributed to Muslim belief about respect of authority in Islamic societies as well as Bedouin traditions (see Mellahi, 2000b). Bjerke and Al-Meer noted that Saudi managers do not tolerate behaviour that deviates from Islamic teaching and Bedouin traditions. Ali (1993) argues Arab tribal values reinforce the concept of absolute right and wrong and 'do not rock the boat' attitudes, and any approach that does not conform to acceptable norms is considered a threat to established authority and organisation stability. High power distance and uncertainty avoidance have resulted in lower tolerance for new ideas, a low degree of initiative for bringing about change, fatalism, unquestioning acceptance of conventional wisdom, and obedience to justified authority.

Saudis are highly collectivist within the in-group (tribe or extended family) and highly individualist with the out-group (non-kin and guest workers). In the out-group ties between individuals are very loose: interactions are limited and the emphasis is on the individual's accomplishment. When dealing with the out-group, managers apply the same standards to all employees and put a strong emphasis on tasks rather than relationships: the relationship between employer and employee is 'calculative'. Within the in-group, however, from birth onward, people are integrated into strong, cohesive groups (tribes and extended families) that protect them in exchange for unquestioning loyalty. Individuals subordinate their personal interests to the goals of their collective, or in-group. Behaviour within the in-group emphasises co-operation, group welfare, duty, security, and stable social relationships. In short, the employer–employee relationship within the in-group is 'moral' and the corresponding managerial style can be best described as directive but welfare-oriented or paternalistic.

HRM policies and practices in Saudi Arabia

What individual firms do is strongly related to the overall nature of the productive system, and formal and informal codifications. As indicated earlier, specific HRM policies and practices in Saudi Arabia vary according to ownership (private or public), and type of employees (Saudi or foreign). In the public sector, the HRM model – predominantly concerned with the management of Saudi employees and managers – is characterised by: lifetime employment; seniority wages; and social cohesiveness rather than competence. In the Saudi cultural context outlined above, tribal ties and friendship are considered more important than the organisation's vitality. Managers seek to employ and promote the maximum number of members of their tribe and relatives. In addition, competition for limited work opportunities in the public sector encourages nepotism (*wastah*) to play a great role in providing jobs through tribal connections. Consequently, those who are not members of the tribe are less motivated to work harder and tribe members may not work as hard since work is guaranteed and reward is not performance-based.

In the private sector, however, the HRM context is itself evolving and the Saudi HRM model is still in the early stage of evolution. The government and management are still looking for innovative ways to recruit and manage the indigenous workforce effectively. So far, there is no universal agreement on the best policies to recruit and retain qualified Saudi workers or how to deal with the issue of wages inequity in the private sector. Reflecting the dualistic nature of the labour market, the Saudi private sector employs two sets of HRM practices – one for Saudis and one for foreign workers. Although the two models differ radically in practice, both models are not greatly regulated by status and laws: there is no law regulating maximum working hours, job security, minimum wages, etc.

HRM practices for foreign workers are rooted in the accounting approach to HRM, which aims at ensuring that production activities are at all times efficiently supplied with the necessary input of human resources. Such resources are essentially no different from any other production factors. HRM practices focus on tight managerial control through close direction and control. Control in this context is more concerned with performance systems, performance management and tight control over individual activities. Employees are managed under an instrumental basis. The goal of control is to reduce direct labour costs, or improve efficiency, by enforcing employee compliance with specified rules and procedures and basing employee rewards on some measurable output criteria. When dealing with foreign workers, the HRM department becomes no more than an administrative function dealing with visas and work permits (*iqamas*), termination and compensation. Salaries are set individually and each employee is treated as an individual rather than as a member of a collective entity. However, pay scales also differentiate between employees on the basis of nationality (Atiyyah, 1996). Al-Qassimi (1987) observed that natives are paid the highest salaries, followed by Americans and Europeans, Arabs, Filipinos, Koreans and, at the bottom of the scale, Indian subcontinent nationals. HRD practices are non-existent. When new skills are required, it is cheaper to acquire new workers rather than invest in the current ones. In addition, selection and recruitment activities are outsourced to specialised agencies abroad.

The above model of HRM is deeply embedded in Saudi HRM practices in the private sector, especially in small and medium-sized companies. Managers are finding it hard to adjust their practices to accommodate Saudi workers, given the latter's apparent reluctance 'to be passive inputs into the production equation'. Rather, Saudis would like to be viewed and treated as 'assets to be developed and nurtured by the organisation'. HRM has long been a neglected function in the private sector. The extensive employment of foreign workers reduced the function to some administrative tasks and hiring and firing. HR managers have to learn new skills to motivate, attract, develop and retain highly skilled Saudi workers. Above all, they have to move from the control paradigm and 'management by fear of sending you home' to a new model better suited to the new workplace reality.

Popular media and government officials often refer to the case of Aramco and often ask other private Saudi companies to imitate this successful case. Although Aramco's successful story provides an insight as to what is required to attract and retain qualified Saudi workers, it could not be generalised to other firms for various reasons. In particular, Aramco is managed by a highly qualified management team who studied at the most prestigious American universities such as Harvard University. In addition, large rich companies like Saudi Aramco, which employs over 57,000 people – over 75 per cent of which are Saudi citizens – is able to offer attractive compensation packages to attract and retain highly qualified Saudis. Furthermore, with a staff of more than 2,000 full-time teachers, trainers and support personnel, the company claims that their training programme is one of the largest of its kind in the world. In 1994 alone, some 9,000 Saudis took part in company-sponsored training. To retain its Saudi workers, the company provides quality rental housing and recreational facilities for family communities throughout the Eastern Province. Many Saudi employees have built their own homes through the company's Home Ownership Program, which provides free developed lots or grants for land purchases as well as subsidised housing loans. Saudi Aramco also provides high-quality medical care for its employees and their dependants, as well as many other services. It is fair to assume that most Saudi companies cannot afford to provide such generous benefits to their employees.

HR challenges and future directions in Saudi Arabia

Historically speaking, Saudi Arabian firms have been heavily dependent on the presence of large numbers of extremely vulnerable foreign workers willing to work for extremely low wages. Given official pressures, and the very real threat of political instability posed by increasing unemployment of locals, firms have to consider ways in which they can gradually move over to a medium to high wage model. However, the highly interventionist nature of the Saudi economy has resulted in a large number of locals having less skills and work ethics and, possibly, productivity, than their relatively privileged status would suggest.

On the one hand, it could be argued that a high domestic birth rate coupled with the freezing of state employment might result in the 'iron whip of hunger' instilling a greater realism amongst this grouping. On the other hand, Saudi Arabia still offers an impressive welfare net for locals who fall on hard times, whilst the omnipresent threat of political unrest in a society dominated by quasi-feudal political institutions makes a significant downward adjustment in locals' wage rates unlikely. In the end, Saudi firms have a number of possible policy options.

The first would be attempts to shore up the current labour market dualism. This would entail firms vigorously lobbying the government to relax affirmative action quotas, pointing out that economic diversification will, in the long term, generate sustainable growth, and greater employment for Saudis, than would abandonment of the current model. However, given the volatile nature of oil prices, the Saudi state cannot always rely on its internal capacity to mop up domestic unemployment, in the face of a burgeoning birth rate. In short, while the difficulties associated with abandoning the current dual labour market model might have prompted the Saudi state to turn a blind eye to those flouting the quotas, it is likely that there will be a gradual tightening up of the system in future.

Second, the productivity of indigenous Saudis could be enhanced by improving the image of skilled manual work and making them feel more welcome in the multi-cultural workplaces, gradually eroding existing stereotypes regarding an ethnic division of labour. The degree to which workers with diverse cultural backgrounds are psychologically linked or attracted toward interacting with one another in pursuit of the firm's objective is of crucial importance. To some extent it depends on the level of social integration, group cohesiveness and the ability of these employees to work together. This requires workers to get to know one another, and to replace stereotypes with more accurate knowledge of each other as individuals, which can result in reduced prejudice, conflict and greater group cohesiveness. A failure to understand and capitalise on diversity can lead to misguided assumptions, poor working conditions, under-performance and discrimination. Put differently, the ignorance of diversity issue and its problems, challenges and opportunities creates an atmosphere that leads to inefficient utilisation of human resources and could lead to the inefficient functioning of the organisation with a resulting negative impact on the corporate competitiveness.

Nevertheless, in spite of the growing importance of workforce diversity, very little empirical research has been done to assess the management of diversity in Saudi Arabia. The need for better management and utilisation of diversity in Saudi Arabia is one of the challenges facing Saudi organisations. As more Saudis join the private sector, it will strongly affect organisations' performance, effectiveness and even survival.

Conclusion

Much of the debate on globalisation has centred on the extent to which national social institutions are capable of determining political and economic outcomes for a population in question (Czaban and Henderson, 1998: 585). The relatively favourable position, at certain historical moments, of oil producers within global commodity chains strengthened the capacity of indigenous institutions in the Gulf States to influence national practices (ibid.). In the case of Saudi Arabia, official policy centred on efforts to dampen the essential volatility of a primary commodity-centred growth regime through diversification, and large-scale job creation within the state sector. This enterprise was underpinned by an historic compromise, whereby private firms gained access to state incentives and were given a free hand in the resourcing and utilisation of foreign workers, in return for investment and limited job creation for Saudi nationals. This was underpinned by a highly segmented labour market, underwritten by formal and informal codes of practice that placed foreign workers in a particularly vulnerable position. However, the attempt at greater stabilisation was only partially successful, in the face of a downturn in oil price in the late 1980s and early 1990s and a high domestic birth rate. This has led to state attempts to reconstitute the labour market into one largely composed of Saudi nationals, which, in turn has forced firms to rethink the manner in which they manage their human resources. The difficulties associated with moving away from a low wage model are not to be underestimated, and, indeed, this has led to official affirmative action quotas being largely flouted. In the end, the viability of a high wage–high productivity alternative depends on coherent human resource development initiatives, and by integrating ethnic Saudis more fully into what will, for the foreseeable future, remain cosmopolitan workplaces, and gradually eroding existing stereotypes regarding an ethnic division of labour. However, the challenges may prove insurmountable without a fundamental reconstitution of political institutions.

References

Abdalla, I. A. H. (1997) 'Construct and Concurrent Validity of Three Protestant Work Ethic Measures in an Arabian Gulf Society', *Journal of Managerial Psychology*, 12 (4), 251–260.

Al-Baik, D. (1996) 'More Jobs for Nationals Urged', *Gulf News*, Business Section, 30 May.

Al-Bar, H. (1978) *Manpower Problems in Saudi Arabia*, Denver, CO: University of Denver.

Al-Essa, G. S. (1983) 'Social Influences of Foreign Nannies on Families', in N. Farjani (ed.) *Foreign Labor in Arab Gulf Countries*, proceedings of a seminar organized by the Center for Arab Unity Studies and the Arab Institute of Planning in Kuwait, Center for Arab Unity Studies, Beirut, pp. 169–81.

Alhabshi, S. O. and Ghazali, A. H. (1994) *Islamic Values and Management*, Kuala Lumpur: Institute of Islamic Understanding Malaysia (IKIM).

Ali, A. and Al-Shakis, M. (1985) 'Managerial Value Systems for Working in Saudi Arabia: An Empirical Investigation', *Group and Organization Studies*, 10 (2), 135–151.

Ali, A. J. (1989a), 'A Comparative Study of Managerial Belief about Work in Arab states', *Advances in International Comparative Management*, 4, 96–112.

Ali, A. J. (1989b) 'Decision Style and Work Satisfaction on Arab Gulf Executives: A Cross-national Study', *International Studies of Management and Organisation*, 19 (2), 22–37.

Ali, A. J. (1993) 'Decision-making Style, Individualism, and Attitudes toward Risk of Arab Executives', *International Studies of Management and Organisation*, 23 (3), 53–73.

Ali, A. J., Azim, A. and Krishnan, K. S. (1995) 'Expatriates and Host Country Nationals: Managerial Values and Decision Styles', *Leadership and Organisation Development Journal*, 16 (6), 27–34.

Al-Iktissad Wal-Aamal (*Economics and Business*) (1997) Special Issue on Saudisation, Riyad, Year 18, March.

Al-Jafary, A. and Hollingsworth, A. T. (1983) 'An Exploratory Study of managerial Practices in the Arabian Gulf Region', *Journal of International Business Studies*, Fall, 143–52.

Almaney, A. (1981) 'Cultural Traits of the Arabs', *Management International Review*, 21 (3), 10–18.

Al Nafii, A. (1993) 'The Fifth National Plan of Development's Orientation towards Employment in the Private Sector', in Al Amala al al-Mowatina fi al Kitaa al Ahli al Saudi (eds) *Employment of Nationals in the Saudi Private Sector*, Conference organized by Institute of Public Administration, Riyad, 12–13 February, 81–96 (in Arabic).

Al-Najjar, B. (1983) *Working and Living Conditions of Foreign workers: foreign Labor in Arab Gulf Countries*, proceedings of a Seminar Organized by the Center for Arab Unity Studies and the Arab Institute of Planning in Kuwait, Center for Arab Unity Studies, Beirut, 169–81.

Alogla, H. (1990) *Obstacles to Saudization in the Private Sector of the Saudi Arabian Labour Force*, Michigan: Michigan State University.

Al-Qassimi, K. M. (1987) *Manpower and Demography in the United Arab Emirates*, Beirut: Oueidat Publications.

Al-Salem, F., Farah, T. and Al-Salem, M.(1979) *Alienation and Expatriate Labor in Kuwait*, Boston: Migration and Labor Study Group, MIT.

Al-Twaijiri, M. (1989) 'A Cross-cultural Comparison of American–Saudi Managerial Values in US-related firms in Saudi Arabia', *International Studies of Management and Organisation*, 19 (2), 58–73.

Anastos, D., Bedos, A. and Seaman, B. (1980) 'The Development of Modern Management Practices in Saudi Arabia', *Columbia Journal of World Business*, Summer, 81–92.

Atiyyah, H. S. (1994) *Working in the Gulf: An Expatriate Guide to the Employment Laws of the Gulf Arab States*, Plymouth: International Venture Handbooks.

Atiyyah, H. S. (1996) 'Expatriate Acculturation in Arab Gulf Countries', *Journal of Management Development*, 15 (5), 37–47.

Atiyyah, H. S. (1999) 'Public Organisations' Effectiveness and its Determinants in a Developing Country', *Cross Cultural Management*, 6 (2), 8–21.

Azzam, H. T. (1993) 'Saudi Arabia: Joint Ventures in the Kingdom', Part I, *Middle East Executive Reports*, 16 (3), 9–15.

Azzam, H. T. (1997) 'Preparing for Global Future', *The Banker*, 47, 72–76.

Badawy, M. K. (1980) Styles of Mid-Eastern Managers, *California Management Review*, 22 (2), 51–58.

Baxter, J. (1998) 'Saudi Heads in the Sand', *Management Today*, March, 30–31.

Bjerke, B. and Al-Meer, A. (1993) 'Culture's Consequences: Management in Saudi Arabia', *Leadership and Organizational Development Journal*, 14 (2), 30–35.

Boyer, R. (2000) 'Is a Finance Led Growth Regime a Viable Alternative to Fordism?', *Economy and Society*, 29 (1), 111–145.

Cooper, J. (1996) 'Putting the Kingdom to Work', *Middle East Economic Digest*, 40 (14), 55–59.

The Council of Saudi Industrial Chamber of Commerce (1993) 'Orientations and Abilities of the Private Sector in Training and Preparing National Workers', in *Al Amala al al-Mowatina fi al Kitaa al Ahli al Saudi (Employment of Nationals in the Saudi Private Sector)* Conference organized by Institute of Public Administration, Riyad, 12–13 February, 197–241. (in Arabic).

Czaban, L. and Henderson, J. (1998) 'Globalization, Institutional Hegemony and Industrial Transformation', *Economy and Society*, 27 (4), 585–613.

Daher, A. G. and Al-Salem, E. (1985) *Manpower in Gulf Arab Countries: A Field Study of the General Situation*, Kuwait: Al-Salasil.

Doumato, E. A. (1999) 'Women and Work in Saudi Arabia: How Flexible are Islamic Margins?', *Middle Eastern Journal*, 53 (4), 568–583.

The Economist (1997) 'Gulf Citizen, No Qualifications, Seeks Well-paid Job', 343 (8012), 41.

The Economist (2000) 'Saudi Arabia on the Dole', 355 (8167), 47.

Gavin, J. (2000) 'Saudi Arabia: The Walls Come Down', *Middle East Economic Digest*, 44 (19), 4–5.

Grahl, J. and Teague, P. (2000) 'The Regulation School, the Employment Relation and Financialization', *Economy and Society*, 29 (1), 160–178.

Hofstede, G. (1984) 'Cultural Dimensions in Management and Planning', *Asia Pacific Journal of Management*, 1, 81–99.

Kemp, P. (1999) 'MEED Saudi Arabia Special Report', *Middle East Economic Digest*, 43 (23), 7–11.

Lumsden, P. (1993) 'Dealing with the Problem of Localisation', *Middle East Economic Digest*, 37 (10), 46–48.

Mellahi, K. (2000a) 'Human Resource Development through Vocational Education in Gulf Cooperation Countries: The case of Saudi Arabia', *Journal of Vocational Education and Training*, 52 (2), 331–347.

Mellahi, K. (2000b) 'Western MBA Education and Effective Leadership Values in Developing Countries: A Case Study of Asian, Arab and African MBA Graduates', *Journal of Transnational Management Development*, 5 (2), 59–73.

Mellahi, K. and Al-hinai, S. (2000) 'Local Workers in Gulf Co-operation Countries: Assets or Liabilities?', *Middle Eastern Studies*, 26 (3), 177–191.

Montagu, C. (1995) 'Making more of National Manpower', *Middle East Economic Digest*, 39 (10), 40–41.

Muna, F. A. (1980) *The Arab Executive*, London: Macmillan.

Owen, R. (1986) 'Migrant Workers in the Gulf', *Middle East Review*, Spring, 24–27.

Parry, C. (1997) *Saudization*. Al-Iktissad Wal-Aamal, Year 18, 39–41.

Saudi American Bank (2000) *The Saudi Economy: 1999 Performance, 2000 Forecast*. 16 February, Kuwait: Saudi American Bank.

Saudi Industrial Chambers of Commerce – Research Section (1993) Methods to Increase the Participation of National Workers in The Private Sector, In Al Amala al al-Mowatina fi al Kitaa al Ahli al Saudi (Employment of Nationals in The Saudi Private Sector) *Conference organized by Institute of Public Administration*, Riyad, February 12–13, 245–311 (in Arabic).

Shaban, A. R., Asaad, R. and Al-Qudsi, S. (1995) 'The Challenges of Employment in the Arab Region', *International Labour Review*, 134, 65–82.

Sirhan, B. B., Al-Bassam, D., Mutai, A. B. A., Kassim, A. A. and Farjani, N. (1983) 'Information File on Foreign Labor in Arab Gulf Countries', in Farjani, N. (ed.), *Foreign Labour in Arab Gulf Countries*, Beirut: CAUS.

Tibawi, A. L. (1972) *Islamic Education: Its Traditions and Modernization into the Arab National Systems*, London: Luzac and Company.

Yavas, U. Luqmani, M. and Quraeshi, Z. (1990) 'Organisational Commitment, Job Satisfaction, Work Values: Saudi and Expatriate Managers', *Leadership and Organisational Development Journal*, 11 (7), 3–10.

Yavas, U. and Yasin, M. M. (1999) 'Organisational Significance and Application of Computer Skills: A Culturally-Based Empirical Examination', *Cross Cultural Management*, 6 (4), 11–21.

Part II

Human resource management in Africa

10 Human resource management in Algeria

Mohamed Branine

Introduction

Algeria, like other developing countries, embarked on radical economic and political reforms in the late 1980s. These reforms were a response to the economic crisis resulting from the fall in oil and gas prices after 1986, and the consequent social unrest after 1988. Credible changes in the economy were, unfortunately, very short-lived and the whole country almost fell into chaos, resulting in destruction of property, fear, uncertainty and terrorism. This chapter is an attempt to present, as far as possible, a useful account of Algeria's experience of socio-economic development and human resource management (HRM). The first section provides a brief overview of the socio-economic and political system of the country. In the second section the labour market and the factors that have influenced it are discussed, and in the third section the two main systems of management, the Self-Management scheme (1962–9) and the Socialist Management of Enterprises (1971–90), are analysed. In the fourth section the functions of HRM before and after the reforms are discussed by examining the policies and practices of recruitment and selection, training and development, reward and remuneration, and industrial relations, as these are the main functions of most personnel/HR departments at present. It is concluded therefore that the problems and the characteristics of managing employees in Algeria are intertwined with contradictory policies, practices and attitudes that have their origins in the cultural, historical, political and socio-economic development of the country.

The socio-economic and political context

Algeria is potentially one of the richest countries in North Africa because of its natural resources of arable land in the north and hydrocarbons (crude oil and natural gas) in the south. Other significant resources include iron, zinc, phosphates, uranium and mercury. However, recent figures released by the Algerian National Office of Statistics (NOS) show that industrial production has declined by about 25 per cent from that in early 1980s and that average economic growth dropped from about 4.4 per cent between 1977 and 1987 to less than 1 per cent between 1988 and 1998, although it did reach 3.5 per cent between 1998 and 1999 (NOS,

1999). It seems that the only sector that is active at present is that of oil and gas production. Algeria is a member of OPEC and has the fifth largest reserves of natural gas and it is the second largest gas exporter in the world. It ranks fourteenth for oil reserves. The hydrocarbons sector provides 97 per cent of export earnings and 65 per cent of the state revenues.

Life in Algeria can be characterized as being strongly underpinned by the Islamic faith, culture and civilization despite also being influenced by more than a hundred years of French colonialism and cultural diffusion. Islam is officially the state's religion and Arabic is the national language. Although open to Western influence, the religious sentiments and cultural values of Islam have retained significant power within Algerian society. Being known as the country of a million and a half martyrs, Algeria is united by Islam and nationalism, regardless of social status, tribal origins or native languages.

The social system has been dominated by extended families and communities which protected their members and cared for the elderly and otherwise needy. Strong emphasis is put on the family as the foundation of society. This strong family orientation has its origins in Islam which values the bond of marriage, having children, obeying one's parents and having respectful and caring family relationships. As in all collectivist cultures the welfare of the group is considered most important. Centralized power structure and a kinship ethos based on the extended family engender a form of authoritarian paternalism. The obligation to family and kin is obviously very significant and it has strong effects on employment and employee relations.

Until the early 1980s the whole economy grew under rigid central control and state ownership, over 70 per cent of enterprises were owned by the state. They were either inherited from the French colonial era or created in the 1960s and 1970s when the economy was booming and oil revenues were high. Most of the national enterprises were large and had monopolies over the production of goods or provision of services in their sectors. They were highly structured, formalized and centralized (Zeffane, 1981a). They were characterized by a wide range of production units, large numbers of workers, high turnover, high levels of investment and rigid hierarchical levels. The growth rate in the 1960s and 1970s was no less than 5 per cent per annum but the emphasis on heavy industry in the 1970s created large state-owned companies which found themselves idle in the 1980s and closed down in the 1990s. The growing size of state-owned enterprises and the diversification of their production made their management poorly integrated. They were in need of structural, organizational and cultural change. By 1980 it was being suggested that in order to have better control of production and better industrial relations, large national enterprises had to be divided into smaller and more specialized units. Therefore a programme for the restructuring of enterprises was introduced, based on a separation between the functions of production, trade and distribution; the distinction between national and local enterprises, in order to have regional decentralization; and a reduction in the size of enterprises. It started by restructuring nineteen national industrial companies into 104 national industrial enterprises. However, until the end of 1986 the restructuring programme was still under way and still some enterprises, although restructured, suffered from problems of management, finance, employment of skilled workers and low productivity (*Révolution Africaine*, no. 1242, 18 December 1987).

The rate of economic growth dropped from 4.6 per cent per annum in 1985 to −1.4 per cent in 1987 and to −2.9 in 1988 (*Algérie Actualité*, no. 47, March 1990) while unemployment increased from 16 per cent in 1986 to 19 per cent in 1988 (*Révolution Africaine*, no. 1266, 3 June 1988: 18). The country was in crisis as high unemployment was met with high inflation and increasing foreign debts. In response to the crisis the government introduced severe austerity measures in 1987. State-owned enterprises were made autonomous organizations that were expected to secure their own financial resources, as they became financially independent from the state. Autonomous enterprises resorted to the reduction of costs through reductions of investments and employee numbers to improve their performance. The programme of enterprise autonomy took a new direction towards a free enterprise economy at a time when the country was in need of national enterprises that would absorb the excessive unemployment. Such measures were followed by a period of social and economic unrest as unemployment increased, essential goods became in short supply and prices rocketed. There were numerous strikes throughout the country and on 5 October 1988 riots erupted in Algiers, the capital, spreading to all other big cities. In response to the unrest and riots, which resulted in hundreds being killed by the government forces, President Chadli Bendjadid announced constitutional changes which permitted multi-party politics. A new Constitution, ending twenty-seven years of the one party system, was approved by referendum in February 1989. New laws were introduced in July 1989 to reduce the state control of the economy and to remove the state monopoly over the national press. Therefore, it was the first time that multi-party general elections were allowed to be contested.

The first round of elections was held on 26 December 1991 and the second round was scheduled for 16 January 1992. In the first round, in which 231 of the 430 seats were won outright, the Islamic Salvation Front (FIS) gained 188 seats and was poised to assume power. The rise in the popularity and the huge support for the FIS were partly an expression of frustration with the country's long history of corruption, mismanagement, injustice, and incompetent and authoritarian government. However, on 11 January 1992 President Chadli was forced by a group of army generals to resign and the High Security Council cancelled the second round of elections. On 14 January a five-member High Council of State (HCE) announced that it would act as a collegiate presidency to be headed by one of the first leaders of the National Liberation Front (FLN), Mohamed Boudiaf, who returned from Morocco after twenty-eight years in exile. These events led to sporadic protests and outbreaks of violence throughout the country. In February 1992 the High Council of State declared a twelve-month state of emergency and in March the FIS party was dissolved. Violence escalated and the state of emergency was renewed for an indefinite period. In June 1992 Mohamed Boudiaf was assassinated by a member of his presidential guard. Despite a number of constitutional, presidential and governmental changes, violence has continued to date. Although much of the killing has been blamed on Islamist groups, the army and other government security forces appear to have been equally responsible for the bloodshed that has claimed more than 100,000 lives and the disappearance of more than 20,000 people since it started in 1992. Significant changes have been made since 1998 but the situation is still volatile. There is now an elected president and an elected parliament in which ten political parties are represented, but the military is still in control of the country's political system and remains very influential in all matters.

As more and more state-owned enterprises go bankrupt, many thousands of employees have lost their jobs. The transition from a planned economy to a market economy has been very slow because of the political turmoil and the associated lack of foreign and indigenous investment. Neither national nor international investments were attracted and therefore the increase in labour supply was not met by the creation of jobs. Today there is a mixture of state-owned enterprises, most of which are in a state of bankruptcy or being privatized, privately owned small and medium-sized enterprises, and a number of joint ventures. The output of the private sector in 1999 was 7 per cent higher than the previous year while that of the public sector declined by 2.7 per cent. Small and medium-sized enterprises have dominated markets in textiles and other light industrial sectors but most of them have been hit by the devaluation of the dinar, high inflation and high interest rates, as well as by terrorism, sabotage and theft. Since the civil concord or the Civil Harmony Act, which was approved by referendum on 16 September 1999, and the relative security in the country, many multinational companies have shown a keen interest in investing in such active sectors as hydrocarbons, telecommunications, pharmaceuticals, construction, and tourism but so far significant investments have yet to materialize.

The labour market

In March 2000 the Algerian labour force was estimated at about 9.5 million out of a population of about 31.5 million. The minimum employment age in Algeria is 16 years. The size of the economically active population rose from 3.574 million in 1970 to 4.854 million in 1980 and to 9.382 million in 1997. Official statistics show that unemployment rate rose from 20.2 per cent in 1991 to 29.2 per cent in 1997. It is currently estimated at 30 per cent of the active population. By the end of 1998 there were more than 65 per cent of those unemployed under the age of 24 years old (World Bank, 1999). There is clearly a youth unemployment problem. For the majority of young people in Algeria the prospect of finding a job has been depressing, and as a result there has been a general sense of frustration among them. Younger and inexperienced people are the most affected in a labour market where job opportunities are very slim and too grim. As many state-owned enterprises are being closed down or privatized, a very limited number of jobs are being created and the problem of unemployment makes potential social unrest imminent if urgent measures are not taken to create new jobs.

The present problems of unemployment are the results of economic and educational policies initiated in the 1970s. The two Four-Year plans (1970–3 and 1974–7) emphasized investment in capital-intensive heavy industry at the expense of more labour-intensive small firm sectors that would have had created more badly needed employment. The state's economic development strategy of industrialization was not labour-intensive enough and led to an increasing gap between the levels of employment in the rural and urban areas as a result of giving so much priority to industry over agriculture. Industrial estates were located on land with fertile soil, reducing agricultural potential and damaging the environment. It was reported in the daily *El Moudjahid* (22 March 1979) that about 251,000 hectares of arable land were being used for industrial sites. According to the national census of 1977, the number of workers employed in agriculture declined from 918,000 in 1966 (then representing 54 per cent of the employed population) to 692,000 in 1977 (then representing 29 per cent of the employed population). Peasant workers with no skills and no qualifications had to look for jobs in industry. Industrial sectors became over-manned but suffered shortages of professional and managerial staff.

While the second quinquennial plan (1984–9) projected an increase in employment by 6 per cent per annum, creating 1 million jobs by 1990, in reality unemployment increased from about 8 per cent in 1984 to 19 per cent in 1988 (*Révolution Africaine*, No. 1266, 3 June 1988: 18). More than 130,000 jobs were shed between 1985 and 1989 (*Révolution Africaine*, No. 1323, July 1989). Recognizing that the country's demographics would make youth unemployment a serious social problem, the government established the Youth Employment Programme in 1988 to provide jobs and training for young people between 16 and 24 years of age. The programme failed eventually to meet its target of creating 40,000 training opportunities and 60,000 jobs each year. Therefore in 1990 two other initiatives were introduced: one would subsidize, by up to 30 per cent of the initial investment, the establishment of new enterprises by young people and the other would guarantee bank loans extended to young entrepreneurs. The latter was relatively successful in helping young people to start their own businesses especially in transport and agriculture but most of the new entrepreneurs found themselves 'working for the banks' as they had to repay the loan with high interest. Also the lack of spare parts, of business experience, of knowledge and skills in actually carrying out the work (especially agriculture), and the lack of support from the local authorities led to the failure of many young people's new ventures. There is a need for companies that would create all kinds of jobs for the increasing supply of labour, for vocational training centres that would produce skilled employees and for policies that would encourage the return to employment in agriculture.

Employment laws and regulations: imposed management systems

The labour market has been regulated since independence but employment regulations in the form of codes of practice and charters have been introduced ideologically without much effective consideration of the needs of employees or the economy. The most significant forms of labour market regulation affecting Algeria's public and private enterprises were the Self-Management system (1962–9) and the Socialist Management of Enterprises system (1971–90). Both systems are discussed below.

Self-Management (1962–9)

On the eve of independence from France in 1962 more than 70 per cent of the economy was based on agriculture, of which some 22,000 farms comprising more than 2.3 million hectares of arable land were left abandoned by the French settlers who had fled the country. There were also hundreds of residential properties, hotels and restaurants, factories and many commercial premises without their former owners (Clegg, 1971; Benissad, 1979). Therefore some 275,979 Algerians, mainly former workers in the abandoned land and properties, occupied them and ran them collectively. They organized themselves into workers' committees, creating a form of self-management. It was not until about six months later that the newly established government of Ahmed Ben Bella intervened by means of legislation to regulate the self-managed enterprises. It issued sets of decrees which became known as the 'March Decrees' of 1963.

The March Decrees established that the permanent employees of each self-managed enterprise had to be represented in a general assembly which had to elect a workers' council for three years. The workers' council had to elect a workers management committee, which in turn elected a president who would work with a state-appointed director (see Figure 10.1). The General Assembly of Workers included all permanent workers over the age of 18 and of Algerian nationality. The workers council, whose members were chosen from among the members of the General Assembly, decided on the purchase and sale of equipment for the unit and saw to its maintenance. It also elected a workers management committee which comprised between three to eleven members and had to select one of its members as president of the unit. The workers management committee was primarily responsible for drawing up the unit's development plan, deciding on work schedules, instituting accounting procedures, producing marketing strategies, and settling disputes. It also had to elect a president to represent the enterprise and to work closely with a state-appointed director. The president of the workers' management committee was expected to call and preside over all meetings and had the right to sign all financial and legal documents of the enterprise. Being appointed by the state, the director had the overall responsibility over the management of the enterprise, including the role of treasurer, chief accountant, coordinator and supervisor of the day-to-day activities.

Self-management was a short-lived experience. It was started spontaneously by the workers but it lost its momentum as soon as it was formally regulated. A study by Chaulet (1971) on self-managed farms in the valley of Metidja (north-west Algiers) reported that no workers assembly had played the 'role of a sovereign organ in production nor was it considered as such' and in none of the farms studied did workers assemblies hold regular meetings (Chaulet, 1971: 149). Also Ottaway and Ottaway (1970: 66–67) reported an Algerian official saying that workers councils 'died in the effort to give birth to management committees, and meetings of the

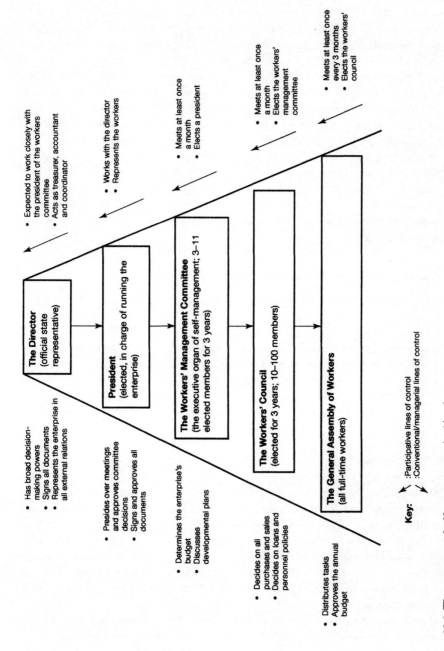

Figure 10.1 The structure of self-management in Algeria

general assemblies rarely took place'. According to Lacks, the directors became 'sterile bureaucrats, displaying a lack of sensitivity to the difficulties of the enterprise by neglecting, for instance, to supervise production, and paying themselves an inflated salary' (1970: 63). Many farms in Metidja and Shlef were taken over by their state-appointed directors who exploited them in their own interest, giving the poverty-stricken peasants no opportunities to participate in management or to share in profits (see Clegg, 1971; Benhouria, 1980).

After the *coup d'état* of 1965 the military government of Colonel Boumédienne argued that self-management would not achieve the country's objectives of socio-economic development. Therefore attention was shifted to the creation of co-operatives for the benefit of war veterans and to the nationalization of foreign companies. The number of self-managed enterprises was reduced, with most of them being converted into small co-operatives. The department in charge of self-management in the Ministry of Industry was closed and in August 1967, nine state-owned companies were created by taking over some of the self-managed enterprises. Therefore by 1969 all self-managed enterprises had either merged into state-owned companies or been transformed into co-operatives and handed over to war veterans.

Socialist Management of Enterprises (1971–90)

The Socialist Management of Enterprises (SME) was introduced through Ordinance No. 71–74, dated 16 November 1971 in a document entitled the Charter and Code of the Socialist Management. The SME charter contained 88 articles divided into nine chapters. It stated that at the level of every unit of operation the workers had to elect a workers assembly from which two members would represent them at a joint management council, with the rest carrying out their participatory role in five executive committees of their units. These were the economic and financial committee, the social and cultural affairs committee, the personnel and occupational training committee, the disciplinary committee, and the health and safety committee (see Figure 10.2). The General Union of Algerian Workers (UGTA) was also expected to play a significant role in the system through its local and enterprise syndicates. The elected workers' assembly at the level of each unit was the UGTA's local syndicate council (*Charte et Code de la Gestion Socialiste des Entreprises*, 1971: 12). A National Commission on the SME (CNGSE), a National Organizational Commission (CNO) and Councils of Co-ordination (CC) were also set up to help implement the Socialist Management of Enterprises in all public and private enterprises in all sectors throughout the country. In 1975 a further set of regulations on how to implement the SME was introduced as The SME Texts of Application (*Textes d'Application de la GSE*, 1975).

The implementation of the SME went through four stages (Branine, 1994) and at each stage a national conference was organized to evaluate the progress made that far. The application of the SME increased steadily between 1974 and 1982. For example, the number of the so-called socialist enterprises increased from 12 in 1974 to 50 in 1976 and to 104 in 1982. However, and despite the increasing

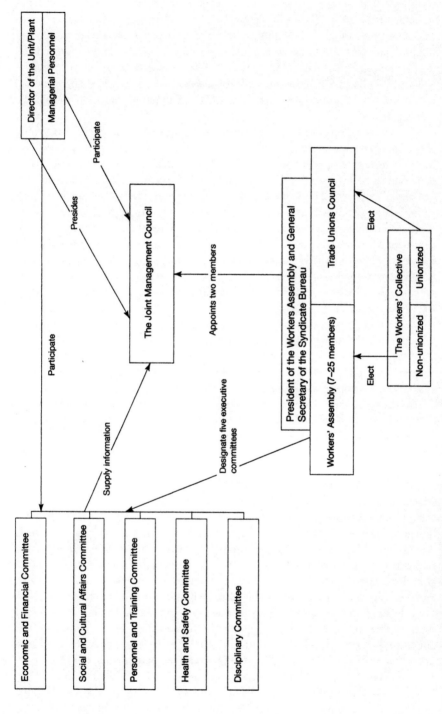

Figure 10.2 The structure of the SME at the unit/plant level in Algeria

number of socialist enterprises, many economically important ones did not implement the SME. For example, by 1979 about 70 large national enterprises and about 320 small and medium-sized local enterprises employing more than 900,000 workers in industrial sectors alone had not yet introduced the SME (Benachenhou, 1980). One of them was the biggest national petroleum company, SONATRACH (*Société Nationale du Transport et de la Commercialisation des Hydrocarbures*), which did not introduce the SME until 1981 and which never implemented the process fully.

Workers were supposed to be involved in the making of decisions concerning their enterprises through elected workers' representatives. In practice, however, and whenever there was any sign of workers contributing to decision-making, it tended to be just consultative and confined to executive matters of social and individual concern. The following factors were conducive to the apparent lack of workers' participation: first, there was a problem of representation as the relationship between the workers and their representatives was not clear. Workers' representatives were expected to hold regular general meetings with workers but it was very often reported that the time at and the ways in which meetings were held did not encourage effective worker participation. There were also cases when rivalries between individual representatives led to informal groups dividing the workers assemblies. Many workers assemblies did not finish their mandate with the same members as they had elected because most representatives had either resigned or were dismissed before the end of the three-year periods (Saadi, 1985: 439). Second, there was a conflict between the role of trade unions council of the unit and that of a workers assembly. Since a workers assembly was expected to represent all workers, regardless of their membership of the unions, there was an overlap between the functions of the unions council and that of a workers assembly. The problematic issue, however, was how to achieve both functions in practice. It was not clear whether it involved combining two functions into one organism or performing one function by two organisms. Third, the existence of the five executive committees was just symbolic. They could not undertake their representative roles because of the withholding of information by management and the weakness of the representatives (Zeffane, 1981b; Saadi, 1985). Fourth, there was a supremacy of management at joint management councils (Zeffane, 1981b). The existence of just two workers' representatives at joint management councils was not enough for them to express workers' views effectively. General managers of enterprises, as presidents of joint management councils, and their management staff dominated discussions during their meetings and restricted information to workers' representatives. Fifth, and finally, such difficulties did not arise only from the internal functioning of the participative system but also came from external bodies representing the state, the party (FLN) and the General Union of the Algerian Workers (UGTA). A number of studies reported that the National Commission of the SME (CNSME), the Operational Commission (CNO) and the UGTA created problems for the implementation of the SME (Boussoumah, 1982; Saadi, 1985). For example, when the CNO was set up to supervise the elections of workers assemblies, the UGTA felt that its functions were being taken over.

This is why elections were seldom carried out without confrontation between the UGTA and the CNO organizers (Bouyacoub, 1987).

Since the early 1990s, as the economy descended into chaos, there has been no clearly definable system of management or employee relations. But there are many millions of people who are being employed, trained and rewarded throughout the country. This means that there is a form of personnel or human resource management that is heavily influenced by the socio-economic, cultural, political, legal and organizational changes discussed above.

The personnel function before and after the reforms

The management of employees in Algeria can best be described as personnel administration rather than human resource management as understood in Western industrial countries. There is no clear evidence of personnel managers' involvement in strategic decision-making or in policy formulation. The formal role of the personnel department does not go beyond the administration of employees' files and record keeping through complicated bureaucratic procedures. There exists a paper-processing job, done almost for its own sake. All terms and conditions of employment are regulated, as mentioned earlier, by government decrees and statutes.

Most companies have personnel departments at their headquarters, with separate divisions or services at regional and local levels. The personnel manager reports directly to the general manager of the enterprise. It should be noted here that the main functions of a personnel department and the bureaucracy involved in the process have their origins in the French colonial administrative system. Despite the introduction of participative management programmes and direct state intervention through ownership and regulation of national enterprises, the French influence is still prominent. This has obviously reflected the kinds of education and training that the Algerian managers acquire but there are also a number of economic, social, cultural and political factors that affect the recruitment and selection of employees, their rewards and their industrial relations.

Recruitment and selection

Although most enterprises use the familiar procedures of recruitment and selection such as advertising jobs in newspapers, reviewing applications, holding interviews and testing candidates, many vacancies are filled through friends and relatives. Generally speaking, the process of recruitment and selection in Algeria is merely a bureaucratic and administrative formality and is neither systematic nor objective. There have been many cases of vacancies being filled before they were advertised. It is normal for organizations to receive unsolicited and speculative applications. It is also common practice to hire new employees without necessarily having vacancies. The latter happens when friends and relatives apply for jobs.

It is very often difficult to get employment without having contacts with people within the organization. Such contacts as acts of favouritism, nepotism or bribery are summed up in the well-known Algerian concept of the 'Piston'. Application forms and documents which are not followed up through the use of the 'Piston' are often easily lost or ignored. The use of the 'Piston' to get jobs, goods and services easily has given many managers enhanced social prestige and strengthened their positions. Friendship and kinship can take precedence over qualifications and skills as managers feel obliged to support their relatives and friends. In return, the employees who get jobs through the 'Piston' have a predisposition not to disagree with those who hired them.

Applying for jobs is a tiresome and time-consuming task which involves paper gathering and undergoing a bureaucratic vicious circle. For every job vacancy the applicant is required to submit a hand-written letter applying for the job, together with a full dossier which includes original or legally certified copies of qualifications obtained, a birth certificate, a residence certificate, a nationality certificate, a certificate of exemption from national service (for men), a certificate of jurisdiction, four or more photographs, and four or more self-addressed and stamped envelopes. Depending on the type of organization, some of them also ask for the birth certificate and the nationality certificate of both the mother and the father. It takes weeks if not months for many people to get the dossier completed because of the delays and obfuscation they encounter when acquiring the above certificates, and finally none of them are returned if the application is unsuccessful. However, if the 'Piston' is in action the required papers would be the minimum and the job would be offered directly.

It should be noted that there is a strong emphasis on a formal hand-written letter and on qualifications. The emphasis on a hand-written letter of application does not mean that Algerian employers use graphology in their selection procedure. It is simply a practice that was inherited from the French bureaucracy or just a way of looking for employees who have neat and legible handwriting. It is also used in some instances as a means of reducing the number of applicants because writing letters by hand may deter some from applying. There is also a great emphasis on qualifications and the degree subject plays an important role in the recruitment of managers because it is believed that the knowledge acquired through education should greatly influence the career of the applicant. For managerial jobs a high priority is placed on language skills, especially the ability to write and communicate fluently in French despite the fact that Arabic is the national language. This is one of the strongest legacies of French influence on Algerian administration and society as a whole, despite nearly four decades of independence. Even the 'Piston' is, according to Clegg (1971: 170), a legacy of colonialism in Algeria which also had roots in the country's indigenous culture and social structure.

After independence it was necessary to appoint some directors without any technical or managerial qualifications because there was an acute shortage of trained managers. For example, by the end of 1963 there were only forty directors qualified to run 450 self-managed enterprises (*Révolution Africaine*, No. 56. 22 February 1964, 9) and by the end of 1964, almost a third of the 2,284 self-managed units

> had no accountants, and most of the existing ones were graduates of a six months accelerated training course. Half of the self-managed farms still had

no directors and had only untrained substitute managers with nothing but an eight week training course behind them.

(Ottaway and Ottaway, 1970: 65–66)

There were also managers who had no managerial qualifications except a rank in the army and some competence in spoken French. They took high positions in the government and became responsible for running public sector enterprises. Using ideological criteria such as membership of the FLN Party or being veterans of the War of Liberation, many managers were appointed to jobs for which they were not qualified. Although more and more managers became available and the level of managerial knowledge has increased in the last two decades, the situation has often become much worse, especially in enterprises where senior managers have built their own niches of sterile bureaucrats from their friends and relatives. The recruitment and selection of administrative staff and new managers have been very crucial for senior managers who wanted only to have those who were ready to follow in their footsteps and to cover up their corrupt practices.

As for the recruitment of manual and unskilled workers, a number of bureaux of employment (similar to UK-style Job Centres) were set up in the 1960s and 1970s throughout the country to help people get jobs. Their main role was to orient and allocate unskilled labour to suitable jobs. In a state-controlled system they were expected to implement government policies relating to employment promotion and allocation. It was expected that through a network of offices throughout the country information on employment and vocational skills could be made available to both employers and job seekers, and therefore it would be possible to establish an effective manpower planning system that controlled the supply and demand of labour. However, they were just bureaucratic centres of corruption and favouritism, providing very little help to job seekers at a time when unemployment was on the increase.

Training and development

The level of training varies from one organization to another even among the state-owned enterprises. There is a tendency to train some and not others and to use training as a reward for employees who may not need it. Selection for training is rarely made on the basis of a training needs analysis or after a performance appraisal. Managerial judgement on who should and should not be on training programmes is the norm and in some cases employees who are put on training programmes may see them just as opportunities to ask for promotion after the completion of training. Evaluation of training effectiveness is formal and carried out at the end of programmes by setting examinations and tests in order to get a certificate as a proof of completing the course.

Education and training are still heavily influenced by the French system. A large number of French teachers and technical assistants continued to work in Algeria following its independence and many Algerians still go to France to obtain further and higher education. As in France, there is a great emphasis on passing examinations. The *baccalauréat* is the examination taken at the end of three years in a secondary school, the *Lyceé*, before being admitted to university. University education has grown rapidly since the 1960s, increasing from one university in Algiers and two *grandes écoles* (*Institut National Agronomique* and *École Nationale Polytechnique*) in 1962 to 14 universities, 13 university colleges and 31 institutes and *écoles supérieures* in 1998. The number of students of higher education has been increasing at a rate of 7.5 per cent per annum. There were 433,000 students enrolled in institutions of higher education for the academic year 1999–2000 (CNES, November 1999).

Training is seen as a cost rather than an investment. Budgets for training are very limited and there is a lack of awareness of the importance of continuous training. It is rare for an employee to actively attempt to enhance his/her knowledge and skills after leaving formal education. There is a clear distinction between school education and vocational training. The emphasis on education rather than vocational training has led to an acute shortage of skilled people. For example, only 7.39 per cent of those enrolled in secondary school education had vocational training in 1998 (Ministry of National Education, 1999). The system of national education has not produced enough skilled people because of the predominance of general education and the marginalization of vocational education and training, and the lack of contact between institutions of education and employers. It is also significant to note that over 92 per cent of those who attended vocational training in the 1990s were young people who had been excluded from general education (CNES, 1999).

Rewards and remuneration

Since 1978 a fixed monthly minimum wage has been guaranteed for all employees by a state decree. The official number of working hours per week is forty-four. The state's national income policy determines the grades and levels of payment in all sectors and the government decides on pay rises in all state-owned enterprises. Most employees are paid on a monthly basis. As well as getting their basic pay, employees get a variety of allowances and bonuses. Under the SME system they used also to get a share of the profits. Today most Algerians also enjoy a relatively comfortable level of public and welfare services which have been provided free of charge since independence. The state welfare system provides for sickness and disability allowances, old age pensions, family allowances and unemployment benefits.

An examination of the levels of income in state-owned enterprises shows clearly that there is a big disparity between managers and workers. The average income of a manager is more than four times that of a worker. In addition to their salaries, managers receive bonuses for responsibility which are up to 70 per cent of their salaries. They also have housing and travelling allowances which are equal to unskilled workers' salaries. Despite the high material incentives given to managers and the privileges they get from their positions, some of them have been involved in corrupt activities. The right to manage meant to some managers a free hand in the funds of their enterprises. Being a *cadre*, however, carries with it many advantages. Cadres have the right to a variety of benefits including handsome budgets for travelling and meals, luxurious company cars (in many cases chauffeur-driven), free housing (flats or villas) and extensive holiday entitlements. On the other hand, they are expected to be committed and loyal to their organizations as well as to the government which appoints them. Therefore such managers are trained to have a strong capacity for dealing with the top-down bureaucracy in the organization and at the same time they give less importance to interpersonal communication and to the needs of employees, customers and suppliers.

The recent reforms have also affected the centralised payment systems giving the power to employers to decide on their own remuneration which is very often related to performance. Merit pay and profit-sharing schemes are less common than in the past because many enterprises have made little or no profits since the 1980s. There has been a move towards linking pay and merit to performance and achievement. In other words, the collectivist approach to rewards and payment has been replaced by a more unitarist one which emphasizes individual employees' contributions and rewards.

Industrial relations

Until the late 1980s the system of industrial relations had been guided by the texts of application of the Socialist Management of Enterprises (SME) system and the General Statute of the Worker (SGT). There were no clear guidelines on the content and format of employment contracts, grievance procedures or the settlement of industrial disputes. For example, Ordinance No. 75–33 of 29 April 1975, concerning employee relations and social welfare, proposed that a process of conciliation was the only way to settle all kinds of dispute (Article 3). In 1978 the practice of arbitration was added in cases where the conciliation process had failed (Article 90 of the General Statute of the Worker of 1978). However, because of the non-specification of collective agreements procedures in the texts of the SME and the SGT, the conciliation process for settling disputes was rarely used in the public sector (Boussoumah, 1982: 631). In the absence of legal dispositions only the rules of common law applied. In many cases the intervention of the Minister, the President of the Communal Assembly, the representative of the party FLN, or even of old and respected employees could overrule decisions and settle disputes between workers and management. The Industrial Relations Law of 1990 regulated the settlement of industrial disputes through third party conciliation and arbitration. It also provided managers with a more flexible framework for administering personnel policies.

Concerning the organization of labour, the struggle of Algerian workers to have their own trade unions started during the French colonial rule. However, with the declaration of the War of Liberation on 1 November 1954 and the creation of the FLN Party, it was necessary to organize the varied masses of the Algerian population to join the struggle for independence. On 24 February 1956 the General Union of the Algerian Workers (UGTA) was formed with a clear aim of contributing actively in the struggle for independence by organizing strikes, sabotage, and so forth. It was stated in the FLN declaration of 24 February 1956, following its leaders' meeting in the Soumam Valley, that the UGTA would take the wage earners from darkness to light, from ambiguity to clarity and from reluctance and hesitation to advancing the revolution. The UGTA played a significant role during the War of Liberation (1954–62) in mobilizing the workers to fight for independence.

In the post-independence period strikes were recognized as a fundamental right for all workers in private and public enterprises (Article 20 of the 1963 Constitution). However, the Code of the Civil Services (*Function Publique*) of 22 June 1966, recognized the workers' rights to unions membership but it did not speak of the right to strike. It was not mentioned until July 1968 when strikes in the public sector were made illegal in a report by the FLN Party on the role of trade unions in Algeria. The report stated that strikes in the public sector were economic crimes against the nation. Therefore both the Statute of the Magistrates of 13 May 1969 (Article 11) and the Penal Code of 1975 indicated, in vague statements, that strikes were acts of sabotage that had to be prohibited. Moreover, the Charter and Texts of Application of the Socialist Management System of 1971 stated that workers' participation and strikes could not occur at the same time because they were contradictory practices. The UGTA had simply been a transmission belt between the one party state and the workers, and was more of an administrative body than an independent organization of workers. It opposed mass strikes and public demonstrations and supported legislation to prohibit strikes in state-owned enterprises.

Following the liberalization of the economy after 1988 the UGTA lost its monopoly over the organization of the workforce and many new and active trade unions were created. The number of strikes and demonstrations increased significantly. According to figures from the Ministry of Labour, the number of strikes in 1989 was at a rate of 250 per month, four times higher than that of the previous year. Every state-owned enterprise had at least two official strikes in the first half of 1990 (*Algérie Actualité*, 12 July 1990: 23–24). In June 1990 a new law on trade union activity was passed. It gave employees the right to form autonomous trade unions. The law ended the monopoly of the one party affiliated trade union UGTA. It recognized the rights of the workers to form and to be represented by any trade unions of their choice. Trade unions can be formed as long as they follow specific guidelines set by the state. For example, they are not allowed to receive funding from abroad but they can form or join international as well as national confederations. Collective bargaining can be practised freely and is protected by law. It also prohibits any kind of forced or compulsory labour. Trade union activity increased at an unprecedented rate between 1990 and 1992. Nevertheless between 1992 and the present (2000) trade union activity has been limited because of the effects of high unemployment, pressures from the state on active trade unionists, lack of investment and low levels of trade union membership.

Conclusion

Until the economic and political reforms of 1988, Algeria's strategy for rapid socio-economic development was based on the ideology of socialism, advocating programmes for workers' participation in management, but the historical experiences of colonialism, the War of Liberation and the post-independence conflicts had led to the emergence of different interest groups. Socialism in Algeria was little more than a mythical slogan produced by a stagnant regime in which indecision led to personality-centred disputes between various leadership factions. It was conceivable, therefore, that workers and managers accepted the 'socialist system of management' only because of its legislative power. By submitting to the will of the predominant legislators, those in managerial positions simply conformed to the inherited and established system of bureaucratic and ideological hegemony. Problems of managing human resources in Algerian enterprises are the outcome of a number of factors including restrictive employment laws, inadequate infrastructure, high population growth, lack of housing, limited training facilities and limited investment. These are the results of contradictory policies that were designed to institutionalize the structure and management of enterprises under autocratic and bureaucratic post-colonial governments. Such contradictory policies, practices and attitudes have their obvious but nevertheless still very influential origins in the cultural, historical and socio-economic developments in the country.

It was the state's industrial development strategy which, while neglecting other sectors of the economy, exacerbated or created the problems of housing, transport and social services. Plans turned out to be difficult to achieve and were very often counter-productive because the planners had been anxious to plan but unable to manage. What was planned for could not be achieved because of contradictions between theory and practice, and between expectations and realities. Social and educational problems were directly related to this imbalance in economic development and to the conflict between an imposed ideology of socialism and the inherited values of Islam, nationalism and paternalism. Such problems affected people's performance and behaviour at work and increased the gaps between what they were formally supposed to do and what they actually did.

Recent reforms in industry and agriculture have been moving towards the ongoing development of a capitalist free market economy, especially as the private sector has become more and more competitive while the public sector has become frail and problematic. As far as human resource management is concerned, all developing countries are being affected by the growing influence of international human resource management as multinational companies spread further and wider throughout the world. At a time when the world is becoming more and more integrated and developing countries cannot advance without having to rely on the transfer of new technology and knowledge from the developed countries, developing countries cannot completely escape at least some domination by the latter. Algeria is no exception to those developing countries that have decided, despite their internal problems, to modernize their institutions and organizations, and to industrialize their economies as fast as possible. Therefore, regardless of what HRM policies are developed in the future, there are challenges which must be met. For instance, clear and simple employment regulations should be introduced to protect workers and their organizations, taking into consideration the impact of multinationals, the influence of the European Union, and the common needs and interests of the Maghreb countries. What is more important here is that no reasonably enlightened system of HRM can exist without genuine political democracy. There is also a need for competent managers who understand, develop and implement adequate employment policies that are neither copied fully from abroad nor imposed unreservedly by the state.

References

Algérie Actualité, Algiers: FLN, published weekly.

Algérie Économie, Algiers: Ministry of the Economy, published weekly.

Benachenhou, A. (1980) *Planification et développement en Algérie 1962–1980*, Algiers: Edition du CREA (Centre de Recherche en Économie Appliquée).

Benhouria, T. (1980) *L'économie de l'Algérie*, Paris: Maspero.

Benissad, M. E. (1979) *Économie et Développement de l'Algérie (1962–1978)*, Paris: Economica.

Benissad, M. E. (1982), 'Démographie et Problèmes Sociaux en Algérie', *The Maghreb Review*, 7, (3), 73–82.

Bennoune, M. (1988) *The Making of Contemporary Algeria*, Cambridge: Cambridge University Press.

Boussoumah, M. (1982) *L'entreprise socialiste en Algérie*, Paris: Economica.

Boutefnouchet, M. (1982) *Le socialisme dans l'entreprise*, 2nd edn, Algiers: ENAP/OPU.

Bouyacoub, A. (1987) *La gestion de l'entreprise industrielle publique en Algérie*, Algiers: Office des Publications Universitaires.

Branine, M. (1994) 'The Rise and Demise of Participative Management in Algeria', *Economic and Industrial Democracy: An International Journal*, 15 (4), 595–630.

Charte et Code de la Gestion Socialiste des Entreprises (SME Charter and Code) (1971) Algiers: FLN publication.

Chaulet, C. (1971) *La Mitidja autogérée*, Algiers: SNED.

Clegg, I. (1971) *Workers' Self-management in Algeria*, London: Penguin.

CNES (*Conseil National Économique et Social*) (1999) *La Relation Formation-Emploi*, Commission Relations de Travail, XIVème session plenière, November, Algiers: CNES.

Ecrement, M. (1986) *Indépendance politique et libération économique: Un quart de siècle du développement de l'Algérie, 1962–1985*, Algiers: ENAP.

El Moudjahid, Algiers: PLN, daily official newspaper, in French.

Entelis, J. P. (1982) 'Algeria: Technocratic Rule, Military Power', in I. W. Zartman *et al.* (eds), *Political Elites in Arab North Africa*, London and New York: Longman.

Etienne, B. (1977) *L' Algérie, culture et révolution*, Paris: Editions du Seuil.

Gestion Socialiste des Entreprises: Charte et textes d'application (SME Charter and Texts of Application) (1975) Algiers: FLN/EPA.

Ghezali, M. (1981) *La participation des travailleurs à la gestion socialiste des entreprises*, 2nd edn, Algiers: OPU.

Jackson, H. F. (1977) *The FLN in Algeria: Party Development in a Revolutionary Society*, London: Greenwood Press.

Lacks, M. (1970) *Autogestion ouvrière et pouvoir politique en Algérie, 1962–1965*, Paris: Edition du Seuil.

Lawless, R. I. (1984) 'Algeria: The Contradictions of Rapid Industrialisation', in R.I. Lawless and A. Findlay (eds), *North Africa: Contemporary Politics and Socio-Political Change*, New York: Croom Helm.

Lazreg, M. (1976) *The Emergence of Classes in Algeria: A Study of Colonialism and Socio-political Change*, Boulder, CO: Westview Press.

Minstry of National Education (1999) *Ministry of National Education Statistics*, Algiers: MNE.

National Office of Statistics (NOS) (1999) *Annual Statistics, 1999*, Algiers: NOS.

Nellis, J. R. (1977) 'Socialist Management in Algeria', *Journal of Modern African Studies*, 15 (4), 529–554.

Nellis, J. R. (1980) 'Maladministration: Cause or Result of Underdevelopment? The Algerian Example', *Canadian Journal of African Studies*, 13, 407–422.

Ottaway, D. and Ottaway, M. (1970) *Algeria: The Politics of a Socialist Revolution*, Berkeley, CA: University of California Press.

Pateman, C. (1970) *Participation and Democratic Theory*, Cambridge: Cambridge University Press.

Révolution Africaine, weekly FLN publication, in French.

Révolution et Travail, weekly UGTA publication, in Arabic and French.

Saadi, R. N. (1982) 'Syndicat et relations du travail dans les entreprises socialistes en Algérie', *Annuaire de l'Afrique du Nord*, 21, 123–132.

Saadi, R. N. (1985) *La gestion socialiste des entreprises en Algérie: essai d'évaluation*, Algiers: OPU (Office des Publications Universitaires).

World Bank (1999) *World Factbook, 1999, Algeria*, New York: World Bank.

World Bank (1997) *World Development Indicators*, February 1997, New York: World Bank.

Zeffane, R. (1981a), 'Context, Technology and Organization Structure Revisited: A Tri-national Study', in R. Mansfield and M. Poole (eds) *International Perspectives on Management and Organizations*, London: Gower, pp. 84–97.

Zeffane, R. (1981b) 'Participative Management in Algeria', in R. Mansfield and M. Poole (eds) *International Perspectives on Management and Organizations*, London: Gower, pp. 67–75.

Further Reading

Adamson, K. (1998) *Algeria: A Study of Competing Ideologies*, London: Cassell.

Bennoune, M. (1976) 'The Origin of the Algerian Proletariat', *Dialectical Anthropology*, 1 (3), 201–223.

Bourdieu, P. (1973) 'The Algerian Sub-proletariat', in I. W. Zartman (ed.) *Man, State and Society in the Contemporary Maghrib*, New York: Praeger.

Entelis, J. P. (1986) *Algeria: The Revolution Institutionalized*, Boulder, CO: Westview Press.

Entelis, J. P. (1999) 'SONATRACH: The political Economy of an Algerian State Institution', *The Middle East Journal*, 53 (1), 9–27.

Mansfield, R. and Zeffane, R. (1983) *Organisational Structures and National Contingencies*, London: Gower.

Marks, J. (1989) *Algeria: Towards Market Socialism*, London: Middle East Economic Digest.

Mortiner, R. (1977) 'Algeria and the Politics of International Economic Reform', *Orbis*, 21 (3), 671–700.

Nellis, J. R. (1980), 'The Algerian Socialism and its Criticisms', *Canadian Journal of Political Science*, 8 (1), 481–507.

Roberts, H. (1984) 'The Politics of Algerian Socialism', in R. Lawless and A. Findlay (eds) *North Africa: Contemporary Politics and Economic Development*, New York: Croom Helm.

11 Human resource management in Nigeria

Franca Ovadje and Augustine Ankomah

Introduction

With an estimated population of 122 million in 1998, Nigeria is the most populous country in Africa. It is a country rich in natural and human resources. Nigeria's population and potential natural and human resource base make it one of the most attractive countries for foreign investment in Africa. With e-commerce, for example, analysts have calculated that Nigeria has a potential 10 million Internet users and a possible 500,000 local web sites (Turner, 2000a). During the 1990s, notwithstanding political upheavals, the uncertain economic climate and erratic power and telecommunications, Nigeria attracted more foreign direct investment than any other African country. The return to democratic rule in May 1999 after a long period of military rule, and with it an active federal government policy of privatisation and liberalisation is likely to increase foreign investments. Under the new policy, more than 1,400 state-owned enterprises are to be privatised.

As foreign firms increase their involvement in Nigeria, they will need to build capabilities and utilise local competencies. Knowledge of human resource management (HRM) and more importantly perhaps, knowledge of the factors that impact on HRM in Nigeria will become increasingly critical to the way they do business in Nigeria and ultimately their success. The way to get things done cannot be divorced from local values, customs, and the overall external cultural environment. In most cases these social, human, and environmental factors are as important as the financial and marketing considerations upon which decisions to undertake multinational ventures depend (Dowling *et al.*, 1999).

HRM policies and practices are carried out within an economic, social, political and legal environment. Thus, there is a need for considerable historical and cultural insight into local conditions to understand the processes, philosophies and problems of national models of HRM (Hofstede, 1993). This chapter, therefore, discusses within a socio-economic context, a number of factors that influence human resource policies and practices in Nigeria and highlights the new trends in human resource management in Nigeria.

The Nigerian Economy

The Nigerian economy has undergone major structural changes since independence in 1960. In the 1950s and 1960s, agriculture was the single sector with the highest contribution to Gross Domestic Product (GDP). At the time of political independence from colonial rule in 1960, livestock, forestry, fishing and cash crops were the major sources of export earnings. The overwhelming importance of oil production in the last three decades has led to a steep decline in and apparent neglect of agricultural production. While in 1962–63 agriculture alone contributed 61.8 per cent to GDP, this figure decreased to 38 per cent in 1972–73. During the period 1990 to 1994, the average contribution of agriculture to GDP was 30.2 per cent.

One contradictory observation is that while the contribution of the agricultural sector to GDP has been declining, the number of persons employed in the sector has continued to increase. Agriculture continues to be the chief employer of labour in Nigeria. In 1984, 56.6 per cent of employed persons were agricultural workers. By 1993–94, the figure had increased to 60.4 per cent. The percentage of production workers, however, fell from 13.4 per cent in 1984 to 8.1 per cent in 1993–94.

Manufacturing was undeveloped in the early 1960s, contributing only 3 per cent to GDP in 1960–61. Its contribution peaked in 1982 at 11.2 per cent but has since been on the decline due, in part, to the Nigerian propensity during the oil boom to import almost everything from abroad. The de-industrialisation of Nigeria that started in the 1980s was conspicuous at the end of the decade and beyond. In 1994, the contribution of manufacturing to GDP was only 6.9 per cent and today it remains at about the same figure. Capacity utilisation has dropped from 31.8 per cent in 1997 to an estimated 30 per cent in the first quarter of 2000. As expected, there has also been a corresponding decline in the number employed in the manufacturing industry. For example, in the first half of 1999 the numbers employed in manufacturing declined by 17.4 per cent compared with the corresponding period in 1998.

The 1970s was the oil boom era. Since then the Nigerian economy has been dominated by the mining and quarrying sector (mainly oil). The sector rose from an insignificant contribution to GDP in the 1960s to 12.9 per cent in 1994. The contribution of the oil sector to export earnings has increased tremendously since the 1960s. The sector's contribution in the 1960s was trivial but rose to 85.6 per cent of export earnings in 1974, to 93.5 in 1984 and 97.2 per cent in 1992. The Nigerian economy has experienced stunted growth since 1960. While nominal GDP grew from 5.6 billion Naira in 1970 to 897.5 billion in 1994, real per capital GDP between 1980 and 1993 was below the 1977 value.

As elsewhere in Sub-Saharan Africa, Nigeria has a large public sector. The origin of government dominance of the economy can be traced to the immediate postcolonial era. As a result of the low domestic capital base at the time, the government set up many parastatals to carry out projects which would otherwise have been executed by the private sector, a practice intensified during the oil boom of the 1970s in post-war (the Nigerian civil war) reconstruction and rehabilitation. This was the beginning of government dominance of the economy. Given that government is a significant player in the Nigerian economy, its policies and actions have a huge impact on the private sector. For example, wage increases in the public sector are usually followed by agitation for wage and salary reviews in the private sector.

With an unbridled government expenditure pattern, corruption and abject mismanagement in the 1970s and early 1980s, Nigeria's economy soon ran out of steam. To address serious imbalances in the economy, the government embarked upon an IMF/World Bank Structural Adjustment Programme. This was a radical programme to address all that had gone wrong with the Nigerian economy since oil became the main source of government revenue. It was designed to 'restructure the economy, expand non-oil exports, reduce the import content of locally manufactured goods, achieve self-sufficiency in food, and give a larger role to the private sector' (Economic Intelligence Unit, 1990: 145). Although the success of Structural Adjustment programmes even in the IMF/World Bank showcases such as Ghana has been questioned, Nigeria's case was without doubt a failure and this can be attributed to a single factor: the military government's inability, or rather unwillingness, to control public spending.

The protracted depression of the Nigerian economy exerts negative pressures on employment and thus on HRM in Nigeria. One result of the economic decline is the massive reduction in the number of job opportunities. There is no reliable statistical evidence about the magnitude of employment and underemployment in Nigeria. According to the Human Development Report on Nigeria, published by the United Nations Development Programme (1996, 1997), the figure may be as high as 50 per cent.

The role of HRM in Nigerian organisations

The growth and development of personnel management in Nigeria, as elsewhere in Sub-Saharan Africa, have undergone significant changes. In the traditional Nigerian societies, the armies and the administration of the kings, the guilds, secret societies and other powerful social institutions had their own methods and procedures for selecting, inducting and training recruits to serve in various functions to ensure good governance of the society. The advent of colonialism, and with it, increased monetisation of the traditional economies saw the importation of foreign organisations based on bureaucratic principles. As local staff were needed to work as messengers, clerks, interpreters and labourers for the colonial administration and the emerging trading companies, the personnel function was one of the first areas to be addressed by British colonialists (Akinnusi, 1991). It must be noted that in Nigeria, as in other West African colonies, where the British adopted the so-called indirect rule system where traditional rulers were made part of the colonial administration, Nigerian chiefs, at least initially, recruited manual labour for the colonial administration. As a characteristic of colonial rule the indigenous workers lacked the academic qualifications and experience to influence decisions which were mostly taken by the expatriate staff (ibid.). Nigeria's achievement of political independence saw a rapid indigenisation – or Nigerianisation – a practice involving the replacement of foreign staff with local employees. This led to a massive drive to employ, train and develop indigenous manpower. The scope of personnel functions in Nigeria was expanded further when in 1974 the government embarked on indigenising the private sector.

One important characteristic of the Nigerian business context is the large number of micro and small enterprises. A large proportion of firms operate in the informal sector. Less than 200 companies are quoted on the Lagos Stock Exchange. Given the size of businesses in Nigeria, it is not surprising that HRM is still at the developmental stage. In the majority of Nigerian organisations, personnel management is still very much an administrative function concerned with recruitment, payroll, and record keeping. In the micro and small businesses, the owner-manager carries out personnel functions. Typically, there are no policies or procedures laid down. As the company grows, he or she may delegate this task to a personal assistant. Relatively few companies (usually medium to large companies and multinational companies) have a formal Personnel or HR department. In these companies, the Personnel Manager typically reports to the Head of Finance and Administration. In very few cases, he or she is a member of the top management. Many companies have not articulated their human resource policies and strategies.

While HRM is a strategic function in some sectors such as oil, banking and consulting, it is in the banking industry that it is well pronounced. The banking industry has experienced dramatic changes in the past fifteen years. In 1998, for example, the government revoked the licences of twenty-six of the forty-eight 'distressed' banks. It has been argued by Hawkins (2000) that the worst of the bank crisis is over and Nigeria's banking industry is now healthier than it has been in the past ten to fifteen years. In terms of personnel in the banking industry, there are two key related issues: downsizing and high turnover. The number of institutions and bank branches continues to shrink with the number of active branches down to 2,200 from nearly 2,500 in 1997 (Hawkins, 2000). In spite of, or perhaps because of, downsizing, turnover, especially among middle managers, is very high in the banking industry. Some banks have turnover rates as high as 80 per cent among this category of staff. Because of the need to attract and retain talented people, the human resource function has become critical to the survival of the banks. In many of the new banks, however, even where the Human Resource Manager reports directly to the Managing Director, he or she is usually not a member of the top management.

Education and manpower planning

Education is an important aspect of human capital development. Manpower availability is a function of the educational system. The period 1960 to 1985 can be described as the golden age of education in Nigeria. Not only did the government establish more educational institutions, thus increasing access to education, but the quality of education was high. Adult literacy increased from 25 per cent in

1970 to 49.5 per cent in 1993–94. Secondary school enrolment grew at 4 per cent per annum during the period 1984 to 1994. By 1997, there were 41,531 primary schools in Nigeria, 6,429 post-primary schools, 45 polytechnics, 58 colleges of education and 42 universities. Student enrolment at all educational levels has increased, for example, university enrolment grew from 40,552 in 1976–77 to 227,999 in 1993–94.

Until the late 1980s, the quality of education in Nigeria at all levels (primary, secondary and tertiary) was high. Recruitment of talented graduating students at university campuses by prominent local and international companies was a common occurrence. Management trainee programmes were designed to provide trainees with specific practical knowledge of the organisation to set them out on promising and rewarding careers in management.

However, chronic underfunding of education since the mid-1980s and with it the deteriorating conditions of physical facilities and the consequent brain drain (especially among academics) have resulted in falling educational standards in the country. Incessant strikes by both students and lecturers or teachers continue to disrupt academic programmes of educational institutions with damaging effect on quality.

The result is that while manpower is readily available (universities still graduate in large numbers), companies are finding it difficult to recruit people with the knowledge base and aptitudes who can contribute meaningfully to company growth and profitability. As noted by Turner (2000b), there is an increasing decline in the quality of Nigerian degrees. Some companies have seen the need to re-design management trainee and induction programmes to, as one Chief Executive put it, 'normalise' the young graduates. In many organisations, the duration of the induction programmes has been increased from three to twelve or eighteen months. At the end of the programme, only those who are successful are given employment in the organisation. With all trainees fully paid while on training, obviously, training costs have increased tremendously.

Recruitment and selection

As with other HRM functions, when discussing the recruitment and selection practices of Nigerian organisations, a distinction must be made between practices in small and medium-sized firms on the one hand, and the large organisations including the multinational companies (MNCs) on the other. The small firms rely on friends and relatives (of the owners and the employees) and unsolicited applications to fill vacancies. The growing unemployment situation has led to an increase in unsolicited job applications.

In the 1980s many companies recruited from the university campuses and polytechnics. However, with growing unemployment among graduates and the number of unsolicited applications, few companies now follow this practice. The use of consulting firms and media advertising is common among the large firms. The challenge is the time and money spent screening the large number of applications in response to an advertisement in the media.

Companies are reacting to the falling educational standards by fine-tuning, sometimes overhauling their recruitment and selection procedures. Many organisations now conduct a variety of aptitude and psychometric tests during the selection process. Since even a first class degree does not mean the graduate has a sound education, a lot of time and resources are spent on selection.

The impact of labour laws on HRM policies and practices in Nigeria

One institution that has an impact on HRM policies and practices in Nigeria is the trade union. According to the Trade Unions (Amendment) Act of 1978, an employer with more than fifty members of staff and whose employees have decided to unionise must recognise that union as the bargaining agent of the employees.

Trade union activity began in Nigeria in 1912, the first union being the Nigerian Civil Service Union. Between 1938 and 1976 the number of trade unions mushroomed to more than 900. However, 54 per cent of the trade unions had a membership of less than 200 each. These unions were small, weak and in many cases, ineffective (Yesufu, 1984). There was no central labour organisation until 1978 when government established the Nigerian Labour Congress (NLC). Trade unions, which hitherto were house unions, were restructured along industrial lines and were affiliated to the NLC. The establishment of a central labour organisation strengthened the bargaining power of the trade unions and created new challenges for employers.

Although since independence in 1960, Nigeria has ratified thirty International Labour Organisation (ILO) conventions and, admittedly, some of these have been incorporated into local labour laws, the legal framework of HRM in Nigeria is provided almost exclusively by Nigerian Labour Laws. In this context, three sets of labour laws are identified and discussed in the following section. These are, first, laws relating to terms and conditions of employment; second, laws relating to employment welfare; and finally, laws dealing with trade union and dispute resolution.

Laws relating to terms and conditions of employment include the Labour Act, National Minimum Wage Act, Wages Board and the Industrial Council Act, and the National Salaries and Wages Commission Decree. The Labour Act, which came into effect in August 1971 is particularly interesting because it incorporated the principles of some ILO conventions into Nigerian law and practice, especially those regarding underground work for women; minimum age and protection of wages. Although the National Minimum Wage Act prescribed a minimum wage, net of all deductions for workers, wages and salaries are a matter for negotiation between the parties.

It is important to note that the Labour Act does not cover persons in administrative, executive, technical and professional positions, all of whom have to negotiate individually with their employers or, where they belong to a union, the union negotiates terms with the employers on their behalf. Such negotiated terms are binding on both parties. It is also worth mentioning that some of the statutes are derived from English statutes or based on English common law and, as a result, the English common law plays an important part in regulating contracts of employment particularly in areas where the Nigerian law is silent.

Laws relating to employee welfare are: the Factories Act, Workmen's Compensation Act, Employees' Housing Schemes, National Social Insurance Trust Fund, National Housing Fund Decree and the Industrial Training Fund Decree (No. 47). Whereas the Labour Act is limited in its application, the Workmen's Compensation Act applies to all employees at all levels in the public and private sectors. The Employees Housing Scheme (Special Provisions) Act makes it mandatory for any employer with at least five hundred employees to maintain a housing scheme for its employees. This is not unusual in Sub-Saharan Africa where, since independence, government and employer housing schemes have been, albeit with little success, the main route to providing adequate housing for employees.

Given that salaries are very poor, a pay rise occurs only after hard bargaining and sometimes violent strikes. For most workers in Nigeria, as elsewhere in Sub-Saharan Africa, therefore, 'fringe benefits', incentives and other compensatory packages associated with work are perhaps even more important than salaries. 'Fringe benefits' including free cars or generous car loans, transport allowance or free fuel, free or heavily subsidised accommodation, furnishing allowance, travel expenses and other emoluments can push overall employer expenditure on personnel cost to astonishing levels when one considers the permeating culture of corruption, waste and bureaucratic officialdom. The following statement by a senior official, however absurd it may seem, illustrates, in part, why the 2000 budget allocated more than 50 per cent of the state's available income to payroll:

> The government will pay more than $200 a night for me to stay at the Hilton because my official residence is not ready. But if I want to make my own arrangements, which would be much cheaper, the allowance is only N6,000 ($60). So, obviously, I stay at the hotel and it costs Nigeria an absolute fortune.
> (Goldman, 2000: 10)

The provision of pensions is another area which impacts on HRM. The National Social Insurance Trust Fund Decree No. 73 of 1993 established a Trust Fund into which employers and employees are to make contributions. The Fund pays retirement grants, invalidity benefits, etc. to contributors. The existence of a private pension scheme does not in itself exempt an employer from making the stipulated contributions to the Fund. In practice, many employees have not received the benefits in spite of the contributions they have made. Thus, employers have private pension schemes in respect of their workers in addition to contributions to the Trust Fund.

The HRM function of training and development is also regulated to some extent by law. The Industrial Training Fund (Amendment) Decree No. 47 of 1990 set up the Industrial Training Fund and makes it mandatory for employers (with twenty-five or more employees), and the Federal Government to make contributions to the Fund. The Fund was established to promote the acquisition of skills in industry and commerce with a view to developing indigenous manpower to meet the needs of the Nigerian economy. Employers are to contribute 1 per cent of their annual payroll. Employers who contribute to the Fund are reimbursed up to 60 per cent of the expenses on training of their indigenous staff provided such training is considered adequate. They are also expected to accept students for industrial attachment purposes.

The final set of laws that impact on HRM are those which deal with trade unions and dispute resolution. Several laws govern the practice of industrial relations in Nigeria. They include the following: Trade Unions Act, Trade Unions (International Affiliation) Decree No. 29, Trade Unions (Amendment Decree, 1996, No. 4) and Trade Unions (Amendment, No.2) Decree No.26 of 1996. Others are Trade Disputes Act, Trade Disputes (Essential Services) Act, Trade Disputes (Amendment) Decree and National Industrial Court Rules.

The Trade Unions Act governs the formation, registration and organisation of Trade Unions in Nigeria and recognises the Nigerian Labour Congress (consisting of twenty-nine affiliated unions) as the only central labour organisation for workers trade unions. It also provides that no staff recognised as a projection of management within the management structure shall be a member of, or hold office in a trade union if it will lead to a conflict of loyalty to either the union or the management. The Trade Unions (Amendment) Decree of 1978 legalised management (senior staff) associations as trade unions. Senior staff unions thrive in organisations that are not responsive to the needs of managers. The motivation to join the union was to act as a pressure group and negotiate salary and fringe benefits with top management. In quite a few organisations, Personnel Managers, who are supposed to represent management in collective bargaining, are members of senior staff unions, and, as a result often find themselves representing management while at the same time negotiating their own salaries and conditions of service.

In 1957, the Nigerian Employers' Consultative Association (NECA) was established. It became the central organisation of employers in the organised private sector. The Ministry of Labour and Welfare influenced its formation in response to government's need for a forum to consult the private sector on social and labour policy matters. Thus, government influenced the establishment of both the central labour organisation and the formation of the national association of employers.

Before the NECA was established, several employers' associations were already in existence but were very weak and labour unions had not been structured along industry lines. Since most trade unions were house unions, bargaining was done between the house union and the employer. Employers' organisations were formed primarily to harmonise terms and conditions of employment of their employees at the industry level. Collective bargaining for the determination of wages and working conditions was moved to the industry level when unions were restructured along industry lines, i.e. bargaining was to take place between the industry trade union and the industry employers' association. Although agreements reached are binding on all employers in that industry, a few items are still negotiated at the organisational level (i.e. between the house union and the employing organisation). However, as pointed out earlier, the government sets the minimum wage which in turn serves as the basis for negotiation in most cases.

The NECA has played an important role in the development of HRM in Nigeria. It provides information, education, training and human resource development services to its members. In the area of industrial relations, the NECA works closely with the employers' associations and member companies in the development of remuneration policies, conflict resolution procedures, collective bargaining, etc. Soon after the trade unions were restructured along industry lines, the NECA took steps to restructure its industrial groups to form parallel organisations to the new industrial trade unions.

Although major decisions that have implications for wages and conditions of employment are made in consultation with the unions at the industry level, powerful unions have forced the management of some companies to go beyond the collective agreement. This is not surprising given the great social inequalities and the high incidence of poverty in the country. For example, some trade unions are making it increasingly difficult for employers to retrench workers. Many companies have had to pay severance benefits much higher than that prescribed in the collective agreement to encourage some employees to leave in order to maintain harmonious relations with the unions. As the economic crunch becomes more severe and companies resort to retrenchment, employees are increasingly relying more and more on unions to protect them from dismissal or at least cushion the effect of such actions on their finances. In one state-owned bank, the union was so powerful that they even influenced the employment of management staff in the bank.

It must be noted that there are wide variations in the power of unions in old, chronically over-staffed and poor performing companies, on the one hand, and those in new or recently restructured organisations on the other. Some employers, especially in the latter group, have made unions irrelevant in their organisations. Characterised by a lean, dedicated and highly motivated workforce, these organisations offer very attractive compensation and benefits packages to their employees. In addition, they have tried to develop and maintain good lines of communication with them. Consequently, employees in many of these organisations have voluntarily renounced union membership and many, in general, have since enjoyed a cordial industrial climate and retained flexibility.

There are about 2 million workers in the public sector, including state and local government employees (Goldman, 2000). Given, therefore, that the government is the largest employer of labour, the government's role as legislator, employer and arbitrator must be mentioned. In the 1990s, state control replaced the principles of voluntarism in industrial relations. In August 1994, for example, the federal military government sacked the executives of the Nigeria Labour Congress as well as members of two vibrant and active unions in the oil industry, the Petroleum and Natural Gas Senior Staff Association of Nigeria and the National Union of Petroleum and Gas Workers, replacing them with government candidates.

Emerging changes in the socio-political environment have enabled unions to regain their powers. Recent announcements by government of its decision to review the wages and conditions of government employees have had a significant effect on private sector collective bargaining.

Culture and human resource management in Nigeria

Perhaps the most important factor that influences HRM in Nigeria is culture. Hofstede (1993) emphasised the need for historical and cultural insights into local conditions to understand the processes and philosophies of HRM in different countries. HRM cannot be divorced from the values, beliefs and norms of a people. As Nigeria becomes increasingly open to foreign investment in an era of economic globalisation, the resurgence of interest in Nigerian cultural values as they affect business has become even more critical.

Many definitions of culture can be found in the literature. Trompenaars (1993) defines culture as 'a shared system of meanings'. Culture influences what we pay attention to, how we act, and what we value. Culture therefore is the commonly held values, beliefs and attitudes of a people (Hofstede, 1980; Trompenaars, 1993).

As Sparrow and Hiltrop (1994) pointed out, HRM practices that are taken for granted in one culture might be considered illogical and unfair in another culture. This is supported by Iguisi (1994) whose study showed, not altogether unexpectedly, that there are profound differences in cultural values between Nigeria and the Netherlands.

In Nigeria, power and authority at the organisational level are considerably shaped by cultural values. This may be particularly visible in relation to the cultural respect for the elderly and the role of women. Respect for age is a predominant cultural value in Nigeria. Through early socialisation, people are taught to respect older people. In the Yoruba culture, for example, an elder sister or brother is not addressed by name; polite and culturally appropriate titles are used. Old age is often equated with wisdom with older people perceived as more experienced, and hence wiser. When they make decisions, a younger person is expected to oblige without any challenge. Generally, Nigerians would rather have an older person as a boss. This creates tension and decision-making problems for leadership in organisations if better qualified and highly motivated but younger people are promoted to higher levels of responsibility (Alo, 1999). It must be noted, however, that respect for age is sometimes translated into respect for positions such that people in higher levels of the hierarchy are regarded as elders.

While Nigerians are not alone in according respect for the elderly, Nigerians are perhaps unique in how greetings are exchanged between the young and the old even in office environments. Wherever they meet, it is the responsibility of the younger to initiate the 'greeting formalities'. Merely saying 'good morning' and rushing to your desk may be taken as evidence of uncaring attitude. One has to ask not only how well the person being greeted is doing, but enquiries must be made of their spouse(s), children and indeed other family members, each of whom may be referred to by name. The greeting formalities may take minutes and when repeated for several employees, as it should, the cost in time may be substantial. A young manager who fails to follow this ritual at work risks being labelled as proud, arrogant and self-conceited, accusations likely to undermine teamwork.

As in most African societies, Nigeria is essentially a male-dominated, masculine society. The attitude to women, which is rooted in the Nigerian culture, also influences the boss–subordinate relationship. The culture ascribes an inferior status to women. Although there is an official policy on equal opportunities in securing employment and in career progression, for most women the reality is very different in the workplace. There is a pervasive lack of acceptability by society of women occupying top management positions (Williams *et al.*, 1993). According to Alo (1999), many male employees have found it difficult to accept women as bosses. Women have had to work twice as hard to prove their competence. Decisions made by female bosses are resisted and fought against by male subordinates regardless of the merits of such action plans.

One of the areas where culture impinges on human resource management is in the area of recruitment and selection. Recruitment is often the most direct channel for injecting new ideas into an introspective and self-perpetuating organisational culture (Williams *et al.*, 1993). There is a tendency to recruit people who belong to one's group – family, village, ethnic group, etc. Sensitive positions are filled with these people and they become the eyes and ears of their patron. While nepotism and ethnicity may be inefficient and even unfair, they also have advantages. The cronies sometimes have a very strong commitment to their sponsor and are often unreservedly loyal. They see the success of the sponsor as their personal success, and indeed as the success of their group. Thus, they put in effort beyond that required by the formal system. On the negative side, managers find it difficult to maintain principles of objectivity and meritocracy in decisions regarding discipline, promotion and performance management. The problem becomes even more acute in matters relating to discipline. It is the norm in Nigeria, as in other Sub-Saharan African countries, for a transgressor awaiting disciplinary action to send a powerful delegation consisting of cultural and local potentates to the home of the manager to plead on behalf of the 'victim'. As part of the plea the manager will be reminded of the economic and social damage the impending disciplinary action will do to the person's family (both immediate and extended), kinsmen, village or even entire ethnic group.

In the Nigerian culture, there is a strong emphasis on the family. Family members support one another. The definition of brother or sister is extensive and elastic. A brother may mean a cousin, a distant relative, someone from one's village or one's ethnic group. Groups are closely knit in this culture. Within a group, such as members of a family or clan as opposed to non-family members, there is a high level of trust. Between groups, the level of trust is lower. In the Nigerian society, you are your brother's keeper.

According to Olugbile (1997), nepotism has been the bane of the workplace in many parts of the world. Among Nigerians it has taken on some quite interesting aspects. In the civil service it is often said that a unit or department very quickly assumes the family and ethnic character of the incumbent head. In some places, the 'ethnic tongue' of the boss (i.e. his local language) becomes the *de facto lingua franca* in the office. The favoured individual is selected over his peers (and sometimes even over his superiors). He is advanced preferentially and is moved to strategically preferred positions in the organisation. Williams *et al.* (1993) have warned that in a system where trust is shown and demanded along ethnic lines, the manager ignores this at their peril.

Culture and compensation systems

Nigerian values and norms have also had a considerable impact on pay and benefits policies in Nigeria. In traditional society, the community (extended family or clan) was closely knit. Cooperation was an important value as illustrated by the Yoruba axiom 'Agbajo owo ni a fin so aiya': unity is strength.

Work in traditional society was organised along family lines; skills were passed from father to son and from mother to daughter. No one hired out labour services, so there was no paid employment. The society had an informal welfare system (Olugbile, 1997), which made it possible for people to contribute according to their abilities but be guaranteed the satisfaction of basic needs. The aged were also guaranteed a means of livelihood.

Many of these traditional values persist in the modern work setting. The organisation is a social context rather than an instrument for gain. The organisation can be likened to a family, which nurtures its members. According to Oloko (1977), 'The beliefs and values of members of these social systems influence a great deal the beliefs and values about reward for effort held by social actors in employing organisations.'

Since 1984, Nigerians have witnessed a rapid deterioration in their welfare. The harsh economic environment as well as the lack of a national welfare system has placed a huge burden on companies. The more proactive human resource managers have introduced policies which take into account the need to show solidarity with employees in good and bad times. For example, burial allowance is paid to employees who have lost a close member of their family to enable these employees give their loved ones a fitting burial. They are also given compassionate leave to enable them organise the elaborate ceremonies involved in the burial, especially of older people.

It must be noted that it is not only in times of crises that employers are expected to show 'generosity' towards their employees. Organisations do recognise that weddings involve huge expenses and elaborate ceremonies. Some amount of money is given to employees who are getting married as a contribution towards the wedding expenses. As Richardson (2000: 208) has noted, 'Enabling the moneyed Nigerian to fulfil his family obligations is, in itself, a testimony of his success and power and therefore legitimises his candidature to office.' Consequently, workers may look up to the organisation for soft loans to build a house, buy a car or even pay rent for their homes (it is common to pay up to two years rent in advance for a home in Nigeria).

Some companies own and operate clinics where employees and their families are given free medical attention, although usually there is a limit to the number of family members who can benefit from this service. Other companies have designated clinics where employees and their families may receive medical attention. Even where there is a cap on the amount of money each cadre of staff can spend on medical expenses annually, many companies assist employees in emergency situations.

Apart from their financial implications, implementing these policies also involves a lot of time commitment from management. Employees expect their managers to find time to attend social functions such as birthdays, weddings, burial ceremonies, etc. The presence of top management at these functions is highly appreciated. It reinforces the family spirit and builds commitment.

The rationale for these policies and practices is that showing you care is very important for employee commitment. A Nigerian is more likely to work hard in an organisation he or she believes cares; an organisation he or she identifies with; an organisation that has a family spirit. The employee feels alienated in a formal, rule-driven, and impersonal work environment.

Human resource managers in Nigeria have learnt to be flexible. For example, wages and salaries are reviewed long before the date collectively agreed upon because of increased transport costs or other shocks in the system.

Culture and performance management

Another human resource practice which has been strongly influenced by the Nigerian culture is performance management. It is difficult for Nigerian managers to accept the Anglo-Saxon concept of performance management with its emphasis on setting specific goals and objectives or giving face-to-face feedback, and newer practices such as peer and subordinate evaluations. These practices are at variance with some traditional values.

In the Yoruba culture, for example, one cannot be critical of a person in his or her presence. Consequently, giving negative or critical feedback – in fact, any face-to-face appraisal – is difficult for many managers. It may be considered an attempt to ruin someone else's career. 'You must be your brother's keeper' is an ubiquitous dictum. Thus, there is very little discrimination between good and poor performance. Because of the lack of objectivity, appraisal information is not reliable. This makes pay-for-performance systems very difficult to implement.

Trends in the development of HRM in Nigeria

The HRM function is evolving. First, the scope of activities the human resource department is directly in charge of is reducing. More and more companies are contracting out services such as staff canteens, staff schools, security services, clinics, staff quarters, etc. It is expected that this will relieve human resource professionals of administrative functions and enable them define their mission, develop clear human resource strategies and become more knowledgeable of their businesses so they can contribute meaningfully to the organisation's strategy.

Although the majority of women work in the informal sectors of the economy, more women are joining the organised private sector. This is partly because of the increase in awareness of the need to educate girls. The male to female ratio of university students fell from 50:1 in 1950 to 4:1 in the mid-1980s. The participation of women is no longer restricted to certain professions (such as nursing or teaching) or clerical jobs. In spite of the cultural challenges, more women are now in executive positions. If this trend continues, female bosses will no longer be a novelty. It should be easier for their male counterparts to accept their authority.

Through education and the other means of communication, Nigerians have been exposed to Western culture. In no other industry has the impact of Western culture been felt as much as in the Information Technology (IT) industry. The organisational culture of the IT companies is different from the culture of most Nigerian organisations. They are owned and managed by young dynamic entrepreneurs. Their organisational structures are flat. There is a greater respect for knowledge rather than age or position. In most of these companies, the environment is informal and everyone is addressed by their first name. Competition for talent is intense. Because of the scarcity of talent in the industry and the consequent high labour turnover, entrepreneurs rely on human resource professionals (mainly consultants) to design very attractive compensation and participatory systems to attract and retain employees.

Another noticeable trend is the search for information and knowledge on how human resources can add more value to the firm. Attendance by human resource professionals at seminars at the Lagos Business School, for example, has increased during the last five years. Consultancy activities in the area of HRM have also increased. Consulting firms (many of which are foreign) and business schools have contributed towards the spread of 'best practices'.

Conclusion

Some key issues emerge from this review of human resource management in Nigeria. First, the socio-cultural norms have some significant impact on specific HRM practices. There is often a greater degree of involvement by management in employees' personal lives. A broader perspective is demanded when considering issues which in a Euro-American context are often simplistic, transparent, and systematic. As noted by Dowling *et al.*, (1999), activities such as recruiting, promoting, rewarding and dismissal are often determined by the culture-specific practices. Modern practices such as peer and/or subordinate appraisals do not sit comfortably within the Nigerian culture where critical face-to-face comments may be misconstrued as personal attack.

Second, there are wider external factors to contend with: the state of the economy, political and other pressures may result in otherwise unpleasant but generally acceptable practices of doing business. As in many societies, in Nigeria, there are basic values and assumptions which influence how people react to various work situations, how they behave in the workplace, and more importantly, outside the workplace.

Third, the federal and state governments together act as the main employers of waged labour and hence are directly involved in the running of trade unions in the country, which sometimes include the firing of trade union leaders. Finally, the cost of labour to employers is often high, resulting from the mandatory provision of heavily subsidised housing, transport and other benefits.

Cultural stereotyping of managers abounds all the world over, but generally is not detrimental to business. For example, as noted by Kanter and Corn (1996), the Swiss are described as 'very orderly'; the Swedes as 'very serious'; the British as 'less emotional, and more deliberate'; compared with the American reputation for fast, and result-oriented decisions. While generally these national characteristics may be obvious in the boardroom, they are less likely to lead to business failures by undermining the fundamentals of human resource management. In contrast, many of the cultural values in Nigeria, as elsewhere in Africa, such as the need to be the 'big brother' for the clan and kinsmen, are potentially prone to abuse and often result in excessive cronyism, nepotism and corruption, vices which new and restructured companies in Nigeria are now doing well to avoid.

References

Akinnusi, D. M. (1991) 'Personnel management in Africa: A Comparative analysis of Ghana, Kenya and Nigeria', in C. Brewster and S. Tyson (eds) *International Comparisons in Human Resource Management*, London: Pitman Publishing.

Alo, O. (1999) *Human Resource Management in Nigeria*, Lagos: Business and Institutional Support Associates.

Brewster, C. and Tyson, S. (1991) *International Comparisons in Human Resource Management*, London: Pitman.

Dowling, P. J., Welch, D. E. and Schuler, R. S. (1999) *International Human Resource Management: Managing People in a Multinational Context*, Cincinnati, OH: South-Western College Publishing.

Economic Intelligence Unit (1990) *West Africa, Cameroon, Cote d'Ivoire, Gabon, Ghana, Nigeria, Senegal: Economic Structure and Analysis*: London: The Economic Intelligence Unit.

FDC Quarterly Report on the Economy, March 1999.

Federal Office of Statistics (1996) *Socio-Economic Profile of Nigeria*, Lagos: Federal Office of Statistics.

Federal Republic of Nigeria (1995) *Annual Abstract of Statistics*.

Goldman, A. (2000) 'Public Sector in Need of a Drastic Overhaul', in *Financial Times Survey: Nigeria*, London: Financial Times.

Hawkins, T. (2000) 'Dead Wood Goes in Shake-out', in *Financial Times Survey: Nigeria*, London: Financial Times.

Hofstede, G. (1980) *Culture's Consequences: International Differences in Work-related Values*, Beverley Hills: Sage.

Hofstede, G. (1993) 'Cultural Constraints in Management Theories', *Academy of Management Executive*, 7 (1), 81–93.

Iguisi, O. (1994) 'Appropriate Management in an African Culture', *Management in Nigeria*, Jan–Mar, 16–24.

Kanter, R. M. and Corn, R. I. (1996) 'Do Cultural Differences make a Business Difference?', in S. M. Puffer, (ed.) *Management Across Cultures: Insights from Fiction and Practice*, Oxford: Blackwell Publishers.

Ojo, F. Aderinto, A. and Fashoyin T. (1986) *Manpower Development and Utilization in Nigeria*, Lagos: Lagos University Press.

Oloko. O. (1977) 'Incentives and Reward for Efforts', *Management in Nigeria*, 13 (5) 59–70.

Olugbile, F. (1997) *Nigeria at Work*, Lagos: Malthouse Press.

Otobo, D. and Omole, O. (1987) *Readings in Industrial Relations in Nigeria*, Lagos: Malthouse Press.

Richardson, P. (2000) 'Management in Nigeria', in M. Warner, (ed.) *Regional Encyclopaedia of Business and Management: Management in the Emerging Countries* London: Thomson Learning, pp. 206–213.

Sparrow, P. and Hiltrop, J. (1994) *European Human Resource Management in Transition*, London: Prentice-Hall.

Trompenaars, F. (1993) *Riding the Waves of Culture*, London: The Economist Books.

Turner, M. (2000a) 'Dreams of Imminent Cyber Take-off in West Africa', in *Financial Times Survey: Nigeria*, London: Financial Times.

Turner, M. (2000b) 'Education Suffers Decay and Neglect', in *Financial Times Survey: Nigeria*, London: Financial Times.

Ubeku, A. (1975) *Personnel Management in Nigeria*, Benin-City: Ethiope Publishers.

United Nations Development Programme (1997) *Nigerian Human Development Report 1996*, Lagos: UNDP.

Weber, H. (ed.) (1985) *Trade Union and Industrial Relations Management in Nigeria: A Manual*, Lagos: Friedrich-Ebert-Foundation.

Williams, A., Dobson, P. and Walters, M. (1993) *Changing Culture: New Organizational Approaches*, London: Institute of Personnel Management.

Yahaya, A. D. and Akinyele, C. I. (eds) (1992) *New Trends in Personnel Management*, Ibadan: Spectrum Books.

Yesufu, T. M. (1984) *The Dynamics of Industrial Relations of the Nigerian Experiences*, Ibadan: University Press.

12 Human resource management in Ghana

Yaw A. Debrah

Introduction

This chapter begins with some basic statistics[1] about Ghana, a West African country with a population of 18.5 million (annual growth rate, 3.1 per cent; average life expectancy, 59 years; national literacy level, 75 per cent). It occupies a total area of 238,537 sq. km and is well endowed with natural resources such as gold, diamonds, bauxite, manganese, iron ore, clay and salt deposits. It is also blessed with a good supply of arable land, suitable for both crop and livestock production, and forestry.

Agriculture is the main economic activity in Ghana, with cocoa the leading export crop. Cocoa is grown in six of the country's ten regions and as an economic activity it occupies 8 million people or close to half the population, mainly as small-scale farmers. Cocoa is the country's second biggest export earner after gold and contributes 13–14 per cent of GDP, 11 per cent of tax and 30–35 per cent of foreign exchange earnings (Wallis, 1999).

In 1999, Ghana had a total labour force of 3.7 million. This is a considerable decline from the 4.2 million in 1982 and slightly higher than the 1970 figure of 3.3 million (Huq, 1989). There is growing concern about unemployment because of the ongoing retrenchment of workers, economic structural changes, and, in particular, the decline in the manufacturing sector. In the late 1970s, manufacturing accounted for about 14 per cent of GDP, in 1999 it was less than 10 per cent. Wage employment exists in almost all industries but, in recent years, the bulk has been in mining and construction. This is due to the former being able to attract foreign investment and the latter benefiting from overseas loans to rehabilitate the country's infrastructure. Ghana is a multi-ethnic country with about six main local languages. English, however, is the official language.

In the economic realm, Ghana has embarked on an ambitious economic and social programme designed to qualify it as a middle income country by 2020. According to the government's development blueprint, known as Vision 2020, it is expected that an annual growth rate of 12 per cent can be achieved by the end of the plan period. But, as Holman (1999a: 3) comments:

> After 13 years of rumbling down the runway of World Bank and IMF aid-backed reforms, Ghana's economy has yet to reach take off. Not only is

take-off – the point at which foreign and domestic investment replace aid flows, and propel the economy into self-sustaining, high rates of growth – still some way off, passengers should brace themselves for what may be a bumpy runway ride in the years ahead.

Although Ghana has made much economic progress since the introduction of the Structural Adjustment Programme (SAP) in the 1980s, it appears those achievements are under threat. For instance, it is estimated that, for the country to achieve the Vision 2020 objectives, it must boost GDP from $7 billion to $43 billion. To achieve this, the country requires economic growth of at least 8 per cent a year (Knipe, 2000: 3). This is a Herculean task in view of the fact that the average 4.3 per cent annual economic growth, achieved in the last decade, was mainly made possible by the support of international donor countries. These donors provided economic aid which, at its peak, reached $800 million a year. But the aid has currently declined significantly and it is not clear whether the original donors would be prepared to pour more money into Ghana's SAP. It is also doubtful whether past levels of assistance are likely to be sustained (Holman, 1999b: 1). Quite apart from this, fluctuations in the prices of cocoa and minerals also seriously threaten growth in the economy and, hence, employment growth. As Knipe points out:

> In spite of the reforms [SAP] and progress towards a market driven private-sector led economy, Ghana is today suffering an economic downturn that could threaten all the gains of the past 14 years. Put starkly, whilst production of basic exports such as cocoa, gold and timber has risen, prices in the second half of last year (1999) collapsed. And the cost of its imported oil has doubled.
>
> (ibid.)

Ghana is now at a critical stage in its attempts to modernize the economy and provide employment to its people but, evidently, there are problems ahead (see Table 12.1). The economic conditions in Ghana have had serious repercussions on employment growth in organizations and, of course, the state of human resource management (HRM).

Table 12.1 Ghana: economic summary

Data	Figure
Total GDP ($bn)	8.12
Real GDP Growth (annual % change)	5.4
GDP per head ($)	407
Inflation (annual % change in CPI)	14.8
Money supply, M2 (annual % change)	21.3
Foreign exchange reserves ($m)	425
Government budget balance (% of GDP)	−8.0
Total foreign debt (% of GDP)	79.8
Current account balance	−411

Source: Financial Times Survey – Ghana, 4 November 1999

Following a flexible application of the theoretical framework set out in the introductory chapter, this chapter sketches the HRM role in both the public and private sectors in Ghana. It begins with a discussion of the origins of HRM in Ghana and moves on to explore the economic and political environment for HRM in that country. This is followed by a description and discussion of the role of national and socio-cultural factors in HRM in Ghana. The next section discusses the HRM functions in Ghanaian organizations and is followed by a section which discusses the industrial relations scene and employers' organizations in Ghana. The penultimate section is a discussion of current issues in HRM in Ghana and the concluding section provides a brief summary of the issues covered.

The historical impact on HRM in Ghana

The Western system of human resource management in Ghanaian organizations has evolved from the systems implemented by the British colonial administration. As such, HRM in Ghana has been heavily influenced by historico-political factors. The British colonial administration, European missionary institutions and commercial enterprises introduced Western labour management practices into Ghana but traditional personnel management existed in some form during both the pre-colonial and colonial periods. As Kiggundu (1991) indicates, pre-colonial Africa had administrative systems; typically small in size and homogeneous in terms of membership. Akinnusi (1991) adds that such administrative systems had personnel functions but were not as formalized and systematized as they currently are. It is asserted that:

> The armies and the administrations of kings, the guilds system and other social institutions had their own mode of selecting recruits, inducting them, maintaining discipline and rewarding employees but the advent of colonialism saw the importing of modern organizations based on bureaucratic principles.
>
> (Akinnusi, 1991: 161–162)

In the British West African colonies, because the British colonial administration relied on indirect rule, whereby British rule was exercised through traditional rulers and customary practices, the personnel function achieved prominence very early in the colonial era (Bourrett, 1963; Kimble, 1965). In line with the indirect rule policy, European traders and colonialists needed indigenous intermediaries in their recruitment and personnel activities. Hence, it was necessary to recruit indigenous labour officers to deal with the complaints and demands of African workers. In Ghana (formerly the British Colony of the Gold Coast) an African was appointed to the post of Assistant Chief Labour Officer in the 1930s after the colonial government set up the Gold Coast Labour Department (Obeng-Fosu, 1991: 2–3).

In Ghana, the process of indigenizing of the Ghanaian economy and organizations, known as Africanization, which followed independence, propelled the HR function to the forefront in the early 1960s. The new government's objective was to replace the expatriate staff with Ghanaians in both the private and public sectors.

Hence, local personnel managers were appointed to fill the posts previously occupied by expatriate staff. Those managers who assumed prominent roles in organizations did not possess the right qualifications and experience. Thus, the image of the personnel function suffered as the managers were ill-equipped to perform it competently.

The growth of the public sector in the mid-1960s and 1970s, as a result of the government's economic development programme, the establishment of public enterprises and the encouragement of joint ventures and foreign investment, greatly increased the number of employees and, as a consequence, the personnel function gained more prominence in organizations. Also, in the immediate post-independence period, the corporatist alliance forged between the Kwame Nkrumah government and the trade union movement resulted in the enactment of various labour laws which required efficient administration and monitoring. In this regard, personnel managers became contract administrators (see Tyson's 1987 typology). The personnel managers assumed this role until the mid-1980s when the government restructured the economy and, consequently, the HR function was faced with new challenges. These challenges will be discussed later.

Economic and political environment for HRM

Quite apart from the colonial influence, the socio-economic development policies of the various post-independence governments have also shaped HRM in Ghana. In the immediate post-independence period (1957–60), Ghana's economy enjoyed annual average GDP growth rates of over 6 per cent, an above average performance for a developing country. During this period, the government structured the economy on a socialist pattern, envisaging the economic transformation of the country into mass industrialization on state capital. Hence, special priority was given to the establishment of factories of varying sizes aimed at producing a range of different products for both domestic and export markets. By the early 1960s, however, the government had initiated an 'Africanization' programme.

Part of this programme was a massive development project. As a result, the public sector saw a huge expansion in employment as new schools, universities, hospitals and factories were built. As more jobs were created in the public sector, more personnel managers were hired but, at the same time, jobs declined in the private sector as multinational companies left Ghana, due to the deterioration of economic conditions. In particular, by the mid-1960s, the socialist industrialization policy had failed to produce positive results. The economy experienced high inflation, a shortage of foreign exchange reserves and a rising external debt service burden. At the same time, mismanagement had resulted in the poor performance of state-owned industrial enterprises. These problems led to political agitation in the country and the eventual overthrow of the Nkrumah government, in 1966, by a military junta – the National Liberation Council (NLC).

As Otoo (1998) has indicated, the NLC's main economic objective was to accelerate the pace of economic liberalization by emphasizing the leading role of private capital in development, with the state playing pragmatic residual and regulatory roles, and a partnership between the state and foreign capital allied with some local partners. Thus, foreign capital inflow, or inward investment, was considered a primary and beneficial engine of growth in the economy. Hence, the government sold part of its share in some state-owned enterprises, such as Lever Brothers (soap and detergents), Ghana Cement Works, Kumasi Brewery, Ghana Aluminium Products, to foreign investors.

In 1969, the NLC handed over power to a civilian, elected government led by Busia, a former Oxford University academic, who sought to establish a Western style of management in Ghana. Like the NLC, it attempted to bury the state-directed industrialization policy and also sold off some public enterprises. Busia continued the policy of encouraging the private sector to take a more active role in the economy. This period then witnessed mass redundancies in the public sector and the increasing prominence of personnel management in the private sector.

The Busia government was overthrown by a military-cum-police junta – the National Redemption Council (NRC) – led by Colonel Achampong, in 1972. The junta reversed the economic and pro-Western policies implemented by Busia's government, moved away from privatization and refocused government policy on state enterprises once again, with implications for personnel management in the public sector. Later the NLC reconstituted itself into the Supreme Military Council (SMC) and tried to tackle the rampant corruption in the country.

However, in 1979 junior officers in the Army led by J. J. Rawlings successfully overthrew the SMC in a coup. The Rawlings government embarked on the running of the country with what was, essentially, a leftist and socialist ideology. But the persistent economic decline and the subsequent chaos have seen the government transform itself into an ardent promoter of privatization and a free-enterprise (market) economy.

Perhaps it is the Rawlings government, which first came to power in 1979, that has made the most significant impact on HRM in Ghana. It initially pursued populist and nationalist policies but it is this government that has made the greatest strides towards a free-enterprise economy. After initially pursuing an economic policy which has been described as bootstrap stabilization, the government, in 1983, transformed itself from a populist/socialist type to a pro-Western style of economic management (*The Economist*, 1990).

In May 1983, the government launched its four-year Economic Recovery Programme (ERP), aimed at addressing economic imbalance and promoting growth through liberalization. The ERP was formulated with assistance from the World Bank and the IMF and had the overriding aim of reducing the balance of payments and fiscal deficits and of bringing external arrears to more manageable levels. It focused on the achievement of the following objectives: lowering inflation through prudent fiscal, monetary and trade policies; increasing the flow of foreign exchange into Ghana and directing it to priority sectors; rehabilitating the infrastructure to enhance conditions for production and evacuation of goods; restoring production incentives to attract direct private investment; restructuring the country's economic institutions; and, increasing the availability of essential consumer goods (Agyekum and Synge, 1993).

The ERP was aimed at enhancing the conditions for growth by focusing on the financial, agricultural, energy, industrial, educational and health sectors. During the initial stages of the Structural Adjustment Programme (SAP), two ongoing activities were predominant: (1) workforce restructuring/retrenchment; and (2) transfer of ownership or liquidation of loss-making public enterprises. The common objective of both strategies was to expose state enterprises to competitive market forces and stimulate a more cost-effective and financially responsible management (Davis, 1991). Unprofitable state enterprises were rationalized, by means of liquidations and privatizations, to reduce the financial drain on the state purse (Abbey, 1990).

As an integral part of the industrial environment, HRM has not been sheltered from the influence of the SAP. In particular, it has led to massive workforce retrenchment and restructuring in the public sector. The main argument behind the restructuring of the workforce was to improve the performance and efficiency of state-owned enterprises and, thus, reduce or eliminate the burden imposed by their poor performance on the economy and the government budget. It was also believed that the state enterprise workforce was characterized by inappropriate skill mixes and staffing ratios and was uneconomically large (Davis, 1991). To correct these problems, over 100,000 workers from the public sector have been made redundant and subsequently, retrenched, resulting in the loss of jobs. Since the privatization programme began, in 1989, 132 state-owned enterprises have been sold off to become 232 privately owned companies. A further 168 are scheduled to do the same. Those already processed have come from the mining, agriculture, telecommunications, road transport and tourism sectors (Knipe, 2000)

The SAP, privatization and the liquidation of public enterprises have exposed weaknesses in the HRM systems in organizations in Ghana. They have drawn attention to the inadequacies of available means for assuring the income security of retired workers in both the private and public sectors. The SAP brought to the fore the tensions involved in the high financial costs of workforce redundancy and the general inability of enterprises to meet their negotiated obligations to workers. It is now known that, in both the private and public sectors, arrangements for providing for workers' retirement benefits were in tatters. As Davis (1991) has shown, the system then in place for retirement benefits included payment of a lump-sum retirement gratuity (as negotiated with the employer) and payment of a social security scheme. Redundant workers were also entitled to redundancy or severance pay. But many organizations could not pay the lump-sum retirement gratuity because this had to be met from current operating income, or revenue, as they came due – and many of these organizations were making losses any way. The immediate problem according to Davis (1991: 998–999) was that the cost of meeting retirement gratuity obligations to large numbers of redundant workers undermines the financial position of the enterprise, thus reducing its capability to rehabilitate other productive assets. Moreover, the arrangements for assuring the income security of retired workers were lacking as the payment of benefits was dependent upon the cash flow of the enterprise in the year of retirement. So if in the year of retirement the organization was in deficit (in the red), then there was the possibility that the retired employee would not be paid the retirement benefit, at least on time.

As a result of the exposure of the inadequacies of the system, the government, in the 1990s, abolished all types of end-of-service awards. This included company provident funds. Currently, the main form of pension arrangement in Ghana is the obligatory contribution for both employers and employees to the Social Security and National Insurance Trust. Some employees, like university lecturers, are, however, on superannuation schemes.

The SAP has also opened up challenges for HRM in Ghana. The government's attempts to woo foreign investors means that HR managers must work hard to improve HRM practices, as organizations are likely to operate in a competitive environment. For instance, the financial services sector has been restructured to improve performance and to attract FDI. In line with this objective, a Stock Exchange was established in Accra in 1990. At another level, transportation, commerce and financial services have witnessed continuous improvement since the initiation of the SAP (Otoo, 1998).

In spite of this grand strategy, there is currently little scope for further development in HRM due to the limited expansion of the economy. According to Turner (1999: 5), despite fifteen years of structural adjustment, Ghana remains fundamentally a rural, commodity-dependent economy. While, twenty years ago, manufacturing accounted for around 14 per cent of GDP, in 1999 it stood at 10 per cent or less. Since 1989, the sector has grown at a mere 2–3 per cent per annum, with manufacturers now facing high interest rates, infrastructure problems, a shortage of foreign exchange and aggressive competition from Asia. As a mainly agricultural economy, any meaningful HRM in Ghana will be limited, essentially, to the large to medium-sized companies in the manufacturing and service sectors.

National socio-cultural factors

As is now abundantly clear, the HR manager's job cannot be accomplished in a vacuum. HRM is influenced by both internal and external environmental factors. These, often, interrelated factors can complicate the management of human resources (see, for instance, Cunningham and Debrah, 1995). In Ghana, the two major external environmental factors that impinge on the management of HR are: (1) the government's predominant role in the economy (economic and political); and, (2) national socio-cultural factors. Apart from these, the influences of colonialism and traditional practices still influence management practices, with traditions and institutions, customs and socio-cultural practices underpinning organizational decision-making. In Ghana, society, traditional practices and culture permeate management in modern organizations. Hence, a complex situation has emerged whereby traditional Ghanaian behaviour, beliefs, practices and attitudes (which often militate against Western modern management systems and practices) seriously undermine organizational performance.

These traditional practices often conflict with economic rationality, making the operating levels inefficient and costly. Consequently, they almost always adversely affect the performance of organizations. They also compromise the integrity and efficiency of the formal bureaucratic system by introducing an element of subjectivity in management practices, such as recruitment, performance appraisal and compensation (Kiggundu, 1988, 1989).

In a society where there is a great deal of respect for the elderly (respect for age), status, and people in authority, there is a high degree of subservience to the elderly and authority figures in organizations (Nzelibe, 1986). Social distance between superiors and subordinates is marked, with a sharp distinction and status difference between management and rank-and-file employees. Workers are expected to do their work and follow management's instructions and directives. Subordinates rarely question or challenge those in authority, not expressing their opinions openly – but there is no shortage of opinions privately. Managers take advantage of this situation to get lower level employees to do personal/non-organizational chores for them. For instance, a messenger in an organization successfully sued the organization for workmen's compensation benefit because he was involved in a motor accident while on an errand for his supervisor during office hours. The suit was successful because, under the law , the injury for which compensation is payable must arise out of and in the course of the person's employment (Obeng-Fosu, 1991: 56).

There is a high sense of collectivism in Ghana which impacts negatively on HRM. Ghanaians are born into extended families which take care of their members. People give help and support to kinsmen and expect to receive help from others when they are in need. Under the traditional system it is not an exploitative relationship. People must be prepared to give help in order to receive help from others. When, however, this cultural issue is extended to a modern bureaucratic organization it borders on exploitation because it is not uncommon for people to harass relatives in managerial positions for favours. In particular, many people coerce their relatives to employ them or their children, regardless of their qualifications or whether there is a vacancy (Gardiner, 1996).

Another cultural/traditional issue which exerts considerable financial pressure on organizations is funerals. A funeral is a major social event and a time for reunion for kinsmen. As such, Ghanaians have long bereavement and mourning periods designed to allow people to travel from various parts of the country to pay their respects. It is expected that organizations will be sympathetic to bereaved employees and allow employees time off to attend the funerals of friends, members of their extended family and kinsmen. In addition, companies are obliged, under the terms of collective agreements, to contribute to the cost of the funeral by buying a coffin for an employee who dies in service or for members of an employee's immediate family. Moreover, organizations are required to provide transport for employees to attend the funerals of colleagues and those of colleagues' relatives. The far-reaching financial implications of these practices become obvious from a successful Workmen's Compensation claim, arising from workers who, under the provisions of a collective agreement, had been selected by management to attend the funeral of a colleague and were involved in an accident while travelling to the venue of the funeral (Obeng-Fosu, 1991: 60).

Also, Ghanaians have a culture of forgiveness which influences management on the issue of transgression and punishment. In the Ghanaian traditional society, there is the tendency for a person who commits an offence, even a criminal one, to beg for forgiveness. This behaviour is often extended to modern bureaucratic organizations and, hence, there is a tendency to beg for forgiveness for infractions of organizational rules. Gardiner comments that, in the workplace, it is considered that:

> regardless of the seriousness of the transgression, whether theft or drunkenness at work, once the transgressor goes to 'beg' all should be forgiven . . . He may even ask a politician or member of government to mediate on his behalf.
>
> (1996: 496)

Such a situation creates problems in the discipline of employees in organizations as, culturally, it is expected that the manager will forgive the transgressor; or be deemed to be a wicked, unfeeling, insensitive and uncaring person. Consequently, Ghanaian managers often fail to invoke disciplinary action against employees for even gross misconduct because they do not want to incur the wrath of the employees and become unpopular in the organization. The issue of respect for the elderly also makes it difficult for a young manager to discipline older subordinates. Moreover, many organizations, particularly in the public sector, base promotion and pay increases on seniority rather than merit or performance.

Another socio-cultural issue that has a negative impact on management is time-keeping. African culture does not emphasize the importance of time and time-keeping in organizational life as most Ghanaians have problems with time-keeping. Thus, lateness is endemic in Ghanaian organizations, with many people always arriving late for work or meetings. This has serious negative consequences for organizational performance and poses a challenge to HRM, in particular, on strategies needed to motivate employees to eliminate this unacceptable behaviour (Debrah, forthcoming).

Although there are both elements of femininity and masculinity in Ghanaian culture, in terms of organizational life, masculinity is emphasized. While the culture encourages people to be concerned about others and places importance on relationships, male chauvinistic behaviour pervades organizations. For instance, male employees often make jokes about the fragility of women and many men cannot reconcile themselves to the idea of working under a female boss. The competence or expertise of women is not, however, doubted and there are no wage differentials between males and females holding the same level of appointment. But, generally, the educational system and socialization practices tend to encourage women to train for feminine jobs such as nursing, teaching, secretarial and catering work. With the predominance of managerial positions being held by men, it becomes difficult for women to find role models and mentors to steer their careers in organizations (Debrah, 2000).

HRM functions

At least in theory, if not in practice, the management philosophy of large organizations in Ghana approaches that of classical management but the bureaucratic and impersonal system of administration of such organizations is challenged by the Ghanaian traditional culture. It is, therefore, extremely difficult for organizations to have undiluted bureaucratic systems: faceless, impersonal and impartial.

On this issue, Akinnusi (1991) explains how environmental factors create inter-group conflict and rivalry, and corrupt the integrity and professionalism of managers, thus undermining organizational bureaucracy. Drawing on the work of Parsons (1951) he explores the influence of particularism and universalism in HRM decisions. Analysis of the HR function in Africa reveals that particularism (where decisions are based on ethnicity and personal relations) predominate over universalism (where the emphasis is rather on personal achievements such as qualifications attained, expertise and competence). There is a pervasive tendency for African managers to act in a particularist manner in selection, performance appraisal, promotion and discipline. In this regard, the transparency of selection and placement criteria is conspicuously absent. Thus, in terms of recruitment and selection, cultural practices seriously undermine all elements of objectivity, as managers often rely on subjective criteria in recruitment and selection.

In this respect, Ghana is no exception. As noted by Fashoyin (2000) HRM in Ghana, as elsewhere in Africa, relies heavily on assertive norms, with HR decisions being influenced by the personal relationships between managers and employees. In such an environment, recruitment and selection are heavily influenced by relations rather than by objective assessment of the suitability of job applicants. He contends that this does not mean that merit is never taken into consideration, but rather that family affiliation and friendship have great influence.

In recent years, as public enterprises have been privatized and the private sector has not been able to expand enough to absorb redundant workers, jobs have become scarce. In fact, in many organizations, the trend is towards downsizing. Consequently, organizations, particularly in the private sector, have effectively stopped the public advertising of jobs and now tend to fill jobs with people introduced to the organization by friends or relatives. It is not uncommon now for over one hundred people to respond to one job advertisement. HR managers indicate that, even for jobs not requiring people with university degrees, they are inundated with applications from graduates. Moreover, HR managers in almost all organizations constantly receive unsolicited applications. Thus, in recent years, organizations have tended to place public advertisements in newspapers only for jobs requiring high level technical training when they find it difficult to get the right people through word-of-mouth advertisement.

In terms of recruitment it is an employer's market with all advantages going to the employers in terms of their power to keep wages low. In an environment of severe job shortages, turnover is almost unheard of and, hence, organizations do not bother about adopting strategies to deal with employee turnover.

In most Ghanaian organizations the responsibility for recruitment and selection is co-ordinated by the HR manager but interview panels are made up of managers from various levels of the organisation. In terms of managerial staff, the final decision to hire a candidate is usually made by top management, while for lower level employees the decision to hire and fire is usually made by the personnel manager.

At another level, the lack of objectivity in recruitment and selection somehow affects job analysis and HR planning. With the exception of a few companies in the private sector, job analysis and HR planning are generally not considered important in organizations. In Ghana, the instability in the political and economic environments makes it extremely difficult for organizations to undertake any meaningful HR planning.

There is very little HR planning as organizations tend to be reactive rather than proactive and long-range planning is not seriously considered. This is because planning departments often lack adequate personnel with expertise in statistics, forecasting, organization development and strategic HRM. So, where any planning is done at all, it is confined to setting general and departmental goals and rarely includes carefully developed strategic plans for translating these goals into realizable targets. There is not much emphasis on strategic HRM and, as such, HR issues are not integrated into organizational strategies. Thus, in Ghana, strategic HRM, as described by Boxall (1992) and Hendry and Pettigrew (1986) hardly exists.

Although training is seen as an important HRM function, there are few opportunities for many employees to undergo training, particularly off-the-job external training. Where there is training at all, it is mainly informal, on-the-job training. In the private sector, few companies have their own well-structured internal training programmes. Unilever is one such company.

Some organizations have their own training schools. These include Ghana Commercial Bank, Standard Bank, Barclays Bank, and Ghana Airways. These schools cater to all employees but it is usually lower to middle level employees that attend their courses. Again, usually, the top management personnel are sponsored for courses overseas or attend courses conducted by private training consultancy companies.

The institutions of higher education also play a significant role. The University of Ghana, Lagon, has had a School of Administration for over thirty years. It offers both undergraduate and post-graduate (e.g., MBA and MPA) degrees. The University of Cape Coast also has a Department of Commerce which offers courses in HRM. Both institutions also offer short post-experience courses. There are other national institutions that also offer post-experience courses to employees, both in the public and private sectors. These include the Management Development and Productivity Institute, Ghana Institute of Management and Public Administration and the Civil Service Training Centre.

In the public sector, many organizations depend on foreign assistance to provide education, and training and development programmes for their employees. Usually these take the form of overseas training, paid for by overseas organizations such as the British Council. Many public sector organizations make use of jointly funded programmes of technical assistance to strengthen the managerial capabilities of the staff in African organizations. Such programmes are sponsored by the United Nations Development Programme (UNDP), the Economic Development Institute (EDI) of the World Bank, and the International Labour Organization (ILO) (Blunt and Jones, 1992). For instance, in recent years, employees from Ghana Airways have benefited from training provided under the Capacity Building Foundation which is supported by the African Development Bank, the UNDP and the World Bank.

Reward/compensation in Ghana for lower level, unskilled and semi-skilled employees is driven by the national minimum wage. For bargainable employees it is determined through collective agreement. So where there is a union, wages are subject to negotiations. Managerial salaries are also subject to individual negotiation but any across-the-board annual increment is negotiated by their associations. In the absence of job evaluation, in most organizations, the main factor in wage determination is the ability of the organization to pay. As jobs are hardly ever analysed and evaluated, the wage structures in most organizations are a haphazard and fertile source of conflict, demotivation and dissatisfaction.

Employers in both the public and private sectors usually raise their wages and salaries when there is a pay rise for civil servants. But managers in the private sector and public enterprises often earn more than high ranking civil servants.

High inflation has brought about a rising cost of living and diminishing purchasing power of earnings. Direct financial compensation for most employees in Ghana is below the cost of living level. Thus, motivation essentially takes the form of financial and extrinsic compensation (salary, bonuses and fringe benefits). It is common practice for organizations to provide employees with accommodation or a rent allowance and to have schemes covering health/medical expenses. Some organizations also provide a car allowance for senior employees.

Currently, all allowances and other financial benefits have been incorporated into the gross pay. This form of direct financial compensation is referred to as consolidated pay. With the abolition of the end of service benefit/gratuity, workers rarely show a high degree of loyalty and commitment to the organization. In such an environment, individual rather than organizational goals drive employee behaviour. Moreover, in areas where there are skill shortages, the few employees with the scarce skill are more likely to be involved in job-hopping because they have no long-term financial security package to tie them to the organization.

Another HR function, although considered important by Ghanaian managers, but which is hardly ever linked to pay, is performance appraisal. In general, reward systems are not conditional upon performance or other organizationally relevant criteria. Perhaps this has a role to play in the low productivity of organizations in Ghana.

In large and medium-sized organizations, performance appraisal is conducted annually, mainly for internal employee relations issues such as promotion and transfers but rarely for compensation purposes. Although performance appraisal is used to assess employees' training and developmental needs, many organizations usually do not have adequate resources to fill the training gaps. Career planning, job design, and personnel research are largely neglected in Ghanaian organizations.

This is because personnel departments are usually poorly, or inadequately, staffed. Moreover, many managers do not themselves have professional training in HRM and, hence, do not possess the skills to carry out some specialist HRM functions.

Industrial relations

Ghana has a long history of trade unionism dating back to the colonial period, but modern trade unionism in Ghana is based on the Dunlopian tripartite system. The Trade Union Congress (TUC) is the main body representing the labour movement in the country. There are seventeen national industrial unions affiliated to the TUC. While the TUC does not, itself, negotiate on behalf of any of the trade unions, it co-ordinates the activities of the various affiliated unions, gives guidance on labour matters and speaks on behalf of the whole labour movement. The congress is represented on a number of boards and committees which deal with matters of direct concern to workers.

In spite of the influential role of the trade union movement in Ghana, many employers still treat trade unions with suspicion. In most private sector organizations, there is managerial antipathy towards trade unions as owners believe that they infringe on managerial prerogatives.

Thus the government has legislation in place to ensure that employees who want to form or join unions can do so without fear or intimidation. Trade unionism in Ghana is based on the freedom of workers and employers to run their organizations and to determine, by collective bargaining, conditions and terms that should regulate their relations without state interference. It is regulated by the 1958 Industrial Relations Act, which was amended in 1959, 1960 and 1962. In 1965, a more extensive Act based on the 1958 Act was passed. This defined and confirmed trade union privileges.

The 1958 Act provided the instruments of collective bargaining. Workers have the right to form a union upon the submission of their constitution and rules to the Registrar of Trade Unions, who is also the Chief Labour Officer. Once a certified union has been issued with a bargaining certificate, it is obligatory for the employer to meet with the representatives of the union for collective bargaining purposes. Certified unions can call a legal strike after fulfilling the procedures listed under the Act (Kusi and Gyimah-Boakye, 1994).

Unions are organized along industrial rather than craft lines. That is, membership is based on the industry in which one works, rather than the occupation to which one belongs. There is no union shop and workers have a choice whether to belong or not to belong to a trade union. There is no regulation in Ghana defining bargainable and non-bargainable employees but the general convention has been that union members are, by and large, workers below management grades. Workers in the senior grades of establishments are usually members of senior staff associations. Although, under the law, such associations do not have collective bargaining certificates for bargaining purposes they are, nevertheless, recognized by the management of the establishments and therefore negotiate on behalf of their members.

In the Civil Service, for instance, most of the workers belong to the Civil Servants' Association. The government periodically discusses, with the association, the conditions and terms of employment of civil servants. Similarly, the Ghana National Association of Teachers (GNAT) is the professional association for teachers. The State Registered Nurses' Association is the equivalent body for nurses. All these professional associations are outside the Trades Union Congress and are recognized by the government.

Single employer bargaining is the predominant mode of bargaining but in some instances multi-employer bargaining is possible. The latter involves groups of employers who are engaged in identical or similar businesses. They usually come together to negotiate one collective agreement with the national union and, as such, any agreement reached is binding on the individual employers in the group.

In Ghana, collective agreements are negotiated by standing joint committees of management and workers. Negotiated collective agreements define basic salary, annual increments and various allowances, as well as benefits and subsidies provided by the employer. A collective agreement covers employees' welfare and social needs. It covers such issues as housing or housing allowance, medical care, education of employees' children, subsidized canteens and free transportation to and from work.

As Davis (1991) has noted, collective agreements cover a variety of benefits or perquisites that are considered as traditional or customary practices. These range from 6–8 weeks' paid annual leave (plus travelling time, expenses, and leave allowance, often equivalent to two months of basic salary), to the supply of a coffin, a shroud, schnapps and beer for the funerals of deceased workers, and the provision of interest free loans for employee purchases of cars or motorcycles and of appliances and furniture.

Although there is labour legislation governing terminations, dismissals as well as redundancies, collective agreements also have provisions for these items. These provide some safeguards for a worker against an employer who might wish to terminate his or her employment wrongfully or without the necessary or required notice. Labour legislation provides for minimum notice periods while provision in collective agreements usually provides longer notice periods and what workers or employers are entitled to claim in lieu of notice.

In general, however, a worker guilty of serious misconduct under the legislation or collective agreement is not, under normal circumstances, given notice but is instantly dismissed. Serious misconduct is variously described in collective agreements. Examples are drunkenness, stealing, fighting and other offences which may be deemed by the establishment to have brought it into disrepute, or undermined discipline (Obeng-Fosu, 1991). The settlement of collective disputes takes the form of conciliation, mediation and arbitration. Procedures for these are laid down under the law.

As a result of the challenges to workers arising from the implementation of SAPs, trade unions have increased their involvement in economic restructuring and other reform issues. In recent years, trade unions have voiced their concerns to the government on the impacts of the SAPs. Moreover, trade unions were actively involved in negotiating terminal benefits with employers, as part of redundancy measures.

At another level, the Ghana Employers' Association also plays a prominent role in HRM. In particular, it promotes cordial relations between employers, on the one hand, and trade unions, employees and the government on the other. It assists its members in negotiations with trade unions. The association also communicates important labour laws, regulations and administrative instructions affecting employers and their workers to its members. Moreover, it encourages consultation between employers and adopts a co-ordinated approach to matters pertaining to the interest of its members. In particular, the association co-ordinates their views and reaction on IR problems, proposed legislation and methods of improving both the climate for, and efficiency of, business affairs. The association is made up of employers from various industrial sectors, including mining, commerce, transport, forestry, engineering, banking and finance, manufacturing, energy, agriculture and fishery, among others.

There are many other associations which influence HRM in Ghana. These include the Federation of Associations of Ghanaian Exporters, the Private Enterprise Foundation, Ghana National Chamber of Commerce, and the Association of Ghana Industries.

Discussion

Although the functions of the HR manager in Ghana are still general administrative and bureaucratic ones, managers are now acting more as change agents (Cunningham and Debrah, 1995). This is necessary in view of the current globalization trend, mergers, and privatization taking place in Ghana. From the 1960s to the mid-1980s, the HR managers in Ghana operated in a growth environment and played the role of administrators of HR policies and consensus negotiators with trade union representatives (Tyson, 1987). This period witnessed some growth, albeit a limited one, in both the public and private sectors. It was also the golden era of trade unionism in Ghana, and HR managers played the role of contract managers simultaneously with that of clerks of works (Tyson and Fell, 1986).

From the mid-1980s, as the implementation of the SAP took hold in Ghana, managing organizational contraction became the most prominent HR function (Levine, 1984). This resulted in the application of new public management-type reforms in the public sector but, increasingly, the related HR initiatives were adopted in the private sector as well. One aspect of this is the increasing tendency to contract out the provision of some services or activities that have traditionally been provided in-house. In the public sector, the rationale for contracting out of public services revolves around the lack of requisite staff, skills, and technical expertise in providing some services, such as complex construction and maintenance works. In other activities, such as cleaning in the water sector, contracting out has been resorted to because of employment cuts in manual and low-skill jobs (Larbi, 1998). It appears that, with decreasing resources, contracting out is seen as a means of improving efficiency and raising additional capital for rehabilitation and expansion of facilities to meet growing demand. Hence, in terms of HRM, Larbi (1998) gives the example of the contracting out of management development and training programmes for senior staff. Also, contracted out are administrative and miscellaneous services such as repair and maintenance of vehicles, office equipment and information technology systems.

It could be argued that, as a result of the implementation of the SAP, managers have come under increasing pressure to adopt the New Public Management (NPM) approach in Ghanaian organizations. Essentially, this management system emphasizes the adoption of private sector management practices in the public sector, strengthening the prerogatives of managers, measuring performance, increasing competitive pressures and cost-cutting (O'Donnell *et al.*, 1999).

Various models of the NPM have been developed. For instance, Hood (1991) identified seven elements of the NPM model. Similarly, Ferlie *et al.* (1996) have also identified four distinct NPM models. Among other things, Hood and Ferlie *et al.*'s models mention the increasing management prerogative in hiring and firing workers and the emphasis on cost-cutting and rationalization. In particular, Ferlie *et al.* refer to such practices as the downsizing and decentralization model, which involves reducing workforce numbers and contracting out.

HR managers in the public enterprises now have to deal with the challenges arising from the SAP and its consequent privatization programme, such as HR issues or challenges emanating from the contracting out of services. This, then, raises the question of the role HR managers in Ghana should play in the downsizing process. Sadhev *et al.* (1999) have reviewed the literature on downsizing and the changing role of HR managers and suggest that the HR manager's role has become wide-ranging, covering the strategic as well as implementation aspects of people management.

Although no research has been conducted into the role of HR managers in the employee management aspects of the SAP, there is some evidence that downsizing and decentralization have forced managers to adopt workforce flexibility strategies. In the public sector, the current trend is to maintain only skeletal staff for minor jobs and contract out major works. Thus, public sector organizations are resorting to labour flexibility strategies. These strategies are undertaken to avoid the financial and management burden of organizing and providing those services directly (Smithson *et al.*, 1997). Ghanaian managers are now acutely aware of the need to differentiate between core and peripheral employees (Atkinson and Meagre, 1986).

It has been argued that HRM in Ghana is still predominantly an administrative and bureaucratic function but, perhaps, the contracting out of services marks the beginning of a watershed in HRM as managers begin shifting from a pluralist to a unitarist perspective or framework. In a sense, indicating a shift from the administrative and control systems associated with personnel management to the strategic and integrative approach more associated with HRM (Walton, 1985; Storey and Sisson, 1993; Guest, 1987 and 1989; Legge, 1995). It is too early yet to judge whether such a transformation is underway but one can be certain that the new initiatives, originating from abroad, in HRM in the public sector in Ghana will soon be used extensively in the private sector.

Conclusion

This chapter has argued that historical, economic and socio-political factors have, in the past, had a significant impact on the HR function and will continue to do so in the future. It is further argued that HR is still very much an administrative and bureaucratic function in Ghanaian organizations. It deals, essentially, with basic issues about employee resourcing, training and development, performance appraisal, and internal employee relations – such as discipline, transfer, and reward/remuneration systems, among others.

In addition, HR managers in most organizations are responsible for IR and employee relations issues. They are responsible for administering HR policies and maintaining cordial employee relations. In unionized organizations they usually meet the union leaders to discuss day-to-day problems, including those affecting conditions of service and dispute settlement. They also form part of the management team during collective bargaining negotiations as they act as advisors to management. With the SAP, privatization and changes in the economy perhaps the HR manager's role will become more strategic in focus in future.

The chapter also indicates that, although most organizations in Ghana follow the Western style of management, managers are confronted every day with traditional practices and customs which conflict with the Western philosophy and rationality of management. These traditions and other socio-cultural issues impose some constraints on managerial efficiency and effectiveness in the HRM arena. The national and socio-cultural factors pose challenges to HRM managers. In particular, these factors tend to move HRM towards a subjective rather than objective treatment of employees. In Ghana, socio-cultural factors make HR managers vulnerable to charges of nepotism and favouritism in the treatment of employees.

Note

1   Statistics compiled from: (a) *Financial Times Survey*, Ghana, 4 November 1999; (b) *The Times*, Focus on Ghana, 18 April 2000; (c) *The Sunday Telegraph*, Ghana: Opening Up the Market, 14 February 1999, (d) www.ghana-embassy.org

References

Abbey, J. L. S. (1990), 'Ghana's Experience with Structural Adjustment', in J. Pickett and H. Singer (eds) *Towards Economic Recovery in Sub-Saharan Africa*, London: Routledge, pp. 32–41.

Agyekum, F. and Synge, R. (1993) 'Ghana', in *Africa Review 1993/4: The Economic and Business Report*, London: Kogan Page, pp. 72–76.

Akinnusi, D. M (1991) 'Personnel Management in Africa: A Comparative Analysis of Ghana, Kenya and Nigeria', in C. Brewster and S. Tyson (eds) *International Comparisons in Human Resource Management*, London: Pitman, pp. 159–172.

Atkinson, J. and Meagre, N (1986) 'Is Flexibility Just a Flash in the Pan?', *Personnel Management*, September, 26–29.

Blunt, P. and Jones, M. L. (1992) *Managing Organisations in Africa*, Berlin: Walter de Gruyter.

Bourrett, F. M. (1963) *Ghana: The Road to Independence 1919–1957*, London: Oxford University Press.

Boxall, P. F. (1992) 'Strategic Human Resource Management: Beginnings of a New Theoretical Sophistication?', *Human Resource Management Journal*, 2 (3), 60–79.

Cunningham, J. B and Debrah, Y. A. (1995) 'Skills for Managing Human Resource in a Complex Environment: The Perception of Human Resource Managers in Singapore', *International Journal of Human Resource Management*, 6 (1), 79–101.

Davis, J. T. (1991) 'Institutional Impediments to Workforce Retrenchment and Restructuring in Ghana's State Enterprises', *World Development*, 19 (8), 987–1005.

Debrah, Y. A. (2000) 'Management in Ghana', in M. Warner (ed.) *Management in Emerging Countries*, London: Thomson Learning.

Debrah, Y. A. (forthcoming) 'Doing Business in Ghana', *Thunderbird Journal of International Business*.

Economist Intelligence Unit (1990) *West Africa: Economic Structure and Analysis*, London: The Economist Intelligence Unit.

Fashoyin, T. (2000) 'Management in Africa', in M. Warner (ed.) *Management in the Emerging Countries: Regional Encyclopaedia of Business and Management*, London: Thomson Business Press, pp. 169–175.

Ferlie, E., Ashburner, L., Fitzgerald, L., and Pettigrew, A (1996) *The New Public Management in Action*, Oxford: Oxford University Press.

Gardiner, K. (1996), 'Managing in Different Cultures: The Case of Ghana', in B. Towers (ed.) *The Handbook of Human Resource Management*, Oxford: Blackwell, pp. 488–510.

Guest, D. (1987) 'Human Resource Management and Industrial Relations', *Journal of Management Studies*, 24 (5), 503–521.

Guest, D. (1989) 'Personnel and HRM: Can You Tell the Difference?', *Personnel Management*, January, 48–51.

Hendry, C. and Pettigrew, A. (1986) 'The Practice of Strategic Human Resource Management', *Personnel Review*, 15 (5), 3–8.

Holman, M. (1999a) 'Still Waiting for Take-Off', *Financial Times Survey – Ghana*, 4 November, p. 3.

Holman, M. (1999b) 'Leadership to Change, Reform to Continue', *Financial Times Survey – Ghana*, 4 November, p. 1.

Hood, C. (1991) 'A Public Management for all Seasons', *Public Administration*, 69 (1), 3–19.

Huq, M. M. (1989) *The Economy of Ghana*, London: Macmillan.

Kiggundu, M. N. (1988) 'Africa', in R. Nath (ed.), *Comparative Management: A Regional View*, Ballinger, pp. 169–243.

Kiggundu, M. N. (1989) *Managing Organizations in Developing Countries: An Operational and Strategic Approach*, West Hartford, CT: Kumarian Press.

Kiggundu, M. N. (1991) 'The Challenges of Management Development in Sub-Saharan Africa', *Journal of Management Development*, 10 (6), 32–47.

Kimble, D. (1965) *A Political History of Ghana*, Oxford: Clarendon.

Knipe, M. (2000) 'The Nation Giving Hope to the Rest of Africa', *The Times: Focus on Ghana*, 18 April, p. 1.

Kusi, T. A. and Gyimah-Boakye, A. K. (1994) 'Collective Bargaining in Ghana: Problems and Perspectives, in Political Transformations, Structural Adjustment and Industrial

Relations in Africa: English Speaking Countries', *ILO Labour Management Relations Series*, No. 78, Geneva: ILO.

Larbi, G. A. (1998) 'Contracting-Out of Public Health and Water Services in Ghana', *International Journal of Public Sector Management*, 11 (2/3), 154–163.

Legge, K. (1995) *Human Resource Management: Rhetoric and Realities*, Basingstoke: Macmillan.

Levine, C. H. (1984) 'Retrenchment, Human Resource Erosion and the Role of the Personnel Managers' Public', *Personnel Management Journal*, Fall, 249–263.

Nzelibe, C. O. (1986) 'The Evolution of African Management Thought', *International Studies of Management and Organisations*, XVI (2), 6–16.

Obeng-Fosu, P. (1991) *Industrial Relations in Ghana*, Accra: Ghana University Press.

O'Donnell, M., Allan, C. and Peetz, D. (1999) *The New Public Management and Workplace Change in Australia*, Working Paper Series, No. 126, School of Industrial Relations and Organisational Behaviour, Sydney: The University of New South Wales.

Otoo, A. (1998) 'Foreign Investment in Ghana', MBA dissertation, Cardiff Business School, University of Wales, Cardiff.

Parsons, T. (1951) *The Social System*, New York: Free Press.

Sadhev, K., Vinnicombe, S. and Tyson, S. (1999) 'Downsizing and the Changing Role of HR', *International Journal of Human Resource Management*, 10 (5), 906–923.

Smithson, P., Asamoah-Baah, A. and Mills, A. (1997) *The Role of Government in Adjusting Economies Paper 26: The Case of Health Sector in Ghana*, Birmingham: Development Administration Group, School of Public Policy, University of Birmingham.

Storey, J. and Sisson, K. (1993) *Managing Human Resources and Industrial Relations*, London: Open University Press.

Turner, M. (1999) 'Dynamo Sector Facing Problems', *Financial Times Survey – Ghana*, 4 November, p. 5.

Tyson, S. (1987) 'The Management of the Personnel Function', *Journal of Management Studies*, 24, 523–532.

Tyson, S. and Fell, A. (1986) *Evaluating the Personnel Function*, London: Hutchinson.

Wallis, M. (1999) 'Cocoa – A Hot Political Issue', *Financial Times Survey – Ghana*, 4 November, p. 7.

Walton, R. (1985) 'From Control to Commitment in the Workplace', *Harvard Business Review*, 63, March–April, pp. 77–84.

13 Human resource management in Kenya

Ken Kamoche

Introduction

The traditional approach to managing people through an emphasis on administrative procedures continues to play a dominant role in Kenyan organizations. Such procedures cover recruitment and selection, wage and benefits administration, setting up training programmes, employee relations, compliance with employment and labour legislation, and so forth. These are the practices at the heart of personnel management. This tradition is even more evident in the large public corporations that are currently being privatized, as well as in the majority of small and medium-sized locally owned firms. The more progressive approaches generally referred to as human resource management (HRM) are mainly to be found in professional firms and subsidiaries of foreign multinational firms.

This chapter takes a critical look at the way the challenges of managing people are problematized, the thinking underpinning the formulation of management approaches, the way these approaches have been shaped by national and other factors. It also considers how the existing management approaches in the country can benefit from more appropriate theories and practices that are now beginning to emerge in the contemporary management literature.

The evolution of management in Kenya

The evolution of management practices in Kenya should be seen in the historical context which goes back to the colonial era and the onset of a capitalist mode of production. The links with Western capitalism are traceable back to the late nineteenth century. According to Swainson (1980), the establishment of a European settler class marked the beginning of a market economy, much of which was channelled into agricultural production. The growing of so-called cash crops like coffee, tea, pyrethrum and sisal, coupled with the absence of any viable natural minerals led to agriculture becoming the mainstay of the economy. To this day, agricultural production and in particular the processing of agricultural commodities employ a large proportion of the working population – about 78 per cent, but agriculture accounts for only about 30 per cent of GDP. Productive activities by indigenous people were systematically stifled by the colonial government which fostered a dual policy of peasant-subsistence and large-scale, European cash-crop production.

Kamoche (2000) argues that this policy was a precursor to the subsequent stifling of indigenous entrepreneurialism and managerial initiative. In industry, the colonial government supported foreign investors while placing all manner of obstacles in the way of indigenous entrepreneurs. Capital only started to move into local hands after independence in 1963. These efforts received some impetus from the campaign of 'Africanization' in the 1960s and 1970s which was designed to enable local people to acquire the means of production and secure jobs. While this objective was, in the main, achieved, in spite of the haphazard manner in which the policy was implemented, it is doubtful whether it made any contribution towards the establishment of administrative and managerial approaches which suited the needs of a newly independent state. The main beneficiaries were politically powerful, already propertied elites who were content to maintain the status quo and indeed worked closely with foreign investors to institute Western styles of management. The importation and unquestioning use of foreign management practices have continued to be an important question in the management debate in Kenya.

In the field of human resources, the flavour has very much been an administrative one, as noted above, involving public relations and patronage. This was particularly noteworthy in the foreign multinationals which responded to the call for Africanization by hiring local people who could negotiate the state bureaucracy. The personnel administrators were responsible for maintaining records, securing work permits for expatriates, pacifying union activists and ensuring a harmonious environment. Much of this activity took place without the benefit of the systematic planning now associated with strategic HRM. As such, the personnel function was characterized by reactiveness and short-termism. As a result, although personnel managers have not traditionally enjoyed the status and financial rewards of their colleagues in finance and marketing, for example, their immense power is evident in their role of hirer/firer. This power has been enhanced in the last decade as unemployment soared to over 40 per cent by the turn of the century.

Key contextual and definitive national factors

This section characterizes some factors which have been shown to have a defining role in shaping managerial thinking and practice in Kenya. Researchers have long realized the importance of environmental and contextual factors in defining and shaping management practice. These factors ultimately impact on the creation and enactment of human resource practices and policies, and it is important that the nature of these factors is understood in order to capture the essence of the human resource challenges.

We characterize a number of these factors, specify their relevance to the Kenyan context, and identify their impact on human resource management. We then demonstrate how these factors contribute to the formulation of a processual HRM approach which we believe has relevance to the broader African context. Such an

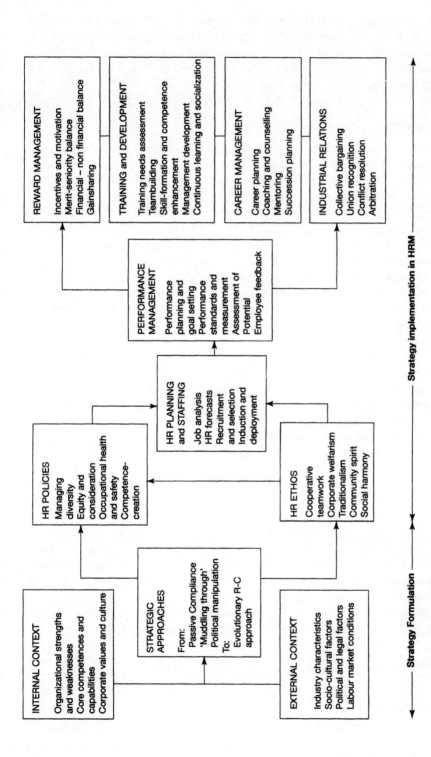

INTERNAL CONTEXT

Organizational strengths and weaknesses
Core competences and capabilities
Corporate values and culture

EXTERNAL CONTEXT

Industry characteristics
Socio-cultural factors
Political and legal factors
Labour market conditions

STRATEGIC APPROACHES

From:
Passive Compliance
'Muddling through'
Political manipulation
To:
Evolutionary R-C approach

HR POLICIES

Managing diversity
Equity and consideration
Occupational health and safety
Competence-creation

HR ETHOS

Cooperative teamwork
Corporate welfarism
Traditionalism
Community spirit
Social harmony

HR PLANNING and STAFFING

Job analysis
HR forecasts
Recruitment and selection
Induction and deployment

PERFORMANCE MANAGEMENT

Performance planning and goal setting
Performance standards and measurement
Assessment of Potential
Employee feedback

REWARD MANAGEMENT

Incentives and motivation
Merit-seniority balance
Financial – non financial balance
Gainsharing

TRAINING and DEVELOPMENT

Training needs assessment
Teambuilding
Skill-formation and competence enhancement
Management development
Continuous learning and socialization

CAREER MANAGEMENT

Career planning
Coaching and counselling
Mentoring
Succession planning

INDUSTRIAL RELATIONS

Collective bargaining
Union recognition
Conflict resolution
Arbitration

◄─── **Strategy Formulation** ───►   ◄─── **Strategy implementation in HRM**

Figure 13.1 A processual, strategic model of **HRM** in Africa
Source: Kamoche (1997)

approach is depicted in Figure 13.1 which shows that before we can begin to design HR practices e.g. for rewards, training and career management, we must appreciate the important impact of the relevant environments, the appropriate strategic approaches and the effect of the culturally defined HR ethos on HR policies. We consider these in the subsequent sections.

The political-economic environment

As the economy teeters on the verge of collapse, it is now becoming increasingly necessary for Kenyans to take a considered look at the national stock of human resources. It is not enough to consider the changing form of HRM or to talk of human capital without taking account of the specific working conditions facing people in Kenya now. An understanding of the context of HRM must, for example, take cognizance of the current state of the economy and in particular the way the economy has been plundered through graft and mismanagement. Kenya has consistently been ranked among the most corrupt nations in league tables prepared by such bodies as Transparency International. The prevalence of graft appears to have been fostered by an opportunistic approach to appropriating public service gains, pressures from the extended family for material support, an uncaring attitude to the utilization of state resources and weak governance structures in which politicians and senior public servants have historically flouted the law with impunity. The latter feature has in turn set a bad example for ordinary people. A culture of low accountability especially in the misappropriation of foreign aid has led to foreign donors freezing aid, especially from the early 1990s, subsequently starving the economy of much-needed financial support. It remains to be seen whether the anti-graft measures now being put in place will have any lasting effect.

The consequence of these developments is that the state has been unable to fund basic education, health and infrastructural development to the required standard, and has had to undertake an ambitious privatization programme which has inevitably led to massive lay-offs and high unemployment in an economy in which the state (and civil service) was previously a major employer. The impact of these developments has also been noted in the private sector. Economic liberalization has exposed the high-cost and inefficient local manufacturers to intense competition from superior imports, especially from South Africa, resulting in factory closures and loss of jobs. A per capita income of only about $310, high unemployment and high inflation have resulted in a declining purchasing power and poverty for many. The near collapse of the infrastructure (e.g. the transportation and telecommunication systems, unreliable electricity supply and so forth) has brought more pressure to bear on production costs which are invariably passed on to the consumer in the form of higher prices.

The destruction of the infrastructure has been blamed on the El Niño rains of 1997–8. Political violence, crime and widespread insecurity have also impacted negatively on a major foreign exchange earner – tourism. The government's failure to improve accountability and implement reforms led to the IMF cancelling Kenya's Enhanced Structural Adjustment Programme. The country currently has a crippling foreign debt of $6.5 billion. These factors have contributed to economic stagnation, widespread poverty (half the population lives below the poverty line) and reduced opportunities for industrial growth. Real GDP has declined from a high of almost 5 per cent in 1995 and 4.6 per cent in 1996 to 1.6 per cent in 1998 and an estimated 1.3 per cent in 1999. Against this backdrop, the urge to secure and retain employment has been sharpened across the board, with the effect that the employers' hand has continued to be strengthened.

The socio-cultural environment

The socio-cultural context is an important consideration in an ethnically hetero-geneous society like Kenya. There are more than forty different ethnic groups, each with its own unique language and culture. This heterogeneity is in one sense an important source of diversity but, unfortunately, it has historically been a source of ethnic tensions which are, for the most part, merely latent. There have, however, been occasions when these tensions have flared into politically motivated 'tribal clashes' and ethnic cleansing which in the early 1990s came perilously close to plunging the country into civil war. The question of ethnicity has impinged heavily on the workplace. It manifests itself mostly through favouritism in recruitment, career advancement and the provision of training opportunities. Although such practices are widely criticized by the intellectual elites, others interpret them in terms of the notion of obligation to close relatives and friends (Kamoche, 1992). Other observers (e.g. Blunt, 1980) see it as an adaptive response to workplace alienation whereby workers from the same rural area come together to give each other psychological and material support in the unfamiliar city environment.

The negative sentiments and acrimony that exist between different ethnic groups constitute the socially undesirable notion of 'tribalism' which, according to some writers, owes its origins to the divide-and-rule policies laid down by the colonial government (e.g. Leys, 1975) and which have continued to be used in independent Kenya. In the era of unprecedented high unemployment and political tension, people have rallied even closer to their ethnic roots in the hope of capitalizing on ethnically sanctioned obligations. The result is that many young people joining the labour market from school or university have very little faith in the ability of the system, either in the public or private sector, to allocate employment opportunities purely on merit. Particularist practices are now widely assumed to be inevitable. Nevertheless, in the wake of increasing criticism and sensitivity about the debilitating effects of particularism, personnel and HR managers, especially in multinational firms, have had to insulate themselves from charges of tribalism and nepotism by striving to formalize procedures in recruitment, promotion and career management. The need for such 'insulation' has also been identified by Blunt and Popoola (1985), who also suggest that managers should be indifferent to kinship pressures, a much more difficult proposition. Kamoche (1992, 2000) found that managers sometimes sought to achieve an 'ethnic balance' at the lower end of the labour market where the homogeneity of skills allows little scope for worker differentiation. Justifying the use of such quotas among office staff would be much more difficult.

The socio-cultural context has also been influenced by the 'African thought system', which, according to Nzelibe (1986), emphasizes ethnocentrism, traditionalism, communalism and co-operative teamwork. Some of the effects of ethnocentrism have been discussed above. Traditionalism is about adherence to long-established attitudes, customs, beliefs and practices which ultimately shape the culture and define the socially desirable norms of behaviour. Communalism stipulates that one does not merely exist as an individual separate from the community but as a member of a community which gives him/her a sense of identity and belonging. Social activities thus evolve around the group, however defined: family, clan, ethnic group and district. This in part explains why it is so difficult for the individual to be 'indifferent to' family or ethnic pressures and for managers to be guided by so-called rational–bureaucratic norms of decision-making. This also demonstrates an important limitation of Western-style HRM.

Communal activities to which the individual is inevitably bound include rites of passage such as initiation ceremonies, marriage, funerals, fund-raising ceremonies (known as *harambee*) to assist those in need and so forth. Communalism thus gives teamwork its *raison d'être* and to a large extent determines the success of work organization, especially where it allows workers to address issues that affect them as a group or community.

In a study of teamwork in a Kenyan firm Kamoche (1995) found that when management first introduced quality circles, they failed. Workers only began to accept them when the agenda went beyond quality and productivity and included personal and work-related social problems. As such, they spent half the time discussing quality problems while the rest of time was devoted to sharing personal or family problems. The opportunity to confide in each other and seek help and advice from peers created a culture of trust in which they felt more willing to devote their energies to the task in hand, in addition to fostering social harmony. This highlighted 'the need to let teamwork emerge from the social context of work' (ibid.: 382). This blurring of the distinction between the worker and the social being is an important aspect of the organizational context in Africa. To conclude this section we note that these socio-cultural characteristics constitute an ethos which stipulates how people wish to be treated in an African organizational context.

Industrial relations

Industrial relations (IR) in Kenya have gone through some notable changes over time. The origins of IR are traceable to the independence movement in which the mass associations that then passed for trade unions were indelibly marked with a political agenda which included a campaign against the 'colony' status imposed in 1920 by Britain, forced labour, identity cards that engendered oppression and so forth (e.g. Singh 1969). The more formalized trade unions that arose in large industries like railways and construction still retained strong political and industrial objectives.

Militancy in industrial relations was sharpened in the 1950s when state suppression intensified but the union movement itself became gradually weakened through legislation and the persecution of activists. Political independence brought with it a much more undefined role for the union movement. With political oppression no longer an immediate threat, the industrial agenda took centre-stage. However, union leaders found they were almost as restrained under the new regime as they were under the colonial era in terms of engaging in certain forms of activity.

For example, the government's policy towards IR was basically underpinned by exhortations to 'exercise restraint' in order to ensure the industrial stability necessary for sustained economic growth. With 'economic growth' as the new post-independence mantra, the role of the state in the shaping of industrial relations became institutionalized. The definitive policy document, the Industrial Relations Charter which had been enacted in 1962, provided for a role for three key stakeholders: the then Federation of Labour, the Kenya Federation of Employers and the Kenyan government. The subsequent 'Tripartite Agreements' signed under the Charter in the ensuing years provided for the peaceful resolution of conflict at the expense of union independence. As a consequence, labour regulation has enjoyed a chequered history whereby unions were restrained from making vociferous wage demands in return for specified labour intakes, the outright banning of strikes, co-optation of union leaders into the political establishment, and so forth.

Labour relations are regulated by the Trade Union Act and the Trade Disputes Act. Disputes are initially referred to the Minister for Labour, who may sub-sequently refer them to the Industrial Court. Terms of employment including minimum wages, working hours, payment for overtime, and so forth fall under the Regulation of Wages and Conditions of Employment Act. Unionization is currently about 40 per cent and the major unions are found in the agri-business, manu-facturing, mining, banking and other services. The Central Organization of Trade Unions (COTU) today constitutes the basic framework for union organization and the protection of workers' rights. Their rival, the Kenyan Federation of Employers (along with the Kenyan Association of Manufacturers) is a much more powerful stakeholder.

Associations like the Institute of Personnel Management and the Kenyan Institute of Management have tried to improve management practice by offering training courses and professionalizing management practice. The union movement has not achieved as much influence on HRM as would have been expected, partly due to the constraints imposed upon unions by the Trade Disputes Act and Presidential decrees pre-empting industrial action. Furthermore, a preoccupation with bread and butter issues has prevented them from playing a more active role in tackling one of the biggest challenges: poor employee relations characterized by poor communications, uncaring attitudes on the part of managers and charges of racism in the case of some foreign and local Asian managers.

The apparent tranquillity in industrial relations in the country is not attributable to any inherent harmony among the three key stakeholders. It is, according to Chege (1988) due to fear of retribution among union leaders who fear arrest for militant activism and ordinary workers who fear being sacked for engaging in industrial action. Thus, adversarial relations between workers and management, a low-trust culture and the high unitarist ethos in management thinking are some noteworthy influences on the shaping of HRM. The degree of participation and empowerment is still fairly low and is not expected to improve in the current industrial climate. High unemployment has also had the effect of tightening controls over labour and encouraging the adoption of more 'flexible' working methods such as casualization, short-term contracts and a limited concern for retention mechanisms.

Questionable working practices are reported to be on the increase. These include the illegal use of a sequence of short-term contracts, and allegations of workers being physically restrained from leaving the premises or being prevented from receiving family and friends in factory lodgings. There clearly needs to be a more humane approach in the use of managerial practices, including paying more attention to such factors as the socio-cultural hierarchy which requires superiors to show consideration to subordinates. This has been shown to be an effective managerial approach in firms that provide a wide range of welfare benefits (including building schools, hospitals and roads) and which invest heavily in training and development (Kamoche 1992, 2000). This study suggested it may be necessary for organizations to contribute to filling the gap that has been created by the failure of the state to provide sufficient infrastructure. It also shows that managers must be aware of the kinds of expectations people have, especially in poverty-stricken communities – they have to be prepared to play an expanded role in contributing to socio-economic development.

The industrial and competitive environment

The formulation of HRM practices needs to take account of the strategic management factors that impinge directly on decision-making and planning. Traditionally in Kenya, and in much of Africa for that matter, these factors have been seen in terms of how to deal with uncertainties that exist in the external competitive environment. This is in part due to the nature and magnitude of uncertainties that characterize the business environment. The volatility of the competitive environment has been recognized as a major obstacle to management on the continent (e.g. Blunt, 1983; Blunt and Jones, 1992; Kamoche, 1993, 1997; Kiggundu, 1989; Munene, 1991). Uncertainties include fluctuating exchange and interest rates, political instability and concomitant social strife, unreliable infrastructure, frequently changing legislation and policies, and so forth.

These problems place a great burden on management's ability to plan and make sound decisions. Within the HR field, the problem is compounded by insufficient and often unreliable information on important questions like demographics and labour statistics. Information asymmetries ultimately imply that decisions may not be optimal. These uncertainties have forced managers to adopt short-term planning horizons and to resort to decision-making mechanisms that, to the outsider, might appear to be highly irrational. One such method identified in a previous study (Kamoche, 1992) was 'management by deciding'. This term was offered by a manager in a car dealership who sought to convey the view that managers were making decisions in an *ad hoc* manner as they confronted the problems, and more importantly, as opportunities and resources presented themselves for problem resolution. This approach echoes approaches such as 'logical incrementalism' (Quinn, 1980). 'Management by deciding' and such other adaptive mechanisms (e.g. muddling through) become an expedient response to a perceived hostile external environment.

The perceived reluctance by managers to engage in long-term strategic planning can also be explained in terms of the helplessness managers experience in the face of seemingly insurmountable obstacles. This is evident, for example, in the problem of 'government interference' in the day-to-day running of organizations. This applies mainly to 'parastatals' but also to foreign-owned ventures in which the state has a substantial interest. The most visible form of interference is in the appointment of politically connected senior executives. Retiring politicians and civil servants who have no business experience have in the past been appointed to head major organizations. In such situations political patronage tends to overshadow economic considerations in decision-making. Rather than engaging in long-term strategic planning, managers might thus find themselves acting on 'orders from above'; such orders may heavily depend on the fortunes of political elites, thus further heightening the instability.

This approach to 'planning' can also be explained from a historical context. Kenyan industry has for many decades enjoyed a high degree of protection. The post-independence policy of import-substitution which was aimed at fostering a sound manufacturing industry merely led to a protected and very inefficient local industry (Langdon, 1987), especially in the form of bureaucratic parastatals which served political rather than economic ends. Industrialists and managers who were guaranteed high prices in a market in which imports faced stiff tariffs perhaps saw little need to plan ahead. The multinational practice of treating subsidiary firms merely as a conduit for strategy implementation rather than strategy formulation has also contributed to the low level of strategic management. Against this backdrop, human resource planning and, by implication, strategic human resource management have not fully taken root.

Applying the logic of the 'matching model' of strategic HRM which argues that human resource strategies should flow from business strategies (e.g. Fombrun *et al.*, 1984), we argue that the short-termism underpinning *ad hoc* strategic planning has fostered an *ad hoc* approach to human resource planning. In the section below we examine how recent developments in strategic management might contribute to the formulation of a human resource management approach which is more appropriate for the Kenyan situation.

Towards a processual approach

The dominant perspective to SHRM has drawn on the industrial organization (IO) model of strategic management as popularized, for example, by Michael Porter (e.g. 1985). In brief, this approach holds that added value is generated in the way firms position themselves and their actions in the external competitive environment.

In its most rudimentary form, the IO perspective proposes that the utilization of resources should be aligned to some specific recipe strategy. This argument provided the cue for the development of SHRM, in particular the 'matching model'. This model was first clearly articulated by Fombrun *et al.* (1984) who, in their seminal book sought to demonstrate how HR practices flow from and are aligned to business strategies. This approach has been widely used in SHRM research, with the work of Schuler and Jackson (e.g. 1987) playing a notable role.

A key weakness of the matching approaches is that we may not know what strategies to adopt since strategies do not necessarily exist out there waiting to be picked or discovered. Various authors such as Mintzberg (e.g. 1985) and Quinn (1980) have also cast doubt on the assumption that strategy formulation is a rationalistic and logical exercise. Instead they demonstrate that the strategy formulation exercise also proceeds on an incremental and piecemeal basis, with strategies 'emerging' in an unplanned fashion. This line of reasoning has important implications for managing in developing countries particularly in turbulent times when standard recipes for problem-solving and strategy formulation are clearly inadequate. Dissatisfaction with the orthodox conceptions of strategy has engendered a search for alternatives.

The resource-based view of the firm (RBV) has emerged to fill the gap created by the IO perspective. Though the intellectual foundations were laid back in the 1950s by Edith Penrose (1959), thirty years elapsed before this concept began to receive critical analysis. From Wernerfelt's (1984) seminal piece, there has been a stream of contributions within strategic management (e.g. Barney 1991; Grant 1991). Penrose argued that firms can be thought of as a 'bundle of resources', or 'potential services' and that differential configuration of internally held resources confers uniqueness on each firm. Within the SHRM debate, this approach has received only limited theoretical development (e.g. Boxall 1998; Kamoche 1996; Mueller 1996; Wright *et al.*, 1994) and hardly any empirical testing (with the possible exception of Boxall and Steeneveld, 1999 and Wright *et al.*, 1995).

Within the Kenyan context, Kamoche (1997) illustrates how the RBV can be applied to an understanding of the role of human resources in strategic management. More specifically, this study argues for a resource-capability approach which is evolutionary rather than static. Such an approach brings together both the individual resources (skills, abilities, etc.) and the organizational capabilities for managing them (e.g. HR practices). We depict the role of this analytical perspective in Figure 13.1. In an organization referred to as Mimea, management were found to have struck a balance between the internal and external environment with particular regard to the importance they attached to the knowledge attributable to organizational members. This firm has been successful in cultivating the strategic value of its employees through a combination of training initiatives and a comprehensive array of welfare benefits.

Management at Mimea have provided mechanisms that facilitate teamwork along a traditional African group ethos which combines the concern for productivity with a social agenda. They also maintain a systematic management development programme which identifies high-potential graduate trainees and subsequently places them on an intensive career development track in the belief that they are the future shapers of the organization's fortunes. Thus, while taking account of the external competitive environment in a highly volatile agricultural sector, management are evidently focusing on the internal environment as a source of competitive advantage. The approach taken in this particular organization is noteworthy for its uniqueness. The extent to which they treat the internally held stock of expertise as a source of competitive advantage is unusual in an economy in which the vast majority of firms are still wedded to the external environment paradigm. The possibility exists, therefore, for managers in Kenya to pay more attention to the unique circumstances that exist within their firms in the way they design and implement HRM practices.

This calls for a radical shift in thinking, especially regarding the role of people in organizational performance, and how managers can best achieve a balance between satisfying corporate objectives and meeting the personal and developmental needs of their employees. The processual approach proposed here (as illustrated in Figure 13.1) thus begins by considering the effects of both the internal and external environments. While recognizing the value of the emergent approaches to strategic planning, e.g. 'muddling through', and 'management by deciding', it proposes a shift towards an evolutionary resource-capability approach. It also suggests that HR policies should be underpinned by an appropriate ethos which is embedded within the socio-cultural context of managing. This processual approach thus gives managers a more appropriate rationale for strategy formulation and implementation in HRM and paves the way for formulation of sound practices which meet the specific needs of people and organizations in Kenya, and indeed, Sub-Saharan Africa.

Conclusions

The Kenyan organizational context evidently calls for a rethink in the approaches currently being applied to the management of people as well as in the existing institutional arrangements within which organizations operate. The adoption of Western management practices, for example, needs to be assessed *vis-à-vis* the organizational realities discussed above and in particular against the circumstances of those upon whom the practices are applied. Scholars in comparative and international management now recognize that the earlier supposed universality of management thought and practice is untenable. This calls for managers and scholars alike to design approaches that are both appropriate and effective, and which are flexible enough to respond to the changing social, political, technological and competitive environments. We argue further that it is not sufficient to focus exclusively on *practices*.

As our discussion on the RBV has indicated, the resources that exist within the firm constitute a potential source of competitive advantage due to the uniqueness of each firm. Thus, while firms may share similarities in terms of size, managerial and financial endowment, and so forth, they differ fundamentally in the quality and configuration of resources. Unutilized or underutilized resources, according to Penrose (1959) constitute an opportunity for 'growth'. This is particularly relevant to human resource management where a potentially vast stock of knowledge, skills and abilities (KSAs) exists, and which the organization may not be putting to optimal use currently. The scope for better and more effective utilization of existing KSAs clearly exists in many organizations in Kenya where the fear of penalty for failure might be preventing employees from exercising their full initiative.

Previously, there was a widespread belief that a clear divide existed between managers whose responsibility was to think and plan, and workers who were merely expected to implement managerial initiatives. However, a heightened awareness of the own abilities, better educational opportunities and an increasingly competitive career advancement culture have given individuals more scope to realize their potential. This opens up the opportunity for managers to re-examine the extent to which existing HR practices in the areas of recruitment/selection, training and career development are facilitating the realization of this employee potential. It is in this regard that the RBV emerges as a robust analytical paradigm. From this perspective, managers have to start refocusing their attention both on the resources and the practices with which to *drive* them, and re-evaluate their current preoccupation with the external environmental context.

References

Barney, J. B. (1991) 'Firm Resources and Sustained Competitive Advantage', *Journal of Management*, 17: 99–120.

Blunt, P. (1980) 'Bureaucracy and ethnicity in Kenya: Some Conjectures for the Eighties', *Journal of Applied Behavioural Science*, 16: 336–353.

Blunt, P. (1983) *Organizational Theory and Behaviour: An African Perspective*, London: Longman.

Blunt, P. and Jones, M. L. (1992) *Managing Organizations in Africa*, Berlin: Walter de Gruyter.

Blunt, P. and Popoola, O. (1985) *Personnel Management in Africa*, London: Longman.

Boxall, P. (1998) 'Achieving Competitive Advantage through Human Resource Strategy: Towards a Theory of Industry Dynamics', *Human Resource Management Review*, 8: 265–288.

Boxall, P. and Steeneveld, M. (1999) 'Human Resource Strategy and Competitive Advantage: A Longitudinal Study of Engineering Consultancies', *Journal of Management Studies*, 39: 443–463.

Chege, P. M. (1988) 'The State and Labour: Industrial Relations in Independent Kenya', in P. Coughlin and G. K. Ikiara (eds) *Industrialization in Kenya*, Nairobi: Heinemann, and London: James Currey.

Fombrun, C., Tichy, N. M. and Devanna, M. A. (eds) (1984) *Strategic Human Resource Management*, New York: Wiley.

Grant, R. M. (1991) 'The Resource-based Theory of Competitive Advantage: Implications for Strategy Formulation', *California Management Review*, 33: 114–135.

Kamoche, K. (1992) 'Human Resource Management: An assessment of the Kenyan Case', *International Journal of Human Resource Management*, 3: 497–521.

Kamoche, K. (1993) 'Toward a Model of HRM in Africa', in J. B. Shaw, P. S. Kirkbride, K. M. Rowland and G. R. Ferris (eds) *Research in Personnel and Human Resource Management*, Suppl. 3, Greenwich, CT: JAI Press.

Kamoche, K. (1995) 'Rhetoric, Ritualism and Totemism in HRM', *Human Relations*, 48: 367–385.

Kamoche, K. (1996) 'Strategic Human Resource Management within a Resource-Capability View of the Firm', *Journal of Management Studies*, 33: 213–233.

Kamoche, K. (1997) 'Managing Human Resources in Africa: Strategic, Organizational and Epistemological Issues', *International Business Review*, 6: 537–558.

Kamoche, K. (2000) *Sociological Paradigms and Human Resources: An African Context*, Aldershot: Ashgate.

Kiggundu, M. N. (1989) *Managing Organizations in Developing Countries*, West Hartford, CT: Kumarian Press.

Langdon, S. (1974) 'The Political Economy of Dependence: Note Toward the Analysis of Multinational Companies in Kenya', *Journal of Eastern African Research and Development*, 4: 123–159.

Langdon, S. (1987) 'Industry and Capitalism in Kenya: Contribution to the Debate', in P. M. Lubeck (ed.) *The African Bourgeoisie: Capitalist Development in Nigeria, Kenya and the Ivory East*, Boulder, CO: Lynne Reiner.

Leys, C. (1975) *Underdevelopment in Kenya: The Political Economy of Neo-colonialism, 1964–1971*, London: Heinemann.

Mintzberg, H. (1985) 'Of Strategies, Deliberate and Emergent', *Strategic Management Journal*, 6: 257–272.

Mueller, F. (1996) 'Human Resources as Strategic Assets: An Evolutionary Resource-based Theory', *Journal of Management Studies*, 33: 757–786.

Munene, J. C. (1991) 'Organizational Environment in Africa', *Human Relations*, 44: 439–458.

Nzelibe, L. O. (1986) 'The Evolution of African Management Thought', *International Studies of Management and Organization*, 16: 6–16.

Penrose, E. T. (1959) *The Theory of the Growth of the Firm*, Oxford: Blackwell.

Porter, M. (1985) *Competitive Advantage: Creating and Sustaining Superior Performance*, New York: Free Press.

Quinn, J. B. (1980) *Strategies for Change: Logical Incrementalism*, Homewood, IL: R.D. Irwin.

Schuler, R. S. and S. E. Jackson (1987) 'Linking Competitive Strategies with Human Resource Practices', *Academy of Management Executive*, 1: 207–219.

Singh, M. (1969) *History of Kenya's Trade Union Movement to 1952*, Nairobi: East African Publishing House.

Swainson, N. (1980) *The Development of Corporate Capitalism in Kenya, 1918–1977*, London: Heinemann.

Wernerfelt, B. (1984) 'A Resource-based View of the Firm', *Strategic Management Journal*, 5: 171–180.

Wright, P. M., McMahan, G. C. and McWilliams, A. (1994) 'Human Resources and Sustained Competitive Advantage: A Resource-based Perspective', *Journal of Human Resource Management*, 5, 301–326.

Wright, P. M., Smart, D. L. and McMahan, G. C. (1995) 'Matches between Human Resources and Strategy among NCAA Basketball Teams', *Academy of Management Journal*, 38: 1052–1074.

14 Human resource management in South Africa

Geoffrey T. Wood and Kamel Mellahi

Introduction

Despite being subject to the same range of pressures commonly associated with globalisation, there remains considerable diversity in the manner in which firms – and countries – manage their human resources. This can be ascribed to variations in accumulation regimes and modes of regulation, themselves products of specific historical experiences (see Grahl and Teague, 2000: 160–178). In this chapter we explore the context within which the South African human resource management (HRM) system operates, and the implications thereof in terms of actual HR managerial practice within the firm.

The South African economic context and HRM

During the apartheid era, the South African economy was characterised by high levels of protectionism, backed up by a range of development incentives geared towards the nurturing of an indigenous industrial sector, with state-owned enterprises dominating key sectors such as steel and transport. A premium was placed on job creation for white workers in the state sector. The desire to heighten racial segregation led to a range of 'decentralisation' incentives, aimed at encouraging firms to relocate to the rural periphery, a policy that proved both costly and unsustainable. The South African economy faced increasing difficulties in the late 1970s and 1980s on account of increasing disinvestment – as a result of increasing political resistance and international pressure – and direct economic sanctions, most notably a fuel embargo. Weeks has noted that, 'From 1980 to the end of 1993, per capita gross domestic product (GDP) rose in only four years, and only in one after 1984, for an annual average decline of almost 1 per cent for the fourteen years' (1999: 796).

The government's continued commitment to the complete political exclusion of Africans resulted not only in continued union militancy at the workplace but also increasing political protests, culminating in the mass insurrection of 1983–7. The latter led to investor flight increasing to unprecedented levels, with a capital outflow of over R8000 million in 1985 alone (CSS, 1996). Unprecedented levels of mass resistance to apartheid both within workplace and township in the 1980s forced unsustainable increases in state expenditure, above all on the security forces, and on separate parallel bureaucratic structures to serve different racial groups. The latter led to unprecedented budgetary deficits, and an inflation rate that approached 20 per cent by 1986 (Harcourt and Wood, 2000). Following the failure of an overly coercive attempt to introduce an incomes policy, the government began to experiment with neo-liberal alternatives, outlined in a 1987 White Paper on Privatisation and Deregulation. The 1987 White Paper called for a range of macro-economic reforms, which were accelerated following the enforced retirement of the last of South Africa's hard-line apartheid rulers, P.W. Botha, and the accession to power of the more pragmatic F.W. De Klerk. In 1989, the Reserve Bank was made independent of direct government control and encouraged to pursue a tight, anti-inflationary monetary policy (Harcourt and Wood, 2000). The removal of the ban on the ANC (African National Congress) and other political organisations in February 1990, and the start of national negotiations to determine the country's political future led the National Party to increasingly assume a lame duck role. However, in 1993, the National Party re-articulated its new-found commitment to a liberal agenda again in the Key Issues in the Normative Economic Model, so as to help differentiate it from the ANC in the lead-up to the first free election in 1994. This document called for a smaller public sector, less taxation, a switch from direct to indirect taxation, a switch from consumption to investment expenditures within the public sector, and a reduction in state regulation of all kinds (Harcourt and Wood, 2000).

During the years in which the ANC was exiled by the apartheid government, its policies were vaguely leftist, incorporating both Africanist and socialist elements. Following the lifting of the ban, the ANC reiterated its commitment to a mixed economy. The trade union movement played a major role in the formulation of the broadly neo-Keynsian Reconstruction and Development Programme (RDP), which served as a major plank in the ANC's campaign in South Africa's first democratic elections, held in 1994. Since the 1994 elections and its accession to power, the ANC has moved steadily rightward, in response to pressures from the World Bank and the IMF, and the business community. In 1997, the RDP was unceremoniously ditched in favour of the neo-liberal Growth, Employment and Redistribution (GEAR) policy framework. GEAR calls for reduced state involvement in the economy, and a greater reliance on market forces (Saul, 1999: 56). The ANC did not consult its Alliance partners in the formulation of GEAR.

Although years of recession were replaced by a modest growth of 1.3 per cent in 1993, 2.7 per cent in 1994 and 3.3 per cent in 1995, the country's growth has begun to slow again (Weeks, 1999: 802). Unemployment stands at over 35 per cent (Statssa.gov.za). Formal employment contracted 1.1 per cent per year in the early 1990s (Republic of South Africa, 1996: Appendix 13).

The rapid phasing out of tariff barriers and investment incentives has resulted in many South African firms facing an acute crisis of competitiveness. This has caused firms to re-evaluate the manner in which they manage and deploy their human resources; there has been a limited experimenting with more flexible forms of work organisation (Smith and Wood, 1998). Unfortunately, as Human and Horwitz (1992: 147) note, many South African managers often underrate the pressures of globalisation, and have a siege mentality, occupying an entrenched enclave at the top of the organisation, far removed from the realities of the shopfloor.

The political context

The February 1990 speech by the then State President, F.W. De Klerk brought into the open a process of tentative negotiations with the major opposition groupings, that resulted in the ending of apartheid, and South Africa's first democratic elections. South Africa is a quasi-federal system with certain powers devolved to nine provincial governments. Provincial governments are elected by means of a separate ballot, with elections being held simultaneously with those for the national parliament. South Africa has, however, re-emerged as a dominant party country; much latent political competition has been subsumed to within the ruling ANC. Opposition groupings tend to have their support bases confined to ethnic minorities, and/or those on the rural periphery. In South Africa's second democratic election held in 1999, the ANC increased its slice of the vote to 66 per cent, up from 62 per cent in the 1994 'liberation election' (IEC, 1999). At the same time, the votes garnered by the former ruling party, now known as the New National Party, dropped from 20 per cent to a dismal 7 per cent (ibid.). The current official opposition, the liberal Democratic Party received just under 10 per cent of all votes cast in 1999, but has yet to gain a significant following among the African community. Its chances of doing so have been greatly reduced following its successful take-over of the demoralised New National Party.

The ANC is in a formal alliance with the South African Communist Party and the country's largest union federation, the Congress of South African Trade Unions (COSATU). Both became increasingly outspoken in denouncing the ANC's gradual shift rightwards. Matters came to a head at the Communist Party's 1998 Congress, where then President Mandela bluntly informed delegates that members of the Tripartite Alliance who were unhappy with the ANC's recent policy directions should refrain from public sniping, or leave the Alliance (*Mail and Guardian*, 3 July 1998). This seems to have rather taken the wind out of the sails of those who were hoping to float an independent socialist agenda while still within the safe harbour of the Tripartite Alliance. Both the SACP's and COSATU's opposition to GEAR has become much more muted, and the leaders of both organisations took great pains to reiterate their support for the ANC-headed Alliance in the 1999 elections. The ANC's commitment to the new right agenda is unlikely to be shaken in the near future. While individual firms have benefited from reduced state intervention – and, above all, greater political stability – it has also meant that they will have to achieve higher levels of global competitiveness if they are to survive.

National culture and HRM

As indicated earlier, managerial positions in South Africa are filled by predominantly white managers (see Table 14.1). Templer *et al.* (1992) argued that the South African track record of advancing blacks into skilled and managerial positions is not very good. SPA Consultant's (1992) study of twenty-three firms in South Africa revealed that blacks occupied less than 5 per cent of managerial posts. Given the historical context and the legacy of apartheid, unions in South Africa regard white-run firms as less credible and trustworthy (Block, 1997). McFarlin and Coster (1999) argued that 'cultural and contextual differences between white managers and black employees contribute to large perception gaps with respect to how employees should be led, motivated, and nurtured'. As a result, managers do not fully understand, or perhaps ignore, black workers' work ethics and values in order to develop congruent HRM policies (Harari and Beaty, 1989). Instead, they apply Western management styles that are incongruent with black workers' values and attitudes (Khoza, 1994). Laburn (1994) noted that management practices in South Africa still reflect Western European colonial power dominated by Western management values such as rationalism, individualism, and autocracy which are incongruent with the co-operative values and communal philosophy of African workers.

Table 14.1 Occupation levels by race in South Africa (percentage)

	White	Black	Coloured	Asian
Management and professional	92.7	3	2	2.3
Skilled and supervisory	77.64	10.74	6.94	4.68
Apprentices and trainee technicians	60.94	30.91	5.82	2.33

Source: Breakwater Monitor, March 1995 report (quoted in Horwitz *et al.*, 1996)

Changes in the South African labour market

The productive system which was operational in South Africa until the 1980s has commonly been referred to as 'racial Fordism' (Joffe *et al.*, 1993: 5; Webster 1987: 217). The 'racial Fordism' system can be defined as the dominance of Fordist methods of production within the industrial and mining sectors, a heavily protected domestic market, combined with a racial division of labour that largely confined the African majority to the lowest job bands. Until the 1980s, statutory colour bars and racially specific industrial relations legislation codified the system. Industrial relations legislation centred on the 1924 Industrial Conciliation Act and Industrial Conciliation Act 1956. These two Acts brought into being centralised industry-wide bargaining forums, the Industrial Councils, which had the power to set wages and working conditions across an entire industry (SALB, 1977: 1–3). Workers could only resort to legal strike action once a complex procedure had been exhausted. However, Africans were not legally defined as 'employees', and, hence, were excluded from participating in the system. The complex and centralised nature of the system, and the relatively privileged position of non-African trade unions led to such unions tending to rely on a few key officials and becoming over-bureaucratised in the process, with shopfloor organisation atrophying.

A number of legislative changes took place during the years 1924–79, most notably, a series of amendments to the Industrial Conciliation Act and the introduction of the Native Labour (Settlement of Disputes) Act. These acts were primarily aimed at shoring up a dualistic labour market, divided between a privileged, generally skilled minority, and an African majority without rights.

In 1973, a long period of apparent industrial peace was shattered by a wave of strikes, which took place in the Durban region. This was followed by a revival of trade union activity. Coterminous with this revival was a nation-wide increase in strike action (SAIRR, 1978; SAIRR, 1979; SAIRR, 1980): it was clear that the old balance that had been achieved was no longer sustainable and that the dualistic system was no longer tenable.

In response to this, the state experimented with a range of reforms. The Wiehahn Commission Report led to the promulgation of the 1979 Labour Relations Act, allowing certain categories of African workers to be represented on the Industrial Councils (Wiehahn Commission, 1979: 31–42). A 1981 Amendment brought migrant workers under the Act, but still excluded farm, domestic and public sector workers. Meanwhile, the Riekert Commission report led to incremental labour market reforms that culminated in the scrapping of the Pass Laws in the late 1980s.

Meanwhile, the gradual phasing out of the colour bar resulted in increasing numbers of Africans moving into higher wage brackets: pay was no longer a direct product of colour (Van der Horst, 1984: 9). In turn, this represented a product of the increasing movement of Africans into semi-skilled occupations, and the growing power of the trade union movement (ibid.: 9). Indeed, despite rising unemployment and the shortage of (mostly white) artisans, the wage gap between Africans and whites narrowed. The Labour Relations Amendment Act 1988, made discrimination on grounds of race and gender an unfair labour practice (Horwitz, 1996). However, Horwitz (1992) noted that the removal of legislated discrimination did not mean pervasive removal of racial prejudice and social discrimination in practice.

Following on democratisation, a new Labour Relations Act was promulgated in 1995, representing the outcome of protracted negotiations between the state, unions and employers. In terms of the Act, Industrial Councils were renamed Bargaining Councils. The new legislation covers not just workers in the industrial and commercial sectors, but also farm, domestic and public service workers (excluding members of the security forces[1]). Previously, workers within the latter categories were excluded from the statutory system of collective bargaining. In terms of the 1995 Act, the Industrial Court has been renamed the Labour Court, and its role somewhat circumscribed. Essentially, within this area, the objective of the Act has been to de-legalise the process of dispute resolution, shifting many of its functions to a new statutory mechanism for dispute resolution, the Commission for Conciliation, Mediation and Arbitration, which has the brief of promoting collective bargaining between employer and employee representatives (Benjamin, 1995: 21). The 1995 Act also makes provision for a Labour Appeal Court, a division of the South African Supreme Court, which not only has the power to hear appeals from the Labour Court, but also 'questions of law referred to it by the Labour Court' (*Government Gazette 16861*, 1995).

On the one hand, it has been argued that the 1995 South African Labour Relations Act is amongst the world's most progressive, with its protection of many categories of striking workers, the organisational rights granted to trade unions, and in its promotion of centralised bargaining (Von Holdt, 1995: 18). On the other hand, despite its stated commitment to promoting centralised bargaining, it is evident that the Act is ambivalent in many key areas. It has been officially recognised that some of this ambivalence is intended to overcome structural rigidities that might impede global competitiveness (Appollis, 1995: 48). Much of the system is based on voluntarism, on a presumed interrelationship between business and labour (ibid.). In the end, it is a system that favours the better-organised unions, who meet the Act's criteria for representativeness at individual workplaces. However, no trade union has the power to bring about centralised bargaining in the teeth of employer opposition. It should be noted that it might be extremely difficult to ensure that the Act is adhered to in more conservative regions, in components of the agricultural sector, and by smaller employers in the smaller urban centres (Wood, 2000). Moreover, by designating individual workers as independent contractors, it is possible for firms to opt out of the Act completely, and avoid having to deal with unions at all. Again, heavily unionised employers would probably be extremely reluctant to jeopardise an established relationship with a union for an uncertain future – at the time of writing, the bulk of firms that have chosen the 'independent contractor' route have been smaller employers and those operating from greenfields industrial sites. Given the political clout of the South African labour movement, it is not likely that, for the foreseeable future, the overwhelming strength of organised labour in the mining and manufacturing sectors will be diluted. It is equally unlikely that individual firms operating in these areas will be able to undercut their competitors through the adoption of labour 'unfriendly' policies. In this sense, it is evident that a dualistic labour market has been reconstituted, although no longer on racial lines, a major cleavage being between unionised, increasingly skilled largely urban insiders, and outsiders. The latter (largely unskilled) grouping encompasses sub-contracted workers, those in temporary contracts, and those located in the rural periphery.

Changes in union organisation

During the 1980s, the independent union movement rapidly expanded, the bulk uniting in a 'super-federation' of trade unions, the Congress of South African Trade Unions (COSATU). COSATU assumed a central role in the opposition to the then apartheid government, and formed close ties with (and ultimately entered into an alliance with) the African National Congress. A smaller body of trade unions formed an Africanist-orientated federation, the National Council of Trade Unions

(NACTU). Today, the bulk of South African workers belong to COSATU. Other union groupings include FEDUSA (Federation of Unions of South Africa) mostly representing workers in the upper job bands, and the regionally based United Workers Union of South Africa. COSATU continued to enjoy an expanding membership in the 1990s, in contrast to most other union groupings, who have had to contend with a gradual decline.

Changes in work organisation

Political and economic reforms represented a product of sustained crises in the existing accumulation regime and mode of regulation (see Grahl and Teague, 2000). As Klerck (2000) citing Joffe *et al.* (1993) notes:

> For both management and workers, so the argument goes, the only way to survive in the new competitive climate is to forge 'social partnerships' on the shopfloor and in society as a whole. The substance of these co-operative relationships form part of an 'intelligent production strategy' in which team-work, flexibility, the abandonment of narrow skills and job demarcations, and a co-operative approach between unions and employers will lead to greater competitiveness.

In other words, the current crisis of competitiveness has certainly caused firms to be more aware of the need to experiment with more flexible techniques of work organisation, even if, in practice this has not always amounted to much (see Smith and Wood, 1998: 479–495). South African firms have had to contend with the challenge of moving beyond comfortable practices of the past engendered by closed markets and an overly interventionist state (Human and Horwitz, 1992: 145), leading to a minority of more progressive firms being willing to explore a range of new HR managerial strategies.

Contemporary HR managerial work in South Africa

Reflecting the new environment, many South African firms have been quick to rename their personnel or industrial relations sections as Human Resource Management Departments. Recent research reveals that what South African HRM managers actually do varies considerably from firm to firm (see Wood and Els, 2000).[2] Commonly, the increased espousal of the 'New HRM' represents part-and-parcel of a shift towards more flexible methods of production. However, it has also provided the ideological basis for progressive reforms, which, in many cases, amount to little more than the adoption of accepted industrial relations practices, replacing earlier attempts at union busting. The latter would include the nurturing of relations between management and employee collectives, collective bargaining-based employment contracts, and temporary truces interspersing disputes over wages, working conditions, and related matters (ibid.).

More broadly speaking, the exigencies of macro-economic adjustment have forced many firms to rethink their managerial strategies, and, in some cases, move away from authoritarian, conservative and rigid practices. However, there is little doubt that in many South African firms, HR departments remain isolated, with staffing issues continuing to be neglected. In these cases, HRM managers commonly perform little more than the traditional personnel administration function, and, in some cases are not accorded managerial status at all (Wood and Els, 2000: 116). Indeed, 'people management' continued to be held in no little contempt among the more conservative employers, with workers being seen more as a problem than a potential asset. Horwitz noted that 'South African companies continue to disinvest in human capital' (1994: 137). Grobler argued that 'although South Africa shows great potential in some areas, it is held back by major deficiencies in the people and management categories. In fact, South Africa's attempts to create the human capital needed for growth are nothing short of disastrous' (1996: 22). McFarlin and Coster noted that South African organisations spend between 0.5 and 1.5 per cent of the payroll on training compared with 5 per cent in Europe and the USA and 8 per cent in Japan (1999: 63).

It is not surprising therefore that within such firms, HR practitioners tend to be isolated, both in formal organisational terms, and with regard to informal power networks. There have been a number of recent changes in labour relations legislation, most notably the promulgation of the Employment Equity Act, which gives central government the power to force firms to adopt a coherent long-term affirmative programme. In the light of this, there is little doubt that these firms may be forced to reappraise their policies for managing their staff, sooner rather than later (Wood and Els, 2000).

In more conservative South African firms, senior managers remain firmly wedded to an autocratic tradition, and are consistently reluctant to share power with more junior sections of management, even if it would enhance their overall viability and competitiveness in the medium and long terms. Although much of HR is partially about creating the potential for 'exploiting the labour resources more fully' (Storey, 1989: 9), firms in this category were reluctant to experiment with new ideas if it entailed any change in existing power relations (Wood and Els, 2000: 117).

In more progressive firms, the central importance of human resources is acknowledged in business plans and corporate statements of strategy. In these cases, the HR function is seen as a 'credible' and legitimate one, with HR practitioners being seen as equals with other categories of managers. However, in many cases, the tasks performed by HR departments are close to those performed by industrial relations departments. As management was gradually forced to adopt more 'modern' employment policies – including trade union recognition – policy shifts were framed in pop-HRM rhetoric (ibid.: 118). However, the latter's research revealed that a number of larger employers have begun to experiment with new forms of strategic HRM. Here, HR managers perform a broad range of tasks, including strategic decision-making impacting on areas not directly related to the deployment of employees. Line management is seen as playing a role in developing individual employees' skills profiles, with the HR department ostensibly providing the strategic vision and necessary support. However, Wood and Els found that in some cases, sections of line management continued to be suspicious of the intentions of the HR department, and make little secret of their preference for a simpler, more conservative era. Moreover, the extent to which the flow of support and ideas from HR departments was simply a one-way traffic to be adopted or rejected by other areas of management was unclear.

It is evident that to many South African firms, the adoption of 'new style' HRM represents not just a potential way of administering a firm's employees, but also an ideology, by which management might demonstrate its progressive credentials.

Lakhani (1997) argues that management have taken HRM terms and distorted it to what they wish to mean. Considerable lip service is often paid to 'people being our most important asset', with closer examination revealing little new in the manner in which a firm approaches both its human resources and its HRM department.

The peripheral position of HR departments within the firm, however, is not simply a product of conservatism on the behalf of general management. There is evidence to suggest that HR departments themselves were often unsure as to what they should be doing. According to one South African practitioner, HR differs from general management:

> Some respond [to not being taken seriously] by wrapping their work in business jargon – we start talking of inputs and outputs, cost-benefit analyses and bottom-line impact training. This is doomed to failure – simply because the language we call 'business' is more the language of other professions – mainly accounting, but also engineering and marketing. And these languages are about things – figures and widgets and products. Our language is about people – it is about feelings and fuzzes and trust and other such 'soft' stuff.
>
> (Lakhani 1997: 11)

This definition differs radically from the accepted meaning of the concept, which is considerably 'harder' and places considerable emphasis on the use of a particular resource in a 'calculative and formally rational manner' (Storey and Sisson, 1993: 17). By emphasising the 'soft' side of their activities, HR practitioners within the firms encompassed by this study both contribute to reinforcing a distinct identity – which may, of course, have definite benefits in the formal, organogram sense – and their own marginalisation.

Thus, despite the fact that HRM is seen as being founded on an integrated vision for managing people (see Dessler, 1994), HRM departments remain distinct entities, in most cases somewhat removed from general and line management. Indeed, in several cases, their work largely remains at the level of corporate philanthropy. This does not mean that the activities of HR practitioners are totally meaningless. In an atmosphere of low trust, high levels of absenteeism may well constitute a form of industrial protest, highlighting a need to review labour relations policies (see Cohen, 1994: 135). However, the latter would be a far cry from activities concerning the strategic deployment of a key resource (see Storey and Sisson, 1993: 17). While of some relevance, what was ostensibly defined as HR work thus remained peripheral, and within a highly traditionalist framework.

In the case of several South African firms which until relatively late employed 'bloody Fordist' methods, HR has provided an ideology to underpin progressive reforms, most of which in practice amount to little more than accepted industrial relations-based practice (Wood and Els, 2000). The latter would include the nurturing of relations between management and employee collectives, collective bargaining-based employment contracts, and temporary truces interspersing disputes over wages, working conditions, and related matters.

Many South African firms have had to directly face the problems associated with greatly increased competition following the phasing out of protectionism, and the ending of state subsidies. This, in turn, has forced firms to rethink their managerial strategies, and, in some cases, move away from authoritarian, conservative and rigid practices. However, others seemed to have done little in this area – the ongoing marginalization of HR departments did not, in these instances, result in management usurping key HR functions in pursuit of an integrated vision, but rather in staffing issues continuing to be neglected, other than in a minimalist and trouble-shooting fashion (ibid.).

Significant proportions of South African firms do not even define HR practitioners as managers at all, but simply 'officers'. Such individuals were excluded from any real decision-making, and had little contact with senior management. In contrast, amongst more 'modern' firms, HR departments have far closer contact with other sections of management, even in areas that had little direct bearing on traditional HR activities. This would seem fairly close to the integrated 'maximalist' definition of HRM. However, even in these cases, it seemed that the flow of ideas from such departments remains strictly one way, offered to central and line management on an accept or reject basis (ibid.). In the end, much day-to-day people management remained in the hands of often-conservative junior sections of line management. Again, this is not necessarily undesirable, given the fact that HR accords a key role to those directly involved with the process of production (see Storey and Sisson, 1993: 16). However, it should be noted that in the Eastern Cape, while formal job reservation was abolished many years ago, junior supervisory functions in many firms remain white-dominated, with, as noted earlier, persistent racial tensions mitigating against holistic, formally rational approaches to the management of individuals at all levels of the firm.

It did not seem that there is a particular pattern of practice associated with large *vis-à-vis* smaller firms. Several relatively large firms with national profiles seem wedded to extremely conservative policies, while others, irrespective of size, appear more willing to experiment with new ideas (Wood and Els, 2000). However, multinational firms seemed to be the most innovative. In part, this seemed to reflect a desire to bolster a progressive image, largely because their presence in the country during the late apartheid era had attracted considerable adverse publicity. Nonetheless, this would also, of course, reflect the firms' international linkages.

HR practice represents a departure from the joint procedure formula, binding together management and unions (see Hyman, 1989: 243). This has led writers such as Guest (quoted in Storey and Sisson, 1993: 18) to suggest that HRM and trade unionism are essentially incompatible. However, in the South African case, employers are legally prohibited from actively seeking to dispense with unions, necessitating some sort of balance to be struck between individualistic employment practices, and traditional collectivist industrial relations principles. This sort of balance clearly continued to elude the firms in the third category, who made free use of HR rhetoric while building relations with the union on conventional IR lines, but is by no means unachievable. For example, it can be argued that it may facilitate greater shopfloor creativity within the 'framework of pluralist management-union jointism' (Ackers *et al.*, 1996: 24). However, the role unions may play in key HR areas such as planning and resourcing has been widely neglected in the literature (Storey and Sisson 1993: 128), and seemed equally neglected in practice. The unusual strength of the South African labour movement has, it seems, necessitated the modification of the HR model, often on an *ad hoc* basis, and based on previous practice. Many South African firms have sought to build on the stability afforded by an existing relationship with a trade union, which had resulted in a body of mutually acceptable practice (Hyman, 1975), gradually updated to meet the cold climate of the late 1990s. In this context, HRM represented not the product of managerial triumphalism over a labour movement in disarray, but rather a possible mechanism for enhancing competitiveness, which, itself, had to be tempered by prevailing realities.

All this highlights somewhat broader issues. Certainly, HR practice in South Africa remains flawed and incomplete in terms of established definitions thereof (see Beach, 1995; Carell *et al.*, 1995; Dessler, 1994). However, it is perhaps too simplistic to ascribe the limited – and traditionalist – range of tasks performed by HR practitioners in South Africa simply to parochialism, or to the presence of effective and militant trade unions. Rather, it highlights a broader issue – while in the West, HRM is associated with the rolling back of trade unions, the South African situation represents a complex package of concepts and practices, which inevitably are subject to adjustment in the light of prevailing realities (see Storey, 1989; Ackers *et al.*, 1996).

The challenges of managing human resources in South Africa in the 2000s

Flexibility and trust

As Boyer (2000: 113) notes, the crisis of Fordist productive methods has forced many countries to experiment with alternative growth regimes. In South Africa, a racial variant of Fordism has gradually been superseded by the increasing adoption of neo-Fordist and/or more flexible methods of production (see Klerck, 2000). This has taken place within a context of democratisation, and the implementation of neo-liberal macro-economic policies. However, the core institutions of a successful equity-based economy such as the United States cannot be easily replicated by labour market deregulation, the phasing out of protective tariffs and cutbacks in public spending (Boyer 2000: 113–14). While South Africa recorded modest economic growth in the late 1990s, the costs of deregulation included ongoing job cutbacks, particularly within core areas of the manufacturing sector.

Moreover, South African employment relations continue to be bedevilled by a climate of low trust, a result of four decades of apartheid. There is little doubt that many employers greatly value the stability accorded to the current labour relations legislation. As Webster (1998: 6) notes, the persistence of racist practices within and outside the workplace in the 1980s led to the emergence of 'militant abstentionism, a refusal to identify with any of the goals of the enterprise, or the concerns of management. This culture of resistance merged with the insurrectionary political climate of the time creating conditions of ungovernability at the workplace.' This deeply rooted ethos of non-collaboration persists in high levels of absenteeism and of strike action, and a general unwillingness to make life too easy for management or their representatives (Harcourt and Wood, 2000). Moreover, workplace protests are not always peaceful. For example, during the annual wage negotiations in 1998, employees of the electricity supply network, ESKOM, ransacked the parastatal's headquarters, with one group of employee protesters even engaging in a gun battle with police (*Southern Africa Report* 31 July 1998). However, the ESKOM outburst – as was the case with the (also violent) Volkswagen dispute of early 2000 – was at odds with formal union policy. The unions continue to represent a stabilising influence in many South African workplaces. As a result, many larger South African employers remain committed to a long-term partnership with them. Whilst significant numbers of South African employers have made little secret of their preference for radical labour market deregulation, many still prefer the current legislative framework, which enjoys a high degree of legitimacy (Webster, 1999: 8). This is particularly so given that earlier attempts to trim back the powers of the unions, in the form of the 1987 Labour Relations Act Amendments, triggered widespread social protests (see Baskin, 1991).

Affirmative action

The above-mentioned Employment Equity Act has placed new pressures on firms to be seen to be taking affirmative action seriously. Currently, in the private sector, managerial positions remain dominated by whites and blue-collar jobs by blacks. While overt racism has been outlawed, there is little doubt that, in practice, racist practices persist in many firms, particularly among smaller employers, especially those located on the rural periphery. This is particularly likely to be pronounced when white workers occupying junior supervisory positions fear that their position may be threatened by future affirmative action legislation, especially in a climate of heightened job insecurity. Unfortunately, the sub-cultures of racism and non-collaboration can be mutually reinforcing. There is little doubt that HR managers will have to take a more pro-active role in stamping out workplace racism in the future, a stance that has already been pioneered by some of South Africa's larger employers.

HRD in South Africa

The challenges facing HR managers include the promotion of more co-operatist employment relations, and greater productivity. In turn, the latter has to be engendered through an increased emphasis on human resource development; the latter need made increasingly pressing by the crisis within official training institutions. In facilitating the development of a country's human resources, the establishment of a coherent qualifications framework by the state – such as the National Qualifications Framework (NQF) in South Africa – can play a major role in skills development. Essentially, the Australian-inspired NQF, established in terms of the 1995 South African Qualifications Act, seeks to recognise prior learning – whether formal or not – and allow transferability between training institutions operating at similar levels. Theoretically speaking, it would be possible for an individual with high levels of practical experience and/or on the job training to transfer to a tertiary educational institution even if s/he failed to meet the normal entrance criteria (as long as her/his earlier training and experience is verified by the South African Qualifications Authority (SAQA)). However, in practice, the philosophy underlying the NQF has run into stiff opposition from many training institutions, and it is unlikely if it will ever be fully implemented.

The 1995 Act has been supplemented by the 1998 Skills Development Act. This encourages firms to take training more seriously (*inter alia*, through the operation of a levy system) and employees to obtain recognised occupational qualifications. However, like much of South African labour legislation, the 1998 Act is primarily aimed at larger employers, with, in practice, smaller businesses falling outside the net.

However, there is little doubt that, as Kochan and Osterman (1994: 42) note, the changing global environment has led to certain contradictory pressures. On the one hand, there is a need to downsize, to encourage innovation through the flattening of the management hierarchy, and to make increasing use of temporary and/or sub-contracted labour. On the other hand, there is a need to increase employee commitment, to encourage teamwork and other more flexible workplace practices, that, in turn require a multi-skilled workforce.

Conclusion

Of all the resources a firm has at its disposal, the human ones are intrinsically the most flexible. They are also less subject to the vagaries of globalisation, than, say technology and the market. Productivity is, above all, about people. And, yet, the human dimension to productivity is, perhaps, the least understood. South African firms have a history of not taking the management of human resources very seriously. Most South African firms – above all, the smaller ones – do not have a dedicated human resources specialist at all. Historically speaking, the emergence of the predominantly African independent trade unions in the 1970s and early 1980s forced many medium and larger-sized enterprises to develop strategies to accommodate greatly changed industrial relations realities. In essence, this entailed the abandonment of, what were in many cases, neo-Victorian employment relations practices and their replacement with accepted pluralist approaches, classically described by Alan Flanders as sharing power with the unions in order to regain it. Although they may have been quick to take the new human resources management rhetoric of the 1990s on board, it is extremely doubtful if the same energy is being focused on evolving new strategies to unlock the human side of productivity, especially among those enterprises that only recently have come to grips with the realities of dealing with unions.

Notes

1 However, members of the security forces are not precluded from joining trade unions. Trade unions are rapidly expanding within the police service, and a trade union has recently emerged in the National Defense Force. It is intended that further labour legislation will be introduced to cover members of the security forces.

2 Most of the points made in this section are outlined in further detail in Wood and Els (2000). Although the findings were based on interviews with managers in Eastern Cape firms, there is little doubt that they have broader nation-wide relevance (see Hofmeyr *et al.*, 1995: 108–114).

References

Ackers, P. *et al.* (1996) 'British Trade Unions in the New Workplace', in P. Ackers, C. Smith and P. Smith (eds) *The New Workplace and Trade Unionism*, London: Routledge.

Appollis, J. (1995) 'The New Labour Relations Bill', *South African Labour Bulletin*, 19 (2), 47–48.

Baskin, J. (1991) *Striking Back: A History of COSATU*, Johannesburg: Ravan.

Beach, D. (1995) *Personnel: The Management of People at Work*, New York: Macmillan.

Benjamin, P. (1995) 'The New Labour Relations Bill', *South African Labour Bulletin*, 19 (1), 15–22.

Boyer, R. (2000) 'Is a Finance Led Growth Regime a Viable Alternative to Fordism?', *Economy and society*, 29 (1), 111–145.

Carrell, M. *et al.* (1995) *Human Resource Management: Global Strategies for Managing a Diverse Workforce*, Englewood Cliffs, NJ: Prentice-Hall.

Central Statistics Services (1996) *RSA Statistics in Brief*, Pretoria.

Cohen, R. (1994) 'Resistance and Hidden Forms of Consciousness amongst African Workers', in E. Webster *et al.* (eds) *Work and Industrialisation in South Africa*, Johannesburg: Ravan.

Dessler, G. (1994) *Human Resource Management*, Englewood Cliffs, NJ: Prentice-Hall.

Government Gazette 16861 (1995) Pretoria: Government Printer.

Grahl, J. and Teague, P. (2000) 'The Regulation School, the Employment Relationship and Financialization', *Economy and Society*, 29 (1), 160–178.

Grobler, A.P. (1996) 'In Search of Excellence: Leadership Challenges Facing Companies in the New South Africa', *SAM Advanced Management Journal*, Spring, 22–41.

Harari, O. and Beaty, D. (1989) *Lessons from South Africa: A New Perspective on Public Policy and Productivity*, New York: Harper and Row.

Harcourt, M. and Wood, G. (2000) 'Is there a Future for a Labour Accord in South Africa', paper presented at the Annual Conference of the International Industrial Relations Association, Tokyo, Japan.

Hirschohn, P. (1998) 'From Grassroots Democracy to National Mobilization: COSATU as a Model of Social Movement Unionism', *Economic and Industrial Democracy*, 19 (4), 633–666.

Hofmeyr, K. *et al.* (1995) 'The Future Challenges Facing South African Human Resources Management', *South African Journal of Business Management*, 26 (3), 108–114.

Horwitz, M.F. Falconer, B. A and Searll, P. (1996) 'Human Resource Development and Management Diversity in South Africa', *International Journal of Manpower*, 17, (4/5), 134–151.

Horwitz, M.F. and Franklin, E. (1996) 'Labour Market Flexibility in South Africa: Researching Recent Developments', *South African Journal of Labour Relations*, 20 (1): 3–40.

Human, P. and Horwitz, F. (1992) *On the Edge: How South African Business Organisations Cope with Change*, Cape Town: Juta.

Hyman, R. (1975) *Industrial Relations: A Marxist Introduction*, London: Macmillan.

Hyman, R. (1989) *The Political Economy of Industrial Relations*, London: Macmillan.

Independent Electoral Commission (1999) *Election Results*, Pretoria.

Joffe, A., Maller, J. and Webster, E. (1993) 'South Africa's Industrialisation: The Challenge Facing Labour', paper presented at History Workshop/SWOP Symposium, University of Witwatersrand, Johannesburg.

Jouvelis, P. (1983). 'Assessing the Registration Debate', *Work in Progress*, 25: 53–56.

Klerck, G. (2000) 'From Racial Fordism to . . . ?: Industrialization and the Social Regulation of Capitalism in South Africa', in J. K. Coetzee, J. Graaff, F. Hendricks and G. Wood, (eds) *Development for the New Millennium*, Oxford/Cape Town: Oxford University Press.

Khoza, R. (1994) 'The Need for an Afrocentric Approach to Management', in P. Christie, R. Lessem and L. Mbigi (eds) *African Management: Knowledge Resources*, Johannesburg, pp. 117–24.

Kochan, T. and Osterman, P. (1994) *The Mutual Gains Enterprise*, Boston: Harvard Business School.

Laburn, P. (1994) 'The Quintessential New South African Organisation', *Human Resource Management*, July, 14–16.

Lakhani, K. (1997) 'This is HR Calling', *People Dynamics*, 9, 11.

Lodge, T. (1978) *Black Politics Since 1945*, Johannesburg: Ravan.

McFarlin, B.D. and Coster, A.E. (1999) 'South African Management Development in the Twenty-First Century: Moving toward an Africanized Model', *Journal of Management Development*, 18 (1), 63–78.

Mail and Guardian (newspaper) Johannesburg.

Republic of South Africa (1996) *Growth, Employment and Distribution*, Pretoria: Government Printer.

Saul, J. (1999). 'Magical Market Realism', *Transformation*, 38: 49–67.

Smith, M. and Wood, G. (1998) 'The End of Apartheid and the Organisation of Work in South Africa's Eastern Cape Province', *Work, Employment and Society*, 12, 3.

South African Labour Bulletin Editors (1977) 'Focusing on the Industrial Council System', *South African Labour Bulletin*, 3 (10), 1–3.

South African Labour Bulletin Editors (1981) 'A Critique of the Act', *South African Labour Bulletin*, 7 (1 and 2), 29–38.

South African Institute of Race Relations (1978–1980) *Race Relations Surveys*, Johannesburg.

Southern Africa Report (newspaper) Toronto.

SPA Consultants (1992) 'Priorities in Human Resources: A Survey in 23 Companies', *The Innes Labour Brief*, 3 (3), 46–58.

statssa.gov.za. Statistics South Africa Website.

Storey, J. (ed.) (1989) *New Perspectives on Human Resource Management*, London: Routledge.

Storey, J. and Sisson, K. (1993) *Managing Human Resources and Industrial Relations*, Buckingham: Open University Press.

Templer, A., Beaty, D. and Hofmerys, K. (1992) 'The Challenge of Management Development in South Africa: So Little Time and So Much to Do', *Journal of Management Development*, 11 (2), 32–41.

Van der Horst, S. (1984) 'The Relationship of Industrial Legislation and Statutory Regulation to Poverty', Carnegie Conference Paper, 133.

Von Holdt, K. (1995) 'The LRA Agreement', *South African Labour Bulletin*, 19 (4), 16–26.

Webster, E. (1984) 'MAWU and the Industrial Council: A Comment', *South African Labour Bulletin*, 8 (5), 14–19.

Webster, E. (1987) 'Introduction to Labour Section', in G. Moss and I. Obery (eds) *SA Review 4*, Johannesburg: SARS/Ravan.

Webster, E. (1998) 'Race, Labour Process and Transition: The Sociology of Work in South Africa', unpublished paper presented at the Annual Conference of the South African Sociological Association, Rand Afrikaans University, Johannesburg, July.

Webster, E. (1999) 'Defusion of the Molotov Cocktail in South African Industrial Relations: The Burdens of the Past and the Challenge of the Future', *Monographs in Organisational Behavior and Industrial Relations*, 25: 19–58.

Weeks, J. (1999) 'Stuck in Low GEAR? Macroeconomic policy in South Africa, (1996–98)', *Cambridge Journal of Economics*, 23: 795–811.

Wiehahn Commission (1979) *Department of Labour and Mines: Report of the Commission of Enquiry into Labour Legislation*, Pretoria: Government Printer.

Wood, G. and Els, C. (2000) 'The Making and Remaking of HRM: The Practice of Managing People in the Eastern Cape Province, South Africa', *International Journal of Human Resource Management*, 11 (1), 112–125.

Wood, G. (2000) 'South African Trade Unions in a Time of Adjustment', *Labour/Le Travail* (forthcoming).

15 Conclusion

International competitive pressures and the challenges for HRM in developing countries

Yaw A. Debrah and Pawan S. Budhwar

Introduction

The exploration of HRM systems in the countries covered in this book leaves us in no doubt about the dominant influence of environmental factors on HRM. Much of the existing literature on HRM and international management has highlighted the extent to which external environmental factors and internal work cultures influence both micro and macro level organisational policies (Jaeger *et al.*, 1995; Kanungo and Jaeger, 1990; Kiggundu, 1986). Predominant emphasis in this area has been on the external environment as an impediment to successful management in developing countries (Kiggundu *et al.*, 1983; Kohn and Austin, 2000). It is suggested that the forces of instability and uncertainty in developing countries' external environment make it an imperative for managers to develop appropriate approaches to managing human resources (Kamoche, 1993). Indeed, the constant changes in the external environment of organisations tend to dictate both the pace and direction of developments in HRM policies and practices at the firm level. Nevertheless, internal factors can equally be important in shaping any firm's HRM policies and practices and hence need serious consideration.

It was with this view in mind that we suggested the adoption of the framework presented in Chapter 1 to analyse HRM practices in a cross-national context (for details, see Budhwar and Sparrow, 2002). The framework asserts that the nature of HRM tends to be 'context-specific' and as such there is considerable diversity in the way 'culture-bound' and 'culture-free' factors impact on, and determine the nature of HRM systems in different countries. Consequently, in an attempt to illuminate our understanding of HRM practices in different countries, it was necessary for each chapter to identify and analyse the main factors and variables that impinge on HRM in that country.

Another objective of the book is to examine the extent to which there are similarities and differences in HRM in different developing countries. But, while it is not possible from the evidence presented in this book to prove or disprove the 'convergence/divergence hypothesis', it is also difficult to argue against the view that there are more similarities than differences in the way national cultures and national institutions influence HRM in different countries.

Hence, in spite of what Khilji (see Chapter 7) calls the 'amalgam of influences' from Western colonial influence to Islamic and traditional cultures on

HRM in the different countries, some of these influences can be co
'cross-national' and have common roots. What emerges from this boo'
three 'models of influences'. These are: (a) religious influences (Islam
Buddhism, and traditional beliefs in spirits, fetishes and gods); (b) traditiun... ..
beliefs (e.g., Confucianism, African traditional practices and institutions, caste in
India, etc.); and (c) Western colonial and modern influences.

The chapters on HRM in Iran, Pakistan, Saudi Arabia and Algeria have, for
instance, clearly shown the influence of Islamic religion on HR management in
these countries. Arguably, of all the factors influencing HRM in these countries,
the Islamic influence is probably the dominant one. Moreover, regardless of the
presence of the unique influencing factors in the various countries, there is some
commonality in the way Islam permeates organisational life in each country.

Similarly, the review of HRM in the Sub-Saharan African countries reveals that
perhaps with the sole exception of South Africa, which essentially exhibits Western
culture in organisations, traditional African culture exerts a strong influence
on HRM. In Ghana, Nigeria, Kenya and elsewhere in Africa, people in organisations still place a lot of emphasis on traditional beliefs such as spirits, witchcraft,
fetishes, and gods (see Gardiner, 1996), traditions and institutions, customs and
socio-cultural issues (Debrah, 2000). In Kiggundu's (1986) view, these traditional
practices tend to have negative effects on organisational performance. In particular,
they compromise the integrity and efficiency of formal bureaucratic system,
injecting an element of subjectivity in HR functions such as recruitment and
selection, performance appraisal, promotion, demotion and compensation. In addition, Ghana, Nigeria, Kenya are all former British colonies, hence there are more
similarities than differences in organisational management practices and systems
as they all inherited similar administrative structures from the British colonial
administration. In this sense, India and Pakistan also inherited some similar
administrative practices from the British.

Like other developing countries, HRM in both India and Nepal is significantly
influenced by national culture and institutions. Hinduism is the dominant religion
in both countries. As Budhwar (Chapter 5) and Adhikari and Muller (Chapter 6)
explain, HRM practices in these two countries is governed largely by social
contacts, based on one's caste, religion, economic status and political affiliation.
Similar to other commonwealth nations covered in this book, British colonial
traditions still exert a strong influence in India and Nepal in the form of numerous
legislation and red-tape-ridden bureaucratic system. Again, in common with other
African countries, the provisions of labour laws are not seriously enforced and,
moreover, the unco-operative and disruptive nature of unions reduces the efficiency
of organisations. However, all these are now challenged and are slowly changing
due to the pressures created by the liberalisation of the economy and the increased
competition.

There is also some commonality in the way national culture and traditions
influence HRM in Taiwan, South Korea and China. In discussing the key
acteristics of Korean companies, Chen (1995) mentions the profound influe
Confucianism on the values, attitudes, and behavioural patterns of K

Confucianism instils a belief in hierarchy and order in society as well as harmonious interpersonal relations. Buddhism is also practised in Korea and as such also influences management practices, albeit it to lesser extent than Confucianism. In addition, there are American and Japanese influences on Korean management. Chen (1995) contends that in spite of the combined effects of these influences, a distinctive style of management has emerged in Korea. This style of management is known as 'K-type management' and its main features include top-down decision-making, paternalistic leadership, clan management, *inhwa* (harmony-oriented cultural values), Korean flexible lifetime employment, personal loyalty and compensation based on seniority and merit rating. Woo-Won (see Chapter 3), however, discusses the rapid changes in the Korean business environment and the growing pressures on organisations to move away from the traditional values and organisational structures.

Warner (Chapter 2) highlights the 'Chinese characteristics' of bureaucratic systems in China. In both China and Taiwan just as in Korea, Confucian values have found their way into management. As such, *guanxi*, face and *renqing* are some of the means of regulating interpersonal relationships in Chinese organisations. Although it is evident that there are some differences in the management practices in the three East Asian countries, some traditional cultures have similar, if not the same impacts on management in all three countries.

Arguably, the issues presented above and in this book in general reinforce our understanding of the impact of national factors (e.g., national cultures, work-related values and external environment) on HRM in developing countries. They have also thrown more light on the influential role of national institutions as well as social institutions such as family, socialisation and internalisation practices on HRM in developing countries. Equally, they have given an indication of how these external factors in turn influence internal HR practices. The accounts presented in this book are by and large consistent with what prevails in the literature. For this reason, we will not dwell any further on these issues in this concluding chapter. Rather, we will focus on a discussion of the major theme emerging from the chapters.

Competitive pressures, economic liberalization and employment in developing countries

This concluding chapter explores the diverse impacts of competitive pressures arising from economic globalisation on HRM in developing countries. Globalisation, here, implies the processes which reduce barriers between countries and encourage closer integration of economic, political and social activity (Frenkel and Peetz, 1998).

According to both Knight (1998) and Lee (1996) globalisation is moving at a high speed and the forces behind its movement include: (a) the pervasive adoption of free market ideology world-wide; (b) the economic expansion in developing countries and the associated world-wide wave of economic globalisation, including the lowering of tariffs and other barriers to international trade; (c) advances in communication technology which have lowered the costs of doing international business; and (d) the promotion of capital and knowledge transfer. It is asserted that the increase in capital flow across international borders has heightened the demand and growth of FDI resulting in rapid growth in world trade. It is also argued that the deregulation of capital transfers and financial markets, as part of the global acceleration in privatisation, has necessitated the adoption of global perspectives in business practices.

Principally, we would argue that economic globalisation and its associated international competitive pressures have the potential to change HRM in developing countries. While globalisation unearths some challenges for HRM in developing countries we contend that it also offers possibilities for the transformation of personnel management into HRM in the developing world.

This argument is supported by evidence from the literature which shows that globalisation has also ushered in new forms of management in developing countries. The global competitive environment has forced governments in developing countries to shed their public enterprises or subject them to private sector management practices. Some public enterprises have been privatised in recent years and are competing vigorously in global markets. Thus, it is argued that globalisation, along with increasing international competitiveness, and new technologies and innovations in production and management, are some of the driving forces behind the changes and new developments in HRM in developing countries (Debrah and Smith, 2000b; 2000c).

As it will become evident from the issues reviewed below, many of the points raised above are in fact occurring in the countries covered in this book. In all the countries covered, enhancing international competitiveness in a globalised era is a national priority. As such, economic liberalisation, deregulation and privatisation feature prominently in every country's restructuring programme. This economic liberalisation and restructuring in developing countries brought on by globalisation have in turn initiated changes in HRM policies and practices. Before turning to an exploration of the impacts of economic globalisation on work and employment, it is necessary to provide a brief overview of the ongoing economic restructuring and liberalisation in the countries covered.

Fundanga (1995) asserts that many of the developing countries that have resorted to privatisation share a common historical background and environmental factors. For instance, for most Sub-Saharan African countries the first two decades after independence were characterised by rapid economic growth. Moreover, they enjoyed favourable terms of trade and high levels of public expenditure in infrastructure and services. The development of import-substituting industries brought in the rise of parastatal companies. Furthermore, many governments moved to nationalise existing foreign companies in their countries and set up state enterprises to carry out various production functions as well as providing services.

These parastatals rapidly dominated the industrial, financial and manufacturing sectors of their economies and acquired important political and economic status and became major sources of employment. However, by the 1980s most of the parastatals were in financial crisis as a result of corruption and mismanagement. The associated inefficiencies rendered most unprofitable and a burden on the government purse.

In the Cold War era and prior to the disintegration of the Soviet Union, many countries managed to get substantial foreign aid from both the East and West and hence were able to prop up these grossly inefficient parastatals. With the end of the Cold War and the emergence of 'donor fatigue', Sub-Saharan African governments suddenly felt pressure from Western governments to abandon dictatorship and democratise their political systems and reduce budget deficits. As part of this democratisation process they were also urged to liberalise their economies. Hence, the introduction of structural adjustment programmes.

The structural adjustment programmes spearheaded by the IMF and the World Bank were made conditional on the achievement of some specific objectives. These included: (a) the liberalisation of the economy by subjecting it to both local and international competition; (b) liberalisation of domestic trade and commerce; (c) reform of fiscal policy; (d) reform of the financial sector; (e) reform of agriculture and industry; and (f) the reduction of budget deficit.

The implementation programme has had significant impact on the management of human resources in Sub-Saharan Africa. In particular, state-owned enterprises have been either closed/liquidated or privatised, resulting in substantial reductions in the number of employees and consequent job insecurity. Some other measures have been introduced to commercialise the provision of services in the public sector and have also ushered in new forms of managing employees. Many of these initiatives have found their way into HRM in the private sector in Sub-Saharan Africa.

Thus, currently, in Sub-Saharan Africa, a tidal wave of privatisation and structural reforms is unleashing its force in all directions. Nigeria (see Chapter 11) embarked on structural adjustment reforms to tackle mismanagement and the consequent economic crisis of the 1970s and 1980 when the country was for the most part under military rule. These problems forced the government to initiate IMF and World Bank-sponsored economic liberalisation programmes. These were abandoned quickly when the consequent short-term hardship required to put the economy on a sound footing started to bite, became unbearable for the populace and led to popular protests. The programmes, however, are on the verge of being revived by the present government. President Olusegun Obasanjo has now secured loans from international organisations such as the IMF to restructure the economy, improve competitiveness, to integrate Nigeria into the global economy and to attract FDI (Wallis, 2000).

Kenya is also in the depths of economic liberalisation (see Chapter 13). The Kenyan programme of structural adjustment has been ongoing for over a decade but was suspended in 1997 as a result of withdrawal of support from international organisations in protest against persistent corruption in Kenya. The Kenyan authorities' inability or unwillingness to control corruption and tackle mismanagement has marred the economic climate and intensified the economic crisis. The restructuring has involved the privatisation of major public sector organisations such as Kenyan Airways. As elsewhere in Africa, the economic restructuring programme has led to massive redundancies of employees and high unemployment in Kenya. But, more privatisation and restructuring are underway as Kenya has recently secured $198 million loan from the IMF to continue the economic liberalisation programme (Turner, 2000) and to meet the challenges posed by global competitive pressures.

Ghana (see Chapter 12) has been hailed by international financial institutions as the success story in Africa in terms of economic restructuring. After years of economic mismanagement and decline, the government embarked on an economic restructuring programme in 1983. The main objectives of the programme were: (a) to promote growth through liberalisation and privatisation of public enterprises; and (b) to attract FDI into Ghana. The liberalisation programme has opened many sectors to competition and encouraged private sector participation in the economy. Just as in other African countries, privatisation led to large-scale shedding of labour as public enterprises trimmed their workforces and became more profit-focused.

Another major African economy currently undergoing transformation is that of South Africa. Wood and Mellahi in Chapter 14 analysed the South African economy under apartheid and the economic crisis stemming from the contradictions within the apartheid economy. The post-apartheid economic transformation is examined. So also is the ANC government's policies on a range of macro-economic reforms which include the reduction in the size of the public sector, a reduction in state involvement in the economy, a greater reliance on market forces and the enhancement of international competitiveness.

Perhaps, of all the countries covered in this book, it is India where the greatest strides have been made in recent years regarding the liberalisation of economy. By late 1980s the Indian economy had reached its worst with problems relating to high inflation, declining industrial production, fiscal indiscipline, high ratio of borrowing to the GNP and very low level of foreign exchange reserves. In response to this crisis, the government devalued the rupee, introduced a new industrial policy and implemented fiscal and trade policies in 1991. In line with these new policies, state ownership in the economy is being scaled down, a structural adjustment programme has been introduced and serious attempts have been made to attract FDI.

Along the same lines, Khilji (see Chapter 7) undertakes an incisive analysis of the restructuring and deregulation of the Pakistani economy. In particular, she discusses the opportunities created in the private sector as a result of the implementation of a comprehensive programme of deregulation aimed at opening up the monopolised public sector services to competition. This essentially means the privatisation of the entire public sector.

In Pakistan, just as in many Sub-Saharan African countries, the initiatives for economic reform – aimed at moving the country towards a free market economy – were external rather than internal. They were mainly due to the influence and pressures of major foreign donors and the World Bank.

Privatisation and deregulation have been important features of the Nepalese economy since the early 1990s. They are essential aspects of the reforms in the public sector in Nepal. Just like Pakistan, the Nepalese government has made vigorous attempts to inject private capital into the economy and in general to revitalise the private sector to enhance the country's prospects in attracting FDI.

Tayeb in Chapter 8 also discusses, albeit in a limited way, the privatisation attempts of the Iranian government since the 1990s. She provides an interesting analysis of the management of the Iranian economy which is run along strict protectionist and statist lines. Tayeb recounts the 'demise' of FDI in Iran in the revolutionary period and the recent attempts to normalise relations with the West and improve the country's chances of attracting FDI on terms acceptable to the Iranians. Hence, the birth of the 'buy-back' contracts under which foreign companies develop certain industries in some identified sectors and the Iranians pay back the development cost within a specified period of time.

Regarding Saudi Arabia, Mellali and Wood (see Chapter 9) paint a seemingly contradictory scenario where, on the one hand, the state still maintains tight control over economic activities but, on the other, seeks to attract FDI. Currently, the Saudi mode of regulation remains a heavily state-centred one as large state monopoly corporations still dominate the economy. But the Saudi government has now realised the need to diversify the economy and to reduce the dependence on oil and petro-chemicals. Accordingly, the government has drawn up plans to liberalise and deregulate the economy. This includes empowering the private sector to take more responsibility and initiative to promote efficiency, stimulate competition both domestically and internationally and to accelerate the economy's integration into the world economy.

Similarly, Branine in Chapter 10 gives an account of the radical economic and political reforms initiated by the Algerian government in the late 1980s. The objective here was to ensure a rapid economic transition from socialist state-owned enterprises to private sector-led economy. The economic crisis resulting from the post-1986 fall in oil and gas prices, along with poor management of the economy and public enterprises under the socialist command economy model, gave rise to the economic restructuring. The symptoms of this mismanagement included high unemployment, high inflation and rising foreign debt. The government's response was to initiate some austerity measures aimed at moving towards a market economy. Hence, state-owned enterprises were made autonomous and expected to secure their own financial resources and to become financially independent.

Facing certain death as a result of the new government policies, the state-owned enterprises responded to the austerity policies by cost reduction measures which principally focused on workforce reduction. As the free enterprise and market economy policies took hold, more and more state-owned enterprises went bankrupt and many employees lost their jobs.

All three East Asian countries covered in this book are currently undergoing restructuring. Warner in Chapter 2 discusses the ongoing restructuring in China. As indicated, enterprise and management decentralisation started in China in the mid-1980s. The objective of this programme was to transform the economy from the one based on central planning to the one based on market socialism. The 1980s and 1990s also witnessed the reform of Chinese industry and its management as the state enterprises were generally inefficient and over-staffed. Since the 1980s the government has actively encouraged the formation of joint ventures, private-owned enterprises and FDI.

In South Korea the 1997 Asian crisis ushered in many changes. As Won-Woo narrates (see Chapter 3), it brought to the fore the importance of competitiveness based on transparency, rationality and capability. Arguably, the forces of globalisation have forced South Korean companies to move towards a market-based economy. South Korean companies are thus undergoing financial restructuring and structural reforms.

Tung-Chun in Chapter 4 discusses the restructuring of the Taiwanese economy in general and the transformation of the personnel function in particular. He traces the beginning of MNCs' investment in Taiwan and their role in the transformation of the agricultural economy into a newly industrialised economy. Tung-Chun asserts that in order to maintain its competitiveness, great efforts are being made to attract FDI and to promote private enterprises.

It can be inferred from the above that economic liberalisation, restructuring and privatisation are essentially responses to global competitive pressures and the need to enhance the performance of organisations in developing countries. In many developing countries such as Pakistan, Ghana, Nigeria, Kenya, Uganda, Tanzania and Zambia, governments were attracted initially by the economic benefits of privatisation such as effective corporate governance, technology transfer and technical know-how as well as the potential of attracting FDI (Bennel, 1997).

In summary, it is worthwhile noting that almost all the chapters provide some evidence on how and why competitive pressures have forced firms to restructure. This form of restructuring involves cutting costs through workforce reduction, the introduction of flexible HR strategies, downsizing, and employment restructuring. Again, the main stimulus for such HR changes is the globalisation of business. As economies and firms are increasingly operating in one global market, firms have found it imperative to develop strategies to respond to competitive pressures. Hence, it is fair to conclude that globalisation is indeed influencing, if not changing, the way human resources are managed in some developing countries (Debrah and Smith, 2000b). This, then, leads us to a discussion of the multifaceted impact of globalisation on work and employment in general, and HRM in particular, in developing countries.

Globalisation, FDI and employment in developing countries

The labour-management literature suggests that under economic globalisation, capital investment, production, marketing, distribution of products and services are increasingly carried out on a 'pan-global' (across all national frontiers) scale in a number of interconnected and shifting locations dictated by MNCs' calculations of where they can derive optimal profitability (see Debrah and Smith, 2000c).

Analogous to this view is the perception that globalisation is associated with increase flow of FDI from developed countries to developing countries with lower cost (including availability of low-cost skilled labour), where investors can reap huge profits. While there is some truth in this assertion, it ignores the role of MNCs from developing countries in FDI and job creation in both developing and developed countries.

Yeung (1999) argues that the internationalisation of business firms from emerging economies has deep historical roots which can be traced back to the late nineteenth century. In particular, transnational banking, trading and other businesses existed in Asia and Latin America as far back as the mid-nineteenth century. South Africa has also had its own transnational companies at least since the early 1900s. Many of these companies invested mainly in their own regions but since the 1960s they have been involved in the globalisation of economic activity through cross-border integration of their operations.

Thus, globalisation is also fostering the development of MNCs from developing countries. MNCs from developed and developing countries both still exhibit considerable influence on the levels of employment in many countries and are significant sources of employment. As such, these MNCs often introduce new working practices which often filter down to local firms. They also develop employment strategies which are in line with their global strategies. The MNCs generally have well-developed HRM systems. It is thus conceivable that as more and more developing countries succeed in attracting FDI, the local firms they work with might emulate their HRM policies and practices. Thus, indirectly the local firms can learn from the MNCs regarding how to transform their personnel management into HRM.

In this respect, then, it is worthwhile noting the emergence of large MNCs from developing countries which are major players in HRM. Table 15.1 shows the leading MNCs based in developing countries. Asia tops the list of the ten largest MNCs from developing countries as it has seven companies on the list. Firms from Hong Kong, China and South Korea dominate the list. There are also some large MNCs from Latin America and Central Europe. Globalisation and liberalisation of economies in the developing world have provided opportunities for firms in developing countries to attract more FDI and with more FDI the impact of globalisation on employment in developing countries becomes more pronounced.

According to the United Nations Conference on Trade and Development, (UNCTAD), flows of FDI by MNCs into Latin America and the Caribbean basin gained 5 per cent to reach a record US$72 billion in 1998. Similarly, Brazil saw its inflows increase by fully US$10 billion to reach US$28.7 billion (UNCTAD, 1999a). The privatised sector attracted approximately 25 per cent of the FDI inflows to Brazil in 1998. Most of the investors were from the USA and countries in the EU. Equally, privatised industries attracted most of the inflows to Venezuela, Columbia, Argentina and Mexico. Privatisation in the service sector stimulated inflows in El Salvador and Guatemala, while privatisation and more traditional investments in export-oriented assembly manufacturing activities stimulated FDI inflow gains for Costa Rica, Dominican Republic and Jamaica (ibid.).

Since 1990, FDI inflows to Africa have overall been increasing. A recent UNCTAD survey has revealed that prospects for increased FDI flows into Africa have improved. This is because many African governments have seriously

Table 15.1 Top 10 MNCs based in developing countries

Rank	Name of corporation	Country of origin	Industrial sector	Foreign assets	Foreign sales	Foreign employees
1	Petroleos de Venezuela	Venezuela	Petroleum	9.0	32.5	11 849
2	Daewoo Corp.	Republic of Korea	Diversified	—	—	—
3	Jardine Matheson	Hong Kong, China/ Bermuda	Diversified	6.7	8.0	—
4	First Pacific Co.	Hong Kong, China	Electronics	6.3	7.4	40 400
5	Cemex S.A.	Mexico	Construction	5.6	2.2	10 690
6	Hutchison Whampoa	Hong Kong, China	Diversified	5.0	1.9	17 013
7	Sappi Limited	South Africa	Paper	3.8	2.4	9 492
8	China State Construction and Engineering Corp.	China	Construction	3.7	1.5	5 496
9	China Nat'l Chemicals Import and Export Corp.	China	Diversified	3.5	11.2	625
10	LG Electronics	Republic of Korea	Electronics	3.2	5.2	32 532

Note: — unpublished UNCTAD estimates. Ranked by foreign assets and sales in billions of U.S. dollars, 1997.

improved their business environment to enable them to attract FDI. Countries which have been mentioned as having created business-friendly environment are South Africa, Nigeria, Botswana, Ghana, Mozambique, Namibia, Tunisia and Uganda. Many of these countries have demonstrated a particular dynamism in attracting FDI throughout the 1990s. FDI inflows into Africa in 1998 amounted to US$8.3 billion and the money went mostly to privatised related businesses (UNCTAD, 1999b).

FDI continues to flow into the Asia-Pacific region despite the recent Asian financial crisis. In 1998, FDI to the Asia-Pacific region was US$85 billion. China received FDI flow of about US$45.5 billion. China not only accounted for well over half of total FDI flows into the region, but was the third largest recipient in the world behind only the USA and the UK (UNCTAD, 1999c). South Korea received its largest ever volume of FDI inflows at US$5.1 billion in 1998. While in South East Asia inflows to countries such as Malaysia, Singapore, and Indonesia declined in 1998, the Philippines and Thailand experienced increased inflow of FDI (ibid.).

There is some evidence that in West Asia plans to expand oil and gas production capacity in Kuwait, Oman, Qatar, United Arab Emirates and Yemen, and the opening up of the petroleum sector to foreign investors in Kuwait and Iran would lead to increased FDI (ibid.). The countries of Central Asia and developing island economies of the Pacific also attracted considerable FDI in 1998. The developing islands of the Pacific alone attracted US$175 million in 1998 and US$146 in 1997. Australia, New Zealand and Japan were the main sources, while several European and US MNCs remained important in the region. In 1998, just over half of the inflows went to Fiji at US$91 million, followed by Papua New Guinea at US$30 million and Vanuatu at US$28 million (ibid.).

Equally, Central and Eastern European countries have been actively attracting FDI. In 1998, FDI by MNCs in this region was heavily concentrated in Poland, the Czech Republic, Romania, Hungary and the Russian Federation. According to UNCTAD, much of Central and Eastern Europe is catching up with the rest of the world in terms of the region's ability to attract FDI (UNCTAD, 1999d).

The impact of globalisation on HRM in developing countries

The ever increasing globalisation trend means the workplace of the twenty-first century will continue to witness the impact of world economic restructuring and liberalisation. This has implications for the organisation of work, employment, labour markets and employee/industrial relations. The trend towards global integration of production and circulation of finance capital is already having immense impacts on the workplace and, as a result, the way human resources are managed. For instance, the recent Asian economic crisis led to some job losses not only in Asia but in other parts of the world as Asian MNCs had to scale down, close their overseas operations or relocate the operations in their home countries.

This is an indication that production and employment are no longer permanently anchored to a particular physical location. As part of the process of internationalisation of production, MNCs can now open production sites at various locations around the globe and production can be relocated easily to suit company objectives (Chaykowski and Giles, 1998). Companies are now increasingly making conscious efforts to design their production and distribution systems as well as their employment strategies to meet the demands and changes in the global economy. These factors precipitate the frequent shifts in the location of employment as existing economic activities change locations and new activities are set up in such places. Thus, in the globalised age, supranational entities such as MNCs in many instances set the employment agenda as the location of production as well as provision of services can be changed quickly (Peel, 1999).

Advances in technology have made it easier for managers to make decisions pertaining to the location of production. The Internet, for instance, provides avenues for organisations to create more world-wide business opportunities (Parker, 1998). For instance, in order for companies located in the developed world to take advantage of lower costs they set up accounting processing offices in developing countries or sub-contract some information processing functions to companies in developing countries (for example, India) which have advanced information technology and skilled human resources (Lamb, 2000).

Globalisation is making it difficult for organisations to shape employee relations policies solely in terms of a national or sub-national government jurisdiction as some international pressure groups can exert a lot of pressure on governments to regulate some areas of employment. A case in point is the pressure on governments in some developing countries such as Pakistan to control child labour in the carpet and garments industries. Thus, with the intensification of the globalisation process we are witnessing major shifts in employee relations in many developing countries (Smith and Debrah, 2000).

As indicated earlier, globalisation and its associated liberalisation and deregulation have precipitated changes to labour markets in developing countries just as in developed countries. One such shift is the near 'demise' of permanent employment. In particular, we are witnessing the rise of the 'insecure workforce' and the disappearance of the standard forms of employment (Heery and Salmon, 2000). Moreover, the emergence of the service economy and electronic commerce and the increasing ascendancy of information technology in the workplace have resulted in an increase in contingent workers, teleworking and other forms of the non-traditional work patterns, even in developing countries. Thus, in developing as well as in developed countries, the concept of the traditional workplace is undergoing tremendous changes both in terms of work systems and the traditional spatial ties to worksites (Chaykowski and Giles, 1998).

With the pressures for change facing HR managers in developing countries as a result of globalisation and international competitiveness, one would have thought that organizations would develop HR strategic responses. But, with the exception of Taiwan and South Korea (and to some extent in India) where HR departments are involved in the formulation of business strategies and HR is closely linked to business strategy, one does not get the impression that there is a movement towards HRM (as understood in Western academic sense) in the other developing countries covered. Generally, the countries covered have not fully embraced an integrated and focused approach to HRM. In almost all the countries, personnel management (PM) and HRM are used interchangeably but often implying a bureaucratic PM system. This is particularly so in the public sector more than in the private sector. Within the private sector, the MNCs are more inclined to adopt a strategic HRM approach than local firms. In the few local firms that have made attempts towards adopting an HRM approach, the whole function has been broadened but not fully integrated into corporate strategy. However, the status and profile of the HR role have been elevated and brought up to par with other business areas and communication channels have been opened up. Khilji asserts that this is happening in Pakistan (see Chapter 7). Similarly, some organisations in Pakistan have adopted 'pay for performance', 'management by objectives' and an 'open appraisal system'.

These progressive developments are in sharp contrast to what exists in Algeria. According to Branini (see Chapter 10), the management of employees in Algeria can best be described as personnel administration rather than HRM. This is because at present there is no clear evidence of personnel managers' involvement in strategic decision-making or in policy formulation in Algeria. Consequently, the formal role of the personnel department does not go beyond the administration of employees' files and record keeping and the monitoring of complicated bureaucratic procedures.

Kamoche paints a similar picture with respect to his discussion of the lack of strategy in HRM in Kenyan organisations (see Chapter 13). In particular, he mentions the perceived reluctance of Kenyan managers to engage in long-term strategic planning. This is attributed to the entrenched nature of short-term bureaucratic personnel management tradition in Sub-Saharan Africa. In this respect, what is happening in Kenya is not very different from what is happening in Ghana and Nigeria. But the South African case is a bit unconventional in African terms because the large organisations can claim to be practising HRM while the local enterprises cannot do so.

In China, Warner asserts that PM is basically a bureaucratic device to run the large state-owned enterprises (see Chapter 2). It is basically concerned with 'bread and butter' activities of recruitment and selection, reward system, disciplinary procedures, etc. He adds that this older form of PM practices is still more common in Chinese enterprises and in other organisations where a decidedly conservative air continues to permeate the administration of personnel. Moreover, PM is still more widely relied on in many joint ventures (JVs). It is mainly in the large JVs and wholly owned MNCs in China, particularly those with expatriate HR managers, that a semblance of HRM is present.

Budhwar in Chapter 5 reports that HRM in India is changing at a more rapid pace than ever, mainly due to the pressures created by the liberalisation of economic policies. HRM is playing a noticeable role in bringing about change in Indian organisations. However, unlike the West, human resource development (HRD) is the preferred term for personnel function. The rapid growth and the usage of the term HRD in India are an outcome of the pressures created by foreign operators (who are equipped with better resources) on local organisations. There is thus a strong emphasis on the development of human resources. However, Nepalese organisations are still struggling to establish formal HRM functions. The strong bureaucratic system is creating hindrances in this regard. But Adhikari and Muller indicated in Chapter 6 that there is some evidence that the personnel function in Nepal is helping organisations to change.

It is clear from the above discussions that economic globalisation has created significant opportunities for some developing countries. Many of these countries have a comparative advantage in terms of labour cost, land cost, and overall operating cost (Zimmerer *et al.*, 1998). In developing countries, MNCs and FDI create employment opportunities. In the same way as local firms, they are a vital source of employment but with increasing economic globalisation and the ease with which firms can relocate their production plants, they can also quickly put workers at a particular location out of jobs. Thus, organisations in developing countries need to develop proactive policies in order to tap the benefits of globalisation to workers and to minimise its detrimental effects on employment. Essentially, organisations must respond proactively to the external environmental pressures by developing internal HR policies and practices which are capable of tapping the benefits of globalisation. We would argue that organisations have a greater chance of doing so if they move away from traditional PM practices and embrace HRM.

This is necessary because the liberalisation and structural adjustment policies have ushered in policies aimed at increasing productivity, reducing costs, improving quality, and reducing over-manning (downsizing). Globalisation and its associated international competitive pressures have precipitated the introduction of flexibility of operations, contingent reward systems, lean production methodologies in a process of ongoing change to underpin efficiency, thereby leading to new challenges to HRM at organisational level, particularly with regard to industrial relations policy and practice (Veersma, 1995).

The rapid developments and the increased reliance on IT in organisations mean that HR managers in developing countries should be ready to develop appropriate HR strategies to cope with the subsequent de-skilling, reskilling and multi-skilling problems, workforce reduction and retention as well as career development. These have significant implications on the management of employees and require organisations to adopt strategic initiatives and policies and to integrate HR strategies into the overall business strategy. With the current bureaucratic PM practices which prevail in most developing countries, it is unlikely that organisations can effectively utilise their human resources to achieve competitive advantage. Developing countries, then, must transform their PM into HRM.

It is for this reason that Kamoche argues that the resource-based view can be applied to an understanding of the role of HRs in strategic management in Africa and might contribute to the formulation of HRM approach which is more appropriate for the Kenyan situation and perhaps all developing countries in general (see Chapter 13).

Conclusion: HRM challenges

Although the chapters in this book have illuminated our understanding of HRM practices in specific countries, they have also thrown more light on the way national factors impact on HRM. An examination of the chapters reveals that in some situations common or similar national factors impact in almost the same way on HRM practices in different countries. Of interest here is the manifold impact of religion and traditional cultures on HRM in developing countries.

Currently, employee relations practices within organizations including internal labour market (ILM) structures in most developing countries are dictated by factors such as social and cultural values, religious beliefs, caste/ethnic-based stratification, political affiliation and economic power. Such ILMs result in the decrease in organisational performance and breed corruption and red-tapism. In the context of the changes taking place in most developing countries in terms of privatisation and structural adjustment programmes, there is now a strong need for HRM systems in these countries to be consistent with rationalised, objective and systematic employment systems. This is already happening in some of the countries covered in this book. However, there is dire need to speed up the process.

Almost all developing nations have established legal structures in the form of relevant labour laws to safeguard the interests of employees. However, in many cases the provisions of the labour laws are not seriously enforced at all which results in the exploitation of employees. Child labour and minimum wage laws are typical examples. Relevant law-enforcing agencies in developing countries need to ensure the serious implementation of such provisions. Moreover, many developing countries do not actively promote equal opportunities, hence the existence of disadvantage on the grounds of ethnicity, gender and age. Again, organisations need to develop policies to tackle these problems.

Moreover, as the global economy expands and competition intensifies, unions in developing countries (e.g., Africa) need to shed their confrontational attitudes which served them well in the independence struggles during the colonial period and adopt a positive and co-operative role. There is also the need for governments in developing countries to curtail if not uproot political influence on trade unions. The trade unions need to be strategic partners with business and industry in order to enhance the competitiveness of their organisations. Any political control can hinder the ability of the trade unions to achieve these objectives.

There is also need to make amendments in the existing labour laws in developing countries. Some of the labour laws in developing countries such as India are less relevant for present business environment. With the privatisation and structural adjustment programmes in place, there is a need to downsize Indian organisations. However, the existing labour laws do not allow such a transition. Moreover, there are no established policies for early retirements to facilitate the process of rationalising the workforce in many developing countries. All these issues create massive challenges for HRM in developing countries.

References

Bennel, P. (1997) 'Privatization in Sub-Saharan Africa: Progress and Prospects During the 1990s', *World Development*, 25 (11), 1785–1803.

Budhwar, P. and Sparrow, P. (2002) 'An Integrative Framework for Determining Cross National Human Resource Management Practices', *Human Resource Management Review*, forthcoming.

Chaykowski, R. and Giles, A. (1998) 'Globalisation, Work and Industrial Relations', *Relations Industrielles – Industrial Relations*, 53 (1), 3–12.

Chen, M. (1995) *Asian Management Systems: Chinese, Japanese and Korean Styles of Business*, London: Routledge.

Debrah, Y. A. (2000a) 'Management in Ghana', in M. Warner (ed.) *Management in Emerging Countries*, London: Thomson Learning, pp. 189–197.

Debrah, Y. A. and Smith, I. G. (2000b) 'Globalization and the Changing Nature of Employment', *International Journal of Manpower*, 21 (6), 446–451.

Debrah, Y. A. and Smith, I. G. (2000c) 'Introduction: Work and Employment in a Globalized Era', *Asia Pacific Business Review*, 7 (1), 1–20.

Frenkel, S. and Peetz, D. (1998) 'Globalisation and Industrial Relations in East Asia: A Three Country Comparison', *Industrial Relations*, 37 (3), 282–311.

Fundanga, C. M. (1995) *Privatization of Public Enterprises: Theory and Practice*, London: Cassell.

Gardiner, K. (1996) 'Managing in Different Cultures: The Case of Ghana', in B. Towers (ed.) *The Handbook of Human Resource Management*, Oxford: Blackwell, pp. 488–510.

Heery, E. and Salmon, J. (2000) 'The Insecurity Thesis', in E. Heery and J. Salmon (eds) *The Insecure Workforce*, London: Routledge.

Jaeger, A. M., Kanungo, R. N. and Srinivas, N. (1995) 'A Review of Human Resource Management Successes in Developing Countries', in R. N. Kanungo and Saunders, D. M. (eds) *New Approaches to Employee Management*, Vol. 3 *Employee Management in Developing Countries*, Greenwich, CT: JAI Press, pp. 243–255.

Kamoche, K. (1993) 'Towards a Model of HRM in Africa', in J. B. Shaw, P. S. Kirkbride and K. M. Rowlands (eds) *Research in Personnel and Human Resource Management*, Supplement 3, Greenwich, CT: JAI Press.

Kanungo, R. and Jaeger, A. (1990) 'Introduction: The Need for Indigenous Management in Developing Countries', in A. Jaeger and R. Kanungo (eds) *Management in Developing Countries*, London: Routledge, pp. 1–22.

Kiggundu, M. N. (1986) 'Limitations to the Application of Socio-technical Systems in Developing Countries', *Journal of Applied Behavioural Science*, 23, 341–353.

Kiggundu, M. N., Jorgensen, J. J and Hafsi, T. (1983) 'Administrative Theory and Practice in Developing Countries: A Synthesis', *Administrative Science Quarterly*, 28, 66–84.

Knight, R. (1998) 'Global Finance – The Great Equaliser in Mastering Global Business: Navigating the Tides of Global Finance', *Financial Times*.

Kohn, T. O. and Austin, J. E. (2000) 'Management in Emerging Countries', in M. Warner (ed.) *Management in Emerging Countries*, London: Thomson Learning, pp. 9–25.

Lamb, J. (2000) 'Recruiters Turn to India for IT Expertise as Skills Crisis Bites', *People Management*, August, pp. 12–13.

Lee, E. (1996) 'Globalization and Employment: Is the Anxiety Justified?', *International Labour Review*, 135 (5), 485–497.

Parker, B. (1998) *Globalisation and Business Practice: Managing Across Boundaries*, London: Sage.

Peel, Q. (1999) 'Walls of the World Come Tumbling Down', *Financial Times Survey: The Millennium – Part 1*, Monday, 6 December, p. 1.

Smith, I. G., and Debrah, Y. A. (2000) 'Globalization, Work and Employment in the Asia-Pacific Region', *Asia Pacific Business Review*, 7 (1).

Turner, M. (2000) 'Death Stirs up Civil Right Fears in Kenya', *Financial Times*, Weekend, 26/27 August, p. 7.

UNCTAD (1999a) 'Foreign Investment Gains in Latin America', http://www.unctad.org/wir/wir1999/index.htm (accessed September 1999).

UNCTAD (1999b) 'Significant Investment Opportunities in Africa Exist: UNCTAD Survey for the World Investment Report', http://www.unctad.org/wir/wir1999/index.htm (accessed September 1999).

UNCTAD (1999c) 'Foreign Investment Flows into Developing Asia', http://www.unctad.org/wir/wir1999/index.htm (accessed September 1999).

UNCTAD (1999d) 'Foreign Investment Flows into Central and Eastern European Countries', http://www.unctad.org/wir/wir1999/index.htm (accessed September 1999).

Veersma, O. (1995) 'Multinational Corporations and Industrial Relations', in A. Harzing and J. Van Russeyveldt (eds) *International Human Resource Management*, London: Sage, pp. 318–336.

Wallis, W. (2000) 'Nigeria Pins Debt Relief Hopes On Clinton', *Financial Times*, Weekend, 26/27 August, p. 7.

Yeung, H. W. (1999) 'Introduction: Competing in the Global Economy. The Globalization of Business Firms from Emerging Economies', in H. W. Yeung (ed) *The Globalization of Business Firms from Emerging Economies*, Vol. 1, Cheltenham: Edgar, pp. XII–XLVI.

Zimmerer, T. W., Alavi, J. and Yasin, M. M. (1998) 'Developing Countries' Strategic Opportunities', *Thunderbird International Business Review*, 40 (3), 315–331.

Subject index

Name index